Praise for *Cross Country*

"*Cross Country* is delightful as history, but it's the tender portrait of
driving home together, enjoying their time just the four of them,
onates on closing the book. America may or may not 'be' the road, b
Sullivans and so many other families, their time there comes to defi
—*New York Times Boo*

"[An] irresistible hymn to the all-American road trip…Sullivan['s] c
ollections make for some laugh-out-loud reading. But he also is a
researcher who enlivens his definitive trip narrative with tasty his
bits about other travelers on the American road stretching back to
Clark."   —*Seattle Post-I*

"In this humorous, wistful, often insightful but always quirky account of one
family's summer trek across the country from Oregon to New York, Sullivan
recalls the disasters, anecdotes and just weird incidents that accrue during a
life on the road…A treat."   —*Chicago Tribune*

"If Jack Kerouac went on the road these days, he'd be sipping a 24-ounce
soda on a 10-lane superhighway…like his bestselling *Rats*, which used the rodents to paint an alternative history of New York, Mr. Sullivan's new book
takes another somewhat prosaic obsession—in this case, highway travel—and
uses it as a historical road map."   —*Wall Street Journal*

"Like Jack Kerouac before him, Sullivan clearly believes that discovery in the
American road sense of the word—meaning the quasi-patriotic reaching of
enlightenment about one's nation via kinetic passage over its breadth—remains a real possibility; minimarts, Wal-Marts, and all. No one is better
equipped to do this than Sullivan. His previous books have revealed him to be
something of an urban Thoreau…So turning the American roadside—with
its blisters of fast-food restaurants, its fungal growth of billboards—into a
thing of beauty is a piece of cake for Sullivan."   —*Boston Globe*

"Sullivan takes us on a propulsive ride. He combines charming personal recollections with compelling musings on the history of American roads, motels,
the Cannonball Run, the coffee-cup lid, and…you get the idea. By book's
end, you'll feel pleasantly tripped out…wide-eyed at all the sights you've seen
along the way."   —*Entertainment Weekly*

"If you ride along with Sullivan—the curious and funny and often very wise
writer of this entertaining, eclectic and eccentric memoir—the days and
miles will melt away like bright and brilliant dreams. And not a single time
will you ask, 'Are we there yet?'"   —*Cleveland Plain Dealer*

"Sullivan's rangy, amusing account of his family's trek from Oregon to New York, gives us Lewis and Clark (and their modern-day impersonators), interstate visionary Carl Fisher, Cannonball Run racer Brock Yates, and those pleasingly mundane highlights (impromptu golf) and headaches (speed traps) of life on the American road." —*Vogue*

"*Cross Country* chronicles a family road trip last summer in a rented Chevy Impala but ends up, guided by the author's rampant curiosity, as a gratifying miscellany of portraits, micro-histories, and minutiae—from the bicycle salesman who founded the Indy 500 to the evolution of coffee cup sip-tops." —*Mother Jones*

"Sullivan is everybody's dad on a long cross-country car trip—setting schedules, getting lost and trying to make the whole experience educational." —*Washington Post*

"Sullivan puts a magnifying glass to the culture born from westward expansion, ruminating on the banal beauty of what is now mostly taken for granted outside our windshields. Like all good road books, *Cross Country* generates the excitement that the idea of transcontinental travel holds: the hope to find something new that we don't realize exists while standing still." —*Playboy.com*

"This is a road-trip ode to all the families who have traveled by car across America. The author's many side trips make for fascinating and funny reading." —*Sacramento Bee*

"*Cross Country* is a mad rush of places, impressions and history cut into bite-size pieces perfect for digesting as a passenger along for the ride." —*Santa Cruz Sentinel*

"Sullivan writes with precision, humor and empathy, his own voice carrying us along." —*Portland Oregonian*

"Mr. Sullivan is an inspiration…[his] digressions never fail to entertain or edify…he channels Walt Whitman's sense of wonder." —*Washington Times*

"[Sullivan] takes us on a journey that's sentimental but also literate, literary, amusing, informative, wicked, self-deprecating and deeply entertaining…a dazzling account of America's most archetypal odyssey, with much social history slyly and wryly inserted." —*Kirkus Reviews* (starred review)

"[Sullivan's] trapped-with-the-family jaunts are authentic and frenetic—just like every good road trip should be—and the teasing details he offers about such things as the origins of the Indy 500 and the coffee cup lid do exactly what a good travel book should do: inspire you to explore." —*Library Journal*

CROSS COUNTRY

CROSS COUNTRY

Fifteen Years and Ninety Thousand Miles
on the Roads and Interstates of America
with Lewis and Clark,
a Lot of Bad Motels, a Moving Van,
Emily Post, Jack Kerouac,
My Wife, My Mother-in-Law, Two Kids,
and Enough Coffee to Kill an Elephant

Robert Sullivan

BLOOMSBURY

Part of the afterword was first published in the *New York Times Magazine*.

Published by Bloomsbury USA, New York
Distributed to the trade by Holtzbrinck Publishers

All papers used by Bloomsbury USA are natural, recyclable
products made from wood grown in well-managed forests.
The manufacturing processes conform to the environmental
regulations of the country of origin.

THE LIBRARY OF CONGRESS HAS CATALOGED THE HARDCOVER EDITION AS FOLLOWS:

Sullivan, Robert, 1963–
Cross country : fifteen years and ninety thousand miles on the roads and
interstates of America with Lewis and Clark, a lot of bad motels, a moving van, Emily Post,
Jack Kerouac, my wife, my mother-in-law, two kids,
and enough coffee to kill an elephant /
Robert Sullivan.—1st U.S. ed.
p.   cm.
Includes bibliographical references.
ISBN-13: 978-1-58234-527-7
ISBN-10: 1-58234-527-9
1. United States—Description and travel. 2. Sullivan, Robert, 1963–—Travel—United States.
3. Automobile travel—United States. I. Title.

E169.Z83S85 2006
917.3'0493—dc22
2006009542

First published in the United States by Bloomsbury in 2006
This paperback edition published in 2007

Paperback ISBN-10 1-59691-137-9
ISBN-13 978-1-59691-137-6

1 3 5 7 9 10 8 6 4 2

Typeset by Westchester Book Group
Printed in the United States of America by Quebecor World Fairfield

for Louise and Sam

CONTENTS

PART IV: *Miles City, Montana, to Minneapolis, Minnesota*
Venture Across America—Knowledge of the Nation—The Expedition Splits Up, Some
Setting Off on Foot—Lost—We Rejoin Our Party at the Kum & Go—On the Island of
Gas Pumps—See America First—The First Time I Saw America—A Message from the
Car—A Brief History of the Automobile in America up to and Including Our Impala—
OK Tire—In the Front Seat, Wondering—A Pleasing Fancy—"I" Is for Interstate—A
Good Cause—Symbol—Expressing the Feeling of the Moment—The Man Who Built
America's First Cross-Country Road (or Tried to Build It)—Totally Falling In Love—
Just a Little More About the Man Who Built America's First Cross-Country Road (or
Tried to Build It)—Great Great Plains—Pal-ship—Journals—Plains Humor—The His-
tory of People Publishing Their Own Personal Accounts of Crossing the Country (i.e.,
Accounts Such as This One)—Santa Fe—Can't Shake That Thing—Earth Lodge—
Inspire—The Point Late in the Day of a Long Day of Driving—Guidebook Reading—

PART V: *Minneapolis, Minnesota, to Beloit, Wisconsin*
Into the East—An Imaginary Doughboy—The Worst Cross-Country Trip Ever, Part
I—Welcome Center—This Land Is Your Land—Coffee—The Worst Cross-Country
Trip Ever, Part II—The Real America—More Than Cheese—Before the Interstates—O
Eau Claire—The Worst Cross-Country Trip Ever, Part III—The Lights of the Dells—
Streamline—Revelation—Not Seeing Wisconsin in the Dark—Lids—Lids Again—
Turnpikes—Passing Madison—The First Motel—Hoping for Holiday Inn Express—To
Beloit—The Worst Cross-Country Trip Ever, Part IV—Psychedelic—Jack Kerouac's
Gas Station—The Worst Cross-Country Trip Ever, Part V—Road Zero—The Worst
Cross-Country Trip Ever, Part VI—The Road Problem—I Can Barely See—The End
of the Worst Cross-Country Trip Ever—Exiting—Check-in—Solving the Road Prob-

PART VI: *Beloit, Wisconsin, to Bellafonte, Pennsylvania*
At the Start of the Day We Are Supposed to Get There—The Modern Breakfast Area—
A Short Digression on Meeting Fellow Travelers in a Breakfast Area—My Breakfast in
the Breakfast Area—The Incident Near the Breakfast Area, in Retrospect—The Face of
the Country—Driving in the East vs. Driving in the West—Over the Road—Go—
Cannonball—Slow Down—Where We Are on the Interstates—Water—Slogans—
Portage—Child Care—Crossing the Fawn River—Forgive Me as We Cross the Fawn
River—Life Line—We Enter Ohio Hearing Sports Talk on the Radio—In Need of

PART I

Setting Out

OFF

WE'RE OFF. We're off across America. We're in the car and we're driving and we're not turning around, even though we usually do, even though we probably have forgotten something. We're crossing the country. We're not the first people to do it, not by a long shot, obviously. There's Lewis and Clark, though they certainly weren't first, even if people think they were— even if *they* thought they were. There are the pioneers in their covered wagons, the wagons that in river crossings were used as boats, the wagons that were stuffed with belongings, just like our car is today. There are the very first people to cross the country in the automobile: the people who, in the early 1900s, thought of driving as a kind of daredevil adventure, as something more akin to camping or hiking or hang gliding, as opposed to what we think of it today (i.e., just getting in the car). And then there are the great underground cross-country racers of the 1970s: the drivers who fought to prevent driving from becoming rote, the otherwise pretty conservative automobile anarchists who, when the price of gas went through the roof, were slowed but not halted, who had to contend with lower and lower speed limits, with cops, with angry truckers. (Truckers, of course, are the subset of cross-country drivers who cross the country all the time, every day.) Yes, we are just the latest in the long list of transcontinentalists. We are gasoline-powered footnotes in the travel- and adventure-related annals of a nation that has as its greatest public works project an ever-expanding system of roads, a crisscross and circling of roads that keeps it from ever sitting still.

We're packed in, the kids in the back, the parents in front, our stuff filling the trunk, piled up around our knees. In our hearts, we're excited. We're excited in the part of our hearts that knows three thousand miles is doable, a snap, three or four or, longest-case scenario, five days, which is about as much time as we have—like many Americans, we have stuff to do, stuff to deal with—and about as much time as we can stand. In our hearts, we're also weary. We're weary in the part that has done this before, that knows three thousand miles is a long, long way, that has been out late at night on a dark road when our eyes have been trying to stay awake and our eyes only wish like all the rest of our tired bodies that they were not driving anymore. We are about to, first, drive on some of America's less-laned roads, some of the not-so-super highways, but we are mostly going to drive on its many many-laned interstates, on the main roads, along with everybody else.

I know that this seems, to many Americans, like the wrong way to go. In our time driving across the country, we have met Americans who posed the following question: "Don't you want to see the *real* America?"

THE REAL AMERICA

THE REAL AMERICA IS ALSO SOMETIMES known as "back-roads America" or "the heart of America" or "America's heartland" or, in shorthand, "America." This is the America that is calculatedly heartwarming, represented by people who are purported to symbolize America—people who are Platonic ideals of Americans: a lobsterman from Maine, a logger from Oregon, a rancher from Texas, the last small farmer living in Missouri.

That America still exists, to some extent: I have seen a pie on the counter of a diner in Wisconsin that caused the phrase "real America" to ring in my head and that also made me hungry.* I have driven on roads in Missouri where, instead of giant, commercially produced signs advertising chain restaurants and chain motels, there were homemade signs advertising organic cattle and wildflowers and signs praising coroners hoping to be re-elected, to be allowed one more term to investigate the local dead. You can see that America, without too much extra effort, but it is a kind of antique-shop America. It's an America that appears in magazines alongside recipes; it's the America where presidential candidates are televised.

---

* Specifically in Osseo, Wisconsin, at a place called the Norske Nook, where we bought way too many pies and then ended up eating them at an interstate rest stop in Ohio, under the fluorescent lights, late at night, with coffee. I have a photograph of us doing so, and the scene is eerie.

But the real America is also the America that Americans generally think they are *not* seeing on the roads they use to cross the country—or for that matter, on the roads they use to commute to work in Chicago or while leaving Saint Louis to visit their in-laws in Omaha or while driving on I-70, formerly Route 66. It seems to me that the real America is the farthest thing from people's minds when they are stopping for some fast food on I-5 in between Los Angeles and San Diego, much less driving from the East Coast to the West. But there it is, the real America, right there. For my part, I have seen America on the superhighways all through my years on the road, traveled its present and looked into its past, and today, grandparents waving good-bye at the window and the kids waving back, we're setting off to see it again.

THE ROADS *ARE* AMERICA

IN THE ROADS OF AMERICA is the history of America. See the nation grow from an unmapped, just-purchased spread of western land to a wagon-train-crossed compilation of territories, to states bound by a few muddy highways, to the modern United States wired with interstates. In the interstates are traces of our first explorations, our impenetrable mountain passes, our old Santa Fe Trail, our pioneers' path to Oregon, our race to California's gold, our first car-happy and nation-spanning private highways. And in the interstates are the paths toward the next America, the one that is always under construction.

See those first roads through young America, those tentative explorations into the unknown, as soldiers and surveyors, trappers and miners push into a West unexplored by white Americans. Then, America breaks away from its eastern beginnings, its coastal fringe: wagon trains lead herds of people to settle the prairies and the plains, to mine the mountains, to farm the fields and work the ranches-to-be. With its national maturation, America champions what it then called Good Roads, the first highways, the aesthetically pleasing parkways that were pleasant to drive, that were the automotive equivalent of a Sunday-afternoon stroll. Then, in the 1950s, America begins its interstate highway system, which itself in turn becomes America, its central arteries, its suburb-expanding and city-smashing nervous system. The interstate system is the centrally calculated roadway of empire, of inland empire, that spawned and fed the military-industrial complex so feared by the interstates' instigator, President Dwight D. Eisenhower, and which also spawned and fed the consumption of fast food, not to mention the automobile industry. Out of this middle age rose the beat poets, who were the midlife crisis of America, who rebelled against the road by taking to it, who did not know that one day their anticorporate Americanism would be taken up by American corporations in roadside ads for mass-produced consumer products that sometimes even featured beat poets. In the fifties and sixties and seventies, interstates destroyed cities and nourished the suburbs, which began expanding forever and ever into what was once the countryside, and then America woke up one day to find that crossing the country—that epic accomplishment that was a dream of America's founders, that was a death-defying feat for the earliest trappers and settlers and explorers, that later was a kick, the thing to do just for the sake of doing it, for a generation of hipsters and, subsequently, hippies—was simple, a snap.

I THINK ABOUT THESE TRANSCONTINENTALISTS when I'm driving cross-country. I think about them and go on and on to anyone in the car who will listen or feign listening or simply look awake. I think of the stories of all the people who crossed before me, from Lewis and Clark to the secret cross-country highway racers of the seventies—crossing the country gives you a *lot* of time to think. And I think not just of where we've already been but also of what we are about to drive through, not any one place but a collection of places all being passed by, all being missed, partly in the impatient attempt to see what we *think* we are looking for when we are driving the road—i.e., the antique-shop America—and partly in the impatience that is a patented American character trait. The America that I see is an America that tells you to keep moving, to move on to something better, to get on the road and keep going, to stop only briefly to refuel your car and yourself but then to keep pushing toward the place that is closer to where you should be, or could be, if only you would keep going. America says move, move on, don't sit still.

When I am on the road, I see the America that is a continual expedition, the never-ending race to the last frontier, rural or suburban or exurban. In other words, America *is* the road.

* * *

WHY ARE WE DOING IT? Why are we crossing the country this time? This time, it is summer vacation. It is summer vacation and after visiting relatives, as usual, and going to a wedding, way up in some faraway, nearly roadless Northwest mountains, after crossing the country once, from New York to Oregon, we are crossing the country yet again, from Oregon back to New York, to get home, to wrap up after six thousand miles, to rest. We are heading from one shining sea to another. We are not heading for the Pacific, as is customary in the history of cross-countrying; we are heading east. Once, when I was young, I headed west; I settled there and lived in the Oregon Country for a number of years. In terms of being young and heading west, I was just like the United States of America, in a sense. Now, I'm heading back into the East, which, for me, is a little like heading back into the past. At least when I head east I feel as if I run into memories, and then history itself. I also feel a little nuts. As far as the American past goes, when I travel east I feel like a deranged driver in the wrong lane of the highway of American history. Aside from getting everybody back safe and sound and in time for whatever it is we all have to do when we do actually get back—get to work, get places, do things that we'd said we'd do with friends and other relatives back in the East—one of my personal goals for this particular trip is to run into some of the larger reasons that I am on the road in the first place, the institutional reasons, or at least some of the reasons that everybody else is. I have spent so much of my life on the road that I almost can't remember why I'm on the road anymore.

OUR FIRST STOP

SURE ENOUGH, just in these first moments, in these first two or three miles, we are stopping. If you are attempting to drive across the United States of America in a manner that will get you to the other side before you run out of money or patience, stopping is the blessing and the curse, the action you most need to avoid, the dream that sometimes seems to be the only thing to do if you are ever going to get there, to make it to your destination. Stopping, like the trip itself, is bittersweet. This morning, we are stopping for coffee and for something to eat. We are stopping in Portland, Oregon, our beginning. We are stopping along the Columbia River, sometimes called the River of the West, other times known as the end of the road for Lewis and Clark. We are stopping and I am paying for the breakfast and wanting to tell the person behind the counter how many times we've set out to cross the country before. I am bringing the coffee and the breakfast to the car—a really late breakfast, as we packed the car all morning and now it's close to ten—and I am looking at the car and shaking my head and thinking about what a long time it is for our son and his sister to sit in the car and about how many times we have put them through this, *we* being my wife and I. Something that I said to my wife just the night before, when we were beginning to load up the car and the kids were already asleep, was "Why do we do this to them?"

WHY (WE DO THIS TO THEM)

THE REASON we do this to them is that, as it turns out, this is who we are. We are people who have crossed the country a lot. This is something we maybe even do too much. When I say *we* in this case, I am referring to my wife and I and our kids. But sometimes the *we* is just my wife and I, because we began driving across the country before we were married, before we ever got involved with kids, when we were cross-country dating, my wife's family on one coast, mine on the other. At first we did it purely to save money; due to the nature of my job, we are never certain about when we are going to leave.* We don't just jump in a car and head out to wherever, like a bunch of beat poets fueled by booze and sex and whatever else (not that I am against booze or sex or whatever else). We're the opposite, in a way: off from the

---

* As everyone knows, if you are buying airline tickets at the last minute, then you might as well buy the airline, especially if you are planning on traveling with a couple of children. If gas prices continue to head the way they have been heading as I type this footnote, and if, geologically speaking, the contents of the earth remain the same, vis-à-vis petroleum deposits, then maybe someday it will be cheaper to sail through the Panama Canal. But, in summary, you can save money driving across the country, and, as far as the country goes, you also see it.

East to get to the West or vice versa, and not looking to revel in the restless, soul-searching, drink- and drug-fueled process but simply looking to get there, and maybe see a little something on the way.

After all this time, our cross-country credentials are significant, if I do say so myself. I have crossed the country on dozens of occasions; I have driven from one side of the United States to the other more than anyone I know who is not a trucker or professional driver of some kind—close to thirty times, as best as I can tell from journals, and receipts, and snapshots, and occasional flashbacks. My total is somewhere around ninety thousand miles, which is about three and a half times around the planet. In 2001, for instance, I made six trips across the country, an eighteen-thousand-mile haul. I personally began my transcontinental driving at twenty-five, a typical age, it seems to me, with my girlfriend, who subsequently married me, and continued it with my wife, who would one day become the mother of our children, and with our children, who would one day complain while driving four and five and sometimes ten days in a row, depending on our cross-country route, which is sometimes a little circuitous (such as on the trip just a few weeks before this one, the trip going west across the country, the trip that took us from New York to Oregon via Texas—a trip that we've done a number of times and that usually runs a little over four thousand miles).

We have crossed the country for grandparent-related purposes, for work, to move—moving being something we often end up having to do for some reason, maybe because we are Americans. We have moved for work and for school, for reasons that to really understand would take more time than I have on a professional's couch. We have crossed the country for weddings in the East and weddings in the West, and once, a few weeks after September 11, 2001, when the World Trade Center and the Pentagon were attacked, we crossed the country when no one was going anywhere, when America stood still for a little while. It was a national fermata, and the interstates were empty and nervous-seeming: America standing still is something that takes getting used to. A few years ago, I traveled across the country by myself, with all our family's belongings in a rental truck, with our station wagon attached to that truck, and with a paranoid sensation hanging over me like the canvas cover of a Conastoga wagon, alone and exposed on the prairie for the first time. Sure enough, I ran into a lot of problems, some of which I did not surmount, to put it mildly.

Growing up in the East, I got in a car every summer and drove to see my grandparents a couple of hours away; like the colonial Americans, I thought the Far West was eastern Pennsylvania. But then it happened one fall day that I met a woman, a woman who was from the West. A few months later, on a spring day that was a little warm and a little cool and just about perfect, we got in a car and went to see her childhood home, all the way across the country. I quit my job and drove off with her—I had never done anything like that, as I am the least spontaneous person you could ever know. That was sixteen years ago. Since then, her West Coast home became my home, and then my East Coast home became her home, and for a while we didn't really have a home at all. We floated between coasts, ourselves and our neither-coasted children, one born here, one born there. We were simultaneously home-poor, or maybe home-free, and thus free to see America. In the case of my wife, she seems to grow stronger the more she sees. In my own case, I feel a little stronger and a little more like a nervous wreck.

A ROAD'S-EYE VIEW

WHEN WE CROSS THE COUNTRY, when we reach the other side, we get a road's-eye view. This might seem limiting, yet I feel that at some point in the trip we end up getting a glimpse of almost all the American landscape's glory. All of America's glory can be divided into two categories: (1) the obviously glorious, such as the Grand Canyon at sunset when there isn't too much smog from all the cars and recreational vehicles people have been driving to see it; and (2) the less obviously glorious, such as an interstate-dissected and beautiful valley in western Pennsylvania, where you are stuck in bumper-to-bumper traffic, where you get out of the car and walk around and talk with all the other people out of their cars, where you mingle with people who have driven from as far away as Alaska, and then marvel that you are mingling with people from Alaska while standing on an interstate highway—where, when you finally get to the next exit, you buy a postcard showing a nearby canyon that is Pennsylvania's lesser-known but also beautiful Grand Canyon, which you never would have guessed was there. I feel as if the kids have seen America almost subconsciously. Trying to understand America while driving across it is like trying to understand a language by playing tape recordings of the language under your pillow while you sleep. The next day, you hear the language and perhaps think you understand it even though you don't.

OFF AGAIN

SO WE GET THE COFFEE and some pastries in downtown Portland, and we're off again, on the road at last.

We take a local side street, named for a member of one of the founding families of Portland, which leads us to a busier local street, likewise named, which in turn leads us onto the interstate highway that separates one part of the city from the rest of the city and that was built on an old historic district that only now people wish hadn't been demolished—a trait of interstate highways around the country. And then we are on that very same highway as it becomes a bridge, a huge bridge with one four-lane deck built directly beneath another four-lane deck carrying traffic the other way, the Fremont Bridge, a bridge named for an American explorer. From high atop the graceful crisscross of interstates and interstate ramps we see the Willamette River, the Columbia, and the Cascade Mountains ahead—the West!

And in the car, I am—like a tour director nobody paid for, like a tour guide nobody can stop, like a human roadside plaque—going on and on about those famous first cross-country travelers, Lewis and Clark, just two among a long line of people I mention. I wish I could control myself; my explications worry me, to some extent. Yes, you, the reader, can put this book down and walk away for a few minutes or even forever, but my family is, at least for a few country-crossing days, stuck with me, trapped.

I try to accommodate them by sometimes not talking, or at least switching topics every day, for the part of me that's not worried thinks the history of cross-country travel is significant, of interest, even. So fear not: When I'm done with Lewis and Clark, not that I am ever done, there are people like the copper kings in Montana for me to rattle on about, not to mention Carl Fisher, the man behind the first cross-country highway, and Emily Post, who, as it happens, was among the first to get in a car and drive across the country. There are the great motel builders of the fifties or the beat poets or the planners who planned the highways and the planners who did not get a chance to. On the other hand, Lewis and Clark were first to cross the country in the nation's popular imagination, and they continue to cross the country today, in the roadside signage and imagery that you run into when you start out with that first cup of coffee in your hand on a day like today.

And even though they were not really the first, even though lots of people had gone before Lewis and Clark when they pushed off in the Missouri River in Saint Louis and headed out to Oregon, Lewis wrote of feeling singular. I, however, feel like one of millions who have crossed America, who cross it every day. Clark was worried about wilderness, about running out of supplies, about Native American populations that he considered very foreign and unknown, while I am worried about the opposite—about being surrounded by people just like me, people in cars, maybe driving a few miles or even a few blocks, maybe driving really fast or angrily. Here in traffic on the bridge over Portland or in traffic even in the middle of the Texas Panhandle or on a stretch of highway in Oklahoma that seems far from anything but turns out to be kind of close to Tulsa, I am worried about civilization, about getting hit by a truck, for instance, especially near Chicago.

And whereas Lewis was often out in the fields alongside his expeditionary team, looking for flora and fauna undiscovered by the scientists cheering him on back east, I'm on the lookout for things we have already seen, for things everyone has already seen, like rest stops.

Yes, rather than feeling like an explorer, I feel like a guy who has seen his family packed in a car, and even a rental car, dozens of times, and thus I feel anxious, imagining all that could go wrong, remembering all that has gone wrong in the past. At the same time, I somehow still feel really good, as if we *were* heading out for the very first time. That is what the road and a full cup of coffee in your hand on the road in the morning will do to you.

A FEW LOGISTICAL DETAILS

I SUPPOSE SOME OF THE PRETRIP logistical details made me feel a *little* like an explorer. I had to think about the car, for instance. I, for one, have never had good luck with cars. Fortunately, my wife has had at least some good luck. When I met her, she had already successfully cross-countryed several times in a 1988 Subaru wagon, the first car we cross-countryed in as a team. For a few years, we crossed the country in a 1992 Toyota Camry; my wife arranged for that car, a car that I could not become emotionally attached to but that nonetheless did the three-thousand-mile job when our children were really young. The car that I was instrumental in procuring was a 1989 Volvo wagon, eleven years old when I paid the guy too much for it. After I negotiated the (bad) deal, my wife picked up the car with our son and they pulled into traffic and the headlights and interior lights began blinking and the horn began honking and it stopped, less than a mile from the guy who had my check. Somehow, we drove across the country in it a few days later. The Volvo always seemed reluctant to make the trip or continue the trip, and yet for some reason I felt good about that car, and eventually became closer and closer to it as it lost its functions, one by one.

Just before we were about to set out this time, on the trip that brought us west to Oregon, I took the Volvo to a garage in our East Coast village to see if they thought it would survive the trip, given that it already had 250,000 miles on it. That garage is a great garage: they make the car work; they don't charge me a lot; in fact, I get to hang out with the father and two sons who run it. In a weird way, I sometimes look forward to breaking down. I asked Harry, the oldest son, to consider whether the car could make it across the country. After spending the day with the car, after checking the engine and everything else, Harry suggested what he considered the most sane course of action. "Look," he said, "you drive it cross country, and if the thing dies on you, then you walk away from it. What do you have to lose?"

With these words ringing in my head, I debated. I went to sleep and had dreams with images resembling the crudely videotaped rescue footage you see on television news, a helicopter lifting a family from a car in a river under a bridge, scored with the refrain, *What do you have to lose?*

I talked to my wife. "I'm leaving this decision up to you," she said, which I translated to mean, "Rent a car."

I decided to rent a car.

Harry was crestfallen. "You're not gonna take the Volvo?" he said. He had, it turns out, driven across the country as a kid with his father and brother, both of whom proceeded to gather in the parts' storage area and recount details of that trip. People remember their cross-country trips; emotionally speaking, crossing the country is a big deal.

The point being that we'd gotten to Oregon from New York state in a rental, an Impala.

I would eventually be pleased that we had rented the Impala, especially on the day when we were driving through Colorado Springs and the interstate was flooded; our old Volvo wagon had holes in the undercarriage and the wipers were mostly for show, and on the day we drove through Colorado Springs, we moved slowly through highway flooding that would have been straight out of the Old Testament if the Old Testament had interstates. Meanwhile, the Christian radio stations, so prevelant in Colorado Springs, played harsh (to me) rock and roll that mentioned Christ a lot, not in the context of a curse, causing me to think the rain was maybe a sign, a message from the heavens regarding my decision to rent a car.

But on the morning of the day I picked up the rental, I was mostly worried about the reception the Impala would receive from the rest of the expeditionary team.

My son, who is thirteen, tested the car first. Already impressed by its fuel efficiency, compared with that of our dying car, he reclined in the back seat and gave it the thumbs-up. "Yes," he said, in a positive manner that indicated to me our genetic and gender similarities. Our daughter was likewise pleased. "I *like* this car, Dad," she said, sweetly.

I also went to the camping store and bought a specially designed, technologically advanced pack for the top of the car. I wanted to buy tons of stuff, as I often do when I am going somewhere. But the pack was very expensive—so expensive, in fact, that when I pointed it out to my wife, I said as much. "If you think we need it, then you should get it," she said. A portion of my husband brain wanted her to say the wrong thing so that I would be liberated, unchained, free to explain to her how her shortsightedness and concern for mere money were about to jeopardize the trip. I commented on the price again but she remained strong.

"I'm telling you," she said when I tried to change her mind, "if you think we need it, then you should get it."

I was assured by the sales staff at the camping supply store that the pack would fit on our rooftop-rackless rental car. Indeed, I bought extra attachments so that it would. It didn't, naturally, and after the first day that it rained, the pack was full of water and I had to rearrange our gear, so that we ended up with a lot more stuff in the car. We went one of the long ways across the country—New York to New Jersey to Pennsylvania, and then through West Virginia for a second and then into Ohio and Indiana and Missouri, followed by Oklahoma, Texas, New Mexico, Colorado and Wyoming, and Utah and Idaho, and finally, into Oregon—and the pack that did not fit correctly on the car began to shred by the time we got to Wyoming. I had to jury-rig it—add extra straps, duct tape, and so forth—just to keep it from flying off, which meant that during the rainstorm in Colorado that I mentioned above, water poured into the car and all over the by-then-irate passengers. It was a little bit of a nightmare.

In addition to the pack, I also bought a fancy compass to mount on our dashboard.

The compass fell off the dashboard about two hours into the trip, in Pennsylvania.

THE NEEDS OF MOTORISTS TRAVELING TODAY'S HIGHWAYS

AS FAR AS DIRECTIONS GO, we did what we have often done—we went to the Automobile Association of America and got a TripTik®. A TripTik is a nine-inch-long-by-four-and-a-quarter-inch-wide flip-top-notebook-like succession of maps that AAA calls "the backbone of your travel package." According to the information on the TripTik that describes the TripTik itself: "The detailed, informative strip maps meet the needs of motorists traveling today's highways." You might think that experienced cross-country travelers wouldn't need a TripTik. On the contrary, the more experienced the travelers, the more information required—precise whereabouts of motels and gas stations so that, if you are out of gas and in between Fargo and Moorehead and not going to make Saint Paul, Minnesota, then you know all your options vis-à-vis price, continental breakfast offerings, and, on occasions when your younger travelers are so desirous, pools. To get our personalized TripTik, which we did when we were in the East, before we crossed the country, we took a train to Grand Central Station, in New York City, to a subway to Columbus Circle—the statue of Columbus watching us as I pointed up Broadway.

"I'm pretty sure it's this way," I said.

"This is why I hate going places with you," my wife said.

We found AAA on the second floor of a small building, and took a number, and sat in the waiting area, where our daughter looked at brochures for cruises to the Caribbean. Our number was called, and we were summoned to the back of the office, to a desk in a row of desks where we would meet what AAA refers to as a travel counselor. Our travel counselor was the person who would put together our TripTik, page by page, one hundred or so miles at a time. "The entire package is tailored to the specific needs of your trip," the TripTik itself says. We felt a little sheepish about asking for a cross-country, round-trip TripTik, as it is pretty much the largest, most time-consuming TripTik. Then, to make matters a little more uncomfortable, we realized that our travel counselor had been about to take off for his break at the moment we were suddenly assigned to him. Over the years, we have come to expect a certain amount of shock from travel counselors when we tell them that we are driving across the entire country; it's like going into a deli and ordering lunch for three hundred. Thus, we greeted this travel counselor as cordially and delicately as we could.

"So where are you going?" he asked us.

"Well," I said, "we're going across the country."

He exhaled. "Well," he said, "there goes my break!" He spun his chair around, and with great dexterity pulled out a map of the United States from his many slots of maps and brochures, and quickly spread it smoothly out on his desk.

Then I mentioned to him that we were driving back as well. He exhaled again. "OK," he said, "how do you want to go?"

We described our route, and as we did, his yellow highlighting pen made its way across the map. As he came to cities and towns, he looked up once in a while to make little jokes and sing snippets of songs; he was getting into it. He gave our daughter a pen shaped like palm tree that advertised a hotel in Florida. When we asked him if he had been to the hotel, he said he didn't travel, just commuted daily from the other side of the Hudson River, in New Jersey. Like most travel counselors I have been counseled by, he was an expert on highways and directions in the abstract. After he had our route, he went away to gather the individual map pages of the TripTik—each rectangular map of a page deliciously detailed with gas station possibilities, with information regarding scenery and rest stops and food and lodging and bail bonds (in case the accident is your or your driving partner's fault, or in case you and your driving partner are Bonnie and Clyde, I suppose), with details about state speed limits and child restraints and studded tires, with teeny snippets of history on the back.

As we waited, we overheard the people in the desks around us planning trips with their travel counselors—trips to the Grand Canyon, to Pennsylvania on a motorcycle, to Canada. Our travel counselor returned and, first, stamped little green arrows on each page of each TripTik. The arrows were to tell us which direction to drive in, and they pointed straight ahead alongside the interstates in the TripTik, which ended up looking like this:

Second, he proceeded to calculate our round-trip mileage. It took him a long time to do so, and as he worked on it, I kept telling him that he didn't have to worry about calculating the total mileage. But he insisted. There was no stopping him by now; he had a kind of preparatory cross-country momentum. Finally, he filled out the blanks on the back of each TripTik: 3,647 to Oregon and 2,900 to get back. As he passed them to us, he was beaming. On the TripTik that would take us to Oregon, he also wrote, "To Oregon." On the TripTik that would bring us back east—the very TripTik that I have in my hands now as we drive off from Portland—he wrote, "Home James!" (I only found out later that the saying was from a 1923 song sung by Fred Hillebrand, "Home James, and Don't Spare the Horses.")

We thanked our travel counselor. He wished us well, and we felt ready, prepared for our adventure, our trip into the sort-of-known unknown. We stopped at the front desk for a few more maps and more guidebooks full of places to stay and see and eat in every state. On our way out of the building, we ran into our travel counselor in the stairwell. He didn't seem to recognize us and he looked exhausted.

REALLY OFF

ON THE BRIDGE OVER PORTLAND, packed in the Impala, with our Trip-Tik opened to the first page, with its stamped, east-pointing arrow, we saw, as I say, the mountains, a preview of the day's scenery. We saw the glacier-covered peaks of the Cascades, the awe-inspiring mountain range noted, of course, by the native people who traded with the early British sailors who subsequently renamed the peaks after themselves, so that, in 1792, W'y'east, was renamed Mount Hood, for Lord Samuel Hood, by William Robert Broughton, who, in his book *Voyage of Discovery*, wrote: "A very distant high snowy mountain now appeared rising beautifully conspicuous in the midst of an extensive tract of low, or moderately elevated, land." Which is what we see today, as we cross over the Willamette River, which Lewis incorrectly assumed to be a river that connected the rivers west of the Rocky Mountains with the Pacific Ocean. We see the beautifully conspicuous mountain. I like to say it aloud: *beautifully conspicuous*!

Of course, I mention some if not all of this to the expeditionary team in the Impala—which brings up the final introductory point, a point I should emphasize in case it is not yet absolutely clear: never go on a cross-country trip with me, for I can't stop rattling on about what I assume or even imagine to be the significance of things, whether things are significant or not, whether the kids want to hear about it or want to sleep or read *Little House on the Prairie* or *Rolling Stone* or just want to relax.

PART II

Portland, Oregon, to Missoula, Montana

OFF IN THE GREAT PACIFIC NORTHWEST

JOY FILLS THE CAR on a day that is alternately sunny, cloudy, and drizzly on Interstate 84. Happiness abounds in the back seat, which may be an overstatement because what I mean is no one is fighting. Yes, we are a little behind schedule, leaving a little later than I'd hoped. Yes, I had a lot of trouble adjusting the expensive cartop pack. Yes, I bought a lot of expensive extra straps to strap it down with and so forth. Yes, we ought to be bored already or blasé, at the very least, given that we have crossed the country so many times, given that we just drove across the country a couple of weeks ago and are now, as I have stated, on our way home. But we are excited to be beginning, to be setting out, to be cruising alongside the Columbia River, the River of the West, and about to enter an area that our AAA map describes as picturesque ("an outstanding scenic route"). And then there is music playing in the car, the first CD choice of the many CD and radio choices. The music is not the historically appropriate fiddle music I have on hand to match what I have in my head as the theme for this first day of five days crossing the country—i.e., the Lewis and Clark expedition; the music is pop music, chosen by my son, but yes, the music is good and everybody likes it, including me, and the musician, a guy named Rufus Wainwright, is, I have learned, the son of a French Canadian folk singer, and Cruzatte, the fiddler on the Lewis and Clark expedition, was French Canadian, so that works for me, that's fine. Cross-country driving joy!

We're out of Portland, the last big city for 2,000 miles: it's 434 miles to Boise or 800 miles to Salt Lake City or 1,291 miles to Denver or 1,700 miles to Omaha or 1,700 miles to Saint Paul, Minnesota, a place we are headed. We're on the edge of the city and the beginning of the country—or what stands for country, these days—when we see our first cross-country-specific facility, the Flying J Travel Plaza. In the language of the interstate, the travel plaza is sometimes called the truck stop, the truck plaza, or the travel oasis; the word *truck* is gradually falling away as more truck stops have become eager to sell to truckers and nontruckers alike, as the interests and needs of truck drivers and non-truck drivers have begun to overlap: Books on Tape, cell phone equipment, little mirrors that help you see a car coming especially if you are in a large, trucklike car. I have never stopped at this particular travel plaza, it being so close to my destination or departure point, depending, but I can say that when I first drove west, when I first passed it, fifteen years before, it was a lonely outpost of automotive convenience. Now it is so crowded by restaurants and chain stores that it's difficult to distinguish between long-distance cross-country travelers and shoppers headed to the store for groceries: Sherri's 24-Hour Restaurant, an RVs-for-sale lot with rows of giant recreational vehicles, a Conoco, a Taco Bell, a Holiday Inn Express, a Wendy's.

It is a veil of commerce marking the separation between worlds, or the nonseparation, for this travel plaza and car-minded environs are the last retail outpost before the scenic area—the Columbia River Gorge National Scenic Area, in fact—where, by law, no travel plaza can exist.

And as we see the gorge, scenic in signage and on maps and *actually* scenic in plain view as well—its skyscraper-tall walls of red basalt run through by the Columbia River, a wide, flat, gray, watery parallel to the gray, flat interstate that races alongside of it—we see the results of that one day, millions of years ago, when a rush of water that was like something described in a myth flowed through the broken ice dam that formed Lake Missoula, a state-sized pool of water that swept through the Columbia's little valley and blew it out, made a gorge. And as soon as we see the gorge, at the moment we are able to look into its miles-away infinity, in the same orgiastic Acadian scenery, we spot that most ubiquitous of Great Pacific Northwest road signs—the sign that marks the beginning of what I shall call our Lewis and Clark leg.

MY PLANS REGARDING LEWIS AND CLARK

IT IS WITH ONLY THE MOST Herculean effort that the highway traveler traveling through the Great Pacific Northwest avoids the thought of either Lewis or Clark. The foreigner, first arriving in Oregon, Washington, Idaho, Montana, North Dakota, and South Dakota, even in Iowa, Missouri, and certain parts of Illinois, could be forgiven if he or she supposed that Lewis and Clark were contemporary elected officials or some ancient and still-worshipped rulers or deities. Lewis and Clark signs are everywhere in the Northwest—specifically the brown road signs that are the size of No Parking signs, each sign decorated with a white-lined drawing of two men, one kneeling, one pointing, one in late-eighteenth-century decorative military plumage, the other in frontier buckskin, both presumably facing west, because westward, in the parlance of the age of the Lewis and Clark generation, is toward empire. In the Great Pacific Northwest, Lewis and Clark signs are as ubiquitous as signs for hospitals—the sign is a brown and white (or sometimes blue and white) icon of history, recreation, commerce, and tourism, even if it doesn't do a great job representing Clark, who was tall and red-haired and gregarious, or Lewis, who was less gregarious, often moody. In my experience, people generally follow the Lewis and Clark trail from Saint Louis to the Oregon coast, where the expedition spent the 1805 to 1806 winter. But it is well known, at least among members of our Impala-driven expedition, that I personally prefer to think about their trip back to Saint Louis, in 1806, when everyone thought they were lost or maybe dead.

And so for this first day of the trip, I proposed—not really seeking any input from the rest of the crew on board the Impala, I understand now—that we follow the Lewis and Clark trail *back* on this return trip home of ours. Aside from that general idea, I had two particular goals. First, I wanted to see a part of the trail they took across the Bitterroot Range of the Rocky Mountains, a piece of the westbound trail that nearly killed them the first winter, when they were lost and without supplies: one of those untouched-seeming Lewis and Clark trails in the middle of the mountains, the kind that you see on television shows or in *National Geographic* photo essays. Second, at the end of this leg of the trip, I wanted to rest our expedition, just as their expedition rested, in the hot springs on the far side of the mountains—in the very spot, just outside of Missoula, where what President Thomas Jefferson called the Corps of Discovery rested and soaked. For them it was a kind of mid-expedition vacation break in the first national cross-country trip. I had this idea that we were going to rest and relax too. We Americans don't just like to read about our history; we like to experience it.

I should point out that while it was by no means the longest day of driving we have ever had in terms of mileage, it felt really, really long due to bad planning on my part and due, also on my part, to a temperament that might be described as Lewis-like, by which I mean moody.

THIS MORNING, AS WE SET OUT, I am very excited, very Lewis and Clark excited, maybe *too* Lewis and Clark excited.

If I had been paying better attention, I would have noticed that everyone in the car is already excited, as much by the Lewis and Clark leg as by the usual cross-country adventure. But foolishly, in order to rouse even more excitement in my party, I encourage our son to read aloud from the journals of Lewis and Clark. By "encourage" I mean I pass into the back seat an abridged version of the journals that I just happened to have on hand and interrupt his own reading. Accordingly, he appeases me and reads as follows: "In this bath which had been prepared by the Indians by stop[p]ing the run with stone and gravel, I bathed and remained in 19 minutes, it was with difficulty I could remain thus long and it caused a profuse sweat . . ."

As it turns out, the boiling aspect of the springs does not appeal to my daughter, and my son expresses a kind of aesthetic/hygienic reluctance.

"I don't want to go anywhere Lewis and Clark were naked," he says. "The thought of their wrinkling skin . . ."

"Gross," my daughter says.

My wife looks over at me. "*You* can go in the hot spring," she says.

A PROBLEM I HAVE WITH THE LEWIS
AND CLARK SIGN

A PROBLEM I HAVE WITH THE Lewis and Clark sign is that, in my opinion, it is misleading, or at least poorly executed. A better roadside marker, while impractical, would include the entire thirty-five- to forty-five-member expeditionary team, making for a huge, billboard-sized, *Last Supper*–like symbol that would depict the women and children and slaves and cabinetmakers and cooks and mapmakers who were either on the trip (Sacagawea and her son, Jean-Baptiste, nicknamed Pompey, and York, Clark's slave, for instance) or involved in supplying, teaching, and feeding those that were (a lot of people in Saint Louis, Philadelphia, and even Pittsburgh). Donald Jackson, the exploration historian, has written, "It is no longer useful to think of the Lewis and Clark Expedition as the personal story of two men. Their story was an enterprise of many aims and a product of many minds."

At the very least Thomas Jefferson ought to be on the sign. Jefferson is the founding father of cross-country travel: he worked for years to set up the Lewis and Clark expedition. In 1783, while serving in the Continental Congress, he attempted in vain to persuade General George Rogers Clark, William Clark's older brother and a Revolutionary War hero, to explore the upper reaches of the Missouri. In 1785, as ambassador to France, Jefferson backed John Ledyard, an explorer who attempted to travel the North American continent in the reverse order of everyone else at the time; he planned to travel first across Europe and then Siberia, but after getting almost all the way across Russia, he was arrested with five hundred miles to go and deported. He then went to Egypt to explore instead, where he was waylaid again and died taking something to ease his upset stomach—he vomited so violently that he burst a blood vessel. In 1793, as secretary of state, Jefferson asked André Michaux, a famous French naturalist, to find "the shortest & most convenient route of communication between the U.S. and the Pacific." Michaux got as far as Kentucky, stopping at the Appalachians, America's first mountain bounder, the great coast-long chain of hills that is still a few days ahead of our rental car.

When Jefferson finally sent Lewis and Clark, he did so in something of a panic. He saw the North American continent as being up for grabs, and he was desperate to beat the British up the Missouri. He was on a summer vacation at Monticello when his New York bookseller sent him *Voyages from Montreal* for summer reading. The book was an account of Alexander Mackenzie's trip from Montreal to the Pacific between 1792 and 1793, in which Mackenzie portrayed a cross-country route as the key to establishing British interests in the Northwest. Jefferson sent a secret message to Congress requesting the funds for a mission to cross the continent. In 1803, he chose Meriwether Lewis, a young man who had been Jefferson's neighbor in Virginia and whom Jefferson himself had trained as a surveyor and brought to Washington, D.C., as his personal secretary. He sent him to Philadelphia, to the Philosophical Society, to train with the most renowned scientific minds in the United States. Jefferson groomed Lewis as the first modern American transcontinentalist.

THE WEST THAT JEFFERSON
THOUGHT HE SAW

WE, BOTH AS TRAVELERS and as citizens, are today accustomed to taking for granted the map of America. We see it as that thing in cellular phone advertisements, that chart illustrating election results, that colorful collection of states on classroom walls. But Thomas Jefferson had to imagine that map. When Jefferson imagined the West, he saw Virginia, or a really big Virginia, a state he loved, a state he saw as a successful noble experiment. "For him, Virginia was another way to say America," historian James Ronda has written. Like many easterners do today, Jefferson idealized the East's gentle-sloped mountain ranges, cut through with navigable passes—"not scattered confusedly over the face of the country," Jefferson wrote in *Notes on the State of Virginia*, his only book. In the East, nature seemed balanced, and nature *was* balance. Jefferson imagined that the mountains Lewis and Clark would discover on the other side of the Mississippi would mirror those on the Virginia side. Like many naturalists, Jefferson considered it very possible that the West would be like the East but *more*, that the West would be an eastern landscape enlarged or engorged with the vitality of nature. "Each step which one takes from East to West," wrote Louis Vilemont, a respected French naturalist of the day, "the size of all objects increases ten-fold in volume . . . The products which one discovers there in proportion as one goes into the interior are more majestic, more beautiful than elsewhere."

Jefferson's thinking about the West also had a lot to do with rivers. Control of streams meant control of the continent and all its commercial possibilities; the rivers were the first superhighways, quicker by far than the scratched-out mountain paths, the dirt river roads, and country traces. "Whoever takes control of the Ohio and the Lakes will become the sole and absolute lord of America," wrote James Maury, a tutor to the young Thomas Jefferson. As the country moved west, Jefferson put his money on the Missouri. "The Missouri is the principal river, contributing to the common stream more than does the Mississippi," he wrote.

JEFFERSON MADE CERTAIN that Lewis and Clark had the best maps of the West available at the time, but the best maps of the West at the time had big gaps about where the West was, precisely the place where Lewis and Clark were headed. Samuel Lewis's 1804 map titled "Louisiana" shows numerous rivers west of the Mississippi, and then a chain of very unformidable-looking mountains, and then a river heading right to the Pacific—the nineteenth-century relative of the fifteenth-century passage to India, the continent-crossing stream that for centuries *had* to be there even though it wasn't. (As early as the 1600s, Richard Hakluyt, a geographer working with the expedition that would end up at Jamestown, Virginia, predicted the existence of a lake just west of the coast of Virginia: "It was Like Enough that Out of the same Lake you shall find Some Spring which run the Contrary way toward the East India Sea.") The map that Lewis and Clark most heavily relied on was drawn by Nicholas King in 1803. It shows several dotted-line rivers marked "conjectural" and hints that the hike from the Missouri to the Columbia River is a quick trip, maybe a day or two. What was actually there were mountains, hundreds of miles thick, with snow and ice, and rivers that were too angry to accept canoes, much less the giant keelboat that the expedition was forced to abandon at the Great Falls in Montana. The first cross-country expedition nearly died in the never-conjectured range now called the Bitterroot Mountains. Significantly, the Bitterroots are the home of our destination, the Lolo Hot Springs, and are the mountains I hope to cross today, or at least this evening.

THE GORGE I IMAGINED

AT THIS JUNCTURE in our first cross-country day, it's worth pointing out that I know what that's like—imagining something before you see it. I know that especially when it comes to the Columbia Gorge, which is where we are now, which is where Lewis and Clark once were. This is a point I am again emphasizing as I push the Lewis and Clark journals once more on the now-reluctant team members in our car by asking questions that I pretend are carefree but that I see now are pretty obnoxious—questions such as "Hey, who wants to read from the Lewis and Clark journals this time?"

The response is silence, except for the car stereo, which is cranked.

Oh, what hopes I still held for the trip in general as a purely positive experience and for the Lewis and Clark leg specifically!

I ask more leading questions regarding journal reading to no avail, so at mile 40 we do not hear this entry for April 9, 1806, apropos as it is to our trip on this first day: "The hills [that] have now become mountains high on each side are rocky and steep and covered generally with fir and white cedar."

Nor do we hear this one: "We passed several beautiful cascades which fell from a great hight over the stupendious rocks which closes the river on both sides nearly."

The beautiful cascades are evident to us too. The thin white ribbons still drape the green and reddish brown cliff walls at Bridal Veil Falls, Latourelle Falls, and then on the left, Rooster Rock, originally called Cock Rock, about which the dictionary *Oregon Geographic Names* tastefully states: "The name is of phallic significance." Lewis and Clark would have passed Rooster Rock both coming and going. It is a tall basalt formation that more recently marked the site of a nudist beach—as I am only three dozen or so miles from Portland, I am still within the zone of intimate, off-the-road knowledge, not that I am saying I've ever been naked or anything.

And at last, with the wide, gray Columbia still on our left and the sun fighting valiantly to break through the muttony-hill-clinging clouds, we see Multnomah Falls. The journals mention Multnomah as "the most remarkable of these cascades." Lewis describes "a perfect mist."

AT MULTNOMAH FALLS WE STOP. Yes, as crazy as it seems here at the beginning when we have plenty of food and fuel and no one is calling for the rest room, we halt the cross-country trip. We do this even though, as I mentioned, we were late in starting, and the thought that we will not be able to accomplish our two simple-seeming goals is already in my brain like a lot of little worms in the wood of a ship's hull.

We take a treacherous left-side-of-the-interstate exit and park briefly in the rest stop parking lot adjacent to Multnomah Falls, the most popular tourist destination in the state of Oregon, due to the fact that it is beautiful and on the side of an interstate highway. We don't pass through the pedestrian tunnel that takes rest stop parkers to the falls and the Multnomah Falls Lodge, where lunch is reported to be served to more than two million people a year. Instead, we stand next to the car, the falls behind us, my wife and

I standing together at my insistence. We turn and face a camera and our son.

FOR THERE IS A FALLS-RELATED STORY that is our marriage's national epic, and we need a picture.

I was young. I had a full head of hair, hair that flowed like a remarkable cascade, or at least flowed. I was at my desk in New York City, where I worked for a travel magazine, though I never actually traveled. It was 1988, on a particular day when I was reading about the interstate highway system, believe it or not, reading about its length and breadth, imagining its extent, imagining what the rest of America looked like or felt like.

And I was reading about a beautiful roadside waterfall, falling 620 feet from the top of a gorge down into a little stream that, as you see when you finally get there, runs beneath the interstate and into the Columbia River. I recall thinking that this might be a good place, a truly beautiful waterfall, not that I, having spent my life in the New York City environs, would know much about giant waterfalls. I had this feeling of calm and promise, which made me do what I perhaps did too much at that particular job, which was get up from my desk and head outside, into the great and wondrous canyons of Midtown Manhattan, for a breather.

Thus, I entered into the elevator, where I gazed upon a woman, a woman who, I learned as we began to speak, had just arrived in New York, after a cross-country trip from Oregon, and who was on that very day wearing a belt that was beaded, a belt with beads that spelled MULTNOMAH FALLS.

"CAN YOU GET US TOO?" I say to our son, as he electronically captures an image of the falls on the other side of the highway, as my wife and I pose together beside the car, as our daughter giggles, as the cameraman smiles.

"Sorry, Dad," he says, while rolling his eyes, in a voice that also rolls its eyes—because that's what he *was* doing, getting us both in, which I would have known if I had been paying attention. His patience, by the way, is like his mother's, solid, practiced, Clark-ian.

In the picture, I am hugging my wife, something I tend not to do in public, certainly not on a highway, but it's one of those times when you have to hug your wife, your body leaves you no choice.

"OK, let's get back in the car," I say next.

In the picture, I am smiling and my wife is smiling and we are only a little sheepish, a little embarrassed, part of the reason our kids are inspired to ask questions relevant to my first encounter with my wife's Multnomah Falls belt, even while I am attempting again to focus on the Lewis and Clark theme, even as we stand just a few yards from a Lewis and Clark sign, the two leaders forever crossing the country, forever pressing on in roadside iconography.

"My friend I do assure you that no man lives whith whome I would prefur to undertake Such a Trip," Clark wrote to Lewis, and that's pretty much how I feel about my wife.

THE NOISE

WE'RE BACK ON I-84, courtesy of the awkward, if not incredibly dangerous, from-the-left-side-of-the-highway entrance ramp, a ramp that caused me to go from a moment of blissful remembrance to a fight to the death with a giant two-trailor truck that doesn't want to slow down or doesn't want to bother with changing lanes or wants to see us die in a fiery plume. I floor the Impala, get the speed up to 65, the speed limit, and enough to pass the truck. And then comes the noise, a big loud flapping noise that I can't figure out at first. The wheels? The road? No, it is the specially designed, expensive cartop pack with the new straps. The expensive cartop pack has begun to flap violently in the wind.

THE ARCH

PLEASE DON'T THINK, BY THE WAY, that our cross-country team has not explored Lewis and Clark's way out west. We have. I have a coffee mug in the car to prove it—purchased at the gift shop in the Museum of Westward Expansion, at the bottom of the Gateway Arch, also known as the Saint Louis arch. We visited the arch on an earlier cross-country trip. It was the summer. We had driven in from Indiana. We didn't really know where in Saint Louis the arch was. We just headed for downtown, thinking we couldn't miss it, which was true. We had trouble parking along the Mississippi River in front of the arch. A security guy drove around in a golf cart, stopping first to send e-mails on his hand-held computer and second to confuse people, with a disgruntled Zen patience.

"Will they ticket if we park here?"

"They gave five hundred tickets yesterday."

"Will they tow?"

"They towed yesterday."

We submitted to the long security-check line to enter the arch—I read carefully the extensive list of particular types of guns and knives not allowed in the arch—and toured the Museum of Westward Expansion. As the National Park Service notes, "Through our exciting exhibits, you can explore the world of the American Indians and the 19th century pioneers who helped shape the history of the American West." We skipped the Odyssey Theatre, where we could have seen a National Geographic film celebrating Lewis and Clark, and instead looked at relics of old Saint Louis, a Sioux war bonnet, a covered wagon, old western farming tools, tools of buffalo hunters and miners. Quotes decorating the exhibit that I put in my journal were from western landscape painter Thomas Moran ("My aim was to bring before the Public the character of the region"), from an unnamed U.S. government official ("The Consequences of the cession of Louisiana will extend to the most distant posterity"), and from an Indian leader ("What! Sell land! As well sell air and water. The Great Spirit gave in common to all, the air to breathe, the water to drink, and the land to live upon"). I had the feeling of walking through the aftermath of a big long raucous party, a party that was good for some people and not so good for others but a lot of work either way. Then we went outside and looked up at the beautiful arch, the incredible 630-foot-high stainless steel ribbon that, I have to say, was a lot more exciting than I thought it was going to be.

"The arch is amazing," I announced repeatedly.

"I know," various members of my family responded comfortingly.

AFTER GAZING AT THE ARCH, we got back in the car and drove to nearby Saint Charles, the very spot where Lewis and Clark had launched their expedition. We ate lunch at a place called Lewis and Clark's: An American Restaurant and Public House.

I chose the restaurant.

It was another one of those situations where I thought I was reading everyone correctly but wasn't, to put it mildly—sometimes an entire trip across the country can be a misreading.

The décor at Lewis and Clark's included tropical fish and a painting of a woman at sea and lots of sports memorabilia; it was not very Lewis and Clark–y. We climbed to the third floor, to a porch overlooking the Missouri, the great wide river's smooth brownness tickled with the raindrops beginning to fall. We looked at the menu. "Well, does this look OK?" I asked, at which point everybody else said nothing, my first clue I was blowing it. (Or was it when they said they didn't want to go there?)

I asked everyone to imagine Lewis and Clark taking off from that very spot, a thought that gave *me* some satisfaction, anyway. That was the last of the satisfaction, though, as I attempted to enjoy my tuna melt while everyone else barely touched what they hadn't wanted: my son's cheese quesadilla, my daughter's soup and salad, and, for my wife, a salad that included a lot of different foods that would not normally come under the heading of "salad" and not much in the way of anything green. I began to get upset and was thinking that the food at this restaurant was a lot better than eating dog, which Lewis and Clark had to eat, but historical references don't always help.

Next, we began to hear the people at the adjacent table go on and on to the waitress about a place called Tubby's.

"*I* was over at Tubby's," the man across from me was saying.

"Tubby's was *great*," another man said.

"Yeah, *Tubby's*," the waitress said, nodding.

The mood of our expedition was, like the sky that afternoon, dreary after we left Lewis and Clark's and drove on Interstate 44 in Missouri. First, we saw a roadside marker that said the interstate was named the Trail of Tears, in honor of the Native Americans who were forced by the U.S. government onto a reservation in Oklahoma, and then we saw another roadside sign that said the interstate was named for Payne Stewart, the professional golfer and Missouri native who died when his chartered Learjet crashed. There were giant road signs with the words ADULT and EROTIC on one side of the highway and GOD and JESUS on the other. That night, we stopped at an old motel along old Route 66, where during the evening, when I was still feeling the effects of having screwed up, I heard something scratching, scratching at the door—a raccoon, a dog, a raccoon-sized rat, or some dog-sized ghost of Route 66, or my anxiety over the previous day.

In the morning, everyone was happier after doughnuts and coffee. I sat in the room for a while and watched a cable television program produced by the Missouri Department of Transportation, a show that featured security-camera-like views of local roads—each road view captioned and speaking to me, the noncommuter, the driver with the commute of all commutes, the continental round-trip. An example:

View To West Sunshine

EVEN THOUGH IT'S AMAZING, WE SHOULDN'T HAVE STOPPED IN THE GORGE

OUR DAUGHTER IS ASLEEP ALREADY. In lieu of reading page after page of the Lewis and Clark journals, her brother, awake, is happily recalling a cross-country trip when he was a toddler and, as he was told once by us, he would burp and excuse himself over and over and over, transmuting from polite to irritating, a test of our cross-country sanity. The gravelly top of Wind Mountain on our left-hand side is lost in a cloud, but the sun is beginning to beat back the perfect mists. At mile 52.6, we pass a logging truck that is stacked with former scenery. In the river a barge that is also full of logs floats downstream.

How amazed I am by the gorge for so many reasons, even though I have seen it so many times! How amazed Lewis and Clark must have been for some similar reasons, especially being, like me, originally from the East—the journal uses words like *beautiful* and *remarkable* and *stupendious*, leading me to think: they must have been blown away!

Also, how I kind of wish we had not stopped at that last rest stop given that we are behind schedule!

Both times coming through the gorge, headed west and headed east, Lewis and Clark were on strict schedules. On the way out, they were worried about getting to the Pacific quickly: they were running out of food, their clothes were rotting, winter was coming. On the way back, they were racing to cross the Bitterroots in Montana as soon as the spring melt came; they wanted to make it down the Missouri quickly so they wouldn't have to spend a thirty-six-degree-below winter on the Great Plains like they did during their first year out, in 1804. They were fed up with living on the Oregon coast after a long, wet winter; they did not get along well with the Clatsop tribe and maybe vice versa. They were tired of eating dog, not being crazy for fish—the tribes referred to the Lewis and Clark expedition as the Dog Eaters. They were low on gifts for the tribes they met, and they weren't doing a good job selling gifts they had. And then, like us, or indeed like anybody on the return leg of a long, long trip, they were anxious to get back, anxious to get off the road.

And yet, all trip scheduling aside, I personally feel that the Discovery Expedition must have felt good coming through the Columbia Gorge. I say this because, first, they were on the road home and, second, because the Columbia Gorge is unlike anything that people who grew up in range of the old East Coast mountains have ever seen, a great blue river in a giant geologic cut—inspiring.

THROUGH THE GORGE

THE GORGE THAT THOSE OF US who are awake see today is a gorge run through by a flat, lakelike Columbia, a fake Columbia, or at least a Columbia reconfigured by human engineering. The Columbia that Lewis and Clark paddled up was a raucous, unruly, glacier-fed stream, fueled by runoff from the mountains of Oregon and Washington, Idaho and Montana, of the Selkirks and the Rockies. Dams began to subdue the Columbia in the 1930s—the dams powered the aluminum factories and the airplane factories that built the airplanes that won WWII. The dams irrigated the high-desert farms and steadied the water for barge transport; they powered the first nuclear experiments that led to an area on the Columbia becoming one of the most toxic in the western hemisphere, the Hanford Nuclear Reservation. The dams made the waters calm, an unnatural scenic naturalness. Even with its river damned, the Columbia is beautiful.

At Bonneville Dam, the road signs emphasize the fish hatcheries, built in an attempt to replace the wild salmon thwarted by the dams with not-so-wild fish—the hatcheries are the concrete conscience of the dams.

After a few minutes, the lush green of the gorge begins to fade slowly away, replaced by a dry sandiness in the softening hills. The river narrows in places, squeezing through islands of rocky gray. Call me biased by the fact that my marriage is primordially mixed up with the Columbia Gorge, by the fact that my children have hiked along the little streams that feed what is the Columbia today, but the view from behind the wheel of the Impala makes me feel like an exclamation point. I am hearing the call of the gorge, the gate into our trip cross-country. I am seeing a view that is beautiful and remarkable and stupendious.

"The gorge is so incredible," I am saying regularly—did I mention that I'm a nightmare to travel with?

My wife is simultaneously road-watching and working on the quilt in her lap. Our son is reading cool rock-and-roll magazines, not that he would call them that, not that I understand what *cool* is anymore—explorations passed on to new explorers. Our daughter is still asleep. The road tires her out, something I understand more and more.

We pass U-Hauls, lots of trucks, RVs, an unidentifiable thing on a long, heavy hauling trailer—a big canister with caution markers all over it that makes me wonder how exactly they haul nuclear waste.

We enter the environs of Hood River, a groovy town that we have visited when not crossing the country but will not visit now; it's a capital of windsurfing—the sail-connected surfboards dart back and forth across the river from cliff to cliff, courtesy of the gorge's wind tunnel. We can see the windsurfers now, moving like fluorescent water bugs. At mile 86, a sign says, WIND GUSTS, and I tell our son about the great and powerful winds of the Columbia Gorge, about how, when he was little and we lived in the West, I read a news report about telephone poles being blown over. "Cool," he says, kindly looking up, nodding.

By the time we come to The Dalles (a settlement whose name is thought to derive from the French phrase for the rocks in the rushing waters, or once-rushing waters) the green is nearly gone from the gorge; the soft hills are corduroy-covered, and because The Dalles is a city, we see chains: Buy-Mart and Pacific Pride gasoline and Subway, the sandwich place, all smashed together. We see more Lewis and Clark signs, of course, and another sign along the highway declares that Interstate 84 is momentarily one with the old Oregon

Trail: the paths of the interstates, as we invariably see while crossing the country, lead to the American past. Now, at mile 91.8 we are passing The Dalles Dam Visitor Center, as well as the gargantuan but less well-marked Dalles Dam.

In the river, water races over the dam's spillways; birds circle for dam-numbed fish. Vice president Richard Nixon spoke at the dam's dedication in 1959. The 1.5-mile-long, turbine-equipped slab of highwaylike concrete changed the river behind it into a 23.6-mile-long lake, named after Celilo Falls waterfall, with absolutely no irony, Lake Celilo.

I've got the radio news on now, and as we drive, we hear that this first day on our cross-country trip is, according to the announcer, the anniversary of the first space landing, America's expedition to the moon.

THE RETURN OF LEWIS AND CLARK

AND INDEED, THE CORPS OF DISCOVERY, the very first cross-country expedition sponsored by the U.S. government, was the moon landing of its day, a scientific and military expedition into the unknown. Jefferson armed the Corps of Discovery with guns, but it was the Enlightenment, a time when documented knowledge was the way to stake and claim territory, and the way that Jefferson planned to claim the interior of the North American continent for his new nation was with the journals and maps of Lewis and Clark, with a full accounting. In addition to Lewis and Clark, the three sergeants were ordered to keep journals, and a couple of privates kept journals on their own—it has been called "the most written expedition of all time." They even brought along waterproof journal containers. Jefferson directed that if the Corps should come under attack from a "superior force," then they should run, not so much for the sake of the expedition's members, but for the sake of the journals. "In the loss of yourselves," Jefferson wrote, "we should lose also the information you have acquired."

But please note: in contrast to the television coverage of the landing on the moon, the journals of Lewis and Clark were not published for years—for a hundred years, America never knew they existed.

* * *

FIRST, AS I HAVE MENTIONED, the corps was late in returning. Missouri was a sight for sore eyes, literally. "A very singular disorder is takeing place amongst our party that of the Sore eyes," Clark wrote, during his last days of the trip back, when they saw white settlers' farms from their boats. They shouted for joy at the sight of cows. When they neared Saint Louis, they heard rumors along the river that they had all died. Then, on September 23, 1806, they stepped out of the woods and arrived in Saint Louis. They bought new clothes and went to a ball, where they were toasted. Jefferson wrote Lewis on the Corps' return with what the president described as "unspeakable joy." "The Length of time without hearing of you had begun to be felt awfully," Jefferson said. Clark's last entry in the journals, on September 25, is this: "a fine morning. We commenced wrighting &c."

Only they didn't, apparently. Then again, the journals were not the kind of journals that we perhaps think of when we think of journals today. Clark, for instance, wrote in a field notebook and then copied his field notes into what he called his journal, often changing things, sometimes for clarity, sometimes for public relations reasons, occasionally messing the dates up. Sometimes Clark copied Lewis's notes and changed things around a little, like a kid writing a school paper out of an encyclopedia. (When Lewis wrote, he was writing under the influence of Alexander Mackenzie's *Voyage to Montreal*, even though *Voyage to Montreal* wasn't exactly what it seemed either: Mackenzie had hired a ghostwriter, to impress potential patrons for future explorations.) In other words, there was a good deal of copying and recopying to do, and millions of words of it was done, but by the time Lewis finally returned, he seemed to have gotten out of the swing of the journals.

Lewis had not written in the journals for weeks after he had been accidentally shot in the buttocks by one of the soldiers on the expedition, Pierre Cruzatte, the fiddler who was half Omaha and half French and an excellent fiddler but also blind in one eye.* Then again, Lewis wrote sporadically all through the expedition. When he rode in the keelboat from

---

* In the first few minutes after the shooting, Cruzatte pretended he had not shot his commander, though everyone figured it out. Lewis did not seem to hold it against Cruzatte, despite the fact that Lewis had to lay facedown in the keelboat on the way back down the Missouri, making his triumphant return to the Saint Louis area, as Lewis and Clark scholars often note, with his rear end in the air.

the Ohio River to Saint Louis, he wrote every day. Then he stopped, not commencing to write daily again until the expedition landed at Fort Mandan, in North Dakota. The notion of Lewis not writing confuses many historians. Lewis knew how important journal keeping was to President Jefferson. He himself had purchased the watertight journal carriers. Why didn't he write?

OUR JOURNALS

YES, OF COURSE, we are keeping journals, of a kind. My daughter is drawing pictures and collecting the business cards of restaurants, hotels, and gas stations.

My son is taking a photograph every two hundred miles or so, à la Ed Ruscha, the pop artist who drove around in a van photographing things with a stop-action camera.

My wife picks up fragments of the natural world, branches, bark, and on a previous trip, a tumbleweed that we once strapped to the top of our station wagon in Montana, to the stares of many Montanans.

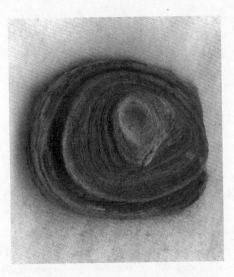

My journal is a journal in the traditional manner of journals, a book with notes, illegible.

THE JOURNALS OF LEWIS AND CLARK FADED AWAY

PEOPLE WHO WERE AROUND two hundred years ago, when the Corps of Discovery returned, might have read the journals of Lewis and Clark if they had had a chance. For a short time, the expedition's cocaptains were heroes. Lewis won appointment as governor of Upper Louisiana, which was just about all the land in the western United States at the time. Clark was put in charge of Indian affairs in the same area. All the members of the expedition were given extra pay and land west of the Mississippi. Meanwhile, President Jefferson was desperate to see the journals in print—this being the Enlightenment, the experiences of the expedition were not knowledge until notes were printed, until diagrams were published, along with drawings, and most important, maps. Lewis published a prospectus, projecting two volumes of narrative and one of scientific aspects; Clark planned to present his map of the unknown West (complete with a conjectured river to California and the Pacific that, it would turn out, did not exist). Lewis found a publisher in Philadelphia. He convinced another publisher not to publish a journal of one of the privates and bought the journals of John Ordway, a sergeant on the expedition. He hired a German naturalist to draw the plants the expedition had brought back. He hired an ornithologist to draw the birds. But, in the words of one eventual editor of the journals, "He seems not to have written a single word of his book."

No one knows why. He went dancing at balls. He sat for his portrait, ran errands for Jefferson, and watched as Patrick Gass, the expedition's carpenter, published his ghostwritten account, titled *Journal of the Voyages & Travels of a Corps of Discovery, Under the Command of Captain Lewis and Captain Clark*, an over-the-top version of the expedition that nonetheless was reprinted in England, France, and Germany. Lewis courted a woman referred to only as "Miss A-n R——h," who apparently rebuffed him. Some historians say Lewis was drinking. Some describe him as depressed. One describes him as having "an identity crisis" at the source of the Missouri, which would be a good place to have one, since he was almost completely lost when he was there. Around the summer of 1807, he disappeared, and didn't show up again until the summer of 1808, in Saint Louis, a year late for the governorship he had been appointed to. He sank in the quicksand of western politics, attempting to broker the differences among the French, trappers, new American farmers, and rival Indian tribes, against the backdrop of separatist movements scheming in the American government. The local military commander, General James Wilkinson, was, unbeknownst to Lewis, a Spanish spy. (Aaron Burr and General Wilkinson, Lewis's predecessor as governor, had plotted with the Spanish government to form a new nation in the American Southwest, and there is speculation that Lewis may have discovered this just before he died.) Lewis was a gifted naturalist but a bad politician. By 1808, he did not respond to even Jefferson's letters.

In 1809, the War Department authorized Lewis to pay a fur trader seven thousand dollars to conduct a mission into Indian territories. Without authorization, Lewis added five hundred dollars, to buy more gifts for the tribes—Lewis knew what it was like to be out on a mission without items to trade, without gifts to smooth negotiations, for he had nearly run out on his way home to Saint

Louis in 1806. The secretary of war attacked him for incompetence. Lewis no longer had Jefferson to protect him. He took the attack personally. In September, he set out to Washington, D.C., to clear his name, writing to President James Madison to say that he was bringing his financial paperwork as well as what may have been the expedition's journals. He traveled with an Indian agent, James Neelly, who later wrote to Jefferson that Lewis seemed "deranged in mind." The men lost two horses. Neelly went to look for them. Lewis stayed in a nearby house. The woman who took him in found him so upset that she stayed in an adjacent building, and during the night she heard three gunshots. There are still suspicions that Lewis might have been murdered, but the last person to see him alive, a young boy, claimed that Lewis had said he was going to kill himself so that his enemies wouldn't get a chance to do it. Just before Lewis died, Clark wrote to his brother: "I fear O! I fear the weight of his mind has over come him."

Here in the gorge, where my own expedition is now, Lewis *was* writing and, it seems to me, maybe even feeling good about his team having survived the winter, though he was beginning to show signs of anxiety. He was beginning to freak out here in the gorge. Perhaps the gorge was the beginning of the end of the journals. To quote the words of the Chicago-based rock-and-roll band that my son now has us playing on the car stereo, since everyone has had enough of the news for the moment: "I can't find the time to write my mind the way I want it to read."

REST-STOPPING WHERE THERE ONCE WERE FALLS

LOOKING BACK IN OUR REARVIEW MIRROR, Mount Hood—the mountain that is the symbol of Portland, of this rain forest section of Oregon, standing above the highest walls of the gorge like a scoop of ice cream—fades into a ghost as we move on toward the Rocky Mountains. The view of Mount Hood tinges my road excitement with sadness—not that the road in general doesn't make me sad a lot of the time, or tinged with regret for moving, for pressing forward to we-are-never-sure where.

But the sky ahead is crisp and cheerful, as the clouds have disappeared. The hills are lower; the gorge walls have become lower, softer, treeless. And as our daughter awakes, we are suddenly desirous of a rest stop, so we pull off at the next one that comes up alongside the highway, alongside the old village of Celilo.

At the rest stop, full of shade trees and parking spaces, one detail above all seems most significant: it is quiet.

We hear the quiet as we de-car for the cinder-block buildings marked MEN and WOMEN. Windsurfers are setting up. We see the quiet before us: the silent sails crossing the whitecapped water.

In a few minutes, we are back in the car, and though our schedule says we shouldn't, just before getting back on the interstate, we drive down a little road into the adjacent village of Celilo.

CELILO COULD ALSO BE CALLED CELILO II. The original village was moved just before The Dalles Dam was finished.* Before it was moved, Celilo was the permanent settlement at the edge of the falls, which were also called Wyam. Celilo was the Times Square of the Pacific Northwest, a crossroads, a place where, when the salmon ran, visitors from all over came to fish and trade and socialize. Celilo Falls was the point in the Columbia where all the water from the mountains and the high deserts of the Northwest was forced into one rocky, thin chute. The falls were where the salmon—on *their* epic journey against the current of the Columbia, up into their spawning grounds—were netted and speared. In the old photos, you see the salmon leaping up, up, up.

DRIVING THROUGH CELILO, we see abandoned houses, and then a few houses that seem as if they might be abandoned but probably aren't, and then a few houses that are well kept. We see trucks parked on the grass beneath the

---

* When the dam was built, the federal government paid to have Celilo village moved to its present location. The Army Corps of Engineers, the agency that built the dam, offered each of the thirty-six villagers up to $4,500 to buy new homes, forgetting about the seasonal visitors from various tribes. Congress decided not to try to find a new place for the Yakima, Warm Springs, Nez Percé, and Umatilla tribes to fish, but to allow the tribes to continue to fish at the old falls, which were now no longer falls but a lake. They also offered a sum of money to each of the villagers that the Army Corps felt would compensate for the loss of fish in the future—i.e., for all time. They offered about $3,500. Chief Tommy Thompson, an elder in the village, wouldn't take the money. County officials considered the village an eyesore—it wasn't what they thought a seasonal encampment ought to look like—and offered villagers $500 more to move at least ten miles away. A lot of the older residents moved away to live with relatives. Some people stayed, in the buildings we see today. An elder asked, "Why did they have to build this dam?"

dry cliffs, trucks that appear to still work, and then fields of cars that probably do not. We see no people, but we do see a large longhouse, where, I have
read, seasonal celebrations still take place. And we hear the soft rush of the
interstate, acting like an echo of the long-silenced rush of the falls.

On our way out, we stop at the shot-up Stop sign and cross the railroad
tracks heading back toward the rest stop and the I-84 entrance ramp. Just as
we do, we spot another roadside historical marker, near a fence that leads to a
boat launch for fishing. At the very bottom the historical marker had been
edited, one word crossed out:

> The loss of Wyam Falls did ~~not~~ mean
> the loss of the Indian way of life.

INTERPRETING

NOT MUCH IS ASKED of us as tourists crossing the country—we are encouraged mostly to eat and sleep, and offered opportunities to shop, relax,
pray, or sightsee, but we are perhaps not often enough offered a chance to interpret, to consider, to compare our view in the present with the view in the
past, or at least our view of the past. Thus, the historical marker that we just
encountered near the Celilo rest stop was full of Corps of Discovery–in-the-
Gorge details, as well as relevant quotes about the westward journey of the
Corps from the journals. The marker mentions Clark's description of the
communal fish-drying methods, for instance, noting that the crew "bartered
hard for firewood." Thus, we consider the Corps bartering hard.

What I want the kids to also consider is that firewood, being so rare in this
nearly treeless stretch of the river, miles now from the Douglas firs of the first
part of the gorge, was stolen by the Corps of Discovery—or taken in desperation, at least, from the tribe's river caches. I want the kids to know that the
crew was at this point on the way back begging for food. The journals talk
about the Indians' "beggary," but they also mention that on one occasion an
Indian chief asked Lewis to control his men, who were annoying the Indians:
"As these people have been liberal with us with respect to our provisions, I di-

rected the men not to crowd their lodge [in] search of food in the manner hunger has compelled them to at most lodges we have passed." I understand that a historical marker is rest stop brief, but it is my nature to point out to my own expedition that the Corps was pretty close to panic at this point on their way home, something that—as I interpret it, anyway—seems pretty understandable when you are so far from home, with so few supplies, coming upon huge crowds of people in what was supposed to be the empty wilderness.

The Corps of Discovery had to carry their boats and baggage across the thunderous falls at Celilo, for example. The previous autumn, villagers helped them get their canoes across the falls, and even caught a canoe when the elk rope the soldiers used broke and the canoe began to fall. But now with the spring salmon run on, the villagers were outnumbered by the seasonal visitors; the falls were packed with people. During the previous autumn, they rested at the falls; as was the case almost everywhere, the residents of Celilo Falls loved the fiddle playing of Pierre Cruzatte. "Peter Crusat played on the *violin* and the men danced which delighted the nativs, who Shew every civility towards us," Clark wrote. But on the way back, the Corps had to work for supplies: in addition to being low on supplies, the expedition needed horses to ride and dogs to eat. And with so many people around, there were security problems. Lewis and Clark blamed the problems on the character of the Indians, but the problems more likely had to do with the crew showing up with a lot of seemingly fancy stuff when a lot of people were around, as well as with the crew not seeming gracious by constantly asking for food. Meanwhile, the expedition wanted to trade for horses but no one seemed to want to make a deal, or at least the Corps thought the prices were way too high. One tribe would take only cooking pots in exchange for horses, even after Clark threw in the hat plume that he wears in all the road signs today and then his sword. Clark wouldn't trade cooking pots; cooking pots were too dear to the Corps.

Lewis described the people in The Dalles as "poor, dirty, proud, haughty, inhospitable, parsimonious, and faithless in every respect," which, as I imagine the situation, is not a bad description of Lewis himself at that moment. Lewis saw someone about to take the iron socket from a canoe pole and punched him out. Clark threatened to shoot the next person who tried anything and, later, threatened to burn down houses. Lewis started making speeches that, chances are, no one understood.

Something I have learned while crossing the country is that no matter how prepared you are, you are never prepared enough. As I set out on this first day, as the pure, parklike splendor of the natural-seeming Columbia Gorge fades from me, as the hills are drying up and I am starting to worry about making it to the Bitterroots in time to experience my Lewis and Clark experiences that I am—yes, I know—too intent on experiencing, I attempt to heed the errors of Lewis and Clark. I endeavor to see them, with their small contingent of armed but starving and homesick troops, passing through crowds of people living their busy, almost citylike lives in a place that the Corps had imagined as savage, to see Lewis and Clark attempt to sell the people stuff they don't want, to see Lewis and Clark threaten them. I see the crew revisiting a place that they thought was going to be as it had been the first time they went through—that is, low-key—but that turns out to be crowded.

Naturally, I am speechifying on this and other points from my front-seat position in the modern, rented cross-country vehicle, the kids tolerating me pretty well. I am saying that there ought be some indication at the Celilo Interstate 84 rest stop—a sign, a note, anything—that Lewis and Clark were freaked out.

There is quiet for a few miles, until my son changes the subject, asking, "Do you think there'll be a place in Missoula that sells old electric guitars."

AN ASIDE REGARDING THE TIME I MET LEWIS

I INTERRUPT THIS DESCRIPTION of the Lewis and Clark leg of the trip only to say that I met Lewis once. He wasn't the actual Lewis, obviously. He was the Lewis re-creating Lewis's trip in the official historic re-creation of the Lewis and Clark expedition, Scott Mandrell. This was 2004, the two hundredth anniversary of the time that the expedition stopped for the winter in 1804, in the Mandan nation—in North Dakota. In the case of the reenactors, they took a winter break from reenacting and returned to their various homes in the Saint Louis area.

I met the acting Lewis at the offices of the Clayton Public School District, where he is based when not on the reenactment trail. He is about six feet tall; his dark hair is speckled with gray, and he has a military bearing. A National Guardsman, he wore a jacket with the insignia of the Old Guard, Third

Infantry, Fort Meyers, Virginia. He was thirty-eight at the time, a little older than Lewis, who was thirty-one when he set out for the Pacific. I drove him to get a sandwich at his usual sandwich shop. He was exhausted after being away for nine weeks on the Lewis and Clark reenactment trail, and when we came to a stoplight, he had to think for a while about which way to turn. "I can't remember where I am," he said. We sat in the back of the shop, where he ordered a chopped-liver sandwich and detailed the progress of the reenactment, which had by that point made it all the way up to the Mandan nation.

I thought I would just hear a little about the smooth runnings of the reenactment, but as I took the first bite of my sandwich, I was startled to hear the acting Lewis say he was considering leaving the historical re-creation of the Lewis and Clark expedition.

"You know, I rode a horse from Washington, D.C., to Pittsburgh, Pennsylvania, to start this trip," he said. "I'm very much about the kinetic aspect of this journey and the physical exertions, and it has become something different for me, this particular group. And it's quite likely that while I might continue to the ocean next year, and they may be continuing to the ocean next year, I may not be continuing to the ocean with the Discovery. Like I say, I have a different agenda than they do. I'm less interested in daily gratification and recognition than I am in the ultimate completion of the entirety of the thing. There's been a lot of emphasis at the end of each day on the potluck dinner at the local historical society or the local daily celebration, and that is really not my ball of wax."

THE REENACTORS' BASIC PHILOSOPHICAL differences, according to Scott, arose from the differences in their reenactment roots—some guys were Civil War reenactors, some French and Indian War and Revolutionary War reenactors. "I'd say the couple of guys who are most hard-core, including myself, really come from the French and Indian era reenacting," he said. "The Civil War reenactors tend to be the kind of guys who argue over whether you have the right buttons. The French and Indian and Rev War reenactors tend to be the kind of reenactors who say, 'Well, it says here they marched twenty miles through chest-deep swamp. Let's go!' And they do it, you know, even though there's no newspaper there to cover it."

Scott began re-creating the Discovery expedition under the tutelage of the late Glenn Bishop, his reenactment mentor, who built a replica of the Corps of Discovery keelboat on which Scott first went up the Missouri in 1996. "It took Glenn thirteen years to build it," Scott said. "He spent thirteen years suffering public ridicule, his own financial pressures. He funded it himself. It was all his deal and he gave us the great gift of being able to ride on it. And at that time we did not even understand the scope of what this thing might become."

On January 31, 1997, at five thirty in the evening, the warehouse holding the first replicated keelboat burned down, and Scott stood in the parking lot alongside Glenn Bishop, who watched the smoldering ruins quietly for a while, then lit up a cigarette, took a big drag, and said, "I was never completely happy with that one anyway."

It was around that time that Bishop chose Scott to be Lewis. "Glenn asked me to act both presentationally and functionally as Lewis," Scott said.

For several years, Scott worked as the managing editor of a chain of suburban Saint Louis papers. "I turned the newspapers into a PR mechanism for the Discovery expedition," Scott said. "Every time somebody from any community in the area got involved, I had a reporter out there." And of course he had been reading the Lewis and Clark journals for years. For the record, Scott believes that Lewis did not commit suicide; he believes Lewis was assassinated, the assassination the work of James Wilkinson, the American officer who was working secretly for the Spanish government—during the Lewis and Clark expedition, Spanish troops were sent out to capture the Corps of Discovery. "Lewis inherited a lot of Jefferson's enemies," Scott told me.

On the first part of the reenactment expedition, he and the other reenactors traveled with a small trailer full of satellite equipment and computer and video equipment used for broadcasting reports to the Clayton Public School District, among other groups, and on the Internet. He worked with several other Lewis and Clark organizations on the re-creation, including the National Park Service, and as a member of the National Guard, he often arranged for assistance from the Guard, for instance, in transporting the large keelboat around dams.

Scott's work in the reenactment caused him to reexamine his attitude toward the Lewis and Clark relationship. "I've changed my opinion, quite frankly, a great deal about the dynamic between the two captains," he said. "Maybe some of it's been influenced by my own experiences with Clark's great-great-great-great-grandson, but I don't think it was quite the ridiculous fraternity that it is made out to be."

The acting Clark, with whom the acting Lewis was experiencing some command-sharing difficulties, was at that time played by Churchill Clark, a great-great-great-great-grandson of William Clark, descended from Clark's firstborn son, Meriwether Lewis Clark. By Scott's way of thinking, at that point in the reenactment, the re-created Clark was more interested in honoring the original Lewis and Clark than in reinterpreting the trip. "He doesn't want to hear anything that doesn't say his ancestor was a superhero," Scott said.

But the big falling-out between the reenacting Lewis and the reenacting Clark began when the re-created Lewis and Clark expedition ran into trouble with the Indians.

THE DISCOVERY CREW HAD ALREADY BEEN MEETING with tribes along the way. But then on September 19, members of a Lakota Sioux tribe came into the reenactment's encampment with signs that said WHY CELEBRATE GENO-CIDE? A man leading the protesters, a Lakota chief named Alex White Plume, said to the reenactors, "We're here to ask you to turn around and go home."

The group was called Stop Lewis and Clark Now. It was organized by some young Indian activists and by some people who had been involved with Wounded Knee—people who saw the expedition as a reminder of the beginning of a war on the tribes of western America.

Similarly, the original Corps of Discovery had diplomatic issues with the Lakota Sioux when they first met them in September 1804. The Sioux controlled trade on the Missouri; they didn't appreciate an armed force coming in to say they were establishing a new trading system. At one point, as the Corps of Discovery was about to press on, the Lakota grabbed the ropes of the boat. Lewis ordered his soldiers to arm themselves; the Lakota pulled arrows out of their quivers and strung them on their bows. The standoff repeated itself on several occassions, until Lewis and Clark finally sailed through.

In the case of the reenactment, the expedition moved past the protesters on September 21, trucking their boats around Big Bend Dam, near Pierre, South Dakota, under police escort. The protesters released a statement: "They spit upon our words and continue to sail into our Nations."

WHEN SCOTT MANDRELL TOLD ME that he was not certain he wanted to go on as Lewis, what he meant was that while he was certain that he still wanted to complete the trip as Lewis, he was not crazy about going along with Clark. Scott felt he had done his best to respect the protesters, observing Native America meeting protocols as best as he knew how, with sage to purify the meeting area, a circular meeting area, and chairs for tribal elders. But Scott felt Clark was more interested in the personal stories of Lewis and Clark than in what Scott saw as an opportunity to talk about what happened to the Sioux and other nations. Also, according to Scott, Churchill Clark continued to refer to Jefferson along the lines of how the original Lewis and Clark referred to him, as the Great White Father, which, as I understand it, really bugged Scott.

Scott ended up not eating in camp much. Sometimes he would skip the karaoke or the build-your-own-ice-cream-sundae parties. "I'd walk up the hill from the river to a convenience store to get a hot dog," he said.

"To me it's a mission," he went on. "I didn't sign up for fun. Native Americans are protesting because of the genocide of their people. I mean, it's not a barbecue. I'm a teacher in a very progressive school district, and I have to think about at the end of the day what it is that I have accomplished, and I cannot simply be a part of what I would characterize as a self-indulgent enterprise."

At our lunch in Saint Louis, Scott was determined to do a more low-key Lewis and Clark, a kind of Lewis as triathlete. "Worst-case scenario, I'll kayak the rest of the Missouri, ride the portage from Great Falls on horseback, run through the Rockies, and then kayak down the Columbia," he said.

After that winter, I read in a newspaper that Scott decided to formally split from the Lewis and Clark reenactment and carry on alone as Lewis. He was determined to reach the Great Falls of the Missouri in Montana under his own power, in a kayak. He said traveling the river made him realize that Lewis and Clark were just average guys assigned to a staggeringly difficult task, not superheroes.

Scott Mandrell kayaked across Montana in June 2005, wearing modern clothes, some made of Gore-Tex, and he took the time that Lewis and Clark spent portaging the falls to return home and visit his two young children and his wife. I was amazed to learn that one of the people who had left the main expedition to accompany Scott on his own pared-down re-creation of the Lewis and Clark expedition was Churchill Clark.*

---

* The person who took over as William Clark for Churchill Clark on the original Lewis and Clark re-creation while Churchill went on with Scott Mandrell was sixty-one-year-old Bud Clark, William's great-great-great-great-grandson, descended from William's third son. (Churchill Clark, forty-one, is descended through William's eldest son.) By the summer of 2005, both reenactments were camping near each other on the Columbia River. *Willamette Week*, a

THE FORGOTTEN TRAIL

IF THE PACIFIC NORTHWEST were a play, then this part of the road that is now before us would be act II, the half that is not full of thick green forest watered by sea-rich clouds but is high desert through which the Columbia River and the Snake River and all the smaller rivers sparkle in the heat of the sun—a surprise ending for most of the Americans attending the show.

The hills in this area are the dusty cut-top buttes of old westerns. Along the edge of the still-huge Columbia River is the occasional green-surrounded farm or green-rectangled vineyard, the water for their greenness sucked up from the river below. On the hill to the left of our car and to the north of Oregon, in a town called Maryhill in Washington, we can just make out a miniature Stonehenge, a gray-concrete replica of the druid sun temple built in honor of the area's World War I dead by James Hill, who also built a mansion just down the river, as well as the railroad from Saint Paul, Minnesota, to Portland. The car moans from the portentious flutterings of the unstable pack. We pass Arlington, once called Alkali, and my wife recalls the time we were driving from New York to Portland in a moving van and our taillight went out and a trucker told us to pretend we thought it was working if the cops pulled us over—a plan that turned out to be too nerve-wracking for me, so we pulled into a motel for the night in Arlington, where, coincidentally, we had pulled in once before when a car in which we were driving west to east began to choke smoke, to gasp.

And then just as Lewis and Clark did on their return trip to Saint Louis, we break off from the trail—in their case, from their trail out; in ours, from the interstate. And instead of trading for horses and leaving the canoes, we transfer from interstate to noninterstate roads, just for a bit, for the only time, in fact, in this trip that we are now thinking will take us four or, at most, five days.

Because, as I announce to our own expeditionary force, Lewis and Clark came out west along the Snake River, but they went home by another way. The other way is forgotten, in that it is not the way celebrated in re-creations

---

weekly newspaper based in Portland, interviewed both encampments at the mouth of the Columbia River. Bud Clark said: "We are the living history group that has the actual recreation of the Lewis and Clark boats." Scott Mandrell said: "Our group has been the group that has really taken the trip."

and so forth. But it is not completely forgotten. In the small towns that are close to or on the trail back, there are the brown and white Lewis and Clark road signs, and, over the past few years, more and more banners have sprouted up. The banners say THE FORGOTTEN TRAIL.

Because we are about to leave the interstate, I'm afraid to say that this portion of the first day of our cross-country trip is not what I personally would define as an absolutely authentic modern-day cross-country experience. We are cheating, in a sense, but we are cheating, in my mind, for historical purposes. We are going to use the back roads—just a little two-hundred-mile or so stretch—to investigate the route that somehow informs all routes today, to go into the mountains that nearly ruined the Corps of Discovery expedition. We are going to the land before the interstates.

We are also hoping to save a little time, or I am. You see, I have always felt that if you could do it right (no bathroom stops, arriving early enough in the day, etc.), the way through the mountains would be quicker than the interstate, which goes way north and then comes down into Missoula. I've never been able to prove it, and I'm not giving too much away by saying that I probably never will, but isn't it the case that long-distance drivers eternally chose to leave the interstate for a more "direct" route that always ends up taking longer? Or it just me?

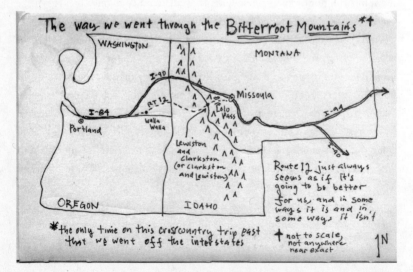

The way we went through the Bitterroot Mountains *†

WASHINGTON

MONTANA

I-90

Missoula

I-84

RT 12

Lolo Pass

I-94

Walla Walla

Portland

Lewiston and Clarkston (or Clarkston and Lewiston)

I-90

OREGON

IDAHO

Route 12 just always seems as if it's going to be better for us, and in some ways it is and in some ways it isn't

* the only time on this crosscountry trip past that we went off the interstates

† not to scale, not anywhere near exact

N

RUNNING BEHIND ON THE FORGOTTEN TRAIL

WE'RE RUNNING BEHIND on the Forgotten Trail, though it's not like we have an appointment or a reservation or anything set up for when we cross into Montana: that's not the kind of cross-country travelers we are—we don't make reservations. We are only late in the abstract sense now—I do not yet realize that the Lolo hot spring that Lewis and Clark and their team soaked in might be closed by the time we get there; I do not yet even realize that it's a commercialized place. Meanwhile, so dry are the hills along the Columbia that the place appears lunar: the river is hypnotizing in its desert-framed blueness. We enter Irrigon, a town named by the editor of the first local paper, the *Oregon Irrigator*, by combining *Oregon* and *irrigator*. Roadside signs include:

> MEET ME AT THE IRRIGON WATERMELON FESTIVAL
> LOOKING FOR GOD—YOU'LL FIND HIM ON BENDED KNEE
> FRED'S MELONS

Umatilla, similarly dry with patches of irrigated lushness, is advertised to drivers entering it as "Home of the Vikings." Once it was home of the Umatillas, who lived here at the meeting of the Umatilla and Columbia rivers until they were moved to a reservation thirty miles away and a large part of their land was given over to a U.S. Army weapons depot, where, as we drive by, the Army is incinerating nerve gases and other kinds of weapons of mass destruction from the American weapons-of-mass-destruction pile. These small towns feature some of the best small signs we will see on the trip—after all, this is not the interstate. There's a sign for a gas station that delivers Mexican pizza. There's the ornately handwritten sign for Lolita's Total Image Salon.

And now Wallula, the very place where I myself first saw the Columbia River—a place that I can still see myself first approaching, my wife driving our tiny-seeming car, me not believing it: a place marked by me with a mental plaque, an imaginary marker. This was the dream river of cartographers and explorers and presidents and merchants and some Native Americans, and though it was not a huge river that ran straight to China or India or anywhere in the Far East, the dream *was* true, in that it was huge and ran to the West, and even to the very end of the West, or the Pacific: *Wallula!*

Sacagawea led the Corps of Discovery here, and I look in the rearview mirror to see our daughter awake and reading, believe it or not, a young adult biography about Sacagawea, the well-known Shoshone Indian woman who traveled with Lewis and Clark, and famously guided them, and translated for them, and fed them on occasion, and saved their equipment when their canoes tipped in the mountains.

In retrospect, I wonder how I could *ever* be even the least bit disappointed in my family's Lewis and Clark receptivity.

And yet when I see her, I can't help myself and I share some information that I have learned about Sacagawea, mentioning that while popular lore talks about her dying in North Dakota, there is a lot of testimony that points to her possibly dying on the Wind River Reservation in Wyoming, where she would have traveled alone, without weapons and supplies and troops.* I also mention that the journal writers refer to the slave and the dog on the trip by name more often than they refer to Sacagawea by name; they call her "squaw."

"Oh," our daughter says, still patient.

Our daughter then shares with me something she read in another book she happens to have on hand, a Barbie reference book, about Barbie, the doll: "Become as knowledgeable as you can by reading books and magazines. Trust your own judgement."

In a manner that in my mind is consistent with a move by the likes of President Jefferson, who collected information, who culled a dictionary on Jesus, who hoped the journals of Lewis and Clark would help him create a great dictionary of Plains Indian languages, our son shows an interest in the Barbie reference book, and then, incredibly, my son is quizzing his sister on the origins of Barbie.

Ah, what just a few hours in a car will force you to do, a few hours without a TV or computer screen, not that we don't pass car after car on the interstates with TV screens dangling from the ceilings, strapped to the back of the parents' headrests! Ah, the benefits of what is today described as boredom but is actually time!

On what is momentarily our Voyage of Barbie Discovery, we learn that

---

* Non-Indian historians have often made light or even fun of these testimonies, calling them "worthless" or "unreliable," possibly because these stories can seem to hurt the Lewis and Clark myth, chip away at the two men's courage, even though they don't necessarily.

Barbie originated in Willows, Wisconsin, a town we cannot find in any of our several atlases, a mystery.

And now our daughter chooses the music for the car, a CD, the sound track to the film *Legally Blonde 2*, a movie about a woman who is shunned because she is overly concerned with her aesthetic appearance but still ends up being respected by the people who made fun of her because she is smart. Initially, there is some concern about this CD choice with some members of the expedition but then there's mild approval as the songs are played in the following order: (1) "America," as sung by Lou Reed; (2) "Power to the People," as sung by John Lennon; (3) a remake of that Buffalo Springfield song with the lyric "Stop, hey, what's that sound / Everybody look what's goin' down," which immediately causes me to remember to study the scenery around us more closely, which in turn means I spot a gray mechanical thing built in the margin of land between the road and the river that is about the size of a single-family house and is an amalgamation of large canisters and valves—a thing I cannot identify, like so many things I see on the road while crossing the country. "Look at *that!*" I say.

"Oh, yeah," says our daughter, who breaks off from the Barbie discussion and goes back to reading.

"Yeah," says our son, who is now reading *The Metamorphosis*, by Franz Kafka.

STILL RUNNING BEHIND ON THE FORGOTTEN TRAIL

ON THE FORGOTTEN TRAIL, we drive between the giant irrigators that look like suburban lawn sprinklers except that they are each as long as a football field, as long as a suburban subdivision; when I see them, I think about flying over them, about seeing their green circles from the air. The one out our window sports an American flag, which feels appropriate. These sprinklers are fed by government dams, by the vast irrigation project that magically greens the dry desert. Then again, American flags are everywhere.

In the little town of Touchet, where one place might sell leftover firewood, or used computers, or offer a lawn mower at a good price, we pass baled hay and alfalfa for sale, the fruit of the hills that now cuddle our car.

THE COLUMBIA HEADS NORTH, and, as we turn east, as we turn inland, we note the number of hills increasing and, along the ridge parallel to the road, a new crop of tall towers—a wind farm, farming the streams of air that invisibly mimic the Columbia:

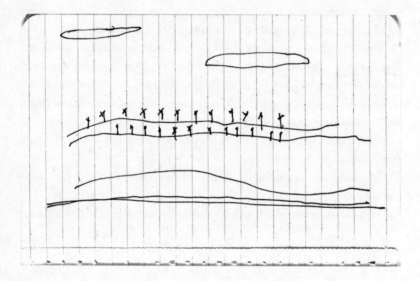

When you cross the country, you are always crossing a new country, a moving destination.

MORE LEWIS AND CLARK SIGNPOSTS, more Forgotten Trail banners, and frankly, a lot of scenery that resembles a place that Lewis and Clark would have seen, as opposed to a lot of the rest of the not-forgotten trip, which is full of dammed rivers and irrigated fields that are nothing like they were, as far as anyone can tell. These hills—that are colored chocolate when the fields are turned and cornflake tan when they are full of grain and, once in while, bright, plant-producing green—are, like a lot of Pacific Northwest vistas, the famous car-commercial landscapes of the TV-watcher's subconscious. These are the roads television commercial directors especially like to use to entice us onto steel and gas-turned rubber wheels—though in the commercials the roads are usually hosed down, to darken them, to suggest a cold morning dew, a cool fall evening. When not out driving across the country, I can be at home watching a baseball game, and on the commercial break, be presented with a car making beautiful turns on the Forgotten Trail.

Somehow then—and I will admit that I am not certain how—it seems fitting to discover that the gas station in the town of Waitsburg is a worker-free institution, a gas-pumping machine that takes credit cards. Coincidentally, an owner of the station pulls up in a truck. As he speaks, a Forgotten Trail banner billows behind him; across the street, the sign of a bar that has lost half its lettering is prevented from finishing its name: WAITSBU—

"Well," says the man, "we can't afford to sell gas *and* pay people—that's how it works." We purchase 14.571 gallons of gas from no one. Happily, the roadside espresso stand, aside from espresso, sells giant sweet onions that are Walla Walla's specialty, and it is womaned.

IT'S SO PRETTY ON THE FORGOTTEN TRAIL, so nice in the middle of the afternoon, that I have forgotten for a moment about the whole Lewis and Clark aspect of our situation—I am traveling without guiding myth. Also, because we were driving so slowly, our expensive but shredded rooftop pack is no longer making any noise.

WHEN LEWIS AND CLARK WERE FORGOTTEN

LEWIS AND CLARK'S ENTIRE TRAIL was forgotten after Lewis and Clark returned, mostly because people forgot about the journals. After Lewis died in 1809, Clark didn't want to edit them alone; he searched Philadelphia for a writer. He finally found Nicholas Biddle, a lawyer and financier who spent three weeks going over everything with Clark. Biddle was done in a year, only to find that the scientist Clark had hired to complete the scientific portion had done nothing. A succession of events slowed publishing: first, the publisher went out of business, then the War of 1812 began, then Biddle finally quit. Clark hired another writer in Boston to finish up. Finally, in 1814, seven years after the expedition had returned to Saint Louis, the journals were published under the title *History of the Expedition Under the Command of Captains Lewis and Clark, to the Sources of the Missouri, Thence Across the Rocky Mountains and Down the River Columbia to the Pacific Ocean.* The book was not, technically speaking, the journals; it was a condensation of all the expedition's writings. The book did not sell, possibly because of all the other versions of the trip that had been published. Clark didn't even see a copy until years later. The actual journals were stored away in the basement of the American Philosophical Society in Philadelphia and forgotten. In the histories of the United States written in the 1800s, Lewis and Clark are barely mentioned, if at all.

History books and television documentaries often make it sound as if settlers raced in after Lewis and Clark crossed the continent, as if American interests immediately spread in their wake. "They went, literally, from the east to west coast and that is what America did in their footsteps," intones the narrator of a recent popular documentary on Lewis and Clark's journey. In that version of the story, Lewis and Clark are nation-building superheros, the nation following behind them like an expectant herd.

But what actually happened after the expedition was not much.

Easier routes across the country were found before the expedition's history was published in 1814. Most of the first people to settle in the Northwest, for instance, were British; they followed not Lewis and Clark but explorers like John Thompson, who, in addition to mapping much of British Columbia, Washington, and Montana, paddled the entire length of the Columbia River, not with an expeditionary force of thirty-five to forty-five people but with his Native American wife—they were pioneering married transcontinentalists. In 1811, an American trading post, Astoria, was established by John Jacob Astor's Pacific Fur Company at the mouth of the Columbia, but thirty-three months later, it was taken over by the British and renamed Fort George. The American settlers came after the furs had all been taken, after the Native American population had been diminished by disease by as much as 90 percent. As opposed to using the Lewis and Clark journals as a guide, the travelers on the Oregon Trail followed the advice of Indians and the so-called mountain men. The West filled with fur traders and trappers who knew nothing of Lewis and

Clark, with people who were French, British, Spanish, Mexican, Iroquois, Tlingit, Russian, Haida, métis, and Hawaiian.

The Corps of Discovery expedition was forgotten until the journals were rediscovered, in the basement of the Philosophical Society in Philadelphia, in the 1890s and published between 1904 and 1906 by Reuben Gold Thwaites, an editor of western travel stories. Bit by bit, more parts of the journals were rediscovered—Clark's field notes, for example, in 1953. The entire collection was not completely edited until 2001, by Gary Moulton. The legacy of Lewis and Clark began in 1900 or so and it adapted to America's needs. In 1905, in Portland, Oregon, the Lewis and Clark Centennial Exposition was billed by the *Oregonian* as a celebration of the explorers who, as the *Oregonian* put it, "blazed the way to profitable expansion of America—in domain, in industry, in commerce, in wealth and in civilization." At the exposition, vice president Charles Fairbanks gave a speech that put even the war in the Philippines in a Lewis and Clark context: "And now the future has much in store for us. Yonder is Hawaii, acquired for strategic purposes and demanded in the interest of expanding commerce. Lying in the waters of the Orient are the Philippines, which fell to us by the inexorable logic of a humane and righteous war." The logo used extensively at the 1905 exposition featured a drawing of a Lewis and Clark arm in arm and with a blond-haired Sacagawea, a Sacagawea who looks a little like Barbie, come to think of it—the three of them are skipping into a sun setting on the western sea.

In the 1920s, the Lewis and Clark story became the story of American businesses such as the Northern Pacific Railroad, which referenced the explorers in their advertising: "Lewis and Clark explored the Pacific Northwest. It is their work which the Northern Pacific has carried forward by pioneering, developing and serving this region." In the 1930s, Lewis and Clark were taken up by populists such as Woody Guthrie, who, in writing songs for the Bonneville Power Authority, described an empire for the people in which the river would, as he sang, "run a thousand factories for Uncle Sam. And everybody else in the world." In the 1950s, the time when the interstate highways were being developed, when everyone with a car was about to be able to cross the country like Lewis and Clark, the Corps of Discovery members were the first Cold Warriors, the representative Organization Men, taking us through the nuclear future to a profitable USA.

THE POINT AT WHICH I REACHED A GOAL, EVEN THOUGH I FELT WE HAD TO KEEP RUSHING

SCENE: In between two dusty green hills on the Forgotten Trail, past the town of Dayton and just before the Forgotten Trail crosses the Snake River, our rental car pulls up beside a large Lewis and Clark roadside historical marker, the marker nearly as big as a pool table, the car blinker blinking, ticking, timing us. The occasional car or truck passes. Remember: we have been on the trail the whole time but we have not seen any kind of actual path, the *precise* Lewis and Clark trail. Rather, we are always merely in the general Lewis and Clark trail area, the vicinity of their path, the path for the most part having obviously been long ago worn away.

DAUGHTER [*reading the historical marker*]: "They had scant—"

WIFE: *Scant.* That means "a little."

DAUGHTER: "They had scant rations of dried meat and dog."

WIFE: I'd only *want* scant rations.

DAUGHTER: "A hospital—"

WIFE: *Hospitable.*

DAUGHTER [*assuredly now*]: "A hospitable Nez Percé Chief Bighorn had come to meet them with the assurance they would find provisions at the Nez Percé camp near the Snake River the next day. The next day the explorers followed 'the road by over the plains,' a branch of the Indian trail that followed up the creek. This east branch can still be seen today across the highway . . ."

ME [*after having sat through the reading of the marker and wanting my daughter to read the sign but also wanting to keep moving, and now reacting with a kind of visible shock to the words* can be seen today: *this is the point I had been hoping for, even if I did not yet know it—a place where I could in fact see a trace of the footsteps, of the old trail, of the first round-trip across the North American continent by a white guy associated with the federal government. Regretfully, I wanted to see something more "authentic," something more like what I thought the trail should look like, something where I wasn't being passed by trucks*]: Can be seen today?

WIFE [*pointing*]: It's over there!

ME [*vigorously pointing*]: That would be *there!*

WIFE [*reading the marker*]: "The southern branch, which went through the Blue Mountains, is visible on the hillside."

ME [*more excited*]: Oh, right there! Everybody see it?

SON [*in back seat, being patient*]: Yes.

DAUGHTER: No.

WIFE [*pointing*]: There.

DAUGHTER: Oh, yeah.

ME [*after I set the blinker, to road reentry, and just as I speed off, too hastily, having glimpsed that centuries-old footpath worn into the side of the dry green hill first by animals, no doubt, then by humans—in other words, that was the substance of trips past, ancient and actual, a transcontinental relic, even if it wasn't precisely what I was looking for*]: OK, let's go!

LEWISTON AND CLARKSTON

IT'S LATE IN THE DAY, too late in the day, near five P.M., and we are just now heading into that last off-the-interstate stretch of the Lewis and Clark leg, into the primordial place of cross-country travel where I am hoping to achieve a greater understanding of Lewis and Clark, or of something. We are off the Forgotten Trail and in the mountains they crossed coming and going. We are heading into the Bitterroots, which thwarted Lewis and Clark and seem as if they are about to thwart me and my goals, including my wish to soak in the those hot springs, to reenact a post-Bitterroot relaxedness, as they did, even if my son now has me thinking of their pruned, early-explorer skin.

OK, so I completely forgot about losing an hour due to the time zone difference, and we are only now arriving at the beginning of the Bitterroots, which is what happens if your first day of driving starts so close to lunchtime.

We are only just arriving in Lewiston and Clarkston, two towns tucked in the Snake River valley at the foot of the Bitterroot Mountains, one in Washington, the other in Idaho, and we are looking for some food (just a snack: we're late) and a bathroom (something clean), and we are, first, in Clarkston. Sometimes I confuse Lewiston and Clarkston, for I have stayed in both places, often at night. Once we stayed in Clarkston, near a manufacturing plant that caused the motel room to smell like a manufacturing plant, and I remember my wife saying, "I wish we'd stayed in Lewiston." Or maybe it happened the other way around. In our AAA guidebook I read that Clarkston has changed its named several times.

Now, as I drive, I am reading signs aloud, as is my habit, sadly, especially when I am either excited or agitated. "Welcome BMW riders," I read from the Sacagawea Motor Inn sign. I recite a sign across the street that says "Fresh-baked lasagna dinner and St. Louis–style barbecue." Everything seems so patriotic, as I duly note—it is truly a miracle that no one has asked me to get out of the car. We cross the Snake River on a little bridge. In Lewiston, I see a place called Meriwether's, and over there is Inn America.

And then my daughter shouts out a sign: "Dad, look, Liberty Mart!"

At my daughter's reading of a sign, I think that perhaps things are changing, that even though I am acting tense and rushing, even though I am sort of shoving it in their faces, the kids are really getting into the whole reverse-Lewis-and-Clark-trail theme. Thus, I praise my daughter, looking back in the rearview mirror, beaming.

"Dad," my daughter says, slowly, carefully. "I spotted that because I have to go to the bathroom."

NEZ PERCE II

IN LEWISTON, we stop at a gas station and convenience store called Nez Perce II. Inside, we find clean restrooms and a tall guy dressed all in denim and wearing a cowboy hat. He strides dramatically to the counter and, through all his time in the store, says only two words.

"Can I help you?" the young Nez Percé woman behind the counter says.

"Six frappucinos," the man says.

Soon we shall be driving alongside the Clearwater River and up into the lands of the Nez Percé reservation. We shall see a land form, a small hill, to which the Nez Percé attributed great significance, and we shall see roadside markers that describe the days when the U.S. military attacked the Nez Percé, among other tribes who frequented this area, who commuted through these hills from buffalo opportunities in Montana to salmon opportunities on the Columbia River. I will feel my heart sink further and further because I will feel I am not achieving anything vis-à-vis my Lewis and Clark goals.

But for now, as I type up my account of my Lewis and Clark experience, I refer to a frequently asked question in the Frequently Asked Questions link that can be had by investigation of the Nez Percé tribal Web site.

In early history were the Nez Perce people peaceful or warlike?
The Nez Perce people were warriors and known for their thought out and intelligent strategies in battle. The Nez Perce people helped Lewis and Clark in their travels in the Northwest. Lewis and Clark recorded how peaceful and helpful the Nez Perce people are, in their journal. For more info you can look up Lewis and Clark journals.

INTO THE BITTERROOTS

INTO THE BITTERROOTS, the 175-mile crossing of this 300-mile-long, 11,000-foot-high range of hills that Jefferson never dreamed of, that Lewis and Clark did not expect, that Patrick Gass, a member of the Corps of Discovery, called "the most terrible mountains I ever beheld." Into the Bitterroots, not on horseback in fear of attacks by humans or bears, in fear of death by cold or starvation, but in fear of being late on Route 12, a road that the U.S. Army's great nineteenth-century builder of western roads, Lieutenant John Mullan, declared to be impossible to build.* This road, Route 12, that Mullan wouldn't build wasn't officially opened until 1962 and it ended at a point just outside Missoula; housewives from Montana took it upon themselves to fill trucks with gravel and extend the road into town. In 1962, a news report stated: "There are no billboards and at present no commercial establishments in its entire length . . . The traveler who wants to savor the qualities of wilderness life and a genuine western atmosphere has perhaps two or three more years to do so."

You can almost say the same thing about Route 12 today.

LEWIS AND CLARK BACKWARD

WHY DID LEWIS STOP WRITING? Yes, he was shot in the buttocks, and he had to lie down a lot, and that made it difficult, if not impossible, to write. But, if you ask me, what surely contributed to his not writing was that the trip did not end up being the way he had imagined it at all, not that he could have imagined it, not that anyone could have.

Even in the first weeks, as Lewis and Clark set out toward the Pacific, as they talked about venturing into wilderness, it must have been a shock for the expedition to see more people living in the Mandan Indian villages in North Dakota than in Saint Louis or Washington, D.C. Those "savages," meanwhile, were farmers and global traders; in the Mandan lodges, there were goods from all over Europe and the Americas, and in the case of some Northwest coast tribes, there were items from Asia. The presence of so many people in the land that Lewis described as unexplored and "virgin" upon taking

---

* Mullan chose instead to build a more northern route through the Bitterroots, which eventually became Interstate 90—a task that required seven years, 120 miles of timber cutting, 30 miles of excavation, hundreds of bridges and several ferries, eighty-eight civilians, five engineers and topographers, two rod men, an astronomer, fourteen general assistants, fifteen teamsters, thirty-two laborers, eight cooks, four packers, four herders, two carpenters, and a man paid to cut grass to feed the livestock. The men carried two weeks's worth of supplies on their backs; they pulled them on hand sleds. In the winter, a man went from one road-building camp to another who had to have his legs amputated after getting his feet wet.

off, must have eventually changed his perception of what it was that the Corps of Discovery was discovering. All the way into Montana, the expedition would camp at spots and believe they were the very first to do so, until Toussaint Charbonneau, the French trader they'd hired to accompany them, would mention that he had already camped there. When they got to the West Coast and paddled the Columbia, they passed mountains previously named by the British. They met Indians who spoke English, carried pistols and tin flasks to hold their powder—Indians who swore in English, spoke of traders from Boston, and wore overalls, shirts, and hats. They met a red-haired Clatsop woman with freckles, and another with a tatoo: J. BOWMAN. Just before they got back to Saint Louis, still in what they were trying to consider unexplored wilderness, they ran into a man originally from Pennsylvania, now of Illinois, Joseph Dickinson, alongside his friend Forest Hancock. Dickinson told Lewis and Clark that he and Hancock had been out in the unknown lands since the summer of 1804. If the Lewis and Clark expedition was like the first trip to the moon, then running into Dickinson and Hancock was like parking beside another spaceship. Lewis was the first U.S. government naturalist to describe scores of species on the plains, even if the species were already known by the Plains Indians, but as far as documenting the cross-country trip itself, some historians argue that Lewis, so well-schooled by Jefferson, realized at some point that he was covering already covered ground.

"Why write?" the historian Thomas Slaughter, has noted. "There could be nothing more of significance to document. They were neither first nor essential to those who would come next."

BACKTRACKING ALONG THE LEWIS AND CLARK TRAIL, you begin to realize that America has always wanted to remember the Lewis and Clark expedition one way—as heading west. You begin to realize that America hasn't thought a lot about heading east, and that as far as Lewis and Clark go, we still think about them leaving as conquerers and we are loathe to think about them coming home another way.

Years after the expedition, Washington Irving visited Clark and wrote that Clark had freed York, the slave who accompanied the expedition, only to have York fail at business and return to his master. It's more likely, though, that York went west to live and did not return—he is mentioned as a hero in one account of a battle between the Crow and the Blackfeet. In fact, Clark, who was frequently upset with York when they first returned from Oregon, threatened to sell York away from York's wife. "I gave him a severe trouncing the other day and he has mended since," Clark wrote in one letter. York often upset Clark when he upstaged the two white commanders on the trip, not to mention all the technology they brought along to impress the tribes with; York was considered magical by many Native Americans, and he appears to have enjoyed this to some extent, except, for instance, when a pack of Nez Percé boys attempted to rub the darkness from his skin with sand. "The Indians much astonished at my servant who made himself more terrible in their view than I wished him to do," Clark wrote in the journals. Yet the National Park Service's Lewis and Clark map refers to York as Clark's "slave and companion."

Likewise, Sacagawea, who was sixteen when Lewis and Clark met her, is described in some accounts as returning with the expedition and staying on and dying a few years later, when it is also probable—and probably *more* probable—that she gave birth six times, raised a daughter and two sons, escaped her slavery, chose her own Commanche husband, made her own trip back across the Great Plains, and lived to be ninety-six in a time when disease was wiping out her neighbors.

On the trail back, you start to think that Lewis and Clark were nice guys sometimes and sometimes they acted like jerks. They made some good decisions and some dumb decisions. They met some Indians they liked and some they didn't. At the end of the winter, they took a canoe from the Clatsop tribe they had been staying with. "We want yet another canoe," wrote Lewis on March 17, 1806, "and as the Clatsops will not sell us one at a price we can afford to give we will take one from them in lieu of the six elk which they stole from us in the winter." What he doesn't say is that the Clatsop thought that the white hunters, having killed the elk and left them unmarked and unattended, didn't want the elk—the rules of the woods as they knew them. What he doesn't say is that when the Clatsop learned that Lewis and Clark were upset about the elk, they brought a number of dogs to the village for the expedition to eat, as an apology, an apology the Clatsop thought had been accepted. Editors of the journals often point out that Lewis and Clark broke their rule about not stealing on only this one occasion, but, according to the journals, the expedition "found" horses that they must have known were set out to graze. According to the journals, Indians stole.

Once, when I was not driving, when I was off the road and in a chair reading,

I found a speech given at a meeting of the National Lewis and Clark Bicentennial Council. The speech said, "Across the two centuries that separate us, we
cannot speak to them. But if we listen hard enough, we can hear their voices
speaking to us—reaching from the past and still calling us toward the next horizon." I'm thinking that I can hear their voices sometimes, but I don't know if
they are calling me to the next horizon. When I hear them, I think I ought to
just hold still, to stay where I am until I can figure things out a little better.

THE LAST STAGE OF THE FIRST DAY OF WHAT WE
ARE STILL THINKING OF AS A FOUR- OR MAYBE
FIVE-DAY TRIP

WE ARRIVE AT THE PUBLIC INFORMATION center for the Clearwater National Forest in Idaho near six o'clock, and the ranger offering public information tells us that the hot springs where Lewis and Clark relaxed are great to
visit but that they are still a few hours away. She also says that for us to drive
on the forest road that had been part of the actual Lewis and Clark trail—
something called the Lolo Trail Motorway—is impossible without a permit, a
reservation, and a car that is not a rented Impala—i.e., an SUV or something
more rugged. In the literature handed out at the public information center, I
read that the Lolo Trail Motorway has been described by the *Oregonian* as "a
cross between a national monument and a joke."

So I put that centerpiece of my grand Lewis and Clark daytrip out of my
head, or try to, with great visible frustration.

Then the ranger mentions that the hot springs might close up before we
can get there. How could a hot springs close, I wondered? I was beginning to
feel like Lewis in the Columbia Gorge or possibly at the headwaters of the
Missouri River—i.e., I was beginning to lose it.

Still, I am determined to try, and my wife is game, while the other members of the expedition are lying kind of low.

"Let's just see how it goes," says my wife—a living fount of hope, as Dante
might have it, though I don't see that, naturally.

Back in the car, I have a map of a few places where I thought the trail came near the highway, and now I am asking my wife to read the map, and then getting upset with how she is reading it, and then she is telling me to read the map for myself. I'm not breaking the speed limit—the rooftop pack still is not making any noise. Speeding would be foolish: on our first trip across the country, we crossed this Bitterroots road going east to west, in the middle of a rainy night, and I can recall seeing, among other wrecks, a police car wrapped around a tree. We have late-summer light now, but I am thinking that I'd better not speed. Instead, I am hunched over the steering wheel, half sullen, half crazed with historic disappointment. My son suggests I calm down—sometimes it's difficult to hear your son rightfully reprimand you. My daughter says, "Dad." Momentarily, I regain composure.

At seven P.M., still light outside, it is quiet in the car.

We cruise up higher and higher through the dark green forest, the green and the Lochsa river lifting my spirits, the late-summer sky more and more calming—something that driving does to me, especially in the woods, is to cause me to realize that in a lot of situations, there's not much I can do. We stop briefly to skip rocks in the river and to use a camping site's comfort station. We listen to an old song about a logger living in a shack in the woods, "The Shantyman." At one point, I think we are maybe close to an area where the trail comes near the road and I go a few yards up a forest road and then I give up, not wanting to get stuck. More disappointment. The AAA TripTik is useless in these hills, in non-interstate land. While driving, I fumble for and eventually find the U.S. Geological Survey map that I had bought at a camping store in Portland the day before, and when I look at it I cannot believe how roaded the woods surrounding us are.* It's seven thirty. It's seven forty-five. It's eight. Then, very suddenly, near the highest point in the crossing, 5,200 feet, we reach the De Voto Memorial Cedar Grove.

---

* Though now I know that there are more roads on public lands like national parks and forests than there are interstate highways. There are 43,000 miles of interstate highway in America, and 550,000 miles of roads on public lands. Obviously, they are different kinds of roads but they are roads.

BORN OF FANTASY

A BEAUTIFUL SPOT, a stand of tall cedars, a riverside glade of green-sparkled light. In all my time crossing the Bitterroots, I have never noticed the DeVoto grove, much less visited it. It is the place where Bernard DeVoto, one of the early modern editors of the Lewis and Clark journals, is said to have come to read and work on his edition of the journals, published in 1953. It is a patch of old-growth cedar trees alongside the Lochsa River, made into a small park, where, after he died, his ashes were scattered.

DeVoto was born in the West, in Utah, and went to the East, to New York, and to Harvard, where he taught. He wrote history and novels and essays on conservation for *Harper's*. One of his first books was about Mark Twain, a book that criticized the literary establishment at the time, which argued that a great American poet was hindered by the American frontier, by the sometimes crass, joke-filled West. Bucking literary trends, DeVoto viewed the frontier, the western way of life, all its songs and stories and hardscrabble ways, as the making of Twain, as part of his genius, rather than something that he sublimated or rose above. DeVoto also wrote about the history of imperial designs on North America, those of the Spanish, French, British, and Americans. When he wrote his histories, he liked to visit the sites and sketch and detail scenes. He drove across the country regularly, to see firsthand the trails and routes that formed the American empire; he worked to analyze the invention of the idea of the United States. "In the Geography of fantasy the English colonies, which in the first moment of settlement began to become the United States, extended to the Pacific Ocean," he wrote. "The usage and expectation that were born of fantasy are the first bud of the psychological component. We completed the continental nation when we fulfilled the fantasy by pushing the western boundary to where it had first been drawn."

We all race out of the car and enter the DeVoto grove and then walk around more and more slowly. The grove is beautiful—right beside the highway but also far, far away. The cedar trees all seem contemplative, the stream knowing.

Calmed now by the grove and feeling that there is no way we were going to make it to the hot springs, so what does it matter anyway, I drive on at a less-frantic pace, and in a startlingly short time come to a roadside historical marker: LOLO TRAIL CROSSING. Somewhere in this vicinity the trail east crossed the modern road.

My son volunteers to read the sign, perhaps to assuage my disappointment. "June 29, 1806: They reported that then they 'ascended a very steep acclivity of a mountain about 2 Miles' crossing this highway here to reach their old trail to Lolo Pass . . ."

"Where did they come through, though?" my wife says, looking up at the almost treeless mountain of dirt.

"I don't know," I say, a little mournfully.

Unlike the footpath we saw a few hours ago on the Forgotten Trail, this path is invisible to us. I am quiet for a while, finally calming down. "Oh, well," I say.

My son takes pictures of the clear-cut valley, the sun fading behind it.

"I'm getting a lot of glare," he said, "like Thomas Cole."

THE HOT SPRINGS

AND THEN SEMI-MIRACULOUSLY, we are at the hot springs, just like that, as if the hot springs had been waiting for me to stop worrying about missing them—we'd been closer than I thought. After we crossed easily through Lolo Pass, and just past the grove and the invisible Lewis and Clark trail crossing, the side of the road was green again. We saw the hot springs in a big clearing just beyond the pass, the hot springs being, in their modern incarnation, little cabins and modern campsites along both sides of Route 12 just as it begins to descend into the valley on the other side of the Bitterroots. Please don't think we see steaming cauldrons everywhere. You'd think it was just a clump of motels if it didn't say "Hot Springs" everywhere.

Yes, there are little cabins all around, various hot-springs-affiliated motels—but there seems to be one main hot-springs-enjoyment facility, the Lolo Hot Springs Resort, which we approach.

I go in with the kids to talk to the guy behind the hot springs counter. He's a nice guy, probably in his early twenties, reading Hemingway, standing and ready to chat—the gatekeeper of the springs. "We don't close until nine," he says. We express relief, which he notices. "You're OK," he says.*

IN THE HOT SPRINGS LOCKER ROOMS, we change into bathing suits. We give little clothes-stuffed wire baskets back to the guy at the front desk and get a wrist tag and towels. Our daughter is now concerned about the word *hot* in hot springs. "I'll put my bathing suit on anyway," our son says.

"They don't have to go in," my wife says.

"I know," I agree.

In the pool, the hot spring hot water was mixed with not-so-hot water to make for an experience that is not unlike a really warm bath. Immediately upon sticking her foot in, my daughter loves it. My son too is pleased. This makes me very happy, and satisfied. For a while, it is just me and the kids and a couple who appear to be in their in their seventies and are floating and bobbing gently in a kind of Fountain of Youth happiness; my wife watches us from a poolside beach chair. No one is really saying anything, we're just soaking, getting prune-skinned. Even though it is almost nine in the evening, it is still light, the sky a soft, clear, beautiful blue. We feel like people who have crossed a mountain on horseback and are now resting.

"This is great," our son says.

"Let's go in the *real* hot spring," our daughter says.

We proceed to the pure hot spring water pool, an indoor pool that features the spring straight up—a room adjacent to the pool into which the spring water is pumped directly.

I wade in with our daughter, who likes the even-hotter water just fine.

In a second, the front-desk attendant walks in and begins to drain the water in the hot springs room to close the springs for the night. We stand there while he does—the water slowly dropping down below my waist and my daughter's shoulders. We talk to a mother and her two children, a boy and a girl, who are also soaking as the water continues to drain. They live nearby, the mother says. She informs us that the proprietor of the hot

---

* My wife is waiting outside, where a man leaving the hot springs looks at her and says, "First time through these parts?" I don't know if it's because she is of Italian origin and has dark hair and olive-colored skin or what, but that happens a lot to her in the West, where, ironically, she is from—people think she's not from there. "No," she says.

spring had recently discovered a new hot spring, even hotter than this one.

"He doesn't know what he's gonna do with it yet, but he'll think of something," she says.

We ask her where we might find dinner so late in the evening, and she lists the fast-food restaurants on the road to Missoula—Subway, Pizza Hut, a truck stop, "café-type places," as she puts it. "Of course you'll have a lot more choices in Missoula," she says, "but then you'll have to deal with the whole rat race!"

With most of the spring drained, we change back into our clothes and head to the front desk to return our clothing baskets. We stand and chat with the gate-keeper for a while, and he talks about how much he likes Ernest Hemingway— he was reading some short stories, I think. "Hemingway was a sexist, machismo, intense guy but he sure had a beautiful way with words," the front desk guy says. He also says that he wants to join the Navy and see the world.

We thank him and repair to our Impala feeling completely relaxed.

IT IS ABOUT A HALF AN HOUR DOWNHILL TO MISSOULA—down a long easy hill that is for me a geophysical relief. We end up staying at a motel we have stayed at a few times before, the Creekside Inn. After I take the pack off the car and scrape dead insects from it, we proceed to the adjacent restaurant. This is how relaxed I am feeling. We are breaking a cardinal cross-country driving rule: never eat late. As we wait for our food, we overhear the conversation in the booth directly behind us. It is being conducted by a couple, a man and a woman, and the man is doing most of the talking, if not every last word of it. He wants to know if the woman has seen a movie that she has not, it turns out, and then he begins talking about, first, the FBI and then, James Joyce. I am waiting to hear how the FBI is related to James Joyce, but all I can make out clearly is this: "You see," the man said, "Joyce had a circular view of life. He wrote *Finnegans Wake*, which is a long novel that starts out in the middle of a sentence and ends in the middle of a sentence." It would take me a while to re-alize that the name of the restaurant we were eating in was Finnegan's.

I go to bed with the road ringing in my ears. All in all—despite things not working out precisely the way I had badly planned, despite me pushing every-one too hard—it has been a good day. When I wake up to begin strapping the even-more-shredded pack to the car, I buy coffee in the restaurant and notice a sign painted on the window that I'd never noticed before: LEWIS AND CLARK CAMPED HERE.

PART III

Missoula, Montana, to Miles City, Montana

HAVING CROSSED THE MOUNTAINS

WE ARISE ON THE SECOND DAY, having crossed the great western mountains, or a good solid mess of them. We awake having made it across the threshold and through the pass, though Lolo Pass, no big problem, really, despite my worrying. And no problem is a lot better than it's been other times when we have crossed the mountains, such as the first time we did it in a rented twenty-five-foot-long truck, going west, when there was ice and fog and snow—that was a time when I thought, What the hell am I thinking driving a truck through the mountains in ice and fog and snow? We arise in the rosy-fingered dawn having soaked in the water of warm springs and relax for a little bit, before proceeding on as a family traveling across the country. We awake with the intention of returning to the interstates, to I-90, which is very nearby. And today it is my hope that we will be less an expedition with a crazed guy in charge, insisting on history-minded stops, and more of an expeditionary team stopping wherever. Yes, this is a fine line, perhaps imperceptible, but a line that I personally can feel on this second morning, when I get a second chance to cool it, to calm down.

Specifically, we arise in a dingy motel room, still tired, from even more-tired mattresses. We are bathed in the woozy daylight that reflects off the green mountains of Missoula. We awake in the thick of cross-countrying, with no turning back: it is as if we have been swallowed by the whale of the trip, like Hiawatha, swallowed in her canoe by the great fish Mishe-Nama. We open the giant curtain on the window to reveal the mountains that surround Missoula, as well as the panorama of local and chain restaurants. Magnificent blue-sky daylight pours in to reveal the paintings of the English countryside on the motel walls. And when I say *we*, of course, I don't mean the youngest people involved in our expedition; I mean, my wife and myself. The kids moan, groan, lash out at our attempts to greet them cheerfully. Our daughter makes a guttural sound that startles me. My son, facedown in the cheap, artificial-fiber-filled pillow, makes several attempts to fend me off, including an empathetic approach, which I just make out, muffled as it is. "Dad, why don't you just give up?" he asks.

A good point, a point that sends me to the door, where I stop, turn around, and grab the keys, which are on a lanyard I wear around my neck, a questionable fashion move that helps assuage my terminal fear of losing the keys, or worse, locking them in the car—my virtually fool-proof plan.

Now, I am off again to the parking lot, to circle the car, and then to Finnegan's, the restaurant from last night, for a cup of coffee, beginning the day where we finished it, like a James Joyce novel. Next, I begin to strap the shredded, moan-making pack back onto the car. As I do, I put the cup of coffee on the trunk for a just a second, at which point I get in the car, forget about the coffee, and proceed to push the button that opens the trunk, a visually tempting button that looks like this:

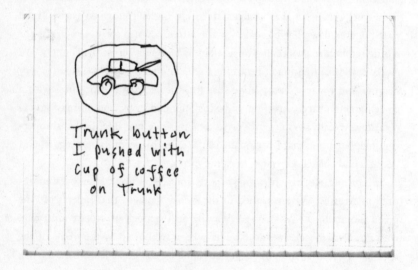

Trunk button
I pushed with
cup of coffee
on Trunk

It is in this way that I accidentally spill the coffee, at which point I head back to the motel room, where I try to act as if I haven't just put the coffee on the trunk and opened it.

In the room, the young people are still not arising.

I'm not rushing anybody today. I pack the car some more. From the balcony, I observe our motel site, makes sketches, though, of course, I would like to get moving at some point.

I step out to purchase and drink another cup of coffee and continue to sketch. If someone had sketched *me* at this moment—out on the balcony, sipping coffee, staying calm, then I would appear unusually relaxed, as if I were anticipating a completely different kind of day. In fact, I am remembering all the times we have moved our family across the country, and I am thinking the United States itself was for a while like a family moving across the country. I retain my relaxed cross-country mode even after checkout, after I find out from the person at the Creekside Inn's front desk that there is some debate over whether Lewis and Clark camped at the site of the Creekside Inn, or just down the road a little.

A NEW EXPEDITIONARY LEAF

I AM ATTEMPTING TO TURN OVER a new expeditionary leaf. What that means is on this, the second day of the trip, I am not making any big plans, à la day one. I am not setting us up for disappointment. Today, I am attempting to take the road as it comes to me, trying to be cool, even though this will hurt us as far as getting home goes, even though I know that in a couple of days people on the expedition, such as myself, will be dying to be home.

So when the kids do eventually get up and get in the car and carve out places to sit in the back seat (from which, as part of what will be my morning preparation ritual, I have scraped away the dead bugs that had fallen from the expensive cartop pack, which spends the night in the car), we drive into downtown Missoula, just a few blocks away, a place we have been many times before on cross-country trips, a place where we are familiar with the food supply, where we will have what will essentially be our last meal before we get to Saint Paul, twelve hundred miles away.

We go to a coffee shop that, to my great geographical delight, is decorated with a large three-dimensional U.S. Geological Survey map of the Missoula area, a map with Lewis and Clark's trip through the area highlighted, and, yes, their trip in comparison to ours is excitingly similar, but of course I don't make a big deal about that today. I just point it out, that's all. Sleepy heads nod in line to buy coffee and hot chocolate and pastries. Outside, cars and trucks are decorated with what appear to be the themes of daily life in Missoula: logging, mining, construction, and recreation, as in kayaking, camping, mountain biking, fishing, and hiking. At the health-food-oriented local market, we buy healthy snacks and healthy drinks and locally brewed Moose Drool Ale (to take home with us, don't worry). We proceed down the street to a couple of antique shops where our son looks at old guitars and my wife and our daughter look at everything else. We stop at a great little bookstore just up from the Missoula train station and buy way too many books, stuffing our car in a fashion that would halt our progress entirely if we were crossing the country the way families first did, when the United States was expanding shortly after the return of Lewis and Clark.

We get on the road late, real late, as far as a typical morning of a cross-country trip goes. We get on the road at an hour that would have caused me to hyperventilate if I were the expeditionary leader I was yesterday. Still, I remain calm. We set out now on Interstate 90—me looking at the soft dollops of clouds floating in the big blue, Montana morning sky, my wife driving.

As we reach a speed of 60 m.p.h., the cartop roof pack that I absolutely had to buy began first to buzz and then to moan, and I almost don't notice.

A FEW WORDS ABOUT MY WIFE AS A
CROSS-COUNTRY DRIVER

MY WIFE IS A GREAT cross-country driver. She has driven in every state in the continental United States, except Alaska. To my mind, one of her most impressive feats was the time she drove all the way across the country when we were moving from the East Coast to the West Coast, about fifteen years before this current trip. I drove a rental truck, carting all our stuff, and she drove a Subaru wagon, filled with our son and a lot of food, toys, and diapers. It was when our son was six months old, and incredibly, she managed to keep him occupied, fed, and happy for the entire trip. I admit that I was not completely certain about the travel arrangements. I drove along behind her in the truck. It was winter, two weeks before Christmas; I remember the holiday-lights festival on the Illinois River that I saw for about thirty seconds as we passed through Peoria on the interstate. We were young, in our twenties, and we could drive for distances that seemed like forever. On a trip we had taken just before our son was born, we crossed the country in two, sleep-deprived days. I was hallucinating when I got out of the car, having ODed on too much bad coffee, having thought I'd seen black and white cows running along I-80.

In traveling from New York to Oregon, we chose to mostly drive on Interstate 80, the least number of miles, and to avoid northern routes that might be snowbound. As we were in the era prior to the development of cell phones, we traveled with cheap walkie-talkies purchased for about twenty bucks at a drugstore in New York at the last minute before heading out. The walkie-talkies worked when we drove the vehicles very close together, otherwise we just heard static, and even when they worked, we had to shout into them. We signaled each other to turn on the walkie-talkies by blinking our headlights. Whenever my wife thought it was time for our son to take a break, we would stop and take a break. My wife pulled over at rest stops to nurse our son, to change his diaper, to buy a snack. I either sat in the car with them or did jumping jacks outside the window. We drove from sunup to sundown, like pioneers on the trail.

One afternoon, in Nebraska, it began to rain. Then the rain began to freeze. Then there was ice everywhere, the road like glass. I drove the truck up close to my wife's car and blinked my lights and then shouted into the walkie-talkie.

"Are you OK?"

"Yes," she said.

"Be careful. It's pretty slippery," I said, as if she hadn't noticed.

"*You* be careful," she kept saying.

The ice got worse. The traffic slowed down way below the speed limit. Then it slowed down to around 25 miles an hour. The traffic was mostly trucks. The trucks began to slide around on the road, as did my truck. I drove even slower. I was holding the wheel very tightly. I had never driven a truck across the country before, and at that moment it was like driving on an air-hockey table. In my journal that night, I wrote, "Heart pounding."

In front of us, trucks began to drive off the road. The trucks would be driving straight, seemingly OK, then they would veer a little left or a little right. Then the front wheels would turn suddenly, and then the truck would be in the ditch alongside I-80, sideways, stuck, tilted.

Seeing this kind of thing happening repeatedly, I got my truck close to the car again, blinked my lights, pressed Talk, shouted. "I'm pulling off up here!" I said.

"OK," she said.

All the trucks were pulling off too; there was a truck stop at that exit. In fact, everyone was pulling off, just near North Platte, along the old Oregon Trail, a way that hundreds of thousands of people had once moved their families and all their stuff across the country—though usually they left in the spring.

WE WENT INSIDE THE TRUCK STOP restaurant and sat around with coffee and finally ordered food like everyone else. Everyone was talking to everyone else, truckers and the few nontruckers alike. Our son was sitting in his car seat on the bench at our table and playing with the tableside jukebox and tableside credit card telephone, as truckers were kindly making funny faces at him, causing him to laugh joyously, as six-month-old children will, even in stressful cross-country situations.

After an hour or so, two state police officers pulled up in the parking lot in a souped-up police car—a sports car with studded tires. The truckers all stood up to look out the window. One police officer made a dramatic entrance. He sauntered in and pulled off his gloves slowly, one finger at a time; it was as if he had just walked through the swinging doors of an old saloon. Everyone watched as he and the other officer sat down. The room was dead quiet. The waitress took his order.

"You write tickets faster than my partner here," he said.

A trucker shouted out. "How are the roads?"

"Sure, the roads are good . . ." he said, as if onstage and so that everyone could hear him. He paused and added, ". . . if you're in the Ice Capades!"

About two hours later, after the police had driven carefully away, the freezing rain let up; the sky began to clear. All of a sudden, one of the truckers who was on the tableside phone shouted to the room: "The road's open!"

"It's all clear past Big Springs," his announcement continued.

Everyone called for their check at once, sending the waitresses into a frenzy. Back in our station wagon–truck convoy, we pulled slowly onto the road. We drove hesitantly, then more confidently, as we could once again see the pavement. In about a half hour, we reached the Wyoming border and all of a sudden there was no ice on the road at all, and the sun was breaking through dark clouds. The road in Wyoming that afternoon was black with an iceless dampness, a benign little mist hovering over it. It was a perfect yellow-striped black that I think of from time to time as a haiku, a pure and simple stroke of perfect roadness.

I pulled my truck alongside my wife's station wagon, blinked. "This is great," I shouted into the walkie-talkie. She waved and smiled and pointed to our son, who was watching a toy that my wife had attached to the ceiling of the car, and then she drove on up ahead, to lead the way.

MOUNTAIN MEN

SURROUNDED BY MOUNTAINS, with Missoula behind us, we cross the Clark Fork River, a wide, sun-happy stream that flirts in view of the Gallatin Mountains and all the hills of the Beaverhead-Deerlodge National Forest, at which point I begin to read aloud from a Montana travel brochure, *Montana's*

Gold West Country, because, let's face it, even though I am acting more relaxed, I haven't changed that much: "Even to the non-history buff, our region's history is impressive and hard to overlook." A history that is impressive to me in this region of the country is the history of the mountain men. The mountain men were the people who traveled to Montana and Wyoming, or even to Nevada and California and various other places around the West—a group of migrating workers who learned the old routes across the country, who mapped them or just remembered them and then led new people across.

One way to look at the mountain men is that they were guys who came to live off the land; another is as the first in a long line of people who came out to trap, to mine, to extract in one way or another. They came originally for the beaver pelts that were valued in Saint Louis and California, in the East and in all of Europe. Mountain men spread up into the rivers of the West, following old animal trails and the trails of the local tribes. Mountain men were not cross-country travelers in the purest, modern-day sense; they did not travel the United States from east to west but mostly from north to south, in part because the United States did not yet stretch all the way from the Atlantic to the Pacific. And they were definitely not the gentleman farmers that Thomas Jefferson had hoped would follow Lewis and Clark and settle the West. They were independent contractors who were not tied to one piece of land but roamed over vast stretches, from valley to valley. There were only about one thousand of them when the mountain men business was thriving.

Between 1820 and 1840, mountain men were spread throughout the West, and like modern cross-country travelers, which is to say like us, they lived by their particular rules and routines. They were not loners, living and trapping in western solitude, as is commonly thought; they were team players. They were mostly French Canadian, and they were either paid a salary by the company they worked for and not entitled to take furs, or outfitted by the company and thus already in debt. They traveled in small brigades for protection; sometimes four or five dozen mountain men would travel by horse up a river valley. They carried rifles, pistols, and black powder. Mountain men did not live in the mountains all year-round; they might also be called part-time town men because they hunted and trapped in the spring and fall, the seasons when beavers were largest, stayed inside during the winter, and summered in places such as Taos, New Mexico, and Jackson Hole, Wyoming—predating corporate executive retreats. The mountain men would meet and recreate and drink to such an extent that they would wind up with debts that would force them to go out trapping again. An old painting of a meeting in a valley in the Wind River between mountain men and tribes from the area resembles an outdoor carnival, a meeting of a lot of people who look as if they hadn't seen each other in years, encircled by the snow-covered peaks of the Wind River Mountains.

The mountain men traveled to western valleys, spread out along streams, then regrouped. They camped high up, and sometimes built defenses. While trapping, they were very careful about budgeting their food and supplies. They carried preserved meats, sugar, bread or flour, and coffee, and they ate what they could find, such as roots. They learned bits and pieces of the languages of the western tribes, just enough to not get killed in a misunderstanding. They adopted the clothing and survival techniques of the Indians; a good way to compliment a mountain man was to mistake him for a Native American. They learned bison trails and Indian trails, the whereabouts of passes and watering holes, and how to read signs of beaver activity. While trapping for beaver, they moved in shallow river water, so as not to leave their scent on the ground. They left traps underwater and baited them on the surface with scents from the beavers' crushed sexual glands. Mountain men rarely took along liquor; they had to stay alert. "Every man carried his life in his own hands," wrote one, "and it is only by the most watchful precaution, grounded upon and guided by the observation of every unnatural appearance however slight, that he can hope to preserve it."

Hugh Glass was a mountain man who was left for dead in the Missouri River headwaters after having been attacked by a grizzly bear. He shot the bear and climbed a tree but the dying bear managed to climb the tree, pull him down and maul him from head to toe before dying on top of him; Glass's throat was punctured, blood was everywhere. His mountain men companions tried to carry him for a while but were feeling susceptible to Indian attack while doing so and, when they were convinced he would not survive, left Glass, taking his gun. Glass crawled for six weeks, eating berries, insects, snakes, and rotting bison flesh. He traveled five miles a day for two hundred miles. After he got to a settlement and recovered, he tried to shoot the guys who abandoned him, but eventually settled for just getting his gun back.

The trapping business began to die out in the 1840s, when the demand for beaver pelts ended—beaver hats went out of fashion, replaced by silk hats. Mountain men began to run out of mountain work, though some of them ended up helping the military expeditions that began to arrive in the West to, first, explore, and to, next, fight the tribes that resisted the invasion of settlers. It was just the time that people were getting on wagon trains and hitting the Oregon Trail, so some of the mountain men ended up working as guides for the settlers, leading people across the mountains, helping them survive, or at least make their way across the country.

CHALET

THE CASUAL OBSERVER watching us casually traveling—lounging late in our creekside motel, shopping leisurely in Missoula, and now pulling off I-90 not far from where we got on—can be forgiven for thinking that perhaps we are leisure-loving tourists, out to explore a very small portion of Montana. Though we are supposed to be crossing the country, today we are commuting merely within river valleys, like, say, Jim Bridger, the Montana-based mountain man who mapped trails from the Oregon Trail on the Platte River up to the Montana gold fields, gold prospecting being a profession that mountain men naturally and easily segued into after beaver pelt collection ended. Bridger helped open up several routes along what was known as the Bozeman Trail, routes that were eventually adopted by the interstate highway system as it runs through the middle of Montana—which is where we are as my wife decides to pull over, citing the need for gas.

Exit 138 is in Bearmouth, Montana, and the sign at the end of the ramp gives us the choice between Garnet, an old mining town that is now a ghost town in these mountains, and a bar that bills itself as a chalet. At the chalet, we purchase gas from a lonely and dusty pump in the hot sun. While pumping, I absentmindedly look down at the dirt between the gas pumps and the chalet to discover a miniature roadside marker beside a rock. The rock does not appear extraordinary in shape, color, or size, and yet it is labeled. "This rock is over 500 million years old," the sign says. "It came from an ancient lake bed ½ mile north of the chalet. At that time the spot where your [*sic*] standing was under 1500ft of water."* It is late in the morning, and I go inside with the idea of buying coffee and perhaps asking about the rock, but when I get to the bar and stand in the midst of video poker games and alongside a woman in her late fifties who is nursing a drink with a guy in his early twenties who is nursing a drink and at last spot a nearly empty coffeepot, the coffee fried, I double back. It is a rare crossing-the-country instance of coffee not singing out to me.

After the chalet, after getting back on the road, after driving between more mountains, after noticing that the mountains were losing their greenness, after passing trucks carrying giant bales of hay that most likely had been taken from the floor of the river valley alongside our car, after following along land that our TripTik describes as "scenic wooded slopes and valleys with mountain views," we spot a tall dark tower in the distance, a smokestack. The smokestack is all that remains of the Anaconda copper smelter. It sits on a hill framed by the hills behind it. We follow the smokestack as if it were a beacon for the town in which it is based, Anaconda, because, while driving, we have decided to stop to play some golf.

Golfing was sort of my idea—I spotted the course in a brochure I picked up on the way out of the chalet. Why did I do this? Why especially since I don't play golf—I don't enjoy a lot of standing around. Why when, even though I am trying to turn over a new expeditionary leaf, I do eventually want to get to the other side, to the Atlantic, or thereabouts, at some point?

"Should we stop at the golf course?" I ask lightly.

"Can we play there?" my son asks in response.

"Sure," I say, trying to sound as if I am not missing a beat.

"*Yes!*" my son says.

"Just relax," my wife says.

---

* I cannot say with absolute certainty but I believe the sign is referring to Lake Missoula, the one-time glacial lake that, when an ice dam broke, flooded out the Columbia Gorge, which, readers may recall, we drove through yesterday, in Oregon. Most exciting for me is that the rock alleged to be from a glacial lake stands next to the ice machine.

WANDERING THROUGH HILLS

INTERSTATE DRIVING IS AKIN to driving in a dream, a dream where you get the feeling that you recognize everything but you don't really, a dream world full of sometimes magical scenery—like these classically wondrous mountains that support the vast blue sky we are driving beneath at this late-morning moment—that is punctuated with oddities, sometimes secretly dangerous, which makes our trip home across Montana, much less the entire country, a little like Ulysses' trip home to Ithaca. And just as Circe suggested Ulysses avoid the Wandering Rocks, those navigational hazards, so she might have frowned on stopping for toxic-waste-site golf. So as we enter the Deer Lodge Valley for interstate-side golf playing, let us look carefully at these hills that are alternately like sun-painted actors in scenic postcards and like a gigantic partially eaten sandwich. Here before us, in the area of Anaconda and Butte, in these valleys that carry us smoothly through the Rocky Mountains, we see hills that have been dug out, scraped away, eaten up by mining interests, with obvious signs of extraction, current or past, such as giant smokestacks or things that belch steam. And then there are the less obvious signs: hills that appear to be hills then as you approach them appear to be hills of striking geologic character and then appear to be not so much hills as huge piles of the remains of hills.

Personally, after so many times passing them, I see these hills as symbols of work, or at least the result of work. In so doing, I often think of Marcus Daly, a miner born in county Cavan, Ireland, who left at the time of the potato famine and showed up in New York City at the age of fifteen and then moved to California to be a miner for a company that eventually sent him to Montana to search for silver, which, as he surmised, often sat on top of large deposits of copper. With the support of the Hearst family in California, Daly bought up a huge silver mine in Montana, and then, at around the same time that the telegraph had become successful and many miles of copper were needed for its wires, Daly established a copper smelter a few miles away from the mine, and the town with the smelter became Anaconda—Anaconda was close to the water of the Deer Lodge Valley, close to copper. Daly then proceeded to buy up forests and coal mines and banks and a newspaper, in addition to politicians. He was said to treat his employees well, encouraging them to join unions, giving preference to new arrivals. When he died in 1900, in New York City, Daly's obituary in the Butte *Miner*, a paper owned by one of Daly's mining rivals, read, "A friend to his friends, to his enemies remorseless and unforgiving. Daly, a father figure, watched over his family, his friends and his employees with a heartfelt benevolence. It must be noted that when he ran the Anaconda Mining Company, he treated his employees better than most corporations of the time."

THE OTHER WAY THAT I SEE THESE HILLS is as an absence, a theft, an act of violence that mirrors the violence involved in the process, and when I am sitting in the car and looking out the window, I think of Frank A. Little, a counterpart to Marcus Daly. Little was an organizer with the Industrial Workers of the World, a labor organization nicknamed the Wobblies. He was born in 1889. His mother was Cherokee, his father a Quaker, and his friends described him as "half white, half Indian, and all Wobbly." He had lost an eye mining, and his health had deteriorated while he was in jail—often in solitary confinement—where he was put when he spoke out in support of free speech. He also spoke out against World War I. "War will mean the end of free speech, free press, free assembly, and everything we ever fought for!" he said. "I'll take the firing squad first!" In Spokane, Washington, Little was forced to work a rock pile for thirty days after reading the Declaration of Independence aloud in public. When he arrived in Butte and Anaconda, he was on crutches, having had his ankle broken while organizing workers in Bisbee, Arizona.

When Marcus Daly died, Butte was a wide open town of a hundred thousand, as opposed to the thirty thousand or so that live there today. Butte boomed especially when World War I broke out; the Anaconda Mining Company produced 30 percent of the copper in the United States and 10 percent of the copper in the world. But a miner in Butte was more likely to be killed than a soldier in the trenches in Europe. As the war continued, copper prices increased; wages did not. Then, production was increased, with no regard toward safety. In June 1917, there was a fire at the Speculator Mine. One hundred and sixty-four men died. On the dead bodies, fingers were ground down to the second knuckle by men who had attempted to claw through sealed hatches. After the fire, the miners went on strike. It was at that point that Frank Little arrived in Anaconda.

Little spoke to the miners, trying to keep them motivated about the strike. The newspapers described both the strike and Frank Little as pro-German and un-American. After a few weeks, six masked men broke into Little's hotel room. His body was found a few hours later hanging from a railroad trestle; he had been beaten and dragged behind a car until his kneecaps were scraped off. The cast on his leg was smashed, a note pinned to his underwear said, "3-7-77," the dimensions of a Montana grave. The police didn't find his murderers. Frank Little's funeral was the largest in Butte's history—seven thousand people attended.*

HAZARDS

AND SO TO GOLF, to walk the bucolic and not-bucolic landscape of a course in Anaconda. In the windshield as we near the course is the 585-foot-tall smokestack, all that remains of Marcus Daly's copper smelter. It calls us from on top of the hills that seem to have been mined (dusty, reddish, lacking visible vegetation) and from the hills that have not necessarily been mined (covered with trees that have not been logged, sometimes covered with summer mountain ice) and from both types of hills blending together. We see a third kind of hill, the hill that appears to be composed entirely of the remnants of

---

* As there are two different ways to think of the hills in Anaconda, there are likewise two different ways to think about Montana and the way it utilizes its land. As opposed to a lot of other western states, Montana has always had a practical, long-term, and cash-oriented streak. In some ways, it can be seen as a state set up to make money for people in Europe and in the East, with furs and minerals and now methane mines. There were no utopian communities in Montana, and Mormon missionaries largely avoided Montana, preferring Idaho and Alberta. In other parts of the Rocky Mountains the scars in the land are from farming on a smaller scale and from the search for water. Montana's scars are often based on large-scale and highly technological industry—huge clear-cuts, completely polluted streams, hill-sized pits. Its nickname is the Treasure State and its slogan is *Oro y plata* (Gold and silver). A result of so much land being worked by so many people over so many years is Montana's often-activist labor force. Also, despite its huge toxic-waste sites, Montana is a state that has worked hard to conserve land, with vast wilderness preserves, with the reintroduction of species, with a penchant for managing large ecosystems. An amendment to Montana's state constitution guarantees the right to a clean and healthy environment.

mining, also called slag. This is a completely black hill, a hill that shines in the sun, that is like a hill of crystallized black glass, a shadow hill.

Also, we smell something.

"What's that smell?" our daughter says.

"Oh, that smells *soooo* bad," says our son.

THROUGH DOWNTOWN ANACONDA, our Impala sails through straight streets of old homes and old storefronts. We take a right turn and proceed on a path off the main street through bleak lots, past rusting cars, through cheatgrass and fields, parking in the lot of a startlingly green golf course, the Old Works Golf Course. It's a Jack Nicklaus–designed course, a place to relax in the valley of wastes with high concentrations of arsenic, in addition to copper and cadmium, lead and zinc, all of which contaminate the health of streams and plants and animals and people living in the valley. We head to the pro shop, at the edge of the millions of cubic yards of rearranged and retreated mining land. We rent clubs and we ask if we might tee up, *we* being our son—our daughter wants to caddie, my wife wants to simply observe, which, given her athleticism seems impossible. I thought I would have to tie her to the Old Works' flag mast to keep her from more than observing the game. I myself plan to not let the golf spoil a nice walk through a remediated toxic area.

Fore!

HERE AT THE GOLF COURSE, we walk simultaneously through a lush green landscape, a re-creation of Scottish splendor, an idyllic ideal of a life-giving glade, and a denuded site, a scene of industrial detritus, of raw earth used and discarded and left for dead. It's a vineyard and a graveyard. In view is the remediated, or at least partially remediated, Warm Creek, a stream once involved in smelting copper, now used to frame a fairway. Ahead I see the green of the greens as they fade into varying shades of less-watered green, and finally unwatered green, native plants and dry grasses, this last layer then surrounded by rubble from the roughed-up hills, the beat-up mini-mountains. I see the paths of slag, the dross of the mining process, an industrial waste, a metamorphic condition that from a distance could be a volcanic beach in the South Pacific.

I see no one around, really, on this bright weekday morning. I see a letter

A carved off into a hill on the course's horizon, which stands for *Anaconda* but, ecologically speaking, brings to mind a Puritan stain.

I see another tall smokestack in ruins a few hills away.

I see my son teed up, his club swing back, the pure white ball lofted, rising, descending, straight ahead, a good-enough shot, though a little close to the sand traps, the so-called hazard—a word that here is a double entendre. The black slag used in the hazards turns the bunkers into black holes.

But I fear not as I walk through the valley of black slag, the reason being that the notice in the clubhouse mentions that the Jack Nicklaus organization sent the slag to a laboratory for testing. When I imagine the slag test results coming back as "negative," I imagine the relief of the golf course designers, of the chamber of commerce officials, of Montana golfers all around Montana. I read about this on the walls of the clubhouse, where I see a plaque for Julius "Buddy" Blume, "whose foresight and work and love of community," the plaque states, "turned a barren valley into the world class Old Works Golf Course."

"The idea of turning Superfund land back to the community is gaining interest nationwide," says an article pinned up nearby.

OUR SON IS PUTTING, our daughter cheerfully playing around with the flag, my wife observing, arms folded, nodding, suggesting. I am wandering up into the beat-up rocks looking down, sketching again.

And then I chat with the greenskeeper, a nice guy tending to native fescues, a guy whose grandfather worked in the Anaconda smelter before it was in ruins, a guy who asks where we are headed and, when I say east, mentions he went to school in New Jersey to study plants. Later, I go back toward the golf course hills to ask the greenskeeper a question but I can't find him. My little eastward-heading team and I—after we all begin to head back to the clubhouse, after looking like surveyors of some kind with flags and instruments and paused concentrated poses—had all of a sudden noticed that the roots of the plants along the edge of the course's creek are a bright fluorescent red, a red that does not seem right to me and even seems a little eerie, under the circumstances, which include toxic waste. I never did find the greenskeeper and nobody else I talked to could tell me why the roots were so red. I'm sure it's completely natural.

SAILING PAST THE PIT

SADLY, WE WON'T BE STOPPING IN BUTTE, a town that we have so often visited, sucked in to see the Berkeley Pit, a.k.a. the Pit. My wife, who is in the navigator's seat again, reads temptingly from our AAA TourBook: "The Berkeley Pit Viewing Stand, open daily dawn to dusk, March to mid-November, is free and provides an excellent view of the old open mine." Sadly, we will not ascend the viewing stand and view the cavity that was unfilled the first time we saw it over a decade ago. We will not view the hole that replaces a mountain out of which 290 million tons of copper were extracted. Once, the pit was two little towns, towns that were bought by the Anaconda Mining Company and then emptied so that the pit could grow to be more than a mile wide, and nearly as deep as the Empire State Building is tall. The mine closed in 1982. Underground pumps ceased pumping water out of the vaults and tunnels. Water filled the hole, forming a kind of lake. Tourists now view the lake, and it's not a lake of rainwater but a lake of water that contains concentrations of arsenic, copper, cadmium, cobalt, iron, manganese, zinc, and sulfate, among other metals, all of which rise up from the old mine shafts,

shafts started in the 1870s, from nine hundred feet below the lake's surface: there are about thirty billion gallons of fluid in the lake by a recent estimate. Once it was called "the richest hill on earth," but now it's a big toxic lake, seeping into the community below. As a perverse tourist site, a place to view an ecological disaster, it is the opposite of a purple mountain's majesty. It is a darkness, an abyss, on which birds alight, and then die.

"Look, the pit," I say.

"Up there," says my wife, pointing to the ruin of the mountain in the sky.

It is not clear that the kids see the pit as we pass it. On the other hand, they do seem to be listening when both of us recount one of our greatest Butte experiences, the time we met a Montana deity, a hero of the automotive world, Evel Knievel. I can't say that much happened to us when we met Evel Knievel but it is the case that my wife and I can't come anywhere near Butte without fondly recalling the episode with a legend of Butte, a legend who is like the Berkeley Pit in that he is a legend whether Butte likes it or not.

CROSSING OVER

FOR WHAT IS A GOD if not a mortal writ large, a mortal transcending? Does not Evel Knievel represent a transcendence, if only when he is in the air on his motorcycle, above the road, above a series of trucks or cars, above America?

Born in Butte in 1938, Robert Craig Knievel is said to have been christened by a local police officer named Mulcahy, who, when Knievel was sixteen and in jail for stealing hubcaps, said, "So, we have Evil Knievel in the cell block tonight!" Later, to avoid offending pious fans, he changed Evil to Evel. He began jumping things in the 1960s and 1970s, initially jumping lions, sharks, and long rows of automobiles or trucks. "I'm not a stuntman. I'm a daredevil," he has said.

According to his authorized biography, Evel worked in the Butte copper mines as a contract miner, as a skip tender and a diamond drill operator. After enlisting in the Army, he ran his own hunting guide service in Montana, and, in so doing, discovered elk were being slaughtered in Yellowstone National Park. In 1961, he campaigned to save the elk in Yellowstone and hitchhiked to Washington, D.C., carrying elk antlers, to appeal to members of Congress and the interior secretary. His idea, which was adopted, was to have the elk that were going to be slaughtered in Yellowstone transported to places in Montana, Wyoming, and Idaho where hunters could shoot them. Evel then sold insurance for a while, but eventually switched to daredeviling, starting out with a five-hundred-dollar jump over a few parked cars and gradually increasing to a million-dollar jump over thirteen buses in England, a jump in which he broke his pelvis. His biography also mentions the following: that in addition to being featured in the movies *Evel Knievel*, starring George Hamilton as Evel, and *Viva Knievel*, starring Evel as himself, Evel had a cameo with Lindsey Wagner in an episode of *The Bionic Woman*; that he considers himself to have revitalized the U.S. toy industry in the 1970s by lending his name to pinball machines and the like; that after his 151-foot jump over the fountains at Caesar's Palace in Las Vegas, he was in a coma for a month; that the winter of 1976 was the winter Evel, during an attempt to jump a tank full of live sharks, suffered a concussion and two broken arms and injured a bystander (a cameraman, who lost an eye); that he established as his successor his son Robbie Knievel after the winter of 1976; that he enjoys painting western scenes; and that there is a river in Arkansas named after him. Discussing his character, his biography notes: "Though having attained super-star status, and genuine friendships with other stars like Elvis Presley, Jackie Gleason and Muhammed Ali, he remained affable and accessible to ordinary working people and children."

Every summer, Butte celebrates Evel Knievel Daze—or at least part of Butte does. Reportedly, many people in Butte would prefer there were no Evel Knievel Daze, because they don't like associating their town with Evel Knievel, while some residents see Evel Knievel as one of them—a mortal god, worshipped by one tribe, abhorred by another. Evel Knievel Daze is a festival that features a tattoo contest, a parade of motorcycles, and an Evel Knievel look-alike contest. (In 2003, the look-alike contest was won by the grandson of Officer Mulcahy.) People who are pro–Evel Knievel Daze enjoy the display of the X-2 Skycycle, a vehicle that is less like a motorcycle and more like a rocket with wheels, which was a jury-rigged driving dream and is the centerpiece of the Knievel legacy. The other part of our Evel Knievel story that our children enjoy hearing as we pass by—indeed, the part of the story that they seem to not believe—is the story of the X-2 Skycycle.

IT WAS ON SEPTEMBER 8, 1974 THAT EVEL KNIEVEL launched the Sky-cyle into the air in an attempt to cross over the Snake River Canyon. The Skycycle was supposed to go up for a while as it proceeded over the Snake River Canyon and then, as it started down toward the flat ground on the other side, a quarter mile away, a parachute was supposed to deploy. Though you couldn't really call it a sport, ABC's *Wide World of Sports* broadcast the jump live. Evel was wearing his white, star-spangled jumpsuit as he entered the Skycycle. The Skycycle waited for a long time at the bottom of an earthen ramp. When Evel ignited the engine, the Skycycle started up into the air, but then the parachute released almost immediately, causing the rocket, which had nearly made it across, to go straight down into the Snake River Canyon, just missing the Snake River, where, people invariably point out, Evel Knievel probably would have drowned.

The earthen ramp from the Skycyle jump is still there, near the visitor center off the interstate highway in Twin Falls. The first time we stopped there on a cross-country trip, I did not even notice the dirt ramp that sent the Sky-cycle into the air—I was too busy studying the state highway map. In Idaho, the state highway map lists the old settlers' trails that crossed that part of Idaho, including the Lewis and Clark trail, the Lolo Trail, the Mullan Road, the Nez Percé Trail, the Southern Nez Percé Trail, the Oregon Trail, the Oregon Trail Southern Alternative, the Hudspeth's Cutoff (a.k.a., the California Trail), the Lander Trail (also to California), the Kelton Road, and Goodale's Cutoff. It's as if Evel Knievel jumped a ghost train of covered wagons, the progenitors of moving trucks or RVs.

The rest stop in Twin Falls is a little ways off the highway and features an Idaho-oriented gift shop. After my daughter bought a gold rush tchotchke at the gift shop, I went out to look at the Snake River, a thin, celery-green stream, from high up on the edge of the steep canyon, and then happened on the plaque that marks the date of the jump and mentions the earthen ramp. Now, whenever we stop there, I see the nearby strip mall expanding with box stores, and each year the stores seem to move closer to the site of Evel Knievel's jump, threatening to overtake it.

THE TIME WE SAW EVEL KNIEVEL, in Butte, my wife and I were traveling with our son, who was one and a half years old, as well as with my wife's friend from college, Mia, who was excited to take a ride to the West Coast. My wife and I were feeling bad about having a guest along on the trip as we pulled into Butte because we had fed our son too much apple juice, a toxic diaper situation. We pulled over at a gas station, legally disposing of the offending diaper, and then drove to have dinner at an Italian restaurant near the airport, Lydia's.

At Lydia's, the waiter seated us in the pleasingly dark main dining room and asked us about our drive cross-country. We ate our dinners happily but at some point the waiter returned to chat with us and suddenly he seemed to think that we were not enjoying ourselves in Butte, which was not the case.

"I'll bet you think this is the armpit of the world," he blurted out.

"No, we don't," I said, proceeding to explain—it was one of those moments when you know you are being misunderstood and there's not a lot you can do about it.

"OK," he interrupted, as if we had put him up to a dare. "Well look over there." With that he pointed to the back of the room. "Do you know who *that* is?"

We all turned around slowly and looked toward an older couple sitting in a banquette by the door—the white-haired man was hunched over as he clutched his drink, sitting silently beside a woman who seemed to be his wife.

"*That's* Evel Knievel," said the waiter, folding his arms and motioning his head emphatically toward back of the room.

As we drank our coffee, we stole glances at the corner, at the man who had jumped over lines of Greyhound buses, over rows of Mack trucks, who, not quite sixty at the time, had broken thirty-seven bones, including one when he fell in a sand trap and another when he fell in a Jacuzzi. To this day I wonder if he was drinking his favorite drink, the Montana Mary, a mixture of beer, tomato juice, and Wild Turkey. Likewise, I wondered if the woman, whom I shall call Mrs. Knievel, was his wife or the girlfriend that he was arrested for beating up in a topless bar. The waiter said it was his wife, and my wife thought it was too.

Later, my son and I got up to leave, and I nervously passed Evel Knievel's table. As I did, our toddler son waved at the couple. Mrs. Knievel stopped us and then pointed to our son. "What a cutey," she said, motioning to Evel. At that moment, Evel Knievel seemed to look up. He seemed to make an effort to focus, to join our world at Lydia's, to cross over from wherever he was. He said nothing and went back to his beverage. We went out into the parking lot and into the car, and our son fell asleep as we all drove on to Missoula, to the Big Sky Motel, and felt we had really experienced something. It was as if we had connected with a piece of America, or a piece of the American dream, but then again for a connection you at least need to make eye contact, and when I think back on the experience, eye contact was not what happened.

HOMESTAKE PASS

LEAVING THE BUTTE AREA, the interstate takes us smoothly through more Rocky Mountains, takes us up with well-graded-concrete grace, up to 6,398 feet, as the road marker precisely informs us, to Homestake Pass, at which point we crest the continent one final time and head down through a canyon of cottage-sized rubbed-round boulders. I shudder as I brake. As I depress the hydraulic foot pedal, I recall crossing Homestake Pass one summer in a truck with all our family's possessions, about to stake out a new home. I shudder even now. How I remember coming straight down from 6,398 feet on I-90 and my son, nine years old then, smelling the smoke that I was trying not to mention, which, as I had feared, turned out to be the brakes, which, as I latter learned from a trucker, were pretty close to being shot. The trucker I learned this from ran up to us at the next rest stop, jogged toward our rental truck, to warn us, given all of the smoke coming off our brakes. "Your brakes are gonna catch fire," said the big trucker, running up to us with his little tiny dog, which he was walking.

"Dad," my son asked, nonplussed, as we were racing down the hill, as I was ready to collapse, "what's your favorite Beatles album?"

How I remember a similar situation later in that same cross-country trip, when we were on the Pennsylvania Turnpike, when there was construction, when trucks had to stay in the left lane, and all the trucks behind me were on our back because my truck could not break sixty, a fact that caused the truckers

behind me to lay on their horns, honks blaring at five- and ten-second inter-
vals. All of this was causing me to freak out, to consider an imminent and
horrible death—a consideration I was again concealing from my son, who
asked another nonchalant nine-year-old question.

"Dad," my son asked, "which do you like better, vanilla ice cream or chocolate ice cream?"

Now in Montana, descending smoothly where once sons and fathers and
mothers and daughters worked like hell to haul wagons up the sides of hills,
we see runaway-truck ramps, a highway feature that also makes me shudder:
to imagine myself, brakeless and heading up into a vehicle-stopping hill, into
a windrow of loose gravel. Next, we pass a giant truck carrying a giant boulder, which seems like an omen but, in the end, isn't, as far as I can tell.

AT THE BOTTOM OF THE PASS, clouds appear in the east and the north,
clouds just beginning to get together, preparing for what will be a big cloud
show if you are passing through rangeland and farmland and see the faraway
valleys and the snow-covered mountaintops to the left and the right and
ahead: cloud shows are a feature of the typical cross-country excursion.

And then, as if I am suffering a relapse of a disease that the doctors
thought I had kicked, I realize there is a Lewis and Clark site of note up
ahead—i.e., just 250 or so miles ahead, well marked, on the TripTik and the
maps. I mention the Lewis and Clark site nonchalantly, as if it doesn't matter
to me whether we visit it or not. It is Pompey's Pillar, a place where Clark
scratched a rock with his name, a place that settlers and soldiers and tourists
often stop at.

AN ASPECT OF INSANITY

AS I'VE MENTIONED, we are not the first family to cross the country: well
known is the story of the families who first crossed the country. These were
the country-crossing families who took part in the overland migrations between 1839 and 1860. Even though I've been back and forth to Oregon

numerous times, I have never bought a wooden wagon, taken it apart to be put on a boat in Saint Louis, and then put it back together, sometimes using it as a boat to cross a river. I have never traveled as little as four miles a day for four or five months straight, assuming things went smoothly, for a total distance of about 2,400 miles—all to get land to farm or maybe to find some gold but always to occupy the territory that America wanted to be American. I have never had to sit down and tell the kids that we are about to *walk* across the continent. Horace Greeley is the newspaper editor famous for telling people to hit the road to Oregon and California, to go west. But before he said that, in the years when people were just beginning to hit the trail, Horace Greeley said: "This migration of more than a thousand persons in one body to Oregon wears an aspect of insanity."

The overland migrations began slowly and then built to a country-crossing frenzy. Lewis and Clark were the United States' first officially sanctioned cross-country team, and they were a small unit, but the overland migrations were a case of a lot of Americans deciding all at once to cross. There were crowds of people at what were referred to as the jumping-off places, where people disassembled their wagons to get them on the steamboats, where they paged through a guidebook that might have seemed knowing and accurate but probably was not. In fact, a lot of times there was no one in a wagon train who knew where they were going; a quarter of a million Americans were often just winging it.

The impetus was money, of course. These were people looking for a fix in their lives; they were taking a chance for something better, and that is something I have done myself in crossing the country. In 1837, there was a national depression. Banks closed. Wages fell by 30 to 50 percent; twenty-thousand people were unemployed. Workers demonstrated in the streets in Philadelphia. The spread of empire also played a part in the crossing; in Massachusetts, a schoolteacher formed the American Society for Encouraging the Settlement of the Oregon Territory, a group intended to establish a Plymouth Bay Colony–like settlement in the West. Also contributing to the giant national move was people feeling "crowded" living on what was then the frontier; one farmer emigrated to Illinois because he had a neighbor twelve miles away. But the real motive was money. In the Mississippi valley wheat prices had fallen so low that steamboats on the Mississippi and the Missouri were burning wheat as fuel. Meanwhile, people only heard great things about the West, which they called the Oregon Country. A diarist quoted a man standing on a box in a public place in the East saying this: "They do say gentlemen . . . that out in Oregon the pigs are running under the great acorn trees, round and fat, and already cooked, with knives and forks sticking in them, so that you can cut off a slice whenever you are hungry."

SO AMERICA LOADED UP ITS WAGONS, wagons that were sometimes called prairie schooners, a name that sees crossing the country like an adventure at sea, which it is in a way. The wagons were like Conestoga wagons but smaller and lighter: four feet wide by twelve feet long. They were loaded up with an average of 2,500 pounds of supplies including beef, rice, tea, dried beans, dried fruit, baking soda, vinegar, pickles, mustard, tallow, 200 pounds of flour, 150 pounds of bacon (stored in bran), 10 pounds of salt, 20 pounds of sugar, and 10 pounds of coffee. They carried cash for repairs, for ferrymen, and for clothes for the first winter in Oregon. It took many families a few years to save up enough to move. According to the diaries of women crossing the country, on most occasions the move was the husband's idea; the thing that kept the women going was the idea of something better on the other side of the continent.

They headed out from Saint Louis, a so-called jumping-off point, resting at Fort Kearny, the first rest stop after three hundred miles, a fort established in 1848 for the overland travelers. They met the Platte River there. The Platte was wide and only three or four feet deep; a diarist on the trail described the Platte as "moving sand." Another said the Platte was "hard to ford, destitute of fish, too dirty to bathe in, and too thick to drink." In the evening, they took the wagon wheels off and soaked them overnight. Women cooked, in wind and rain, using weeds for fuel, or using buffalo manure, which burned clean and without scent. The men walked alongside livestock shouting *giddyap, haw, gee,* and *whoa.* Dogs barked constantly. The temperature inside the wagon reached 110 degrees by midday on the Great Plains. After a few days, the tan or brown canvas that covered the wagon was white, bleached by the sun.

To follow the trail, settlers spotted markers made with rocks; they looked for wheel indentations, for carvings, for large rocks marked with axle grease. Letters were posted on the rocks, notices, directions for people. There was always a temptation to try a shortcut; parties would see a piece of paper on a rock that described a possible trip-shortening route and then take it, then get lost or nearly die. Lucy Hall Bennett, a thirteen-year-old, wrote in her cross-country diary that her family had taken a shortcut described by a man named Meek. "After several of our party died, the men discovered that Meek really knew nothing about the road," she said.

"The westward emigration is a history of false starts and near disasters," one historian wrote.

The typical day on the trail often included men arguing, men fistfighting, lost children, broken axles, disabled animals, rain, and encounters with Indians—on the trail, families were always behind schedule, always being held up. When they got to the South Pass, a broad open plain that gently traversed the Rockies, they knew they had crossed the Continental Divide when the water began flowing westward.

But they made it to California, after passing through fifty miles of Nevada sands, their oxen succumbing to exhaustion, their cattle bleeding from their mouths and noses. They made it through seventy-five miles of slopes in the Sierras, using winches and chains to lower the wagons down the other side. They pressed on to Oregon, making their way through the Snake River Canyon, where Evel Knievel would one day jump, or attempt to jump. The migrators would follow the edge of desert, pulling themselves through the Blue Mountains and then to an "evil branch of the Columbia River." When the cliffs were too high to cross, they hired Indians to paddle them. Some tied things to pack animals, some just left everything and walked. "It was," wrote a diarist, "not a trip for the faint hearted; perhaps it was only for the fool-hardy."

AND THERE WERE SO MANY DIARISTS—more than at any time in American history, with the exception of the Civil War.

"I write on my lap with the wind rocking the wagon," wrote Angeline Ashley.

The women described the men being run over by cattle, children being run over by oxen; the women wrote about the Indians, who were not the problem that storytelling later made them into. On the contrary, the women describe the Indians as helpful. Indians did kill emigrants, and vice versa, but Indians most often acted as guides; the women travelers traded with the local tribes, often trading pancakes for moccasins. The women did not mention in the diaries when they were pregnant, but they often were. Mentioning pregnancy was considered inappropriate: the diaries merely mention that a child had been born. One teenager wrote about a wagon overturning one rainy day, with her mother and her mother's newborn inside. "A tent was set up and Mother was carried into it, where for a long time she lay insensible. The wagon was righted, the things loaded in, and Mother having recovered[,] we drove on." And yet the death rate on the trail was no worse than in the eastern cities, where cholera was rampant.

Sometimes, the diarists wrote about moments of happiness ("A fiddler comes down from the other camp to see if a dance on the turf cannot be started . . . Mr. Upton got down the melodeon and played some—we danced a while and went to bed") but more often the diarists wrote about death, with men and women dealing with death differently. Men, watching for graves, marked the number of people who had died. Women, on the other hand, gave detailed descriptions of graves and gravestones and always noted the grave's condition. "We find two names on the one headboard . . . These graves were dug in the soft prairie & were dug full of holes [by wolves] and one headboard was slipt off." The idea of burying a loved one on the trail was most upsetting to the families. "We couldn't Bear the thought of leaving his little body among the sands of this wilderness surrounded by Indians and wolves," a mother wrote. This family treated the body with camphor. They carried it as far as they could. Most people planned to return to exhume a body, and they sometimes did, only to find that the body was gone.

"No one who reads the diaries of women on the Overland trail can escape feeling the intensity with which the women regarded loss of life," one historian of the trail has written.

THE OVERLAND MIGRATIONS wound down slowly. For a very short time toward the end of the first overland migrations and before the first continental railroad, people crossed the country by stagecoach—though I would point out that, to my mind, crossing the country by stagecoach is a little like crossing by train: the stagecoach is not under the control of the typical cross-countryer a la a car or wagon or Volkswagon camper van. The stagecoach had been an important part of the development of the young United States; stagecoaches carried newspapers for low rates, helping make the American people in the eighteenth century the largest newspaper-reading populace in history up to that point. Stagecoaches had already begun to fade away in the East, due to the development of the railroad, when they had a second period of dominance in the West, just after the Civil War. But the stagecoach as a cross-country instrument was killed in 1869, when the cross-country railroad was completed.* The train was quicker and easier for families but settlers still

---

* During the time that people crossed the country in stagecoaches, the preeminent stagecoach was the Concord coach, a nearly indestructible mixture of iron and wood, first manufactured in Concord, New Hampshire, in 1827, and needing little change for seventy-five years. The wood was steamed and shaped; the designers' structural model was the strong but light and thin-walled egg. The coach was painted red and shined with varnish; the underbody was painted yellow to hide the dust. The Concord pioneered a suspension system of leather straps, called thorough-braces, of which one rider said: "It, the body, consequently dances in the air like a balloon, giving a certain kind of variety to the monotony of the journey." The coach was four feet, four inches wide, on average, and a little bit taller. The driver sat five feet in the air. Inside were three rows of seats; the back and front rows faced each other, and the middle seat had no back but a leather strap that could be strung from one side of the coach to the other. The windows were covered with leather curtains; the interior was lined with russet leather or enamel leather or plush. The door almost always featured a hand-painted picture, often of a famous person or a landscape. The coach held nine people inside and, if necessary, another twelve on top, in addition to the driver, who sat above the boot, which contained mail or gold. In 1877, a newspaper published the following tips for stagecoach riders:

- When the driver asks you to get out and walk, do it without grumbling.
- Don't flop over on your neighbor when sleeping.
- Don't ask how far it is to the next station until you get there.
- Don't discuss politics or religion, nor point out places on the road where horrible murders have been committed.

Stagecoach passengers were allowed twenty-five pounds of baggage each, and most chose to bring clothes, blankets, water canteens, and weapons. An armed guard rode alongside the driver if the coach carried valuables, which it often did. Foreign visitors noted that American stage-coach drivers were likely to talk to the horses, which foreigners considered unusual, and that, when drivers came to a stream or even a river, the drivers would stop, stand to look upriver and downriver for a second, and then race across with unnerving abandon. There were many noted drivers, including Charlie Parkhurst, who was known for his bravery and for his lifelong disguise: at his death, he was discovered to have been a woman. The drivers were also likely to talk to the passengers. "This tedious travelling was by no means to our taste and we should possibly have lost our good humour, had not the arch whimsicality of our driver, who was called Captain White, furnished us with abundant matter for mirth," one British traveler commented. Mark Twain noted that he heard the exact same stories over and over from different drivers. Some-thing that completely amazed many European visitors was that the drivers often ate alongside passengers. Likewise, when stages stopped at taverns, Europeans were also amazed that tavern owners, humble and innocuous in England, were prominent figures in the United States. "The hotelkeepers of the country are the noblesse of the district," said a British stagecoach patron.

It took about twenty-five days to get from Saint Louis to California, with stops several times a day, sometimes at taverns, but more often at stagecoach stations, crude shelters where the horses or drivers were switched—the precursor to gas stations. The food served at the stagecoach stations was usually bread, beans, pork, and cornmeal porridge, or mush.

found it less expensive to travel by wagon. One of the biggest reasons the wagon trains stopped was that many able-bodied men headed to war; for a while, the Union Army posted Confederate prisoners to fight the Indians who were beginning to resent the new settlers imposing on their territories, among other things; the Army called the Confederate prisoners "galvanized Yankees."

Of course, wagons weren't the only way to cross overland; some crossers used handcarts, which looked like covered wheelbarrows, and pulled their belongings themselves. The usual wagon into which this mass migration of cross-country travelers packed all their worldly belongings was about the size of an SUV, though maybe a little smaller.

Imagine 250,000 people, getting up and hopping in their SUVS and putting them in neutral and pulling them across America, with oxen—pulling them over creeks and rivers, up hills and mountains cliffs, as their children die, as their friends take shortcuts that mean they are never seen again, as people fade away in forests, in deserts.

TUMBLEWEED

HOW DO WE RECALL our cross-country trips? How do we remember them? Are they recounted in songs like those that recount the original cross-country trips—"Cumberland Gap," "The Colorado Trail," "I'm Going to the West"? Will we one day speak of them to our descendants as they in turn listen in rapt attention? Or will we forget all about them? As our family travels across the country today, the interstate highway in southern Montana late on this summer afternoon is a painless, hardship-free drive through the flat bottom of valleys, long gorgeous green valleys, divided by the interstate, and we see a valley that is at once familiar and unfamiliar, like so much of the interstate landscape. In the category of familiar, we see the exit with the gas station that is where, years and trips ago, the kids took a photo of my wife and me with a tumbleweed tied to the top of our old beat-up station wagon—a memory sighting.

When I am old and come upon this photo—if, that is, I should become old and also not lose the photo—I will attempt to recall that we had just come from the Prairie County Museum, which is based in an old bank building in Terry, Montana. We were driving east to west. We were looking for gas off the interstate, and looked into the door, whereupon two women in their late sixties greeted us enthusiastically, as if they had not seen museum visitors for a long while. I will recall that the women toured us through room after room of what seemed like all the stuff that had ever been used for anything in the county, stuff that many people might not have thought was museumworthy, such as bottle tops and old cans. After spending an hour going from room to room, we thought that was it, that the tour was over. It was then, I will remember, that the women said there was one more thing to see, downplaying it.

When I look at the photo of the two of us standing by the old car, I will remember that, even though we had just been planning on quickly stopping for gas, we figured we might as well see this last exhibit, at which point we entered into a room that featured beautiful photographs by a woman who moved to Montana and photographed the farmers and ranchers: Evelyn Cameron, who lived from 1894 to 1928. We had to rush through this last room, and then the women running the museum walked us out to our car.

Mostly, though, when I one day look at the photo of my wife and myself, side by side, I will see the tumbleweed and remember, not even where we found the tumbleweed precisely, but I will remember that when the two women saw the tumbleweed that my wife had strapped to the top of our old station wagon, they began to laugh. They thought that strapping a tumbleweed to the top of a car was hilarious—and we came to equate it with someone driving around a city with garbage strapped to the top of their pickup truck. A story they had to tell, if they felt like it.

I suppose it is most likely that if my wife and I are the last of our generation, no one will even care that we drove across the country—perhaps crossing the country by car will be forgotten, perhaps it will be de rigueur. We will be the opposite of the so-called pioneers. But at this moment in our current cross-country trip, upon seeing the gas station off the exit and having the memory sighting, I remember that we stopped for gas that day here at mile 249 on Interstate 90, and our kids took a photo of me and my wife and the car with the tumbleweed, a photo I still treasure.

RUBURB

JUST NEAR THE SETTLEMENT OF MANHATTAN, Montana, we come to fields full of new homes—hundreds and hundreds of them, as if the area were the end of a twenty-first-century migration: large boxy homes with flat featureless front sides. These new homes were not in this valley when we began crossing the country years ago, when there were just valleys with little homes and little towns. These homes seem designed to resemble log cabins, though they are without logs and clearly not cabins. And then come the new and not-yet-completed homes, wrapped in plastic, backdropped by mountains, incongruous to the non-Montana-native, who thinks all Montana will resemble a national park, as opposed to a giant suburban housing development that is settled alongside the highway.

Near Belgrade, a town in the middle of Montana that once had a population of six thousand, we are now completely surrounded by streets of population-swelling new homes—homes that look like ranch houses for giant ranches except they are on small pieces of property, the giant ranches having been subsumed by them all. Now, our son has switched to reading a book that I bought earlier in Missoula, a book that was on the bookstore's front table, a picture book, in fact: *A Field Guide to Sprawl*. From the entry marked "Leapfrog":

> Like the children's game where one player crouches down and another player vaults over the first, leapfrog development skips over empty land. It may move beyond existing town boundaries to avoid local land use regulation . . . When leapfrog development is both remote and dense, it may be called a ruburb. Rurban was coined by Walter Firey in 1946 for urbanized rural area.

Here we are in the mythic West, driving through land that was once crossed by people following herds of buffalo and then by mountain men carrying pelts and then by wagon trains and then by military expeditions attempting to wipe out the native people who followed the buffalo and now by people who build near interstate exits, as is the modern settlement pattern, not so much a stop on the trail but, strangely, an end.

SQUEEGEE

THE BLUE IN THE SUMMER SKY is darkening now, the clouds playing finger-puppet on the floor of the great valley. The second cross-country day is waning as we pass Bozeman and then a little later Livingston, where the interstate picks up the Yellowstone River, or the river picks up the interstate, where the housing lets up, where we stop, as we often do, this time for a quick dinner at a restaurant that bills itself as "New York–style," though its walls are covered with photos of Montana. Then we get gas at Town Pump, where I fill up with gas and nostalgia, for it is at Town Pump, as I recall, that our daughter first cleaned a windshield with a squeegee. Considering squeegees, I reflect on the passage of cross-country time. When our son was two and we crossed the country, I wrote this in my notebook:

Stop
5 min gas
5 min coffee
20 min clean windshield

At Town Pump, when our daughter was a toddler, I lifted her to the windshield and to the back window of the car, watched her enjoy the thrill of walking on the dust-covered hood, the excitement of the brownish squeegee water, the joy of the squeegee itself, the kick that one can derive from the squeegeeing process, especially as it applies to the removal of the remains of splatched bugs, gross, disgusting bugs. In the old days, I applauded her work (while holding her steady), as did her mother, as did her older brother, and thus, she returned to her car seat proud. I waited until she fell asleep or retired to the women's room with her mother or was otherwise distracted so that I might repeat the squeeegee process and actually be able to see out of the windows, toddlers not yet having developed the most refined squeegee skills, of course.

Now, as a more mature squeegee-er, my daughter crawls on the car and squeegees on her own, which delights and saddens me, and to a lesser extent makes me wonder whether insurance would cover the hood. At Town Pump, she soaks the window with the squeegee's sponge and then—

"Wait!" she says. She asks that the car's power be turned on. After some hemming and hawing, I comply. She takes the driver's seat, starts the wipers. They wipe meticulously, thoroughly—a genius stroke!

I WOULD JUST LIKE TO POINT out that if we had needed to fill up with gas and it was 1907, before there was much in the way of windshields, we would have hoped to have run out of gas in Seattle—as opposed to Montana—where in that year the first gas station appeared, with a glass gas gauge and valve-controlled hose. If we had run out in 1909, it would have been nice to have been near the first "drive in" station, operated by the American Gasoline Company in Saint Louis, which was a small tin shed housing barrels of oil and two converted hot-water tanks and a garden hose. The first gas pump is often credited to Sylvanus F. Bowser of Fort Wayne, Indiana, who in 1885 modified a water pump and so impressed his first customer, Jake Gumper, that Gumper quit his job as a local grocery store owner and worked for Bowser, painting over the pump the words FILLING STATION. The pump was refined, the tank buried underground, bells added (one clang per gallon), and, in 1912, a globe of glass placed on top of the pump to allay the gas customer's fear of being cheated. Customers wanted to see the gas—so badly, in fact, that gas companies added dyes, to distinguish their fuels: Texaco sold green gas, Sunoco blue, Esso red.

Gas pumps were usually on curbsides until the 1920s when fire ordinances forced them to move away from more and more oncoming traffic: by the thirties, car companies were selling cars on credit, with cars becoming what has been called "the backbone of the nation's consumer-oriented culture." Gas companies bought land to put pumps on, accompanying the pump first with a shed and then a houselike building. The house was built to blend in— people didn't want gas stations in their towns, and gas stations tried to stick out and hide at the same time. Subsequently, gas stations began to mimic pyramids, windmills, pagodas, castles, wigwams, and mosques. In Philadelphia, the Atlantic Refining Company built a gas station that looked like a Greek temple. In Albuquerque, a Tydol gas station was designed to look like an iceberg. In New England, gas stations were designed to resemble the Massachusetts State House; in California, Spanish missions.

The gas station as selling point, the gas station as a place that you would visit repeatedly like a neighborhood restaurant or a church, was pioneered by

Henry Dawes, who resigned from the Coolidge administration to run Pure Oil. Pure Oil stations were built in an English cottage style. Dawes was obsessed with the suburb, with the idea that cities, and particularly apartment buildings corrupted. Dawes himself lived in a two-story Greek Revival neoclassical mansion in Evanston, Illinois, which called itself the "City of Homes" and the "Gem Suburb." He had what one historian called a "singular disregard for highly individualized forms of expression, such as music or poetry." He patented his cottage-style station, which included a restroom for men accessible through the front office and a restroom for women accessible in the rear. He once lent one of his cottage-style gas stations to a department store in New York as a centerpiece for a show involving toys and midgets. He photographed his own stations when he traveled and obsessed over them being clean. "In these days of an educated public alarmed against venereal diseases, it is not going to be the brand of oil and gasoline the automobilist thinks of as he approaches a station, but, judging from the exterior of the station, what kind of toilet might be inside," *Pure Oil News* reported.

As cars streamlined and as the nation streamlined in the thirties, so did gas stations: The car began to symbolize the future, and car-related industrial architecture too began to forget about yesterday, and design almost strictly for tomorrow. Gas station designers such as Norman Bel Geddes and Walter D. Teague, an industrial designer who also designed cameras for Kodak, planned variations on the Bauhaus-influenced oblong box—often covered in white porcelain. In the 1930s, gas consumption slumped due to the Depression, but it increased again in the late forties. In 1955, car registrations doubled and demand for gasoline increased 80 percent. With limited petroleum reserves in Texas and Oklahoma and California, oil companies began drilling in the Persian Gulf, in the oil fields of Kuwait, Saudi Arabia, and Iraq. Gas companies tried to make gas burn cleaner in the sixties when air pollution standards were introduced, and at the same time began giving away free things at stations—such as toys and cash. Gas companies also built motels at highway interchanges. Pure Oil had a three-way partnership with Travelodge and Quaker Oats, owner of Aunt Jemima restaurants. In the sixties, self-service gas stations caught on. (A chain of twenty self-service gas stations in Indiana was closed in the 1930s because the state fire marshal didn't like the idea of people handling a flammable liquid.) The 1973 oil embargo caused the business of selling gas to be less about service and more about appealing to people through low prices. Meanwhile, in 1973, Exxon posted the highest net profit ever earned by an American corporation, $2.4 billion.

The predominant gas station style of today is a remnant of the gas station of the sixties—specifically, Texaco's Mattewan-style station, named for Mattewan, New Jersey, where it was introduced in 1964. It featured gas pumps with a flat canopy over them and a detached station with a mansard roof, the mansard roof being a remnant of Louis XIV's Paris (named for his chief architect, Jules Hardouin Mansart) as well as being the roof that was adopted by the majority of roadside establishments beginning in the sixties. The canopy was born at the time in the sixties that service stations began to fade away. In 1970, new stations were mostly giant canopies with little sheds or restrooms attached. But the gas station began to die in the seventies, when convenience stores cut prices on gas and increased prices on food, beer, milk. Pumps initially appeared in front of Handy Andy's, Little Generals, and 7-Elevens. In retaliation, petroleum companies built food stores, Chevron built C-Stores, Mobil built Mobil Marts, Exxon built Exxon Stores, and Sun built Stop-N-Gos. Competition with convenience stores killed gas stations. The gas station became the convenience store that sold gas, a coffeelike, essentially daily convenience that was not so convenient as it was essential. Then, in the nineties, gas stations began to combine with fast-food outlets—I recall buying an egg sandwich and a tank of gas at a McDonald's somewhere near Buffalo, Wyoming, around 1991, and then driving, and then thinking about the proximity of food and gas, and then subsequently feeling sick.

OUR GAS TANK FILLED—credit card scanned, digital readout, thermagraphic printing of receipt—and our windshield cleaned, we pull out of Town Pump and, after a brief team discussion, are now officially planning on stopping to see Pompey's Pillar, the rock that William Clark signed when he was on the way back to Saint Louis, a rock that a lot of other people have signed too, such as trappers, soldiers, settlers, and the native settlers who saw it first but didn't sign it until they discovered it had been signed with pictographs by the people who saw it after them. We are headed there but, as I mentioned, if we don't make it, we've already done our share of Lewis and Clark–related activity, so no big deal.

BIG TIMBER

WE ARE IN BIG TIMBER, in the shadow of the eleven-thousand-foot-plus Crazy Peak, in view of the snow-covered Crazy Mountains. Or we are passing through Big Timber on the I-90, anyway. In passing through Big Timber, I recall that one of the best and worst times that my wife and I ever had as a cross-country team was punctuated by a stay in downtown Big Timber itself. It was a time when we were moving west, part of our own personal great western emigration. It was a reluctant move, not because we don't like the West—like I say, we like a lot of the country, an unfortunate trait that makes a permanent settlement area difficult to choose. We had just found ourselves in circumstances that did not give us a lot of choice, as far as finances went, and we had just moved east across the country a few months before, and, in a nutshell, we were tired of moving and didn't want to do it anymore, much less spend money on another twenty-five-foot-long rental truck. The kids were already out in Oregon, as my wife had flown out to her parents' with them and then flown back solo to make the crossing with all our stuff, as well as me. Our friends helped us pack our things into a rental truck, and it was just me and her, in the truck, alone together in a cross-country vehicle for the first time in many years and planning on making the best of a difficult time, or at least making good time.

So we started out, me making some wrong turns in New York City, taking the wrong way out, finally getting in a tunnel and then on a highway out of town, at which point we played a cassette tape of songs that a neighbor had put together, a tape that was supposed to make us happy but managed to make my wife so happy that it made her sad, which made for tears on her side of the truck, which caused a sad, driving-away happiness all around.

But then we just drove, drove into New Jersey, drove into Pennsylvania, on I-80, to the town of Lamar, where, exhausted from packing late the night before, we went to sleep early, getting up early and getting an early start that would have been even earlier if I had not spent about an hour looking for the keys, which I had left on the floor of the cab of the truck—it was after that trip that I began wearing the car keys on a lanyard.

The trip went fine after that until we ran into trouble with thousands of bikers as we entered Minnesota. Unbeknownst to us, we were about to attempt to find a motel room during the Sturgis Motorcycle Rally, what I like to think of as the largest motorcycle festival known to man—a motorcycle festival involving some three hundred thousand bikers the year we were passing by it. It's a festival that began in 1938 when a Sturgis, South Dakota, motorbike shop owner hosted a biker race and stunt competition that included Evel Knievel ramp jumps and head-on collisions with cars. The festival was a big deal to the motorcyclists who had come from all over the country. To us and our truck it meant that there was pretty much no way we were ever going to find a motel room.

YOU CAN'T DRIVE VERY FAST in a truck filled with your life in stuff. You do better than the four or five miles a day that settlers did in 1850. You do the modern equivalent, which is only a few hundred miles a day. We were initially looking for a place to spend the night just past Sioux Falls, South Dakota, in the town of Mitchell, where we have often stopped to see the Corn Palace, an actual palace actually made of corn. We were traveling through swarms of motorcycles or, more often, being passed by swarms of them. When we got to Mitchell, we began a routine that lasted for a couple of hours; pulling up to motels, entering the lobby, finding no vacancies. Outside each motel there were motorcyclists partying; they would look at us as we pulled slowly into the motorcycle-filled parking lot, our twenty-five-foot-long, beat-up, unprofessionally driven truck perhaps menacing to their shiny, well-loved cycles. At one front desk, the clerk looked at my wife sadly and said, "Honey, there aren't any rooms from Sioux Falls to Rapid City." By which she meant that there was not a room in the entire state.

We pulled off at the next interstate exit. No rooms. We had the disagreement that we always have: I argue that we should phone ahead. My wife never likes this idea. She prefers to remain uncommitted to a room reservation in case we can end up traveling farther than we had estimated. I have never had anything against bikers, but this particular gigantic herd of bikers was beginning to get on my nerves. My wife, relenting, began phoning ahead to places, and people on the phone told her that up ahead there were no rooms either. It was late now, close to eleven. Finally, we came to Plankinton, population 226, a town I had never noticed before. We drove a few miles off the road, not actually seeing any town. We came to a little cluster of white wooden cabins, which are popular with pheasant hunters, as I realized the next day, just before dawn, when pheasant hunters started up their cars. The person in the office said we could rent one for the evening. The room my wife inspected was lacking in amenities. It did not lack a smell that smelled like a couple of pheasant hunters had spent the last few days in the room chain-smoking, among other things. (My wife had asked me to ask the clerk for a nonsmoking room but I could see that the clerk was smoking so I didn't bother.) The door to the room would not lock and barely closed. We couldn't tell what was outside in the black darkness. We proceeded to have a disagreement about the room, which no one won. We went to bed upset and left at first light.

The morning revived us and made us more pleasant, as mornings on the road do. We knew we had a long way to go to pass the booked motels of the bikers. We traveled amid more fleets of cycles, the lead biker cutting through packs of migrating monarch butterflies. (A biker told us that the lead biker always takes all the butterfly hits for the biker pack.) We passed Rapid City and then Sturgis, where, at the exit, hundreds of bikers just kept pulling off, as if swarming. Now, we were traveling into the oncoming bikers. The Great Plains became the Black Hills, and we took lunch across the Wyoming border, in Sundance, an Old West–type town, known as the place where Harry Longabaugh, a.k.a. the Sundance Kid, won his nickname while sitting in jail for horse stealing. We were near Devil's Tower, a landmark on trails west. We ate at the Aro Family Restaurant, whose Devil's Tower dessert was described in our AAA guidebook: "a decadent Devil's Tower dessert of brownies, ice cream, chocolate syrup with a dollop of whipped cream." Inside, the place was filled with bikers, big muscular men in leather pants and leather vests and tight T-shirts, and women also muscular and dressed similarly.

I was not dressed in leather, and my wife wore a summer dress that to my mind attracted the stares of the bikers—yes, I was getting into a state again, but it's just that these guys weren't particularly friendly to nonbikers who had been traveling among them for several days. I wanted to get out of the Aro Family Restaurant, even though it seemed like a good place to eat, even though my wife was loving her grilled chicken sandwich; frustrations in this move across the country were compounding. We didn't have time to find another place to eat and this was going to be our meal for the day. We ordered, and I tried my best to leer at a couple of people and look tough while finishing my Devil's Tower dessert.

We drove farther westward, as fast as we could, which, thanks to the regulator on the truck engine, was between 63 and 65 m.p.h. We ended up driving a little over six hundred miles that day, a tremendous amount for nontruckers in a truck, especially at top speeds of between 63 and 65 m.p.h. When night came, we couldn't find any rooms again. Finally, we pulled into Big Timber, Montana, very late and, taking a chance, drove away from the highway motels and into the old town and walked straight into a beautiful old railroad hotel with a room that was the opposite of the night before—a big comfortable bed, antique furniture in excellent repair, perfect. We were so relieved that, exhausted, we went across the street to a little bar.

As parents, we do not get out much and we hardly ever go out late for a drink in a bar in Big Timber, Montana; it was our first and only time ever stopping at a bar while crossing the country. The place was packed with non-bikers; the guy next to us told us about all the celebrities whose ranches were nearby. I had a couple of beers, my wife had a glass of wine, and we listened to great music on the jukebox and laughed and got to bed way, way too late after successfully crossing the street. I'm not really going to get into it but I will say that our night in Big Timber was one of the greatest nights of our cross-country married life. In the morning, we had breakfast in the hotel dining room, surrounded by bikers.

THE SUNSET IS COMING, THE SUNSET IS COMING

THE SUNSET IS COMING, the sunset is coming, and we pick up speed, because, what the heck, we might as well see Pompey's Pillar if we can. That's what I'm saying. I'm saying that kind of thing over and over—the problem with me and the low-key approach is that I'm not very convincing. But we press on. In fact, Pompey's Pillar is mostly a Clark site, it being his signature on a rock. And as Lewis and Clark–ologists will tell you, Lewis and Clark split up on the way back: Clark followed the Yellowstone, as we are doing, and Lewis and a small party went north to make contact with a tribe in northern Montana, the Blackfeet, on a diplomatic mission he botched, killing an Indian teenager. It is sometimes said that Lewis and Clark only made really big mistakes when they split up, something I can absolutely sympathize with from my own cross-country experiences. When they split up, after crossing the Bitterroots on the way back to Saint Louis, Lewis wrote: "I could not avoid feeling much concern on this occasion although I hoped this separation was only momentary."

According to our TripTik, Pompey's Pillar is a national landmark. As I read this, fear grips me that the pillar might close soon.

But just to reiterate, despite the fear that is gripping me, I'm *saying* I'm OK with the place being closed. It's only about a mile off the interstate, not a big trip—we won't waste any cross-country time. I catch myself from banging the steering wheel.

"We'll just see where we are," says my wife, like Penelope in her steadiness.

"Right," I say, my voice still sounding sort of relaxed, my body hunched over the steering wheel, gripping, racing.

The thing is, the sunset is coming. And to make matters more dramatic, the sky is really performing now, the white, fluffy cumulus clouds have all herded together and gone gray, semi-ominously. The clouds are stretched out in low packs, backdropped by high-up white streaks. In the middle of Montana, there are always cloud theatrics for the driver who is crossing the country; this is the place where the wind rushes over the Rockies on its trip east. Here are the rocks in the American wind stream, the clouds the white water.

As we pass through Billings and its great fields of oil refineries, the steam and smoke and belching flames from the refineries seem to blend with the clouds, the clouds slowly choreographed, the sound track now being our CD of "Fanfare for the Common Man," by Aaron Copland: a minor-keyed fanfare. And now, in the lee of the far-off mountaintops, we see the lenticular clouds that are like flying saucers, seeming to spin in the high currents, their edges lit with color from the dying sun. The Impala speeds beneath a swirling, reddish orange roof of clouds that looks like something made by computerized special-effects designers, something done on cue, when the script calls for intense cloud drama.

I'm not saying anything, and I'm not at all certain, but I think we may be making it. Besides, the clouds are keeping my mind off of Pompey's Pillar, and I'm spending a lot of time saying, "Look at the clouds *now!*"

POMPEY'S PILLAR

A MERE TWENTY-THREE MILES from Billings, we take the exit for Pompey's Pillar and then the side road to Pompey's Pillar and then, following signs, drive to the gate for Pompey's Pillar. And we pull up to the gate to see it being closed by a park ranger *at that very moment*. The ranger then looks at us and, I don't know, maybe sees the shredded pack on top of the car, but for whatever reason reopens the gate and lets us in, the last visitors for the day.

"Lock yourself out," she says, smiling.

We wave, drive in slowly. I am joyous, and as far as I can tell, everyone else is pretty impressed.

"Can you believe this?" I begin to say, over and over.

"It's a sign," my wife says.

"It's a freakin' miracle," our son says.

AND THERE IT IS: POMPEY'S PILLAR. It's a big butte, 150 feet high and composed of sandstone, and on it is William Clark's signature, said to be the only remaining physical evidence of the Lewis and Clark expedition, as if brown and white road signs weren't enough. Clark named the butte "Pompeys Tower" in honor of Sacagawea's son, whom he had nicknamed "Pomp." Nicholas Biddle, the first editor of the Lewis and Clark journals, wanted to make the tower sound more classical and changed the name to Pompeys Pillar, à la Pompeii's Pillar.

We get out of the car slowly, greet the rest of the rangers who are still smiling and being extremely cool given the lateness of the day—it's about nine at night, and still light late in the summer on the northern plains. We proceed to the top of the butte. We climb up wooden stairs and along a walkway that looks out over the Yellowstone River in a completely sprawl-free zone. We walk toward cameras and motion detectors and postings that protect and guard the signature; signs everywhere implore people to stay on the path. Later the guards will tell us that when people climb off the trail and attempt to get closer to the signature and set off the motion detectors and the alarms, the trespassers inevitably tell the police and guards and rangers who are immediately summoned to the scene: "I didn't see the sign."

At the top, a little out of breath, standing 150 feet over the Great Plains and looking out on so much of the country that we are crossing, we see first the signatures that surround the signature and then the signature itself, covered in Plexiglas and locked in a case, a most precious graffiti:

Willam Clark (signed)
1806

PHYSICAL EVIDENCE

HOW FAR CLARK, as well as Lewis, had traveled as the first transcontinentalist—two years and four months and eight thousand wilderness miles, all told! How far all the people whose signatures crowd around his had traveled! How far we have all traveled, moving as a family, as an overland migration of two and then three and four, even if we are only up to 1,026 miles today! How successfully have we navigated our own national loop, so far!

Upon descending the butte, we would talk to a ranger who was half Crow, half Italian (southern) and married to an actress originally from the East—or who at least acted a long time ago at La MaMa, an experimental theater in New York City. "I'm a mongrel," he said. He also told us that the Crow side of his family had owned the farm that the butte and its signatures were on; that a man had bought the land around the butte and opened it to the public, and subsequently passed away; that it was closed for a while then opened again by the federal government, which now owns the land.

But at this moment, while still on top of the butte, right there near the signature, mere yards from the physical evidence, I take a photo of our kids and the Yellowstone Valley and the softening sky, and then release the kids from their pose. The sun is just about to set, and the clouds that have been building all day are finishing things up with timpani rolls of blue and cymbal crashes of orange, with stringlike flutterings of red toward the horizon's edge. It is a sun setting with all the pyrotechnics of a storm but without the storm. Just standing there, I project much happiness into the sky. Then I take a picture of my wife, and as I look through the camera, I think that time seems to be standing still at the end of this day. I am happy we are together on the road again and, to be honest, she looks really, really beautiful.

THE LAST ROOM IN MILES CITY

WE DRIVE ON FOR two more hours and pull into Miles City, not able to find a vacancy. I had hoped to stay at the Holiday Inn Express, a Holiday Inn Express that I had stayed at while crossing the country alone a few years before—it was new at the time and I had found it to be clean and the staff amiable. But it is booked solid. Likewise, so are a few other places. We end up at a Super 8 behind the Holiday Inn Express, looking down on it from on top of a hill, jealously. I am trying to think of something nice to say about this room we enter as I type this account of the end of our second day crossing the country but I can't. It's past eleven P.M. This room, as far as I can tell, stinks. The mattresses feel like plywood, and the room itself is in the basement of the motel, the windows up high, looking out on who knows what. I open the door, look around, throw the bags in, our son helping. My wife enters.

"How does it look?" she says.

"I wish we could have stayed at the Holiday Inn Express," I say.

Our son collapses on the bed.

Our daughter is looking around, with a kind of on-the-road motel excitement. All of a sudden she shouts from the bathroom. "Look at this," she says. She comes running out, holding up a perfumed rectangle. "French-milled soap!"

PART IV

Miles City, Montana, to Minneapolis, Minnesota

VENTURE ACROSS AMERICA

IT'S EARLY, TOO EARLY, just after sunrise, five thirty in the morning, and as I stand on a rise of land—looking out over Interstate 94 and Miles City, Montana, and the Great Plains and the small grove of chain restaurants and chain gas stations beside the highway off-ramp in the distance—I sip the littlest sips of the really bad complimentary motel coffee, my key dangling from its lanyard. The sky is awakening, a few clouds fringing a perfect bowl of blue, and I look north to see the Holiday Inn Express where I had very much wanted to stay last night but did not, due to there being no vacancies. In this early moment of precious prehighway contemplation, my back calls out to me, reminding me that I slept on a sheet-covered board. I look east, the way we are headed. I take more delicate sips of the complimentary coffee, because, although I want, and even need, this coffee to wake me up this morning, it is truly very bad, bordering on criminal. I wonder: Will we make more miles today than we did yesterday, which was, from a miles standpoint, a very bad day? Will we be able to get our supplies together and ourselves together and into the car and eat some breakfast and get on the road by six thirty or seven? Will the children be able to wake up or even speak to us before, say, noon? For today we will leave the West, and, in so doing, we will cross the Great Plains.

We absolutely need to make better time on this, Day Three, because even though we drove three hundred miles on Day Two, with me being semirelaxed and all, we also ate a late breakfast and—I still can't believe it—played nine holes of golf, two things you can't be doing if you ever want to make it across the country in a fashion that doesn't take weeks, let's face it. What does it matter if we take forever, if we sail the interstate seas for weeks and months, seeing the sights of America, or what you can see from the big roads, for an entire summer, rather than just four or five or, tops, six days? First of all, unlike Lewis and Clark, we're not federally funded, and every time we dawdle, it increases the amount spent on the road trinity: gas, food, and lodging. Second, we've got stuff to do besides sit in the car, in the areas of friends, relatives, and work. But the most important reason has to do with the nature of the trip itself. We are beginning to get desperate to get home. The road is making us a little crazy. Don't forget we've already driven across the country once this summer. This is the way back. We have already driven four thousand miles. This is the hard part, the trip down the mountain, the potentially unglorious return.

Thoughts of our total distance, thoughts of the distance ahead—thoughts such as these cross my mind as I savor a few seconds of the morning time before my family is awake. The morning in the parking lot is the time when you feel as if the day ahead is out there and knowable, right in front of you, even though it most likely isn't, the time when the day presents itself as something that could be pretty good, kind of like the complimentary coffee.

The parking lot is three-quarters full, and, because we checked in late, our rented Impala is parked far off in the area that is not so convenient to any of the motel's doors. The Impala rests patiently beside the small truck of a Montana exterminator, and a tailless cat moves around the rear wheel of the exterminator's truck and slinks off into weeds. The painted side of a rented truck, a U-Haul parked a few cars away, advertises a state that we will pass through in a few more days, should the trip proceed, should the rest of my party wake up. (And I'm not talking about my wife, who, when I am out with the pack, is showering with French-milled soap). The side of the rental truck refers specifically to New Jersey, saying, "Where will U go next?"

Where I go is our room, where, amazingly, people do wake up, where soon there is packing and showering and an early-morning viewing of the daily baseball report on ESPN. At 6:25, my daughter accompanies me to the front lobby, where we partake in the complimentary breakfast and appropriate an additional cup of really bad coffee for her mom. As we pass through the long, bare hall, a man in his late sixties works to open a door with a magnetized plastic card. He is swiping the card through the door lock mechanism—swiping, swiping, swiping until, at last, with a click and a sigh, it opens. His wife hovers over him.

"Oh, I more or less had it the wrong way," the man says, examining his magnetized card.

"More, yeah, more," his wife says, pushing him into the room.

My daughter and I return to the check-in area of the motel and see that we have fallen into a pack of senior citizen travelers, a little crowd of people in their seventies who seem as if they are not displeased to suffer bad mattresses: there is an air of happy productivity, of planned and measured movement, as people consume watery juice, spongy toast, and English muffins, as well as lots of mushy little non-English muffins.

"See you next time," a woman says, as she drops off her key.

The clerk is less talkative.

The key-returning woman has a lot to say about her travel plans. "Probably next summer," she continues, "and I'll probably be retired by that time— oh, well. You aren't going to change anything like the last time I was here?"

The clerk smiles and nods and doesn't seem to answer, yet the key-returning woman is still talking as she stands alongside a rack of postcards featuring images of Montana. The postcards say, "Montana is . . ." and then allow the pictures do the talking; the pictures talk of the gorgeous valleys that we traveled through yesterday, the ones filled with momentous clouds, as opposed to the flat mountainless plains that I looked on from the parking lot this morning. The woman is also standing alongside the Super 8 map of America, which displays the geography of the United States in relation to Super 8 locations.

Such maps remind me of those drawn by Charles Preuss, the Civil War–era mapmaker, who accompanied John Charles Frémont, known in his day as the Trailblazer and probably the most famous explorer at the time of the Civil War. Frémont was a semirenegade explorer. He followed orders from the U.S. military and, semi-illegally, from his father-in-law, Senator Thomas Hart Benton, a key proponent of Manifest Destiny, as well as the cross-country railroad and the removal of the Indians. Mapping new trails and new mountain routes near and even into territories claimed by the Spanish—territories that politicians like Benton began to claim were rightfully American—Frémont ended up capturing the public imagination, in part because the public imagined the nation being as big as possible. As Frémont's cartographer, Preuss drew the new America—those maps, meanwhile, being a practical application of the nation's view of itself.

Preuss also made maps expressly for the sake of emigrant settlers, most practically, a seven-segment, 1846 map of the Oregon Trail; they are the Trip-Tiks of American expansion, in that they show only the road and its immediate travel-applicable environment. Preuss's maps remind me of Captain William Clark's daily dead reckonings, his river-bend-by-river-bend description of the Discovery Expedition's path along the Missouri River. Thus (for me, anyway),

Preuss's maps are even akin to directions that Internet sites give out today, directions in mere "rights" and "lefts" and mileage specifics, pure directions devoid of context, directions that, in leading us today to our hoped-for destination, Saint Paul, Minnesota, would say nothing about the change from flat, ocean-bottom-like plain to the glacial-pothole-covered prairies of Minnesota. When exploring or emigrating or driving as fast as you can (within reason) across the country, you see what you want to see, and the Internet gives us interstate-style directions: directions that merely consider speed and distance and the essentials of the food and lodging industries.

Oh, how I wish I carried a map that told us what we were seeing out our window or how many of the people we were passing were crossing the country or crossing from one side of the state or the town to the next. Don't even get me started on our own personal need for directions on where to live and how to proceed in life in general.*

IN THE LITTLE SUPER 8 LOBBY, people are filling their coolers with ice from the ice machine that has a sign on it asking that people not fill their coolers with ice from the ice machine, people who look bright and cheery, as well as people who look as if they slept on the interstate last night. Because the muffin is "complimentary," I am eating it and simultaneously meditating on the phrase that is a slogan of the Super 8 motel chain: *Travel is just the beginning*. It is a phrase that appears initially to be Zen-like and then, sort of like staying in a basement on the Great Plains, is not Zen-like at all.

Back in our room, our daughter has her turn at the TV—cartoons. Like a cartoon character, I return to the parking lot to reattach our pack to the top of the car, hauling it out of the back seat, swearing, as is now my established way, here at the start of Day Three. As I wrestle with the pack, I wonder some more, the wonderings in roughly this order: Will we make it to Saint Paul tonight? Will the pack shred away? And what will I next allow myself to spend a lot of money on that will not work, at least for me?

---

* In the meantime, I make due with the TripTik, and, just for fun, when I get home, check for Internet-generated directions, which say only this about the road from Miles City to Saint Paul, Minnesota: turn and merge and drive a total of 706.01 miles along I-94 and, then, in the words of MapQuest.com, "End at Saint Paul, MN US." The computerized directions add, somewhat disconcertingly, the following: "Total Est. Time: 10 hours, 15 minutes."

The writing-covered U-Haul truck again speaks to me at the dawn of Day Three, the side of the truck exhorting, imploring me, cheering, maybe not knowing how literally I might take it: "Venture across America."

KNOWLEDGE OF THE NATION

BEFORE THE CIVIL WAR, people did not venture across America for fun; tourism was local, and besides, there was not much of an American nation to cross. People didn't venture across America unless they were moving their lives across America, or going to work across America. Wealthier Americans traveled to Europe, or, on what were some of the first semi-long-distance tourist trips, to places like the Adirondacks or the White Mountains in New Hampshire. Around the time of the Civil War, people began to cross America for fun, or what was billed as fun. Sometimes, fun was a number of business-people or politicians crossing the country in a train or a stagecoach and then, when they got home, telling people to cross the country for fun.

This was the mode of travel for Samuel Bowles, the editor of the *Republican*, in Springfield, Massachusetts. One of the most influential editors of his day, Bowles went all around the country writing long dispatches in which he talked about how terrific going all around the country could be. He wrote books such as *Our New West: Records of Travel Between the Mississippi and the Pacific Ocean* and *The Pacific Railroad—Open; How to Go; What to See*. In 1865, he set out across the country with Schuyler Colfax, Speaker of the House of Representatives and chairman of the House Committee on Post Offices and Post Roads, as well as various reporters and officials, a trip that was published as *Across the Continent: A Summer's Journey to the Rocky Mountains, the Mormons, and the Pacific States.* Bowles was promoting the railroad across the country, even if the railroad did not completely cross yet: from Nebraska to Colorado, he had to take a five-day-long stagecoach ride along the Platte River. Bowles called the Platte "the natural highway," and his stagecoach's path is roughly the same path of Interstate 80 today. Bowles saw the crossing of the country as redemptive. "The Continent is spanned, the national breadth is measured," he wrote. "How this republic, saved, reunited, bound together as never before, expands under such personal passage and footstep tread; how magnificent its domain; how far-reaching and uprising its material, moral and political possibilities and promises!"

Bowles was a pioneer in the notion that the only way to know America is to see it. "There is no such knowledge of the nation as comes of travelling it, of seeing eye to eye its vast extent, its various and teeming wealth, and above all its purpose-filled people," he wrote. He believed that crossing the country would heal the rifts of the Civil War—putting, he said, "the great sections of the Nation into sympathy and unity."

"It marries the Atlantic and the Pacific," Bowles continued. "It destroys disunion in the quarter where it was ever most threatening; it brings into harmony the heretofore jarring discords of a Continent of separated peoples; it determines the future of America, as the first nation of the world, in commerce, in government, in intellectual and moral supremacy."

He was also a pioneer in the notion that Americans ought to skip Europe. The Americans who visited Europe for the Grand Tour saw ruins, museums, the principal cities, and Bowles and his companions were recommending an American version of the same. Colfax wrote as much in a public letter to Bowles: "If our people, who go to Europe for pleasure, travel, and observation, knew a tenth of the enjoyment we experienced in our travel under our own flag, far more of them would turn their faces toward the setting sun." Bowles and Colfax called the new kind of traveler "the Across the Continent Traveler."

BOWLES AND HIS FELLOW ACROSS-THE-CONTINENT enthusiasts were attempting to cast a hassle-filled, exhausting journey through often-inhospitable lands as a pleasure trip. For his own part, Bowles, riding in a stagecoach in the company of the Speaker of the House of Representatives, was being guarded by horse-mounted U.S. Army soldiers as the coach went through the lands of Indians tribes with which the U.S. Army were at war. At a breakfast that was plush, given the circumstances, in the company of a U.S. Army general on the Great Plains, Bowles ate canned chicken and oysters off tin plates and drank "coffee with the brownest of sugar and the most concentrated of milk, all in the simplest and most barren of border life." Bowles thrilled at the telegraph lines that had just been built across the country. "We had a special privilege of reading the news as it ran East and

West, and so we were up with the world, though so far out of it in all material circumstance."

He was traveling from Fort Kearney, which is today Kearney, Nebraska, to Denver, which is still Denver, a five-day trip across the Plains to the Rockies that now can be easily accomplished in a day or so on Interstate 80. His five-day trip across the stretch of the interior is coincidentally just about the same distance as our own across-the-country trip, which is, also coincidentally, pretty much through the same portion of the interior, longitudinally speaking. Of course, on our trip, we're doing it backward.

"We passed on to and through the great Central Desert of the Continent, stretching from the far distant north to the Gulf of Mexico," Bowles wrote.

Sometimes, Bowles had to work pretty hard to make his travels sound attractive. Up to that point, settlers were mostly passing *through* the Plains, leaving the Plains to the Native Americans; first the railroad and then the Great Plains settlers and all the subsequent across-the-continent travel would change that.

"Yet not a desert, as such is commonly interpreted—not worthless, by any means," he goes on to say. "The soil is fat, indeed, compared with your New England pine plains. It yields a coarse and thin grass that, green or dry, makes the best food for cattle that the Continent offers. It is, indeed, the great Pasture of the nation. This is its present use and its future profit. Now it supports the machinery of the commerce of the two great wings of the nation, that it both separates and connects. Then—when railroad shall supersede cattle and mules—it will feed us with beef and mutton, and give wool and leather immeasurable. Let us, then, not despise the Plains; but turn their capacities to best account."

THE EXPEDITION SPLITS UP, SOME SETTING OFF ON FOOT

BY AROUND SEVEN, we are prepared to depart. The ripped-and-getting-more-ripped-by-the-mile pack is on top of the car, the luggage from the room lugged, and a decision is made for our party to split up—my daughter and I will stay at the motel with the car and the gear while my wife and son walk the mile or so north to the convenience store where we will later rendezvous. They set out to walk beneath the highway. I have an urge to compare us to Lewis and Clark when they split up on the way home in 1806, but luckily I suppress it.

As is the case in prolonged space travel, exercise is difficult on the road, and on some trips, by the time we land on the other coast, I feel as if my system is beginning to shut down, as if I am an inert material, like lead. Still, we try to exercise, and we have developed some expertise in that area. My son and I threw baseballs during the summer of 1999, me crouching with our beat-up station wagon as a backdrop in parking lots, him comparing West and East Coast teams. When my daughter was two, we played soccer at a rest stop in Utah; when I put the soccer ball back in the car, it was covered with white dust. In a parking lot in Sioux Falls, South Dakota, at a Ramada Inn that was way off the road and way too expensive but the only thing we could find one night when a huge thunderstorm was about to get us, we all tried jumping rope, with limited success. In Texas, on the old Route 66, a woman walked my wife a long way from the front desk to unlock the glass room that the motel staff referred to as the exercise room. It contained a stationary bicycle. In fact, the stationary bicycle seemed *really* stationary. The woman was out of breath when she made it to the door of the exercise room. She opened the door slowly. A horrible moldy smell rushed out of the glassed-in space, a smell that seemed to have checked in to the motel months before. "Ha," the woman joked, "I guess no one's been using *this*!" She volunteered that she did not need to use the exercise room herself as she got so much exercise walking around the motel. The complimentary breakfast at that motel featured a huge sweet bun sitting in a pool of buttery sugar. My wife couldn't look at it and even the kids skipped it for toast and juice. I ate the entire thing, and eating it was something like exercise. The woman serving it was thin as a rail. "It was delicious," I said to her. "Really?" she said. "I've never tried it."

TRAVELING ON FOOT ANYWHERE near an interstate is always hazardous; these roads descended from foot-friendly trails but are now the province of fast-moving swaths of rubber and steel. Walking alongside an interstate is like escaping into a lion cage at the zoo: you suffer for the diminutiveness of your species. In pondering the difference in scale between life and interstate life, I am reminded of the following short excursion from what served as an overnight base camp three trips ago when we were on Interstate 70, which begins in Pennsylvania and gets you through Ohio, Indiana, Illinois, Missouri, Kansas, Colorado, and part of Utah, at which point you have to finish crossing the country via Interstates 15, 80, or 84 to the Pacific.

The base camp was a motel in Cloverdale, Indiana, a small town between Terre Haute and Indianapolis. The Cloverdale motto is "Small Town Pride, Focused on the Future." Technically, the motel was in Cloverdale, but more accurately it was in the interstate off-ramp portion of Cloverdale, where the atmosphere was more truck stop than small town and the motto might have been "Focused on the Highway." Late at night, we checked in to a motel that was approximately one hundred yards away from the interstate, lugging our bags through the newish lobby and into a room looking out on the service road; we went to sleep in the glow of gas station and convenience store lights.

I woke up early and attempted to cross the service road to buy coffee, a bottle of water, and a newspaper at a convenience store.

I walked through a gravel parking lot where trucks were parked overnight, their engines rumbling, keeping their cabins air-conditioned; walked for a few yards along a drive-through path for a fast-food restaurant (noting all the rat poison dispensers behind the restaurant); crossed a one-way, two-lane street that was carrying traffic off the interstate; crossed another one-way, two-lane street with traffic heading onto the interstate; proceeded up the service road, which took me back toward another fast-food restaurant; headed into the convenience store attached to the gas station, watched people getting in and out of their cars for a minute; then returned following a similar route, avoiding one fast-food restaurant because I couldn't stomach its smell so early in the morning. At each road crossing, I would pause, waiting for speeding traffic to pass, to endure the quickly increasing and then decreasing wail of wind and engine sounds. At each road crossing, I would experience the sensation in my knees that marks the presence of fear. The walk was completely car-friendly.

It was an arduous trip, a harrowing trip, the interstate-obsessed terrain acting as if I were not even there, the cars seeming not to notice me, given that I am not a car. I felt slight, or even more slight than usual.

And after I returned, my wife attempted to go for a walk—just to stretch her legs and get some exercise, as she is attempting with my son today in Montana—and, on that occasion, she couldn't figure out a way to walk to anywhere. She ended up walking around and around the parking lot, circling past the still-sleeping trucks, their engines snoring, their exhaust choking her.

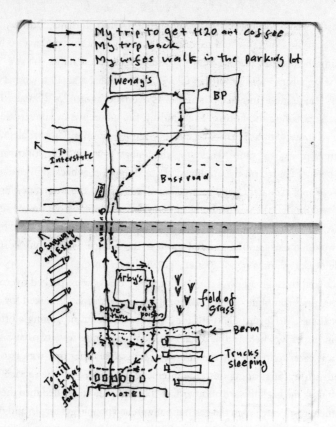

LOST

IN THE SUPER 8, my daughter wades through the coffee sippers and the ice cooler fillers to smilingly return the key to the front desk, greeting, stretching, getting on tiptoes to reach up, up, up and, yes, successfully return the magnetically charged plastic card that is not really a key at all. We leave the Super 8 parking lot, pass the Holiday Inn Express, which, as I have mentioned, I had so hoped we would be checking out of today, and now we are looking for the rest of our party.

And now we are not seeing the rest of our party.

WE ARE DRIVING SLOWLY. We cross under the interstate and we leave the gas-and-highway-oriented area of Miles City and, judging from our surroundings—specifically, an old and about-to-be-closed-down-looking supermarket—we are closer to the old town, the town named for General Nelson Miles, who came to this land at the confluence of the Yellowstone and Tongue rivers in 1876 to attack Crazy Horse, who was camped there but got away. It seems to me that in the West, in the places where interstates run through small towns or no towns at all, the gas-food-and-lodging-selling settlements are the descendants of the small wooden towns that sprouted up alongside the railroad, towns that, when the railroad faded, faded too.

We drive a little farther down the road, expectantly. We think we see our traveling companions but no, that was not them. We turn around. Thoughts that I have lost my wife and son in the middle of the country are beginning to make cameo appearances in my mind but are, fortunately, overshadowed by the glorious morning, the sunshine that spreads out on this strip of national and regional chain stores. Down here near the interstate, it's a hive of pretravel industry, of long-western-drive foreplay. In gas station attached to convenience store after gas station attached to convenience store, there is an early-morning, in-and-out, "fill it up" or "top it off" or "pull it around back to check the tire pressure" frenzy. It is a wide vista of people putting things in their cars and in their mouths, of people opening and closing the doors of cars with license plates that are sometimes from Montana and nearby North Dakota but mostly *not* from Montana— the activity reminds me of animals stopping at a watering hole in the middle of some dry savanna.

And then we rejoin our party, as they are entering a Kum & Go.

WE REJOIN OUR PARTY AT THE KUM & GO

KUM & GO IS A GAS-SELLING convenience store chain that operates slightly more than four hundred stores in Arkansas, Colorado, Iowa, Kansas, Minnesota, Missouri, Montana, Nebraska, North Dakota, Oklahoma, South Dakota, Wyoming, and Wisconsin. Sure, you can read in the local papers about a Kum & Go being held up, and once in a while people coming into a Kum & Go and tying up the person working behind the counter. That kind of thing happens in roadside gas-selling convenience stores. But this is a quality roadside convenience store: in 1997, *Convenience Store Decisions* magazine named Kum & Go the top convenience store in the United States. Kum & Go began as a gas station in 1959 in Hampton, Iowa. It was named Kum & Go at a meeting of the families of the two owners in which everyone threw out different names for the chain that would simultaneously reflect the nature of the business and use the last initials of the two principals and founders, W. A. Krause and T. S. Gentle. "With hard work and foresight, Mr. Krause and Mr. Gentle saw no limits," a company history reports. "In 1963, Krause and Gentle converted gas stations into convenience stores with fuel and merchandise. The concept was based on their desire to further serve customers. The Krause Gentle Corporation was the third Iowa company to receive a beer license for convenience stores."

Inside the Kum & Go in Miles City, my wife is unable to find any nonfat milk for her coffee and makes do with milk that is 2 percent milkfat—being on the road, or perhaps more accurately, sitting still in a car for close to a week, makes you feel like you have to be neurotic about your health. My son is unable to locate any rock-and-roll magazines and makes do with an orange juice and a new appreciation for the number of magazines relating to hunting and fishing and cars and guns.

Meanwhile, I grab a coffee and pay for it and am the first back in the car, and as I slowly peel back the plastic coffee lid, I sit calmly and recall the last time we all woke up in this area of the Great Plains.

It was four years earlier, the time my son and I were driving in a truck and my wife and daughter were in our car. We were in separate vehicles but we kept each other in sight continually and, as usual, communicated by walkie-talkie. We were a very small cross-country convoy. Late one night, the men of the party found it necessary to stop in Custer, Montana, for gas. We were practiced country-crossers by then but we did something we'd never done before or since: we split up while driving, my wife continuing on the interstate while I exited, looking for gas. My son and I found a pump at a closed gas station that took a credit card. It was my very first credit-card-only-pump experience, and at the time, getting gas in the dark and empty station, it felt slightly illegal.

When we got back on the road, I thought we might have lost my wife and daughter for good: we were in an unpopulated and (at that point in time) un-cell-phone-tower-covered area where the plains and the star-drenched night sky laughed at cell phones. So we used our walkie-talkies, this model being more advanced than the cheapo pair we had first crossed the country with; they were not professional trucker-quality walkie-talkies or anything, but they were pretty good and worked well in flat areas, such as the Great Plains. I had a sinking feeling as my son and I drove on. "Hello, hello—do you read me? Over?" I said over and over into the walkie-talkie. My son, who was ten at the time, took turns doing roughly the same. "Mom?" he said. "Do you *read* me, Mom?" After about an hour, I heard a voice—at first faintly and then stronger as it repeated the same thing over and over: "Exit 93!" Exit 93!" The voice was that of my wife, who was standing at a Great Plains–facing window of a motel at exit 93. She was checked in and talking out to us in the dark flatness. "I hear you," I said over and over.

Now, every time I come to that rise of land, that slight hill that looks out on eastern Montana and all of I-94 ahead, that precise place where my wife's walkie-talkie signal came through, I think of that time and can't believe we found each other.

ON THE ISLAND OF GAS PUMPS

AT KUM & GO, with Kum & Go coffee in hand, I pull up to the gas-pumping island, as people insert credit cards, open gas tanks, squeeze pump handles, as they say nothing at all. I look around to see that the Subway sandwich shop that is built into the Kum & Go has a special on buffalo sandwiches: "delicious

roast bison." It is an example of diversity within monotony, a nationally or-
chestrated regional nondelicacy. I see the morning light hitting the diesel gas
pump back where the truckers are fueling and wish, as usual, that I were a
landscape painter—to capture this pure light that causes the entire convenience store and gas station to appear golden, like a promise! I look down at
the pump handle and realize that even it has something to say, for it is a pump
handle label that recommends the Kum & Go bottled-water brand, sold under a pure-sounding name: Highland Natural Spring Water. The water
comes from Liberty, Illinois, something I learn when I subsequently take the
advice of the gas pump handle and purchase the water when I reenter Kum &
Go to pay for gas. Indeed, from the island, everywhere I look something is either for sale or recommending something for sale, such as the Kum & Go air
fresheners, which are combination air fresheners and wind chimes: "Express
yourself with air chimes, a soft soothing chime for your car rear view mirror."
And even though I don't like air fresheners, even though I am not one to buy
wind chimes, I am thinking of getting wind chimes at this moment, of actually spending money on them, because that's the kind of morning it is and because there's something about these air chimes. In the words of the British
sailor describing Mount Hood, they are "beautifully conspicuous."

Now my wife exits Kum & Go and heads to our car, holding a couple of
bananas and a cup of Kum & Go coffee and a Kum & Go 2 percent milk container. When I see her, I start the car, driving slowly, setting off from the gas
island, driving a few yards south, then a few yards east, meeting her at the side
entrance of Kum & Go, where all the garbage cans are. As I lean over and
push the door open for her, I can see a framed-by-the-car-door view of more
labels and brands, with very little of the earth itself in sight.

I see a Kum & Go banner, a FedEx box, an ice machine, a forest of four-
story-tall highway signs: Exxon Plaza, Econolodge, Town Pump, TouchFree
Car Wash, a sign that melds together KFC and A&W—commerce as chemical notation. Then, as the kids take their seats, my wife hands me a coffee, and
I turn to place the coffee in the car cup holder and, in doing so, notice a man
coming out of Kum & Go and realize that he is the man who was having trouble with his motel room key. Highway recognition! The Man Who Was Having Trouble with His Key gets in his car, a LeSabre, with Wisconsin plates,
after kindly holding the door for the Kum & Go customer exiting behind
him, who does not acknowledge him. We will not see the Man Who Was

Having Trouble with His Key again that day, even though I suspect we are heading the same way, on to Wisconsin, and somehow I sense this as I see him consult with his wife, as I see him flip down the sunglass attachment on his nonsunglasses. I sense that this is another person who I have gotten to know the tiniest bit by walking down a hall he was in at a very early hour but am never going to see again, a companionship of place.

I will see Wisconsin, though. I am looking forward to seeing Wisconsin, and as we pull away from Kum & Go, I say, "I can't wait to see Wisconsin."

After I say that, I realize that there aren't many states that I don't feel that way about, though, as opposed to my wife, who has driven to every state in the continental United States, I have yet to drive through Mississippi or North Carolina.

"Banana anybody?" says my wife.

SEE AMERICA FIRST

LIKE MANY ASPECTS OF THE FORMULATION of what we today call America, travel at the end of the nineteenth century was promoted with a mixture of religious zeal and commercial scheming—i.e., to sell stuff. People began to cross the country—and to promote America as a place to cross and see—at the same time that the United States was developing an idea of itself as a modern industrial nation state, as a place that made and then sold stuff and could also sell itself as a place as well. America went from seeing itself as a collection of states to seeing itself as one nation, a nation that could be explored and understood via a railroad coach or a series of tourist hotels. In 1906, a conference of businessmen, politicians, and various kinds of promoters met in Utah to launch a campaign to promote a new kind of national tourism. "The movement that you strive for in this conference will make better citizens of the tens of thousands of Americans who are now living in ignorance of their own land, will through the agencies of school, pulpit and press bring to you men and maidens of the land a vision of the regions they know nothing of which are yet under the dominion of the flag we all revere," the governor of Utah said. The campaign's motto was "See Europe if you will, but see America first."

At the See America First conference in Salt Lake City, as at their conferences elsewhere, the America Firsters touted statistics: between 1904 and 1905, Americans had spent $250 million touring in Europe, money that could have been better spent here, especially in light of World War I. They worried that easterners were becoming "effete" due to their interest in Europe: "They are not educated about our throbbing West. They do not realize that some day out of this great West will come a Shakespeare, a Byron and the nation's greatest statesmen." The America Firsters equated the East and Europe with elitism, wealth, and culture. The America Firsters equated the West with freedom, democracy, and nature, even if corporations were amassing millions by logging and mining the West, even if corporations were building hotels pretty much just for upper-class tourists, even if corporations were fighting to stamp out organized labor. They vowed to build a tourist infrastructure of hotels and roads. Editors, business leaders, and even Theodore Roosevelt pledged support. At the dawn of the magazine age, they started up publications such as *Western Monthly* and, later, *See America First*, which was published in the Pacific Northwest, to, in the latter's words, "make more enthusiastic Americans, to show the East what the Great West is and the West what the East has." The America Firsters got together regularly to lecture each other on how great America was and what a waste of time and money it was for Americans to go to Europe—you can almost see their heads nodding. They believed that money spent in America would make for better American wagon roads, hotels, homes, and products, as well as, argued one delegate, "more fervent and intense patriotism without the artificial stimulus of war."

"I know men who have never been west of Buffalo, New York, yet who go frequently to Europe, perhaps once a year," a promoter wrote in 1915. "Such men would become better citizens were they to see the west."

RAILROAD COMPANIES WERE VERY SUPPORTIVE of seeing America first. They used their expertise in eastern tourism to spearhead the new national tourism. The Southern Pacific Railroad started a magazine called *Sunset*, which featured western scenes. In 1870, Jay Cooke, a promoter for the Northern Pacific Railroad, became interested in a little-known area of waterfalls and valleys called Yellowstone. He published descriptions by naturalists and hired Thomas Moran, a popular landscape painter, to paint scenes from the valley. When Congress voted on establishing Yellowstone as the first national park, *The Wonders of Yellowstone*, an illustrated, railroad-sponsored brochure, was handed out to each member, each natural feature labeled with otherworldly names: Giant's Thumb, Jupiter Terrace, Devil's Frying Pan.

The idea of Glacier National Park, in Montana, was a result of public relations work on the part of the Great Northern Railway. Louis W. Hill, the railway's chairman, was the son of the founder, and in always-flattering magazine and newspaper profiles was described in terms like "no Wall Street railway president." One account marveled that Louis Hill could "make a living and reputation as a musician, a landscape painter, a chauffeur on difficult roads." There was a lot of marveling; he was treated like a natural feature himself. He was described as "the Man Who Is Building a Great National Park" and compared to Christopher Columbus as the discoverer of "altitudinous America." Hill hung a huge billboard depicting a scene from Glacier National Park in downtown Saint Paul, Minnesota, where he established an early version of the publicity office that touted the park around the United States: Hoke Smith, a former reporter for the Minneapolis *Journal*, paid reporters to write stories or sent out his own stories for papers to publish or sometimes wrote letters to editors asking questions about Glacier. "After the story is prepared it is merely a matter of clerical help to get it out and distributed to the proper papers," Smith wrote. Like a stage designer, Hill cast the east side of Glacier National Park as a balm to city life, highlighting western themes as well as Pacific and European themes; the lobby at the hotel was decorated with logs, Japanese lanterns, Blackfeet rugs. Waitresses wore Swiss outfits (despite tourism officials' mixed feelings about the Swiss) and a Japanese couple served tea. He described the park as "everybody's park," though what he meant by "everybody" was people like him, white upper-class Americans; he doted especially on industrialists and their families when they visited, sending gifts to their rustic rooms, which were only rustic-looking.

Originally, "everybody" had also included the Blackfeet Confederacy—the Piegan, the Blood, and the Northern Blackfeet tribes—who had lived on the land. (They were the same people that Lewis had gone to meet without Clark, killing a young warrior.) The government and the railroad had moved them to adjacent reservations, and then the railroad talked about them as if they were the park mascots; Hill had them camp in teepees near the hotel and escort guests from the train to the hotel. "The Blackfeet is a friendly Indian, and the tribe has already endeared itself to hundreds of tourists who have visited Glacier National Park," park literature assured visitors. Louis Hill once sent several Blackfeet to New York via train to attend a travel and convention show. It's hard to tell whether the Indians did it on purpose or because Hill wanted them to or some combination of both, but the Blackfeet refused hotel suites and set up camp on the roof of the twenty-five-story hotel, to the delight of guests and reporters, and, presumably, Hill. "Hot room no good. Want plenty of outdoors," one Indian reportedly said. The Indians visited the Bronx Zoo, the New York Aquarium, Saint Patrick's Cathedral, the subway, and the beach, according to the *Brooklyn Eagle*. On the ferry from the railroad terminus across the Hudson River, Chief Three Bears was said to have prayed to the skyline of Manhattan. The *New York Times* wrote, "The venerable Chief thought the skyscrapers were monuments of great departed warriors."

At one point, Hill tried to copyright the phrase "See America First," so the Great Northern Railroad would own it, but his lawyers told him that was impossible.

THE FIRST TIME I SAW AMERICA

WHEN I FIRST SAW AMERICA, I saw it with my girlfriend, whom I will herein call my wife, and we were on that very first cross-country trip (which I mentioned previously), and we were in her car, and we left our little apartment in New York City. I brought along a Super 8 camera, to document us seeing America first, though mostly me seeing it first, since my wife, being from the West, had already seen a lot of it. I still have the film; I looked at it the other day with the kids, who watched it the way scientists would watch a film about a lost species. At the time that I filmed it, I was concerned that I would not have enough film to cover our entire trip; I was thinking that America was even bigger than it is. As a result, I filmed everything we saw very quickly, the final cut being a document of us seeing America first that is a jittery, rat-a-tat-tat newsreel-like portrait of America, a brief summary of which goes like this: Quick shot of Pennsylvania mountains, blurry. Quick shot of grocery store in Ohio—ditto rest stop in Illinois. A too-quick pan of the elevated trains in Chicago from the window of the car. A long series of photos of the prairie from the car, my wife pointing at the prairie. Three-second scene after ten-second scene of the old-timey roadside advertising for Wall Drug, a roadside attraction in South Dakota that is known for advertising free ice water. A ten-second scene of my wife drinking free ice water. At Mount Rushmore, I filmed all the tourists, thinking I had an ironic detachment, even though I didn't. I attempted an experimental joke sequence that featured my wife "climbing" to the top of Mount Rushmore—while watching it, the kids didn't think this scene was as successful as I did. I filmed my journal on the porch of a log cabin that we rented outside of Yellowstone—probably the longest scene in the film, for whatever reason. I filmed my wife coming out of the shower at the log cabin we rented one night on the old back road into Yellowstone, a brief, toweled scene that would not get me a PG rating. I panned the mountains in Yellowstone over and over—I was thrilled to see them, and, generally, I could not believe how beautiful America was and how much there was of it to see—but never for a satisfyingly long enough time. The footage ends shortly after my wife shoots the best scene: a long, luxurious shot of the winding road that took us out of Idaho and into Oregon, where I subsequently tried several unsuccessful out-the-window-of-the-car shots of the Columbia River and the mountains, which I thought of as the most true American vistas I had ever seen. I kept looking at our atlas, at the map of the entire country, not believing I'd crossed the entire thing.

A MESSAGE FROM THE CAR

FINISHED REFUELING AT KUM & GO, I am on I-94 again, pulling out of Miles City on this sunny Day Three morning, and immediately I get a chance to let a giant chemical truck pass—it is covered with so many large FLAMMABLE stickers that it seems like the right thing to do, yielding to a highway monster.

The toll-free number that accompanies the slogan (SAFETY AND COURTESY ARE MY GOALS) begs me to call it but I'm not going to waste cell phone minutes—a good thing, because when I do get home and do call the number and hear how many thousands of truck companies the toll-free-numbered driving-safety-monitoring business monitors, it does not make me feel very good, frankly. My wife is quilting. Our daughter is showing off the mosquito bite she received on the top of Pompey's Pillar in the evening of Day Two and making notes in her journal, describing William Clark's signature at the top of Pompey's Pillar, drawing the container that enclosed the signature and the case's lock. My son is reading a Lawrence Ferlinghetti poem, "Challenges to Young Poets": "Be naïve, innocent, non-cynical, as if you had just landed on earth (as indeed you have, as indeed we all have), astonished by what you have fallen upon."

We enjoy juices, muffins that remind me of wallpaper paste, more coffee, my second-to-last cup for the morning. My daughter arranges her seating area for the day—a green book light for the evening, a pink pencil with a pink fluffy fluff ball where the eraser would be, her journal, some magazines. My son does not arrange his area; at least the method of organization is not clear to me: all his stuff is around his feet. Then, the two of them, having eaten, having passed up their trash, having been up so late last night looking for a room that, as it ended up, was—I can't let it go!—*not* a Holiday Inn Express, begin to fade, to fall asleep. One minute into the news on the radio and our daughter is slumped over toward the seat divider, leaning dangerously close to our son. (As parents traveling the shortest of distances know, the seat divider is crucial to in-car harmony; it sets the territorial boundaries that keep peace in the back seat and thus in the car. That they might be touching—hair on head to side of arm or elbow to elbow—while simultaneously asleep is no matter.) Our son fades thereafter: his legs crossed, his pillow strangled in the seat strap, his arms folded, as if chairing a meeting of teenagers, his sweatshirt hood all we can see.

Meanwhile, in the front seat, we say what I imagine millions and millions of driving parents say when they gaze into the back seat to see their children sleeping.

"Look at them," I say.

"I know," says my wife.

AND YES, THE TECHNOLOGICALLY ADVANCED rooftop pack that I assumed would soothe me as I drove, would take away cares rather than add to them, that pack is making sounds that resemble the noises uttered by the buffalo that once roamed the Great Plains when the buffalo were not roaming but attempting to reproduce. I pull on one of the straps that I now have running through the interior of the car—to the disappointment of my fellow travelers—and that adjustment quiets the pack, somewhat.

We are just over a thousand miles into our trip, one third of the way through, and the land here on the Great Plains is beautiful rangeland; the short, eaten-up or chemically treated dusty green grasses roll in waves that sometimes offer views of infinity.

The clouds are few and high-up; the sky like the blue inside of a turtle's shell.

We're going. We're moving. We've got a hundred miles of Montana left. We're trying to make Saint Paul, where we're hoping to have dinner with a friend we always stop to see in Minnesota when we are going through Minnesota on our way back across America—a little cross-country ritual. We've got to cross North Dakota, and we're approaching its border. We're following the Yellowstone River. And now, in this heady, progress-making moment, I look down at the dashboard to see that I am receiving a message in what the Chevrolet dashboard designers have deemed the Message Center. The message is one of the scariest messages that you can get while on a cross-country trip, as far as I'm concerned, and it relates precisely to the reason that I rented a car rather than take our own. The message reads:

Check Engine

A BRIEF HISTORY OF THE AUTOMOBILE IN AMERICA UP TO AND INCLUDING OUR IMPALA

IN EUROPE, PEOPLE HAD BEEN WORKING on the idea of something along the lines of a car for a long time, beginning, by some accounts, in 2 B.C., when a steam engine was made by a Greek inventor in Alexandria. In England, in the 1780s, James Murdoch, an assistant to a steam engine maker, invented what he called "a steam carriage," a steam-powered wagon. He managed to drive it in circles in a storeroom but decided not to patent it after listening to his boss at the steam engine company, who suggested that a steam-powered wagon would depress the market for steam engines. A gasoline engine was patented in France by Jean Joseph Lenoir, who, in 1862, drove a four-wheeled, gas-powered vehicle into the French countryside, a fifteen-mile round-trip that was pretty much forgotten after its three-hour duration. The gas-powered engine was perfected by Gottlieb Daimler, in Germany, who built a motor-powered car that beat out that of his competitor, Karl Benz, whose car, unlike Daimler's, could only go forward, not in reverse. The French used Daimler's engines to make more cars and referred to them as self-moving—i.e., *automobile*.

The Duryea brothers were America's first automakers, as well as familial archrivals. Charles was a mechanic in Springfield, Massachusetts, and Frank was a toolmaker at an Illinois bicycle shop. They got together a thousand dollars and built a two-cycle gas engine with a top speed of eighteen miles an hour that, except for its rear-mounted engine, looked just like a horse-drawn carriage. When they first drove their car on the streets of Springfield, in 1893, people were amazed, even though the car broke down after two or three hundred feet. "The thrill was not to last," Frank wrote about that first American road trip, "for I now noticed the engine was beginning to labor heavily and slow down." At the dawn of the idea of the car, the idea of racing was preeminent. The brothers entered their car in the first car race in the country, sponsored by the *Chicago-Times Herald*, a fifty-two-mile run from Evanston to Jackson Park, Illinois, in snow, slush, and mud—there had been a blizzard three days before. Frank drove, averaging seven and a half miles an hour, and they won, beating Benz's car by an hour and a half. They won again in races in America and Europe. They built thirteen different models of cars but fought over every detail until finally the business folded. Initially, only Charles was given credit for the invention of the car; in 1948, ten years after Charles died, Frank was given co-credit by the Smithsonian Institution, and Frank, to the unending protest of Charles's children, tried to say he invented everything except the steering wheel.

For a while, car manufacturers fell into two groups: bike manufacturers that built motorized bikes that featured elements of carriages, such as the Duryeas, and motorized carriage manufacturers whose carriages featured elements of bikes, such as Studebaker and Buick. Manufacturers settled on gas power because it had a better range than battery power and because a gas-powered car was lighter than a steam-powered car. Cars were expensive, costing over $1,000, until 1900, when Ransom Eli Olds proposed a $650 "small runabout" that he would call the Oldsmobile. The Cadillac Motor Company sold a more reliable car, the Model A, for $750. Henry Ford began making cars in 1896, as an employee of the Detroit Motor Company. He started his own company in 1900, and in 1905 released the first Model T, nicknamed the Tin Lizzie, a car that was considered homely and not at all fancy and, by 1916, when the price dropped to just $345, very affordable. Farmers loved it because its wheel clearance was higher than that of most other cars and it could make it through mud and ruts.

The genetic history of our rented Impala begins with William Crapo Durant, a high school dropout who got a job at his grandfather's lumberyard and then started his own cart-making business, becoming the largest cart maker in America in 1890. Durant recognized that carts were about to be replaced by cars and built a giant car-making facility, which he named General Motors. He bought out a lot of car companies, including Buick and the Olds company. He spent so much money that he lost control of General Motors, until he got together with Louis Chevrolet, started the Chevrolet Company, and subsequently made enough to win back control of GM. The Depression hurt him again and he got out of cars and into bowling alleys, bowling being a sport he thought would sweep America, which it did a little, but not in the ways cars were about to sweep America.

After World War II, Americans wanted their cars to seem less like horse-drawn carriages and more like jets. They wanted fast engines—fast like impalas, the reddish, African animal noted for its leaping ability as well as for the long curved horns that mark the male (and our rented trunk). Initially, the Impala was the top model to emerge from Chevrolet's Bel Air line, featuring, according to the company, "curves where before there were lines." It had big fins on the back and, on the rear, what were called cat-eye lights. Engine-wise, it had a 348 V-8 putting out 315 b.h.p., not that that means anything to this cross-country driver. The Impala became one of the first so-called muscle cars, used by a lot of teenagers for illegal drag racing. In 1964, the Pontiac GTO became more popular—it was lighter and faster and cost less. Meanwhile, just as the Impala grew out of the Bel Air, so the Caprice grew out of the Impala. By the 1990s, the height of our own cross-country travelings, the Caprice was a favorite of police forces, as well as a favorite of cab drivers. The popularity of the Impala faded and it then went through a redesign and then made a minor comeback: today, as we cross the country, we shall see police cruisers that are Impalas. The Impala we drive is a taupe-colored, sleek but still (to me) lumpish-looking, four-door, full-size relative of a drag racer, its huge V-8 engine now suggesting, as I just mentioned, it be checked.

OK TIRE

IT'S JUST THE OIL! And it's just an automotive recommendation from the Message Center. No big deal. The Message Center suggests in its message that it merely wants us to consider changing the oil when we get a chance, which we will when we make it across the country. It's optional. That's all. No major malfunction, which is great news. My heart is beating regularly again.

While my heart had been beating irregularly, I had been recalling past breakdowns. On a trip across Montana in 1994, for instance, when we drove off the main highways with the kids to see if we could find an underground nuclear missile silo—a side trip that is more difficult than it sounds if you are certain there are nuclear missile silos in the area but are not at all certain what a nuclear missile silo looks like—we found what we thought was a silo, right across from a cute little bed-and-breakfast on an old dirt road, on which we picked up a flat tire. It ended up being kind of fun waiting around at Don's OK Tire on Main Street in Lewiston to get it fixed the next day. In 1990, we broke down just outside Lowell, Massachusetts. We were heading north before west, and we spent two days and several thousand dollars waiting for a timing-belt repair, which was not fun at all, especially with a two-month-old, who sat with us on the interstate while we waited for the truck on what the repairman later referred to as "dead man's curve," so named due to the fact that people who broke down there were difficult to see by passersby and often hit and killed. (On the first U.S. roadways, before the invention of federally regulated highways signs, a dangerous curve was often marked with a hand-painted sign of death in the person of the grim reaper.) We have stopped for repairs at stations in Oregon and Washington, and, I think, once in Ohio. A message on the Message Center at this point in our trip to change the oil makes sense given that we have had the car for nearly four thousand miles' worth of driving, having driven it from the East Coast to the West Coast and now about a third of the way back again; it's about due for an oil change, though the oil is not low—I checked it this morning. But they will change it when we get back—or at least I am not going to worry about it. Everything will be OK for now. The Message Center in my brain is blinking *Don't worry*, over and over again. Rare is the occasion when I am not filled with worry of one kind or another, such is the kind of traveler I am, but I come closest to the state of worry-free-ness in a rental car, when I am paying someone else to have car worries for me. It's one of my favorite ways to see America.

IN THE FRONT SEAT, WONDERING

IN THE FRONT SEAT, we are consumed in the view, in the mere thought of the Great Plains miles to cover. Once again, it is a landscape that we know and do not know, that is familiar from so many passages yet still a mystery. In the front seat, we are like sailors in a ship set on course, the wheel held firm, the sails full of wind, a course set by the highway gods, and the TripTik. In the front seat, we drink coffee, quilt, drive, look at the Message Center of the Impala, which will be flashing CHECK ENGINE for the next two thousand or so miles. We listen to Montana radio stations. We listen knowing that there is less local Montana radio, given that local radio stations are being bought out by radio station companies.* We hear the story of the goats that had escaped the night before in Helena, Montana. Apparently, the town leased the goats from a goatherder, who herded with one dog. The goats were supposed to eat

---

* Frequently reported in discussions of the state of radio is the incident in Minot, North Dakota, when toxic chemical tanks overturned and the local radio stations did not report evacuation procedures to the local populace because the stations were automated, people-less.

what are considered weeds on Mount Helena. Weeds such as Dalmation toadflax, leafy spurge, and spotted knapweed. But the goats escaped and were now roaming through town, soon to be captured. Joe Dooling, the goatherder, reported receiving only one complaint. We imagine the herder and Mount Helena, and feel its relative proximity while seeing just the Great Plains, the goatless Montana road. Then, coincidentally, we pass a big sign for DuPont Cimarron, a chemical that also kills weeds like Dalmation toadflax, leafy spurge, and spotted knapweed and, if you are not careful, can destroy whole pastures, among other things.

Mostly, though, I sit up close to the steering wheel, the way I like to sit. I look out at the culverts and the little dried-up ponds and wonder how you would make a life on this land if you settled in it, if you stopped moving—wondering is a major occupation of the transcontinentalist. Here, I wonder how I would do it. Over the years, in the newspapers I found in motel lobbies, in books and magazines, I've read about the declining population of the Great Plains—in 2003, in a long report on the fall in income and population in the area, the *Fargo Forum* reported that sixteen thousand people ages twenty to twenty-five left the state in the three previous years. But as a mere cross-country traveler, I have little or no clue about the prospects for a good life in this land: a car trip makes for an interested detachment—though once while stopping for coffee on a cross-country trip in 2001, I met a young woman who was between twenty and twenty-five years old and from the part of the Great Plains through which we now travel. This woman was studying agriculture in college in North Dakota and looking to take over her family's farm, even though her grandfather was against the idea of a woman running his farm. She talked about how she and her boyfriend, on weekend nights, would drive around together in a truck and check the fences on all their grazing land, and then call it a date. Every time I race impatiently across the vastness of the entire Great Plains, I think of her patient circles, sometimes jealously, sometimes not jealously at all.

In lieu of traffic negotiation of any kind, in lieu even of giant chemical-toting trucks, I look out at these hills that hypnotize. I see the ruins of pumps and farmhouses and settlements of one kind or another—little traces, little scars and scabs. I see alkali on the rocks, the harsh remnant of undrinkable water. I look out and wonder about exits that exit to no visible settlement. I imagine possible histories that align with the nomenclature on the signs—I imagine old stories that I will never know: Bad Route Road, Pleasant View Road, Whoop Up Creek Road.

IN 2000, WITH NINE YEARS of crossing the country under his belt, my son complained about this portion of the drive. "There's just *nothing*," he said. I explained to him how I had grown to love this part of the trip. In 2001, he was quiet for a long time when we hit the Great Plains, quiet and awake. Then, as if we hadn't stopped talking over the year that had passed, he said, "Dad, I think I see what you mean about the Dakotas."

A PLEASING FANCY

AMERICANS FIRST BEGAN TO TRAVEL AMERICA in large packs just after World War I. It was a time when the car had begun to be ubiquitous—Ford was producing one Model T every half hour. It was a time when patriotism had intensified and European vacations were on hold. There was, on the one hand, a kind of anti-European rhetoric in the air, or anti-Swiss rhetoric, as far as vacationing went. "The department of Commerce and Labor statistics show that $290,000,000 was left in Europe last year by American tourists," wrote Elizabeth B. Gentry, chairwoman of the Old Trails Road Committee of the Missouri Daughters of the American Revolution. "Switzerland is not an agricultural country, but is supported by its crop of tourists; the nation practically exists because Americans prefer the Alps to the Rockies." On the other hand, the federal government began creating national parks and then recommending them, in the satisfied company of railroad and tourism promoters. To run the parks, President Woodrow Wilson hired Stephen Tyng Mather, a former *New York Sun* reporter and executive of the Pacific Coast Borax Company who was known by his admirers as "a genius of publicity." Mather pitched the parks to Americans as useable, rather than useless scenery. According to *Glimpses of Our National Parks*, one of Mather's many brochures promoting the parks: "Every person living in the United States ought to know about these eight national parks and ought to visit them when possible, for, considered together, they contain more features of conspicuous grandeur than are readily accessible in all the rest of the world." Visiting the parks, it was further argued, would also help Americans know other Americans, through in-park mingling. Apparently, there was a time when Americans, while on the road, mingled—this being as opposed to now. "One sits at dinner, say, between a Missouri farmer and an Idaho miner, and at supper between a New York artist and an Oregon shopkeeper," said a 1922 National Parks Association pamphlet, *The People and the National Parks*. People poured into the parks, and the parks were very quickly overcrowded. People piled into their cars and set out to cross the country, to discover America and become Americans. In the mid-1920s, estimates for the number of people auto-camping ran between ten million and twenty million. In 1917, *American Motorist* published what it called "A Motorist's Creed":

> I believe that travel, familiarity with the sights and scenes of other parts of the country, first hand knowledge of how my fellow-men live, is of inestimable value to me and will do more to make me patriotic and public spirited than daily intimacy with the Declaration of Independence.

As the number of cars in America moved into the millions, touring in an automobile became more than just driving. It was a reinvigorating cure for urban living. It gave, in the words of one tourist at the time, "vigor and strength to the hundreds of thousands who have lost them in their mad and pathetic chase for wealth, or a livelihood, in the crowded cities of the East and Middle West." "The nation needs a tonic knowledge of the physical thing called America, a love of the body Columbia, an inspiring sense of the nobility and splendor, the epic sweep and the intimate beauty of the land to whom our forebearers gave their devotion and we claim our home," said an editorial in the *Chicago Tribune*. "An acquaintance with the mere physical quality of the country west of the Alleghenies would notably assist a deeper understanding of the American Spirit. The east should go west as the west goes east." Touring was—like taking a train trip when the railroads were promoting railroads—patriotic.

Travel into the West and the western parks also inaugurated an American style of contemplating history, a style that continues today: to stand where before stood someone else, the way that I had attempted to stand with my family where Lewis and Clark stood, or at least where they had bathed in hot springs. "One cannot refrain from wondering at the task that was before the venturesome pioneers of the late 1700 and early 1800 periods when Lewis and Clark and other pioneering heros [*sic*] first negotiated this stretch of the then virgin country that is now passed so swiftly and so easily," a journalist wrote.

The other related trend that traveling across America ignited was that of comparing what the landscape was then and what it is now, a trend that continues today and inspires observations that are often wrong. In a 1926 *American Motorist*, a driver wrote: "It is sometimes a pleasing fancy to identify yourself with the first men to come this way . . . In some respects, the Maine Coast of that day couldn't have been very different from what it is at the present time."

THE VERY FIRST CROSS-COUNTRY car trips taken by Americans in America were trips that people were not certain they were going to complete. The first attempt across via automobile is thought to have been made in 1899 by John D. Davis and his wife, Louise Hitchcock Davis, a reporter; they ended up in Chicago after three months. The first successful trip was in 1903: Horatio Nelson Jackson, a doctor from Vermont, made a fifty-dollar bet that he could cross the country in a car. He proceeded to buy a car in San Francisco, hire a mechanic to drive it, share some of the driving with the mechanic, and, in sixty-three and a half days, pulled into New York City. Twenty-three-year-old Alice Ramsey, who left from New York City with three friends, did her own driving and a lot of her own engine maintenance in 1909. Ramsey was sponsored by a car company hoping to encourage women to drive cars. A lot of the first trips were part publicity stunt; Horatio Nelson Jackson learned after he set out that two car companies sent out cars to try to beat him to New York. The champion of early cross-country car travelers was A. L. Westgard, who had driven the country several times to find suitable routes and, eventually, to lead trips, little cross-country caravans.

Westgard was known as "the Pathfinder." He drew his own maps; he charted his own courses. And, as John Charles Frémont was allied with Senator Benton, the senator pushing America's Manifest Destiny, Westgard was allied with the American Automobile Association, the association pushing the use in America of cars. In photographs beside his car on the Great Plains, Westgard wears an oilskin coat, a hat; travelers stand round him as he directs the ropes and pulleys that haul cars across a stream. Westgard's first trips ran from New York to Florida or New York to Los Angeles. He was made a special agent by the federal government for his work in mapping roads. At the time, the roads of America were a mystery to the potential driver, a twentieth-century version of the mystery that Lewis and Clark faced. The roads were all local; except for a few old stagecoach routes, there was little need for a map for anyone who did not live there and travel by horse or foot. Westgard's tours were team adventures. He gave prizes for driving skills. In 1911, a tour took twenty-six men, ten women, and four children from Atlantic City to Los Angeles; Westgard called it "The Trail to Sunset." "There was no trouble of any magnitude encountered, no illness en route," *Motor Age* reported, "and the physical condition of the members of the party was better at the end than at the beginning."

After a while, the trip across the country went from being an adventure to a tourist trip. Westgard set up gas and oil stations in remote stretches, which encompassed most of the trip. Pamphlets highlighted scenes: *Lake, River & Mountain Scenery, Grape Vineyards, Splendid Farms, Ranch and Farm Country, Mexicans, Adobe Houses, Pueblo Indians, Colored Cliffs, Apache Indians, Copper Mining, Desert Valley & Mountain Scenery, Orange Groves.* By the twenties, driving cross-country was just another fad in a fad-rich nation, a trip that anyone could take, no tour guide necessary. "The trip through the heart of America is coming to be known as the great American pilgrimage," *American Motorist* said in 1924. "No American can motor from New York to San Francisco without gaining a new conception of the lives of his fellow citizens, a knowledge of his country that will widen local horizons and stifle seasonal prejudices, and achieve a pride in and an appreciation of his United States that can be gained in no other way."

"I" IS FOR INTERSTATE

WHICH IS TRUE TO SOME EXTENT—at least, you appreciate that you *can't* appreciate all of the United States. And anyway, the kids are still asleep, so they can't appreciate the two-tanker truck full of Nutra-Lix that is slowly pulling past us, its name like ancient Greek to me, until I get home and realize it is a dietary supplement for cattle made by a company that, when I peruse its promotional literature, I see includes this testimonial from a customer whose farm I must have driven by but will most likely never see: "We like to use Nutra-Lix in the fall when the grass is dried out and right before weaning. This helps keep our cows in good shape. When we put them out for weaning, they go right to feed since they were already on the Nutra-Lix, and they wean real nice."

THROUGH OUR WINDSHIELD THE HIGHWAY anchors the view: a perfect double line of road straight through dark green waves, the green of the waves lightening as the morning light intensifies. This view of the roads in South Dakota is a highway haiku, a pure and simple symbol of the road and of the expansiveness experienced. But the symbol is deceiving or obscure, because the highway is at once expansive and restricting. The white-striped road down the middle of the countryside through which you are driving works as the opposite of a picture frame. Rather than squaring off a panoramic vista, it is a giant "I" through the world, a car- and road- and driver-centered view.

And now a sign that acutely describes the absence of what is normally expected from a sign:

No Services

A GOOD CAUSE

IS RADIO MORE INTIMATE in the car? Yes, I believe it is. I feel as if I am eavesdropping on the people and places of the Great Plains as I drive. I listen and look for signs of what I hear in the view, as I sit motionless while in seventy-mile-an-hour motion. I hear life as the people who are not just driving through the Great Plains know it. I hear, for instance, these commercials, aired within just five plains-crossing miles:

MALE VOICE, SOUNDING EXCITED, ANIMATED, ENTHUSIASTIC:
Old-fashioned summer-blowout sale is on now. They need to make

room for new merchandise arriving daily, and they're offering *huge* savings on summer clothing, excluding French dresses. Save 40 percent on fashions by Tommy and Lulu, Nancy Boland, and many others. You can also save on your favorite summertime accessories, such as fun handbags and flip-flops. Don't miss the summer blowout sale going on now at Gold Fashions in downtown Williston. Gold Fashions, for the best-dressed woman.

MALE VOICE INTENT ON SOUNDING REASONABLE, ASSURED, CALM: Most Montanans want to see a healthy mining industry in this state, one that creates good jobs and additional tax revenues for education and health care. All agree, however, that if there is to be mining in Montana, it must be well regulated and environmentally safe. Under I-147, new mines using cyanide, a necessary tool in gold mining, must meet stringent new regulations before they can be permitted. I-147 requires new mines to include a primary synthetic liner, a secondary liner, and a system for leak detection and recovery. These are only a few of the new environmental requirements in I-147, all enforced by the state, not the industry. I-147. Isn't it about time we started bringing jobs into Montana instead of driving them out?

MALE VOICE, SOUNDING EXCITED, KIND OF LIKE THE FASHION-AD VOICE: American Cancer Society Relay for Life is coming up August 13 and 14 from seven P.M. to seven A.M. at Sydney High School Track. Just as last year, it's going to be a great team event to help fight cancer . . . It's going to be a lot of good fun that night, and it's all for a good cause. We were successful last year; hope to make it doubly so this year. These reminders brought to you by Moose Lodge 239 at Williston, Dennis Water Well Drilling, Western Cooperative Union, and your branch here at Sydney's very own Power 95. It's twenty-one past with the weather check straight ahead . . .

SYMBOL

THE WEATHER TURNS OUT TO BE GOOD straight ahead, due east, where the road through Montana becomes the road through North Dakota, the state sign announcing the state's boundaries, a quick note to those moving beneath the unending sky. We see a sign for an exit called Home on the Range and then the exit itself, which seems to lead to more of the same range, until we see the low breast-shaped hills covered with the words HOME ON THE RANGE, written in rocks, a roadside sculpture. In this stretch of North Dakota, we will see several giant roadside sculptures, the kind of giant sculptures we see on occasion while crossing the Great Plains. The largest will be at exit 72 on I-94. It is, according to *The Guinness Book of World Records*, the largest scrap metal art sculpture in the world—a sculpture that is ten stories high and half as wide as a football field is long and titled *Geese in Flight*. *Geese in Flight* sits on a hill at the intersection of I-94 and State Route 21; it was designed, welded, constructed, and raised by farmers, high school students, and family members of its creator, Gary Greff. Greff is a former teacher and principal at public schools around the Great Plains who grew up in Regent, the town thirty miles down Route 21, where Route 21 ends. An untrained artist whose mother helps him sketch the figures, Greff works for farmers in the winter and on giant sculptures along the road from I-94 the rest of the time, reportedly living on fifteen hundred dollars a year. He completed his most recent sculpture at the age of fifty-five, in 2004—a giant bass called *Fisherman's Dream*. Greff's other giant sculptures are called *The Tin Family*, which depicts a giant man, wife, and son held up by telephone poles; *Teddy Rides Again*, which features Teddy Roosevelt on a horse and is made of used oil well pipes; *Pheasants on the Prairie*, which features five pheasants and is constructed of wire mesh once used to screen gravel; *Grasshoppers in the Field*, featuring six giant grasshoppers made from old gas and oil tanks; and *Deer Crossing*, featuring deer jumping a fence that was made from old oil tanks. Greff calls the scrap-metal-art-decorated stretch of Route 21 "The Enchanted Highway" and got the idea for the sculptures in 1989, after watching drivers stop to see a strong-man constructed of hay bales built by a farmer. The sculptures are intended to draw people to Regent, in hopes of enriching Regent's economy and preventing further population decline: since 1995, one fourth of the residents have died or moved away, leaving the total population at approximately two hundred. Greff has had the on-again, off-again support of the town, with nearly everyone in Regent eventually deciding he was crazy until around the time that U.S. Senator Byron Dorgan helped him raise eighty thousand dollars at a breakfast in Washington, D.C. Greff hopes that one day Regent will be "the metal art capital of the world," a capital that would include a dinner theater, café, and motel. So far, there is only an Enchanted Highway Gift Shop, featuring Enchanted Highway Frisbees and thimbles, and a store selling metal art, opened by Greff's brother.

At a ceremony marking the completion of *Geese in Flight*, Greff spoke to an assembled crowd, saying, "Yes, I have a vision, to make North Dakota a destination for tourists. I know if I had a family, if I said to my kids, 'Well, we're going to North Dakota to see the wide open spaces,' they would probably say, 'No way.' But if I said we were going to North Dakota to see the world's largest metal sculpture and then from there we're going to go into a theme park where you can see five more sculptures and you can ride the waterslide, then you will say, 'Let's stop in North Dakota and make it a place of destination.'"

Greff has also been quoted as saying, "I guess maybe I'm out to prove that any community, if you really want to survive, you can survive. If nobody tries, we are a community that's gonna be extinct."

"I think Gary symbolizes hope," a local teacher told a reporter.

We gaze out at the scrap metal geese flying through the scrap metal sunset. Though we have stopped there before, this time, with the kids asleep, we press on. But just as people feel compelled to decorate the naked vista that is the Great Plains, so I try to capture the essence of the giant sunset with geese in my journal but cannot.

And for that matter, what can capture this one long corridor, from about Billings, Montana, to Fargo, North Dakota, this interstate passage that on the one hand seems like nothing, but on the other hand is like a multivolume discourse or like a long explanation of something that seems simple but isn't, familiar and changed like the face of the ocean to a sailor.

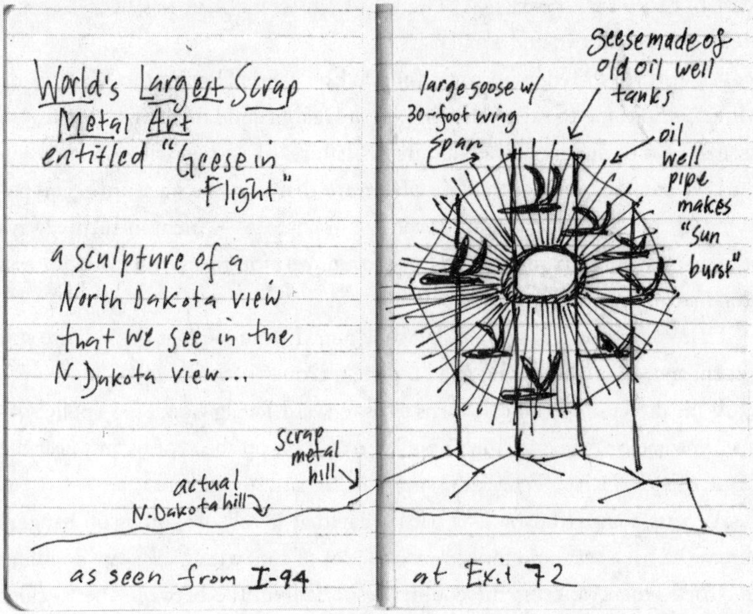

Handwritten notebook sketch, left page:

World's Largest Scrap
Metal Art
entitled "Geese in
        Flight"

a sculpture of a
North Dakota view
that we see in the
N. Dakota view...

scrap
metal hill↓
actual
N. Dakota hill↓

as seen from I-94

Handwritten notebook sketch, right page:

large goose w/
30-foot wing
span

Geese made of
old oil well
tanks

oil
well
pipe
makes
"sun
burst"

at Exit 72

EXPRESSING THE FEELING OF THE MOMENT

AS WE ENTER THE AREA of the Painted Canyon, the little valleys between
the little hills suddenly become deeper and more arid, and the land begins to
look as if it has been baking. We pass a roadside Painted Canyon scenic-view
stop, a scenic-view stop where I have pictures of the kids from several crossings, where I might take a photo of the kids again, for cross-countrying comparison purposes, if they weren't still sound asleep. Even asleep, they seem so
mature as cross-countryers, so mile-savvy, so used to it, so prematurely well-
miled—road-worn since infancy. The Painted Canyon is so-called badlands,
those eroded hills that President Roosevelt described as having "a curious
fantastic beauty all their own," even though General Alfred Sully, a western
military man, called them "a part of hell with the fires burned out."

But marking any one view as *scenic* is a redundancy, if you ask me, or at least unnecessarily restrictive. The way I am seeing it, it has been a scenic view for the past two and a half days.

We also pass Medora, a town founded by a Frenchman, the Marquis de Morès, who came to raise cattle in North Dakota and failed; his story always seems fresh to me, untainted despite his failure, like a recurring dream, each time we stop and look at the fine silverware that is in the museum accompanying his out-of-place, twenty-seven-room château—which, in turn, always seems so far away from France—each time we stop to use the Medora rest stop bathroom.

That said, I check again, looking back quickly, and see that the kids are still asleep, and, thus, there is no need for the marquis' bathroom.

As my driver's head quickly turns to its forward-facing view, I see a police officer in what looks like an Impala pulling over a car up ahead of us, just near the Little Missouri River. I check my speedometer and slow down.

We pass a car from Indiana with a bar that is full of clothes on hangers across the back seat, and indeed we see a lot of cars with back seats doubling as closets when we cross the country, especially in the between the Rockies and the Alleghenies. And now we are passing a bus that is not a commercial bus and not a rock star's bus, a bus that seems more like a cruise ship at sea but is just someone's bus, and it is towing a large SUV.

On second thought, we, the expedition leaders, decide that we *do* need to stop, that we unasleep adults must visit a restroom, soon, come to think of it, and we choose the Painted Hills rest stop on I-94, a combination rest stop and visitor center just inside Theodore Roosevelt National Park: here in the less-populated part of the interstate-flushed West, the national park seems to be riding on the coattails of the rest area. We stop even though the kids are asleep, and we see no need to wake them up. While there, I pick up a brochure that I read a few nights later, in a motel in Wisconsin, when I can't sleep. It notes that a plant called leafy spurge—just one of sixty-eight exotic species that have invaded the twenty thousand acres of native Great Plains habitat—had been choking all the native grasses out of the park until the park rangers began killing the spurge with chemicals and the nine million Aphthona flea beetles released in 2003. I read about the buffalo herd south in Yellowstone with a disease that farmers worried might hurt their cattle, even though the pro-buffalo people argue one might be worried about the buffalo catching a disease from the cows. I also read that Roosevelt once said he would never have achieved his presidency if he had not been to North Dakota and shot a buffalo. While there, while utilizing the restroom as well as the water fountain at the rest stop and pausing in the never-pausing stream of interstate traffic, while as near the buffalo as I will ever be, I am not aware of the herd at all.

BUT BEFORE I UTILIZE THE RESTROOM at the visitor center—in the moments when I am oblivious to the extent of invasive species in the area, as well as to herd issues—in my own invasive and herdish way, I stand alongside the car and, like the drivers on either side of me, inspect the standing-still car rather than talk or communicate with the other drivers in any way. And then I watch my wife get out of the car, enter the restroom–visitor center, leave the restroom–visitor center, and walk briskly toward an informational sign, passing a park ranger emptying trash bins, with whom she appears to chat briefly. Next, she looks down at the sign and then looks out on a huge and beautiful canyon, and pauses, appearing to reflect.

Like relay racers wordlessly passing a baton, when my wife gets back in the car, I jog to the same sign, and I look out on the landscape that I hadn't been able to see from the parking lot: I look into a valley of sands and dry grasses and eroded buttes that appear to have been made in part by seaside children dripping wet sand from their hands. I read the plaque:

Painted Canyon—the name itself evokes the image
of color and light playing across the face of a wild and broken land.
Of the countless individuals who have stood transfixed at this canyon
rim—Native Americans, fur traders, a cavalry general, a man who would
become the 26th President, naturalists, travelers, and writers—all have
tried to express the feeling of the moment.

When I return to the car and ask my wife about her trip to the edge of the canyon, she expresses to me the feeling of the moment. Apparently, the ranger had kindly asked her how she was, causing her, in turn, to ask him how he was, at which point he happily responded, "Dazed and confused, as usual."

THE MAN WHO BUILT AMERICA'S FIRST
CROSS-COUNTRY ROAD (OR TRIED TO BUILD IT)

INITIALLY, THERE WAS A PROBLEM when people set out in their cars to cross the country at the urging of the federal government and promoters: there were no roads. As cars were largely developed by bicycle makers, the impetus for roads largely came from bicycle riders. A good example of a bicycle rider who began driving cars and eventually built a road is Carl Fisher, builder of bicycles, of cars, of Miami Beach and Montauk, and of the Indianapolis Motor Speedway. Carl Fisher was the man behind the Lincoln Highway, the first transcontinental road, dubbed in its time (even though it probably wasn't ever finished) "America's Main Street."

By the end of the 1860s, when they were all the rage, bicycles were called velocipedes. They were nicknamed bone-shakers. Cartoonists made fun of people falling off bicycles all the time, of bicyclists getting stuck in packs behind horses and carriages, of bicyclists crowding onto the very few paved roads. Most bicyclists lived in cities; they toured into the countryside on the weekends. As a group, they petitioned for better roads around the city and into the country, establishing, by the 1880s and 1890s, what became known as the Good Roads Movement. (The Good Roads Movement is sometimes considered an extension of the Country Life Movement, which saw roads as a way to improve rural life—first, by making better farm-to-market routes, and second, by improving access to city cultural and entertainment offerings for rural residents; farmers hoped roads might stop young people from moving to the city.) Better roads mostly meant roads that were paved. Prior to paved roads, road care was executed primarily with a "drag," or "road scraper," a split log that worked like a snowplow and was dragged down a road by horses, scraping the mud flat. When cars came along, farmers were often called on to pull them out of ditches, mud, and streams that cars were not able to ford—farmers thought that cars, like bicycles, were a horse-scaring fad. Prior to Henry Ford making the car affordable for almost everyone, indeed, driving was a patrician hobby; in 1900 there were only twenty-three thousand registered cars in the United States, and seventeen million horses.

Europe, meanwhile, had lots of roads, built during the time that America was busy simply settling the West. Two British engineers, John L. McAdam and Thomas Telford, developed one of the first modern road surfaces, stones covered with a layer of bricks or broken stones, later called macadam. (The coating of crushed stones with bitumen or tar was later called tarmacadam, or tarmac.) In 1824, portland cement was reinvented near Cornwall, England, the secret of cement having been lost during the Middle Ages, and a one-block-long, eight-foot-wide section of road was paved with concrete in Bella-fontaine, Ohio. (We saw what is still billed as the one-block-long section on the two occasions we crossed the country via Bellafontaine.) There were four miles of brick pavement laid in 1893, near Cleveland, Ohio. In 1898, Los Angeles was the first city to spray oil on its roads to hold down the dust. And the first concrete highway was laid down in Michigan in 1909, a one-mile piece near Detroit. But according to a 1904 census, there were only 108,000 miles of gravel road, 38,000 miles of road made of things like stones or sand or shells, and 1,997 miles of dirt road—only about 200 total miles suitable for cars.

BEFORE HE BEGAN BUILDING THE LINCOLN HIGHWAY, Carl Fisher made his name as a bicyclist in clubs with names like the Flat Tire Club and the Zig-Zag Cycling Club. Fisher was a stunt bike driver; his crowd of bicyclists were known as "speed kings," men who would eventually graduate from riding fast on bicycles to riding fast in cars—men such as Barney Oldfield, the first person to drive sixty miles an hour in a car. To win a place on a racing team, Fisher had to learn to fall off a bike going thirty miles an hour. When he was not racing, he worked at his bike shop with his brother, repairing flat tires for twenty-five cents each and eventually manufacturing and selling bikes. "Fisher was a master salesman," said a friend. "You couldn't be with him more than half a minute without feeling that life was a pretty damn exciting proposition." Fisher convinced a bike manufacturer in Toledo to sell him 250 bicycles at cost, which he sold at his shop in Indianapolis, a bustling town of 169,000 in 1900—its population having doubled in the past twenty years. At the time, Indianapolis was, in the words of Indiana historian John Bartlow Martin, "the best place." There were, as was less frequently cited, as many brothels in Indianapolis as there were in New York.

Fisher specialized in publicity stunts. Once, he rode around town on a twenty-foot-high bike, startling people on second floors. He hired a balloonist to make one hundred small balloons, each with a free-bike coupon attached; people used shotguns to shoot them from the sky. The people of Indianapolis loved Carl Fisher; the police found him problematic. On one occasion, he advertised in the papers that he planned to throw a brand-new bicycle off the top of the city's tallest building and would offer a new bicycle to whoever brought the frame back to his bicycle shop. The police announced that if he went through with the stunt, he would be arrested. Fisher in turn announced the date of his bicycle drop and the time, noon, causing the police chief to go nuts. At nine A.M. on the morning of Fisher's bicycle toss, ten policemen surrounded the building, along with crowds of people. It looked as if the police chief had thwarted Fisher. Then, at noon, a bicycle came crashing to the ground—Fisher had slept on the roof with the bicycle. The crowd cheered as people rushed to claim the mangled frame. The police raced up the fire escape, but Fisher snuck down a back staircase. Later in the day, police raided Fisher's bicycle shop. A sign inside said: "You can come see me in the police station. I just gave myself up." The charges were dropped. "Publicly, the police chased him, but privately, many were his friends," one of Fisher's biographers explained. "Even though his successful antics made them look incompetent, they felt lucky that he had not chosen a life of crime." Sometimes Fisher paid a fine in advance, before he was arrested.

In nonpublic life, the inventor of the first coast-to-coast highway was relatively shy and quiet, a creature of habit. He wore loud, and often mismatched, sports coats. He always ate at Horace "Pop" Haynes's restaurant, often three times a day, always ordering steak and potatoes; he ate with the likes of Barney Oldfield as well as Eddie Rickenbacker, the soon-to-be World War I flying ace. Fisher liked to hire people he thought were smarter than he was. "I have a great many men working for me whom I consider have more brain power than I," he said. When he was not talking, people assumed he was thinking of a stunt or commercial opportunity. When he had a new idea, he would say, "I have a new hen coming off." He hired a lot of secretaries to take down ideas. Frequently, he married his secretaries or had extramarital affairs with them. He surprised his first fiancée, and all of Indianapolis, by marrying a fifteen-year-old who was not his fiancée and who described him as having a "dark magnetism" and a "strangely beautiful face." He then surprised his new fifteen-year-old wife with his leather pillow, embroidered with the phrase "A woman is only a woman, but a good cigar is a smoke."

AS THE BICYCLE CRAZE TURNED INTO A MOTORCAR CRAZE, Fisher fell in love with cars. By 1900, his bike shop had become an auto dealership, and he was transferring his publicity skills from bikes to cars. He pushed a car off a roof—this time with the consent of the police—and the car landed upright, bouncing. (Fisher had spent a lot of time practicing with models and adjusting the tire pressure.) He participated in the very first car races, ramshackle affairs often run through towns and villages. Horrifyingly, he does not seem to have known or cared that his eyesight was bad. "Carl's limited vision may have contributed to his daring bravado," one of his relatives wrote. Jumping ditches, he did not see his terrorized passengers, and in races, he tended to run into things, including spectators, who occasionally died. During a race in Zanesville, Ohio, his brakes failed in a turn; he ran through a fence and mowed down a group of fans, ending up in a chicken exhibit. He killed or injured fourteen spectators, and yet the *Columbian* magazine extolled him as having "a national reputation."

As it happened, people were dying in races all around the country, and Fisher finally realized that American cars weren't very safe. At dinner at Pop Haynes's restaurant, he sketched out a plan for a three-mile racetrack on a napkin, the design that would become the Indianapolis Motor Speedway. He had trouble getting financing because bankers were not so excited about cars and racing; a rumor had it that Indianapolis bankers had discouraged Henry Ford from moving to their town. Fisher raised money with balloon races ending at the racetrack site. He built the track with crushed stone and asphalt. When things fell behind schedule, Fisher ordered twenty-four-hour crews to work. During construction, one man died in a vat of boiling tar. At the first race at the new track, spectators crowded to the edges of the road and police pushed them away. A car crashed, killing the mechanic and two spectators. Fisher hired an engineer to design a safer track. After weeks of tests, the engineer decided to use brick with concrete barriers. Three million paving bricks were in place in sixty-three days. The first race was on a winter day, December 17, 1910. It was so cold that a racer wore a stocking cap over his face and cut holes in it to see. The racing lasted for several days and the drivers broke records. There was only one broken leg. To increase race attendance,

Fisher decided to make it a once-a-year race of five hundred miles, an unprecedented distance.

The Indianapolis 500 became America's most famous racing event because of its high purse and because it was held only once a year. Eddie Rickenbacker said that 70 percent of all mechanical improvements on cars were developed at the Indianapolis speedway—a percentage that is probably too high. The aspect of automobiles that was mostly invented at the Indianapolis 500 was speed. Most race teams who specialized in engineering small, fast cars based themselves in Indianapolis. Detroit was the city of engineers of cars that were large and roomy and good for driving families around. Because large cars were more successful in the long run, Detroit was more successful as a car-manufacturing city than Indianapolis. One family-utilized safety device that was developed at the Indianapolis racetrack, however, was the rearview mirror. A racer, Ray Harroun, wanted to race alone, without a mechanic. The other racers protested, saying that he would create a safety issue—at the time, mechanics rode in the cars and watched for cars approaching from the rear. Harroun welded a steel-framed mirror to the front of his car. Harroun won the race, though he did so by keeping his speed down and avoiding pit stops. The other racers said he had cheated by using a rearview mirror.

Carl Fisher developed his own kind of safety device for cars, the Prest-O-Lite safety light. It was a safety device in that it was a light that attached to the car for night driving; in that it worked with compressed gas, it was like a bomb. A worker in Fisher's shop had bought the patent for the device but could not sell it as a light to car manufacturers, who thought it was not safe. One of Fisher's associates tested it by taking the canister to the West Washington Street Bridge and throwing it down onto the rocks of the White River. The canister did not explode. Fisher became a partner in the Prest-O-Lite company. As the head of that company, Fisher mostly traveled the country dealing with lawsuits, most regarding the Prest-O-Lite factories, which would often explode. When an Indianapolis factory next to a sauerkraut plant blew up, sauerkraut sprayed all over a nearby hospital. Fifteen Prest-O-Lite factories across the country exploded. Carl invented a code to keep the explosions secret when company officials sent messages from city to city. The code for the Bayonne plant blowing up was "Bayonne gone at ten thirty." The code for the Omaha plant blowing up was "Omaha left at four thirty." Eventually, they developed a technology that kept the gas safe: they put asbestos in the tanks—not knowing about asbestos causing cancer. In 1911, Fisher sold the company to Union Carbide, the company that owned the chemical plant in Bhopal, India, that exploded in 1984, killing thousands of people. At the time that Union Carbide bought the Prest-O-Lite company, it was reportedly not as interested in the Prest-O-Lite light as it was in the Prest-O-Lite gas.

TOTALLY FALLING IN LOVE

NO, THE NOISE OF US STOPPING, of us opening and closing doors, of us rest-stopping did not wake up the kids, for we are pulling out of the rest stop/national park visitor center and on the road and sailing. We sail through a stretch of what seems like empty openness, then drive through a cluster of signs marked FOOD—GAS—LODGING, and then, as the kids remain asleep, my wife reads from the AAA guidebook about Fort Lincoln, which reminds my driving-delirious mind of Abraham Lincoln, which reminds me of the Lincoln Highway, which causes me to remember the time we stopped in Indianapolis, hometown of Carl Fisher, while crossing the country—another thing we do when we drive is remember, often remembering other times driving, a vicious cross-country-driving circle.

What happened on that trip was my wife read restaurant listings from the AAA guidebook and we quickly picked one that sounded good and jumped off an exit a few blocks from downtown, ending up at the old Indiana Oxygen Building, where gases such as oxygen and hydrogen were once produced. We sat in the dining room, a room that was once the office of the director of the gas factory. I wondered if a former owner of the Indiana Oxygen Company would have known Carl Fisher, if there would have been some kind of gas connection. The food was great; it was fresh and even organic. The waiter chatted with us about Indianapolis.

After we ordered, we sat through that moment of euphoric quietness that comes after driving and talking and driving for, say, five hundred miles, and then sitting somewhere that is not the inside of a car. In that moment, we could not help but overhear the man at the adjacent table. This man was balding in a loud sports coat and purple turtleneck, which was inappropriate for the summer weather, and he was wearing a wedding ring while talking to a woman who was very much not wearing a wedding ring.

Somehow, the dinner arrangement seemed illicit. The kids could tell, and were, like all of us, embarrassed that we were in earshot of this guy. The man in the sports coat was looking deep into the woman's eyes and leaning across his organic greens and holding her hands over the bread and butter. He only averted his deep, passionate stare momentarily, to say hello to the people at the table on the other side of the room who asked him about his mother. "She's great, thanks," he said. Then he turned back to the woman and looked her in the eyes again and after a while said, "I am so totally falling in love with you."

Over the next twenty-five hundred miles, this phrase was repeated in the car on many occasions (and in numerous intonations), according to my journal.

I am so totally falling in love with you.

JUST A LITTLE MORE ABOUT THE MAN WHO BUILT AMERICA'S FIRST CROSS-COUNTRY ROAD (OR TRIED TO BUILD IT)

AS WE DRIVE, as we move on, my wife suggests that I am perhaps going on too much about Carl Fisher, and I feel for her on this account, so I will now in desperation confide this last bit about Carl Fisher to the reader alone. But fear not! We're still moving, still driving—we're making time in North Dakota, the kids *still* asleep, the radio turned to local news, weather, events. We're cruising through what would be the waistband of America if America was standing up and the East Coast was its head and the West Coast was its feet and it was overweight. But before I say precisely where we are on the road, I'd like to mention that in 1910 Carl Fisher decided he would build a road across the country.

Farmers, at the time, were still skeptical of roads; they wanted to get their goods to market but they still saw roads as places for, in the words of one critic, "city dudes to run their gas buggies over." Driving was "an idle sport." But soon driving graduated from sport to business. Like many businessmen, Carl Fisher saw good roads as good business: one of the first rural concrete roads, in Michigan, near Ford's factory, paved in 1908, cost ten thousand dollars a mile to pave, but lasted twenty years and cost twenty-five dollars annually to repair. Freight cost one to eight cents a mile to transport on concrete, as opposed to between eighteen and thirty-five cents on a rock road. Fisher wrote to leaders around the country, including Teddy Roosevelt, who supported a coast-to-coast highway, and Henry Ford, who was not initially keen on the idea, though Ford's son Edsel was. Cement companies also supported it, as did tire companies and car companies and booster organizations in the western states. Also behind the idea of cross-country highways was Charles Henry Davis, a third generation road builder from Massachusetts who was president of the National Highways Association and who had made a map with A. L. Westgard, "the Pathfinder," titled *100,000 Miles of Road Proposed by the National Highways Association*. Davis wrote, "May our beloved land be gridironed by National Highways."

Fisher first dubbed the proposed road the Coast-to-Coast Rock Highway, and established a national committee using such slogans as "Good roads for America" and "Tightening the Union" and "It can be done—let's build it before we are too old too enjoy it." He raised a million dollars in thirty days and renamed it the Ocean-to-Ocean Highway, and then finally, on the advice of Henry Joy, president of the Packard Motor Car Company, the Lincoln Highway. Joy thought Congress would donate money if the highway was seen as a tribute to Abraham Lincoln. (Rejected road names were the Fisher Highway, the Jefferson Memorial Highway, and the American Road.) The route itself was debated, though San Francisco was always assumed to be the end point, since the road was planned to be finished in time for the Panama-Pacific International Exposition in San Francisco in 1915 (it wasn't). Some of the proposed routes touched on the historic trails of America. "Root from your hearts the miasma of commercialism, which, in its fever and fury, blinds your eyes to the upper and higher aim, that of uniting hearts and hands across this great country of ours, to build a National Monument that will ever be pointed to as the Old Trail's Road . . . over which marched civilization, opportunity, religion, development, and progress of our grand America," wrote Mrs. Hunter M. Merriwether.

The not-so-historically minded were interested in connecting towns and cities for business purposes. Fisher organized a cross-country trip on July 1, 1913, to scout the route from Indianapolis to San Francisco. Led by W. D. Edenburn and John Guy Monihan, two experienced cross-country drivers, the participants drove in seventeen touring cars, with a supply truck following, along with telegraph company representatives, members of the Royal Automobile Club of England, reporters, and a AAA field representative, as well as the Pathfinder, Westgard. Each car had the following:

- 1 pick or mattock
- 1 pair of tackle blocks
- 600 feet of ¾-inch rope
- 1 barn lantern, hung on the rear tire carrier, to be lighted if the car's regular lights failed, so the following driver would see it and keep in line
- 1 steel stake, 3 feet long and 1½ inches wide at the top, tapered to a point for use as an anchor to pull the car out of the sand or mud
- 1 full set of chains
- 1 sledge
- 12 mud hooks
- 1 four-by-six-foot tent, envelope-type, made especially for the tour
- chocolate bars in cans and beans in cans, all stowed under the rear seat
- 4 African water bags, kept filled at all times

They drove across county roads and sometimes through fields, cutting cattlemen's fences and repairing them; they dressed in khaki suits and high boots. Citizens of Indianapolis lined the streets to cheer them on. Price, Utah, built a road so the expedition would come through the town. They tried to cover 150 miles a day, but kept having to stop to have lunch with the entire population of small towns. Bishop, California, prepared a camp where people brought free gas and the local bank president cooked a meal. Twelve hundred cars escorted them into Oakland, California.

The route that the Lincoln Highway promoters settled on was not new but

based on improved sections of old roads, a palimpsest. It was funded through
the development of seedling roads that were built by Henry Joy in Illinois,
Iowa, Nebraska, Wyoming, Utah, and Nevada. The seedling roads were
smooth concrete strips, less than a mile long. People would look at a seedling
road, touch it, drive it, take their pocketknives to it. Joy built the roads just
outside cities, where there were only mud roads, suckering the farmers, in a
way, by contrasting what might be with what was, as if roads were a cure-all
in an old medicine show. Lincoln Highway promoters referred to the
seedling roads as Ideal Sections. In Lake Country, Indiana, an Ideal Section
was completed in 1922. It cost $166,655.16, paid for by the state, the county,
and U.S. Rubber, a tire company interested in the manufacture of roads. It
was one and a half miles of forty-foot-wide, four-lane highway, paved with
steel-reinforced concrete, ten inches thick, and built to withstand over five
times the expected traffic; it featured underground wiring and landscaping,
and was supposed to feaure a five-thousand-dollar campground, courtesy of
Edsel Ford, that was never finished. In the end, the Lincoln Highway started
in Times Square in New York City, went through New Jersey, Pennsylvania,
Ohio, Indiana, Illinois, Iowa, Nebraska, Wyoming, Utah, Nevada, and California, and ended in Lincoln Park, San Francisco—some parts were new
road, some old road dubbed new.

The Lincoln Highway helped set off a frenzy of named highways, which,
like the Lincoln Highway, eventually became numbered roads: the Jefferson
Highway from New Orleans to Texas, which became U.S. 90; the Boston
Post Road from Boston to New York City, which became Route 1; the Santa
Fe Trail from Independence, Missouri, to Santa Fe, New Mexico, which be-
came U.S. 56 and 66; the old Oregon Trail from Independence, Missouri, to
Oregon City, which is now U.S. 30 and 26; the Yellowstone Trail from
Boston to Seattle, now U.S. 20, 12, and 10; and the Redwood Highway from
Grants Pass, Oregon, to San Francisco, now U.S. 99 and 101. Of all these,
the Lincoln Highway, decorated with red, white, and blue markers, was the
first and best known—the I-80 or I-95 of its day, as a recent Federal Highway
Administration report stated. In 1940, NBC broadcast a Saturday-morning
dramatic show called *Lincoln Highway* that was, according to *Tune In Yesterday*,
an encyclopedia of the radio era, "a morning show of big-time quality featuring top stars of Broadway and Hollywood who usually were only available
for prime-time evening shows." The show's introduction left the mistaken

impression that the highway had ended not in San Francisco but in Portland, Oregon. It was sponsored by Shinola, the shoe polish company.

CARL FISHER ALSO WENT ON TO BUILD THE DIXIE HIGHWAY, a route to the resort he was developing called Miami Beach, though he never liked the route—as the federal government soon would, Fisher and his partners debated designing a route through cities and a route avoiding them, resulting in what Fisher called "a four-thousand mile wandering pea-vine." He developed Miami Beach as someplace to drive to in the winter. He attempted to develop Montauk on Long Island, using a medieval theme. (A meeting house and the almost skyscrapers that he managed to get up before he ran out of money are still there.) He continued to use publicity stunts and added elephants to his repertoire. But the Depression drove him to bankruptcy and to drink. One of his wives said, "Life with Carl was an unending succession of records set and building accomplished, but tormenting to the nerves of those who raced and those who built." When a friend asked Fisher why he didn't just retire, he replied, "Damn your soul."

His last wife divorced him and married a minister. Afterward, he lived alone, poor, and tried to sell a Frederic Remington painting after losing twenty-five million dollars on the stock market. He drank beer by the case during the day, and at night he read in bed beneath portraits of Lincoln and Napoleon, his heroes, with a beer and a can of peanuts. "I used to make my dreams come true," he wrote to a friend. "I can't do it anymore. I'm only a beggar now. The end can't be far away."

The Lincoln Highway was never entirely completed, and by 1923 the association considered disbanding. Sometimes the Lincoln Highway was merely an old road marked as the Lincoln Highway. Boys stole the red, white, and blue highway markers laid out across the country. The Boy Scouts subsequently volunteered to put up new signs, concrete markers with a portrait of Lincoln. The government had to help finish the route, which was eventually numbered, 40, causing the public to complain. A 1925 *New York Times* editorial lamented: "The traveler may shed tears as he drives the Lincoln Highway, but how can he get a 'kick' out of 46 or 55 or 33 or 21?" In *The Lincoln Highway: Main Street Across America*, Drake Hokanson wrote: "This was the Fisher idea, a road for the whole nation as an example to all and a path for all—a democratic ideal that lived on in the words of songs, the

names of little hotels and streets, a chain of concrete markers, and the restless psyche of America."

In the 1980s, Hokanson looked for traces of the Lincoln Highway and reported it almost gone. In 2003, my family went looking for it on a cross-
country trip and found an Ideal Section in Dyer, Indiana. One afternoon, we
parked at the town library, where I went inside with my daughter and checked
with the reference librarian, who kindly called the town historian, who told
the librarian to send us up the road about a half a mile, where we eventually
found the plaque: IDEAL SECTION. There is no sidewalk; you can't visit the
Ideal Section easily as a pedestrian. We drove on it a couple of times, each
time straining to read the plaque, and then proceeded on until it merged into
an interstate highway where the traffic was heavy, intense, scary. As a matter
of fact, the Ideal Section doesn't seem so ideal anymore; it seems like another
road.

GREAT GREAT PLAINS

THE PROGRESSION OF MY FEELINGS toward the Great Plains while driving across the country for years and years—a progression of feelings that in
some ways mirrors how I have felt about crossing the country itself these
same years—has gone like this: (1) awe, during the initial crossings, at their
sheer existence; (2) frustration that they are so wide and big and seem to take
forever to cross; (3) a return to a kind of awe, an awe that is more appreciative
than the first awe, an awe that becomes a three- or four-hundred-mile medi-
tation on their flatness, the flatness itself being for me, as I have already
stated, mesmerizing, especially given that the interstates cross them as quickly
as possible, that the interstates have little or no interest in contemplation: on
the interstates of the Great Plains, we are back to the time before railroad
promoters and land speculators wanted us to reconsider the Plains and maybe
even live there. And even after driving them for hundreds and hundreds of
hours, the Great Plains still surprise me. In 2002, when we were down in
Texas in between Abilene and Amarillo, we realized my son had accidentally

left his brand-new camera in the breakfast area of a motel in Abilene—or, more specifically, I had accidentally forgotten to check to see that he had not left his brand-new camera in the breakfast area of the motel in Abilene, which, of course, was now many hours behind us. I stopped to use a pay phone in an old phone booth, and I remember looking out of the old phone booth and suddenly realizing I was seeing the flattest plains I had ever seen, covered with cotton but appearing to my eye as absolutely, fantastically flat. Beautifully conspicuous!*

Here in the Dakotas, the flatness is not that of a tabletop but that of the surface of an ocean while calm, of a soft, rolling sea, and a sea is what the Great Plains were before they were the Great Plains—a shallow sea between the West and the East that disappeared eventually and became green backyard lawn, a collection of soft sediments in between the Rockies and the uplift in the Ozarks that is only occasionally interrupted by things like Devil's Tower in Wyoming and the Black Hills in North Dakota. The Plains were where dinosaurs roamed, as well as herds of animals such as horses and eventually bison, which were hunted by Indians, until the Indians were hunted and bison replaced with cattle and farms, to make the meat and potatoes, as well as soybeans, corn, and wheat, that the new America desired.

Through my mind's eye, I see the Impala as if I am a bird or a helicopter news team reporting on nonexistent traffic: I see the Impala as it rolls along the grasslands and former grasslands and lands that have been occupied and unoccupied over and over—a slowly moving dot on the bottom of the old ocean floor.

Through the windshield, I see another Impala, or at least I think it's an Impala, but, anyway, it's a cop at the top of a hill.

I slow down and am cool, or think I am cool. *God*, I think, *please let me be cool!*

On our first trip across the country, both my wife (who was not yet my wife but about to be) and I got tickets crossing the Great Plains, not realizing how fast we were going. I was stopped just before sunset by Officer Haler of the Wyoming Highway Patrol. He clocked me at 77 m.p.h. in an area with a speed limit of 65, and he fined me ten dollars, which I paid on the

---

* In the phone booth, I called the manager of the motel, who, incredibly, found the camera and FedExed it on to us at our next stop, in Austin, Texas. Boy, was my son happy.

spot. I noted in my journal at the time that Officer Haler might have been mistaken for a tourism official had he been any nicer. He told me about the pronghorns on the side of the road, about water restrictions in town—not that I knew where the town he was talking about was. He remembered going east once himself, to Fort Dix in New Jersey in 1959, to serve in the military. He also called me "pardner." "I'll bet you thought you were the only man alive, pardner," he said. That was true. He seemed to have previously observed the phenomenon of the easterner driving for the first time into the West. "Drive fast in Montana," he said.

The next day, the woman who would soon be my wife got a ticket in Montana. I watched her and the police officer chat in the police car as they sat in front of me. She came back and showed me her ticket, for five dollars. I asked her how she managed to get a ticket for only five dollars. "I asked him if I could touch his gun," she said. That was not the case—she was joking—but for many years I believed that she had asked to touch his gun. I tend to be very serious as far as breaking road rules goes. Additionally, the policeman seemed as if he would have been extremely amenable to her touching the gun.*

As for the cop that I was worried about a second ago, when I noticed him, it turns out that I'm cool.

AS WE NEAR A TOWN this morning while inching at a great speed across the Great Plains, the succession of events goes as it always goes when you approach a town on the interstates crossing the Great Plains and indeed a lot of the Rocky Mountain west. First, I notice that the reception on our cell phone, which is mostly without reception on the Great Plains, suddenly increases.† The same thing happens with radio signals, and sometimes when you push the button marked SEEK on the digital radio tuner while on the Great Plains, the radio tuner will automatically digitally seek over and over in the infinity of

---

* Recently, when I was compiling this account of our most recent cross-country trip, my wife said to me: "You don't think I'd ask a policeman to touch his gun, do you?" I had to think for a minute but I decided that she probably wouldn't.

† When cell phones were just becoming ubiquitous, I suggested to my wife that we might want one for cross-country-driving safety. So we got one, took it on a trip, found that you could barely use it between Portland, Oregon, and Saint Paul, Minnesota, got home, and paid an astronomical bill for the one time we got through to a grandparent who couldn't hear a word we said. In many parts of the cross-country excursion area, that's how it still is with cell phones, though now when you are talking to someone you can't hear, at least you can clip the phone right on your ear.

weak reception. Next, I spot a faraway cell phone tower. Then traffic picks up just slightly, which sometimes means there are more than three or four cars in sight. Then comes the thicket of roadside billboards that pitch the town in advance: WATER PARK AND SLIDE, CHARCOAL THICK BURGERS, DISCOVER RICHES ALONG THE TRAIL. Then we see the thicket of towering signs that marks, in this case, roadside Dickinson, North Dakota, the interstate face of the actual Dickinson. Additionally, there are a few grain silos, the few indications to the road traveler that the motel, gas, and fast-food industries are not the only ones. Near the exit, we come very close to the motels and restaurants, and then everything happens in reverse, the signs facing the other way, the cell phone tower fading, reception fading into a signal-free flatness again.

PAL-SHIP

THE KIDS ARE STILL ASLEEP. Without consulting them, we make a decision not to stop, to drive as long as we can while they are asleep this morning, at which point the Impala's Message Center summons me again, messaging me for fuel—a first request, nothing urgent, nothing that I can't handle. We pass many retired tractor trailers converted into roadside signs, a landscape feature in this area that is, like most of the salient landscape features, not mentioned in our guidebooks. We pass a field of retired underground gasoline tanks. We pass a road perpendicular to the interstate that is filled with more giant metal sculptures. We pass the town of Richardton. A sign says, OVER 40 FAMILY BUSINESSES. The number forty on the sign is removable. We pass more and more flat fields surrounded by hay. We pass Hebron, "The Brick City." I look for bricks. I do not see any bricks. Now, there is movement in the back seat. I look back: the troops remain asleep. We begin to pass cars with passengers who appear to look at our license plates and then make gesticulations indicating that—and, yes, I may just be full of cross-country excitement at this point in Day Three—they are impressed with how far away from our license plates' origin we are. People seeming (to me) to be impressed with our plates is a driving-on-the-interstates-of-the–Great Plains

phenomenon. When this happens, we feel a certain amount of pride, for people can tell that we are crossing the country.

Now, we are passing a large recreational vehicle, a model called the Dutch
Star. The Dutch Star is on the scale of a tractor trailer, or maybe on the scale
of the state of Delaware, and it is towing an SUV with a boat attached to the
top. It has Florida plates. I wasn't certain the Dutch Star was a mobile home
when I first saw it, in part because, while crossing the country, I keep hearing
from truck drivers—in idle conversation in truck stops and rest stops—that
the U.S. military is involved in transporting U.S. military equipment in unmarked vehicles of one kind or another, that that is the reason I no longer see
the military convoys that I used to see on the highway as a youth, lying in the
back of my parents' station wagon and reading books about war. But then, not
too long before I took off on *this* cross-country trip, I picked up a copy of
MotorHome magazine and read about forty-foot-long motor homes that are
considered relatively small. As a result, when I get close to the Dutch Star, I
think, Yes, that is a motor home. After the Dutch Star, we pass an SUV with
Seattle plates with a really terrific-looking pack on its roof, a sexy streamlined
pack that is not shredding in the wind or moaning, one that seems to have
given the owners their money's worth. We wave. They wave back. We are
pals, friends for just a moment! Fleeting friends on the road across the country! Fellow transcontinentalists—or so it seems, each sealed in our cars, except that in our case, our windows are open because personally I dislike
air-conditioning and prefer to feel the wind racing through the car, even
though we have to just about shout to say anything!

JOURNALS

THOSE FIRST PEOPLE CROSSING THE COUNTRY in cars thought of
themselves as high-class gypsies. Their cars wore banners: KANSAS CITY TO
LOS ANGELES or OCEAN TO OCEAN or JUST A LITTLE DUSTY or PARDON OUR DUST.
They put tin cans on their radiator caps. Train travel was restrictive; driving
allowed people to camp wherever they wanted, to the chagrin of farmers. In

the teens and twenties, magazines published articles on what was variously called motor gypsying, motor hoboing, nomadic motoring, gypsying deluxe, autotramping, and motor vagabonding. "You are your own master, the road is ahead," one report said. "You eat as you please, cooking your own meals over an open fire; sleeping when you will under the stars. Waking with the dawn; swim in a mountain lake when you will, and always the road ahead." *Motor Camping Book* promised "Thoreau at 29 cents a gallon." John Burroughs, the preeminent naturalist of his day, went on an autocamping trip with Henry Ford, Thomas Edison, and Harvey Firestone, the tire manufacturer. They took a lot of stuff with them, like everyone who went motoring; stuff was strapped all over the cars. *Outing* magazine wrote: "The car or trailer is M'Lord autocamper's castle." Magazine articles targeted to men emphasized the conquest of miles, large engines, speed, and the driver's technical mastery, while articles targeted at women emphasized things like the "soft-glowing campfire" and "the silver radiance of the summer moon playing on the sands."

In the motoring camps that soon popped up, people talked about comradery, which they called "pal-ship." They shared information about traveling, about the roads, the ruts, the mud, which was called "gumbo" or "toothpaste"; they talked about what they had seen and people they had met. For residents of the coastal cities, traveling through the Great Plains was like traveling through an unexplored country, an uncharted land. Vernon McGill took a trip in 1921 from Chicago to L.A. and reported that you didn't need to take a gun on a cross-country excursion. City residents were shocked that cowboys in Wyoming understood carburetors, that there were telephones in North Dakota—the kind of shock that hits easterners as they cross the country even today. The motoring camps were, according to the *Saturday Evening Post*, "one of our greatest modern let's-get-acquainted institutions." A New Yorker traveling across the country described "a comfortable feeling of solidarity with America" and wrote, "Having seen Americans, the ordinary rank and file of this land, we have no desire to be known as New Yorkers."

The camps were looked at as leveling devices, a balm for the war between the city and the country that was especially intense in the 1920s. In the camps, everyone wore the same thing, dusty clothes. People didn't use names; anonymity was cherished, and they referred to each other by license plates or nicknames such as the Woman with the Long Skirt, the Old Gent, and the Busybody. Men would gather round each other's equipment, much of it invented: collapsible beds, front seats that converted into beds, a back seat that had a refrigerator, a truck that was a kitchen. (Experienced campers often ridiculed the overequipped campers who did not know how to use their gear.) Women even went on trips with other women, the car offering a freedom not necessarily available in nonmotoring society.

In 1928, Kathryn Hulme privately published *How's the Road*, an account of her trip from New York to San Francisco with her friend Tuny, short for "Petunia." Like many motorists, Hulme named her car Reggie, short for "Reginald." The two women had access to places usually reserved for men— garages and stables, for instance—and they got to do things that women did not normally do. Hulme described her hair as "smoothed down with a bacony hand, that had ridden bare through dust storms and hung over smoke and had sometimes been rudely jammed up against the black greasy housing of Reggie's underside during various tinkerings." They camped on open prairie alone and entertained two cowboys. In Choteau, Montana, a blacksmith invited them to watch him work in his forge. "He found a rod," Hulme reported, "scanned it critically, seeming to see through its rusty stiffness, the curving bracket he could make of it. Then he thrust it in the live coals of his forge. He pumped the bellows and a spurt of red sparks shot up the chimney. And while the rod heated, he led us around his shop, exhibiting specimens of his wrought-iron workmanship."

Travel quickly got easier, and, paradoxically, less exciting. A car could make 125 miles a day in 1916, 170 in 1920, 200 in 1925, 240 in 1928, 300 in 1931, and 400 in 1936. The faster and farther they went, the less motorists tended to engage in leisurely sightseeing over greater distances. "It is amazing how quickly Americans became accustomed to their cars and the road," writes Warren James Belasco, a historian. "In a way, this had been an aim of early gypsying: to be at home on the road, with all the easy familiarity of a world traveler. Yet the familiarity meant that motorists soon took the road for granted. Motoring emerged as a means to get somewhere rather than as an end in itself." Soon came the traffic jams around national parks, litter along the roads, billboards deemed unattractive. In just over a decade, the car went from being a cure to an ill. Belasco continues: "The view of roadside America as a tawdry bazaar was well established by the early 1920s."

PLAINS HUMOR

ASIDE FROM THE CLERK WHO SOLD US FOOD and water and milk and
juice and coffee this morning in Miles City, Montana, and aside from the
ranger sweeping up trash at the rest stop–national park visitor center in
Medora, North Dakota, we have not spoken to anyone but each other for
several hours. And now we are barely doing that; nothing personal, we're just
hypnotized by the view, the endless driving, as we are somewhere just outside
of New Salem, North Dakota. We are hypnotized as well by the radio station
playing a recording of a Swiss youth chorus: a sorrowful song, a melancholy
hymn with a lush melody that blasts nicely in the front seat of the Impala, in
that decent-but-not-great, stereo-in-a-rental-car kind of way, and makes us
feel even farther away than we are. The music does not play in the back seat
because I have adjusted the so-called fader to play the music only in the front
seat—a great tool of parents and young people alike, and a phrase appropriate
to the quality of cross-country scenery: *fade*. As Lewis and Clark allowed the
men of the Discovery Expedition alcoholic beverages only on special occasions, such as holidays and the day they made it to the Pacific Ocean, so we
limit the use of personal music-listening devices with headphones and emphasize the communal use of the stereo while driving thousands and thousands of miles in the car. As we, the commanding officers of our annual
cross-country expedition see it, car time is a social time, a time when Americans are together, for short or long periods, as opposed to the times that they
are apart—in day care or at school or at work, or commuting in the car. We
talk in the car. We fight in the car. We fight a little more in the car. We play
games in the car, such as what we call the alphabet game, wherein the players
search for all of the letters of the alphabet on road signs or anywhere at all on
passing cars. We play games I don't even have crude names for, such as the
game where we think of two word clues that are hints to two words rhymes,
if that makes any sense at all.* We read. We stare out the window. Or in the
case at hand, we drive and listen to the radio in the front seat while in the
back seat, for about three hundred miles, we sleep.

---

* Example car-rhyming game clue: crazy automobile. Example correct answer: bizarre car.

The Swiss youth choir makes the view of the Great Plains even more romantic—the roll of dry grass is like the long chord of the young voices—until the pack on the top of the Impala begins to freak out again and I have to pull over and rearrange the straps, and as I pull the straps tighter, I swear under my breath, repeatedly. The interstate is being made new as we near Mandan, North Dakota. Nine men man a road grader, pouring concrete around a half-buried metal frame, the road spilling out into more road. Then, to my great and semiprofound delight and the comforting head nodding of my quilting wife, the radio broadcasts an entry from the journals of Lewis and Clark, an entry from the corresponding day two hundred years before, July 22, 1804, the day that the expedition met Indians for the first time since setting out from Saint Louis. I am ecstatic, to say the least. I cannot imagine the restraint I exhibit in not waking the kids. The radio announcer speaks magisterially:

> Today, Captain Clark writes: "Set out very early with a view of getting to some situations above in time to take equal altitudes and take observations, as well as one calculated to make our party comfortable in a situation where they could receive the benefits of the shade. We concluded to delay at this place a few days, and send for some of the Chiefs of that Nation to let them know of the changing government, the wishes of our government to cultivate friendship with them, the objects of our journey, and to present them with a flag and some small presents."

Very shortly after hearing the above journal entry, I see a highway billboard advertising Mandan, North Dakota, exit 157: PROVIDING GUIDE SERVICES, 1804. And a few miles later: LEWIS & CLARK SLEPT HERE 146 TIMES. Again, a smile breaks out across my sunburned-even-through-the-windshield face. If Lewis and Clark stopped there, then yes, so will we—as long as we're making good time this morning. Just quickly. Lewis and Clark spent the winter there once. I'm just thinking maybe half an hour.

THE HISTORY OF PEOPLE PUBLISHING THEIR OWN PERSONAL ACCOUNTS OF CROSSING THE COUNTRY (I.E., ACCOUNTS SUCH AS THIS ONE)

IN THE BEGINNING OF CROSS-COUNTRY TRAVEL BY CAR, the thing that was almost as common as cars driving cross-country was cross-country road memoirs. There was *Retracing the Pioneers from West to East in an Automobile* by Hugo Alois Taussig in 1910, and *Story of an Automobile Trip from Lincoln, Nebraska, to Los Angeles* by Paul H. Marley in 1911. "Strangely, when established writers took to publishing their motor memoirs, they were often as naïve and boosterish as the raw amateurs," one historian of the road has written. My favorite road memoir is by Emily Post, the writer most known for her etiquette guides but who was also an early cross-country traveler. Her account of crossing the country is called *By Motor to the Golden Gate*, and it originally appeared as a serial in *Collier's* magazine. She wrote her book when cross-country travel was still a novelty, and the thing I most enjoy about it is that she approaches all the towns and all the people and the road with a kind of skeptical optimism that sometimes is even pleasingly unskeptical.

Post was born Emily Price, in Baltimore, in 1872. Her father was the architect who designed the first gated community in America, Tuxedo Park, New York. Her mother was a stock investor. Post married Edwin Post, a businessman, and had two sons. His extramarital affairs made the papers. She divorced him and began to make a living by writing—novels and short stories in the vein of Edith Wharton and investigations for *Collier's*, a top muckraking magazine of its day. In 1921, she was asked to write a book on etiquette: *Etiquette in Society, in Business, in Politics and at Home*, a manners manual that was eventually ravenously consumed by new immigrants and upwardly mobile Americans. She subsequently wrote a column on etiquette in *McCall's*, an early women's magazine.

But before that her editor at *Collier's* sent her on a trip across the country. (Her car broke down in New Mexico, and she ended up taking the train from the Grand Canyon to California.) Her story complemented another story written by another reporter crossing the country for *Collier's* by train. Whereas the other reporter interviewed prostitutes in Cripple Creek, Colorado, Emily Post interviewed wealthy tuberculosis patients who were in

Colorado Springs, Colorado, for a cure. "Death is the one word never mentioned," she reported. "If by chance they speak of one who has gone, they say he had 'crossed the great divide.'"

EMILY POST LEFT THE EAST for the west in the spring of 1915, when her friend Frank Crowninshield, editor of *Vanity Fair*, told her the western mountain passes would be clear. The trip cost her $1,800 and took forty-five days, twenty-eight of them spent driving. Her friends told her that the Lincoln Highway was just an imaginary line, like the equator. She went to the offices of AAA in Manhattan, and a clerk suggested she just take a vacation in the mountains in New England. She went again to AAA and met with A. L. Westgard, who recommended a Ford instead of her European car (because European cars were low to the ground). "You won't find Ritz hotels every few miles, and you won't find Central Park roads along the way," Westgard told her. "If you can put up with that you can go—easy." She took her son out of college to drive, telling his professors that he would learn more driving across the country than he would at Harvard. Her cousin also came along, possibly at the last minute. They packed a European car, which was too low to the ground, too full of stuff; a day out she sent back a silver service. "One would have thought we were starting for the Congo or the North Pole," she wrote.

As they drove up Fifth Avenue toward Albany, their first stop, they waved to friends and told them they were headed to San Francisco. "No really, where are you going?" the friends said.

LIKE US WITH OUR ROOF PACK, Emily Post had problems with her gear. "In every way my clothes are a trial and disappointment," she said. But on the whole she describes a trip across a country where cities are far apart, where each new section is like a new universe, where the lack of roads makes the localities seems especially local, and, thus, quaint to the tourist. "Plunging into an uninhabited land is not unlike plunging into the surf," she wrote. "A first shock! To which you become accustomed, and find invigoratingly delicious. Why difficulties disappear, and why that magic land leaves you afterwards with a persistent longing to go back, I can't explain; I only know that it's true."

She meets towns and cities as if they were people. "Cleveland, 'the Sixth City'—and she likes you to . . . know her rating—is currently prosperous-looking and in many ways beautiful . . . The whole city impresses one as having a nice fat bank account and being in no hurry to spend it." She loved the coffee in Cleveland, as opposed to the food she ate near South Bend, where she stopped for a chicken dinner, advertised in a Blue Book: "Mrs. Seth Brown. Chicken dinners a specialty." Post recounted her meeting with Mrs. Seth Brown and the chicken dinner, which was not actually chicken.

"What y'want?"
"Do you serve chicken dinners?" I asked
"D'ye see it advertised?"
"Yes, in the Blue Book."
"Y'c'n have dinner," she said

"Chicken dinner" was greasy fried fish, accompanied by cold potatoes, sliced raw onions, pickled gherkins, bread, and coffee. "We ate some bread and drank the coffee," Post wrote. "If we had been blindfolded it wouldn't have been so bad."

She took the meal in stride, like everything else. For me, this is the best thing about Emily Post's trip, and, in a way, the best thing about all those first cross-country travelers: they looked forward to being inconvenienced. They seemed to know intuitively that the road was work, that work paid off, if in strange and sometimes imperceptible ways, kind of like in life.

In Post's case, she was with her family. She was on a trip that she wasn't sure about. She was giving it her best upper-class–New York shot. "There is one consoling feature in such an incident, that although it is not especially enjoyable at the time, it is just such experience and disappointments, of course, that make the high spots of a whole motor trip in looking back upon it," Emily Post wrote. "It is your troubles on the road, your bad meals in queer places, your unexpected stops at people's houses; in short your misadventures that afterwards become your most treasured memories."

EMILY POST LOVED SEEING NEW PLACES, or seeing any places at all, even when she was uncomfortable—uncomfortableness being something I personally feel is necessary for the most successful cross-country trips. In Chicago, she was amazed by civic pride and checked into what was described as "America's most perfect hotel" by the hotel in the description. "Nearly all of

Chicago's prominent citizens are self-made—and proud of it," she wrote. "Millionaire after millionaire will tell you of the day when he wore ragged clothes, ran bare-footed, sold papers, cleaned sidewalks, drove grocer's wagons." She loved Chicago, mostly because of the way it loved itself. "I don't think I can explain this personal and sudden liking that I have for Chicago. Once in a very great while one meets a rare person whom one likes and trusts at first sight, and about whom one feels that to know him better would be to love him much. To me Chicago is like that."

Post was traveling during, meteorologically speaking, one of the wettest springs the Midwest had ever seen, and she met a lot of mud on the early dirt roads: "The highway itself disappeared into a wallow of mud! The center of the road was slightly turtle-backed; the sides were of thick, black ooze and unmanageably deep, and the car was possessed, as though it were alive, to pivot around and slide backward into it." When her car broke down in Rochelle, Illinois, Post stayed in what was not America's most perfect hotel by a long shot and, to her own surprise, loved it, getting to know the fire chief, someone she would only have met driving across the country. In *The Tourist: Travel in Twentieth-Century North America*, John A. Jakle writes that early motoring "encouraged different forms of social encounter."

"Twenty-four hours in a town like this and we feel as though we knew it and the people intimately," Post said.

She thought America was amazing, even though she missed Manhattan. She loved that department store clerks pushed shoppers around in wheelchairs in Ohio, and middle-of-the-street parking in the wide streets of Omaha. (She compared Council Bluffs and Omaha to Brooklyn and Manhattan.) On the Plains, her party saw a cowboy come galloping over the plains with a lariat; they saw horse-drawn covered wagons. They crossed a river in their car. They slept outside. In Trinidad, New Mexico, they met motoring tourists who had a banner on their car: "Kansas City to Los Angeles." Outside Santa Fe, they met a woman on a horse, riding out of nowhere, who accused Post and her party of being from Europe or New York or Boston, all the same. "What can you get over there, I'd like to know, that you can't get here?"

THE DEPRESSING PART OF EMILY POST'S cross-country report comes when she arrives in the Southwest, where she visited with Indians. Seeing the

Indians was what tourists did in the Southwest. The Southwest was "America's Orient." Tourists were encouraged to imagine themselves on an expedition, coming in contact with exotic people. "The Red Man of America appeals intensely to the imagination," one guidebook said. "All that is wild, primitive within us is aroused when we reflect upon the care-free life which must have been before the white man's coming."

Emily Post stayed in a hotel owned by Fred Harvey, an English immigrant who opened his first hotel in Topeka, Kansas, in 1876, and built several more along the Santa Fe railroad; Harvey hired young waitresses and dressed them in crisp black and white uniforms—Harvey Girls. He encouraged the meeting of tourists and Indians. He bought and sold Indian artifacts, and hired Indians to perform dances as trains dumped tourists off and shuttled them out. He hired architects who created the hotel architecture that still lingers today: an amalgam of Southwest and pueblo styles and railroad commercialism, pleasing to the tourist.

She goes to see Indians who entertain guests at the hotel—"entertain" in this case meaning that the Indians lined up for money while the hotel was running the tourists in and out. She described it as "frankly a vaudeville performance." In fact, her passages on Indians are the only passages in the book that are not gracious. She seems to have a lot of disdain for the Indians, though of course she is no different from nearly everyone else traveling through Santa Fe at the time. She was disappointed with the dress of the Indian women, especially. "Only one wore the blanket costume as it is supposed to be worn," Post wrote, adding, "the men were more picturesque." She gets upset with an Indian who thinks she took two pictures of his child and, thus, wants to be paid twice—two quarters. "Personally I feel rather embarrassed on being told to look in upon a group of swarthy figures who contemplate the intrusion of their privacy in solemn silence," she wrote. At another point she reported at length on the laziness of the Indians, via a conversation with an employee of Fred Harvey. Like I say, I understand that her editors may have agreed with her in her disdain for Native American culture, but I had hoped for more; she wasn't much of a muckraker as far as the third-class treatment of Indians was concerned. When she turned to etiquette writing, she once said this: "Manners are a sensitive awareness of the feelings of others. If you have that awareness, you have good manners no matter what fork you use."

SANTA FE

ON THE WESTBOUND TRIP that preceded the one I am now describing—the trip, that is, that took us from the East Coast to the West Coast via New Mexico—we stopped in Santa Fe. In preparation for not eating food of any substance, much less quality, for a thousand or so miles, we had a big lunch of beautiful and healthy-feeling southwestern food at a restaurant downtown. Emily Post has said of road food: "After many days of it you feel as though you have been interlined with a sort of paste." Our southwestern meal was the opposite of that, a perfect antidote to all the saltines we had eaten over the past few days. After lunch, we walked around leisurely, observing the town that has always been a stop—on the old trail, on the train route, and now on an interstate, I-25, which runs a little ways out of town. We walked to the old governor's mansion, the oldest public building in America, and my wife and daughter bought handmade jewelry from a Native American guy, an artist, who, after they paid him, smiled and packed up and walked away. Then we went to the Georgia O'Keeffe Museum. To our shock, it was closing—once again we had forgotten about a time zone change. I pleaded with the staff person, and she let us in, begrudgingly. I felt guilty about pleading with the staff person, and made the kids uncomfortable as I began to race them through, but the guards were especially nice and told us to take our time. Naturally, the kids then fell in love with Georgia O'Keeffe, especially my daughter, who had already fallen in love with Santa Fe.

"When I grow up, I'm going to live here," she told us.

After the museum, my wife got the idea that we could see Georgia O'Keeffe's house on the road north, out of town—my wife had been there when she was a kid, when she fell in love with Georgia O'Keeffe, this being when Georgia O'Keeffe was still alive. I was skeptical. A guidebook said you had to book three months in advance for a tour of Georgia O'Keeffe's home, as if, for us, that had happened or was ever going to happen. My wife became semiconsumed with her intent to see O'Keeffe's house, her ability to become semi-consumed probably a reason I married her, as I think of it now.

"How did you find her house then?" I asked, anxiously. It was going to be dark in two hours.

"I don't know. It was known," my wife said.

"What do you mean 'It was known?'" I asked, my tone maybe a little intense.

"Dad, lighten up," my son said.

My daughter said, "Dad."

In my opinion, we had no idea where Georgia O'Keeffe's house was, or very little idea. "I know exactly where it is," my wife kept saying, even though she offered no details. Thus prepared, we set out for Georgia O'Keeffe's house. We drove along another highway being constructed—a state road transforming into something along the lines of an interstate highway, the trend in most of America. We drove through pueblos. We drove up into the hills and ended up passing through canyons that looked precisely like Georgia O'Keeffe paintings: you could open the pages of the book we had bought at the museum and match them to the landscape, as if they were pages from a guidebook. There were buttes made of layers of colors, rocks sculpted by giants—abstract nature. And the darkening sky dramatically lit the roadside gallery, and, yes, made me a little more anxious about our destination, which we did not even know, for crying out loud.

My wife held in her hand a book with a photograph taken from the window of Georgia O'Keeffe's house, our only clue, and soon we arrived in Abiquiu, where my wife, like a human divining rod, was pointing and nodding, recollections of her youth coming back to her. We looked around and, sure enough, saw the hill in the photo. "There it is," she said. She also said, "Just calm down." We saw a house on the edge of a hill. We drove up the narrow road into the tiny settlement. The part of me that was not flipping out was amazed at the perfect practicalness of the small adobe houses, of the communal grazing area in the village and villages all around—the Spanish-American architecture of the Southwest is to me the opposite of a modern housing development and its meaningless private parcels, its hollow references to Tudor England or to various colonialisms. The other part of me, the part that was flipping out, was concerned that we were about to be arrested for trespassing.

I WAS DRIVING ABOUT TWO MILES AN HOUR, thinking we were headed somewhere that would get us in trouble, thinking that I was steering through dangerous waters—my wife tends to take us places that I, as opposed to our kids, am reluctant to visit.

"I just feel like we shouldn't be doing this," I said.

"Stop worrying, Dad," my daughter said.

"Dad," my son said again, with emphasis.

Then I saw the graffiti on a trailer: TOURISTS NOT WELCOME. That was it for me. Panic. Now, my wife was shaking her head, perhaps wondering how she had ever ended up traveling with me, of all people—I don't know. She grabbed her camera and got out of the car.

I could feel the kids once again rolling their eyes as I locked the doors. My wife walked to a beautifully flowered fence—and from there saw Georgia O'Keeffe's house. At that moment, I saw a villager. I saw the villager see, first, our car, then my wife. My wife took a photo of the flowers on the fence, unaware of the villager approaching. My wife turned around. I feared what would happen next.

"Dad, it's OK," my daughter said.

My wife smiled at the villager. The villager smiled back. They waved to each other.

"She's dead, honey," my wife said, as she got back in the car. "She would love you to visit her house."

WE CONTINUED DRIVING NORTH THAT EVENING. After Georgia O'Keeffe's house we were attempting to see a church that Georgia O'Keeffe had famously painted, Ghost Ranch—a public place, I had been assured. We were planning on spending the night in Taos, so this was out of our way, and there I was once again trying unsuccessfully to be relaxed with what looked like a big storm coming. This is my modus operandi: to freak out and then attempt to seem like I never freak out, like a bank robber trying to chat calmly with a teller. We were looking at a back road to get us to Taos—the thinnest road described in our atlas, and on our TripTik, not described at all.

We drove and drove into lonely canyons, the sky turning stormy, until even my wife became concerned and we turned back toward Santa Fe to follow more-major-looking routes north to Taos. We got lost. It began to storm. In the downpour, I asked a policeman for directions. I got lost again. We arrived in Taos at close to eleven and stopped first at one motel that had a country-western band rocking in the lobby and then at another with an old bunch of cabins, where a note on the manager's door said the manager would be back in ten minutes—after twenty minutes we left. Eventually, we said what the heck and checked into the Taos Inn in the heart of tiny downtown Taos, a pricey place. It was beautiful, an art deco inn from the thirties. A guy who was about twenty-five set us up in our room and brought in a cot for our son. As he was working, he told us that he had driven across the country once—to Boston, where he studied the fiddle.

In the morning, we drove north again, this time through winding New Mexican forest until we caught up with the interstate. It was the very spot where Emily Post had hit a huge storm of hail and rain and had fed her son hard-boiled eggs as he drove in the open car. Coincidentally, we hit a really bad storm there too. As usual, I was having some pack problems, and, as usual, I ended up running the straps through the windows, something you are not supposed to do, except that I had a very serious pack problem. The water followed the straps into the car, water running along the straps above us all, water falling in large drops and small rivulets. In a very short time it was essentially raining in the car. Everyone got wet for a long time. People said things such as *What a nightmare!* and *I can't believe this is happening!* I was very frustrated, to say the least. Still, as Emily Post noted, the biggest mishaps sometimes make for fond retellings and, as far as the time it was raining in the car goes, we will all treasure the memory, maybe.

CAN'T SHAKE THAT THING

THE DESCRIPTION THAT EMILY POST, early car-crosser, used when she was where we are today, was this: "The interminable distance was in itself an unforgettably wonderful experience. It gave us an impression of the lavish immensity of our own country as nothing else could."

I feel similarly—there is pleasure in the plains' sometimes unmarked infinity, a pleasure tinged with the danger of remoteness, and now, with my dashboard's Message Center asking me to seriously consider gas, I am noticing the roadside signs that have sprung up. And then our TripTik—a vestige, of course, of the first A. L. Westgard AAA maps that Emily Post carried—indicates that there will be gas at the next exit. On a bluff to the south of the interstate, there is also a giant cow, representing, again according to our Trip-Tik, the area's dairy industry.

I follow the giant cow, it stares off toward the north and east, a docile monster. Off the exit, I come to two gas stations, stop, and choose the cleaner-, newer-looking of the two. As I fill the tank, my wife sees a tall guy, dressed in jeans and a white cowboy shirt and large cowboy hat, get out of a Camaro and tip his cowboy hat to her, a human interaction that is not just human but also seemingly western as well—I almost wish I had a cowboy hat, and I could tip it to people in the gas station area. I go inside the convenience store and use the restroom, where something happens.

USUALLY, IT IS SAMENESS ON THE HIGHWAYS, sameness, distinguished by newness or oldness, but once in a while, within the sameness, you en-counter a highway novelty, something that is different even though it will probably one day be the same. So it is in the restroom, as I cast my eyes for the first time on the enMotion towel dispenser, a thing of on-the-road recycled-paper-towel-dispensing beauty, or at least the nicest restroom towel dispenser I have ever seen.

My hands dry from the paper towel that is automatically dispensed, I come out of the bathroom semi-ecstatic. I compliment the clerk on the towel dis-penser; she thanks me warily. I send my wife to the restroom while I sit with the still-sleeping, if you can believe it, kids in the car. "Wait till you see the bathroom," I say. I instruct her to place her hand beneath the paper-towel dis-penser and see a recycled paper towel electronically delivered to her. She comes out, also impressed.

After we arrive home, in the days ahead, I will get in contact with a man who happened to be at a meeting in Connecticut when his boss suggested the idea for the machine. It was the year 2000. It was a time when the paper-towel-dispensing industry was looking to find the next big thing in paper-towel dis-pensing. A design company in Boston had made a more-pleasing version of a towel dispenser for the James River Paper company, a curvy thing, streamlined and a long way, visually speaking, from the first dispensers you would have seen on the road—whereby towels were distributed with a coat hanger. This all-new dispenser ran on flashlight batteries, the sensitivity adjustable, the batteries last-ing for months: it addressed people's on-the-road interest in not using levers or handles—it addressed their hygiene-motivated interest in not touching.

In an office in Chicago—located approximately twenty-five hundred feet from I-94, *the very interstate we are on now*—employees and contractors of the Fort James paper company, which was soon to be bought by the Georgia Pacific paper company, watched a corporate demonstration video, highlighting the electronic dispenser. The video featured a song by MC Hammer, "Can't Touch This," as well as the song "Put Your Body in Motion." The words *in motion* appealed to the executives, though people at the meeting knew that the legal department would find those words difficult to trademark. Thus, using the language of branding that is not really a language but more of a melding or streamlining device that often has the secondary effect of removing all meaning, they chose the term *enMotion* as a name for the dispenser—a word-like name that like many such names often takes away all meaning.

In the car, as we pull out of the station, the kids are, after several hundred miles, now waking up. Rustling, talking, brief quick shouts, bursts of expeditionary friction. On the way out of the gas station, my daughter, still groggy, looks out the window and sees a red car and makes a cross-country observation. A great cross-country observation. "Red cars," she notes, astutely, "always have a lot of teenagers in them."

EARTH LODGE

IN HALF AN HOUR, everyone is wide awake and we arrive, fresh from the interstate, in Mandan, North Dakota. We drive through tree-lined streets of neat little houses, and then into downtown Mandan. We are across the river from Bismarck. Mandan is to Bismarck as Brooklyn is to Manhattan. Bismarck is also the state capital of North Dakota, a city named for Germany's chancellor in hopes of luring German settlers. We pass the Lewis and Clark Hotel, now apartments. We pass many Chinese restaurants, and we drive a few miles south to Fort Lincoln, the onetime U.S. cavalry post from which General George Armstrong Custer set out to the Battle of Little Bighorn. Fort Lincoln is built adjacent to the site of the On-a-Slant Indian Village, where Mandan people lived from about 1575 to 1781, where Lewis and Clark camped, where they met Sacagawea, whose biography for young people my daughter has now completed.

Yes, it was a little farther from the interstate than I expected. But as usual, we were just planning on a quick stop, a momentary diversion.

We head straight for the village, crossing an old bridge, to see the earth lodges, which are, aside from being a site of cultural, anthropological, and ethnological importance, a big hit with our kids.

"These are amazing," our son says. "Can you imagine?"

I refer to Clark, who wrote thusly in his journal, not having access to any kind of computer program that would aid him in spelling: "Their Houses (also Cald. Lodges) are built in a Circular form of different Sises from 20 to 70 feet Diameter and from 8 to 14 feet high, Supported with 4 Pillars Set in a Squar form near the Center neat the hight of the hut."

I refer also to George Catlin, the nineteenth-century artist, and better speller, who painted a room in an earth lodge and showed it to be as practical as it was, for lack of a better word, cozy—though perhaps I say that because I stayed in such a bad motel last night: "The lodge . . . was a room of immense size."

It occurs to me that building an earth lodge is the opposite of moving, of driving across the country. Building an earth lodge means you're not going anywhere very soon.

WE CERTAINLY AREN'T GOING ANYWHERE because we stumble onto a tour, which, I should know by now, always takes longer than you expect. Our tour guide is a non-Indian in her thirties. We met her alongside a plaque that describes the history of the village. "As for the plaque, I will warn you that most of the information is wrong," she says. "It was put up in 1956 and based on archaeological research done in 1937."

She is also a bit of a comedian, her trademark line being "So that worked out pretty nicely." Examples: "The Mandan herded bison off of the cliff, so that worked out pretty nicely" and "I hear the big advantage is you only have one mother-in-law, so that worked out pretty nicely."

We see how the Mandan in this village farmed, using nitrogen supplied by beans, using squash to hold moisture in the ground, harvesting salt from alkali on the plains. We hear about their coast-to-coast trading network, about how women owned the property and only men were allowed to hunt.

"Then again," says the tour guide, "hunting isn't the safest job in the world."

She makes a fake throat-slit sign with her hand.

Our tour guide tells us the lodges were constructed by women, except for the communal lodge, which was built by men. "I like to say that's why they took so much longer," she says. She mentions that women rarely spoke at communal meetings. "But when they did, everyone listened, so that worked out pretty nicely."

AT THE SOUTHERN END OF THE VILLAGE, where it overlooks the Missouri River, we go into a lodge that features an exhibit about this very village being rebuilt. In it, I learn about the New Indian Deal, something I had never heard of before and that I read about when I got home. The New Indian Deal happened during the presidency of Franklin Roosevelt. It was proposed in large part by a man named John Collier, the Indian Affairs commissioner at the time, and it encouraged the renewal of Indian cultural traditions, as well as a renewal of representative government on reservations, tribal autonomy, and land acquisition policies (or reacquisition policies). Previously, the U.S. government sought to strip Indians of their Indian-ness, to Anglo-ize them and Christianize them; the federal government sent young Native Americans to English-only schools, for example. Collier sought to give young children a bilingual education. He believed that the communal aspect of Native American culture ought to be emulated by American society. In retrospect, Collier had some patronizing and romanticized notions about Indians, and historians have mixed feelings about him today. In his time, he was labeled a communist—people associated communism with any mention of the word *communal*—and he resigned. Subsequently, federal funding for reservations was severely cut.

But before Collier resigned, the Mandan earth lodges were rebuilt, under the guidance of Mandan elders. In the lodge, a video display talked about a local woman who found them again falling down in the 1980s and worked to fund the rebuilding of the New Indian Deal rebuilding. She was a Mandan elder and storyteller named Regina Schanandore.

WHEN WE LEAVE THE LODGES, we walk over to Fort Lincoln, where General George Armstrong Custer had been based, and we meet with the cavalry reenactors, who are hanging around one of those cool old canvas tents, the kind you see Abraham Lincoln and U. S. Grant sitting outside in old photos of the Civil War; the reenactors seem hot in the sun in the old wool uniforms. We buy some postcards and a Lewis and Clark key chain. And then we trudge back to the car and then back toward the interstate via downtown Mandan, stopping at the old train depot, which has been converted into a place called Five Nations Arts, a store filled with traditional arts and crafts made by members of the five Mandan tribes. And, as we all jog back to the car, I am coming to the realization that we have spent way too much time at Mandan if we are even going to make it across the country.

INSPIRE

NOT THAT WE DON'T STOP at the native arts and crafts store on the way out of town, the point at which a small road coincidence happens. Our son is looking around at the Mandan art, as my wife and daughter are hovering over earrings that they eventually buy. And I am thinking about Emily Post and Indians and reading a magazine called *Inspire*, a North Dakota magazine published, according to the cover, "For Women—About Women." The cover story is about Amy Mossett, the nationally recognized Sacagawea expert. The article features photos of her dressed as Sacagawea while standing alongside several people, including the governor of North Dakota, the U.S. senators from North Dakota, her daughters, and Scott Mandrell.* The article describes Mossett's childhood home (along the Little Missouri River in the North Dakota Badlands) and her hobbies (gardening), and the last line is a quote from Mossett: "This incredible young woman left us with certain legacies. I really think that Sacagawea intended for certain people to go on a journey with her. She has taken some people on an incredible journey, and I truly believe I'm one of them. It's been a life changing experience, and I'm humbled and tremendously thankful for it."

As I finish reading the article, I look up and happen to see a young man who appears to be of Native American heritage talking to a woman behind

---

* The same Meriwether Lewis reenactor I met in Saint Louis, by the way.

the counter near the CDs. I also hear a flute on the loudspeaker. After he leaves, I am inspired to asked the woman behind the CD counter about the flute—it sounded great. "That's Matt Schanandore playing flute. He was just right here," the woman says.

Later, when I call up Matt Schanandore at Fort Lincoln, where he works in the marketing department, he referred me to his Web site, which describes his ancestry as European, Native American, and Hispanic—his native heritage being of the Mandan-Hidatsa tribes of North Dakota and the Oneida tribe of Wisconsin. He told me that his first album was traditional Native America flute music, while his second album featured flute and piano, an instrument his grandmother taught him. He dedicated his albums to his grandmother. "Her story of culture lost, culture sought, her presentations about the Indian culture, pointing to herself as a soon-to-be extinct species, led him into stressing that we, too, learn the culture," a Great Plains newspaper reported. Schanandore said his grandmother had volunteered her time to care for the lodges for many years. "It really was her dream to see the village restored again," Matt said.

As we are looking for the road back to the interstate, I slowly put it together that I had just seen Matt Schanandore, grandson of the late Regina Schanandore.

"Do you know who that was?" I eventually say to everyone in the car. I began to elaborate but that was when I really began to understand the situation regarding us and Minnesota and the time.

THE POINT LATE IN THE DAY OF
A LONG DAY OF DRIVING

THERE COMES A POINT late in every day of driving that began really, really early—in today's case around seven A.M., even—at which you have just had it and you can barely drive anymore but you're driving anyway, you are just not going to stop. We've already driven four hours and we have about five to go. We've already covered more than two hundred miles. We've already spent

close to three hours looking around Mandan—which I refuse to believe because it seemed more like forty-five minutes—when we really should have
been moving, especially since we played golf on a toxic-waste site the day before. We must now move, book, rock and roll.

We get back in the car, vowing not to get out of it.

"OK, we really can't stop anymore if we're going to make it to Saint Paul
tonight," my wife says.

"Let's just *get* there," my son says.

"So that worked out pretty nicely," says my daughter.

GUIDEBOOK READING

WE DRIVE AND DRIVE and drive over the Plains as it becomes a prairie full
of green farm fields, and we read and quilt and listen to music, and rather than
stopping to see the sights, my wife shouts out not-so-illuminating passages
from the AAA guidebook about them. The windows are down, warm air rushing in, the pack on top of the car making strange sounds again, but we're not
adjusting it—an experience of America:

Jamestown! Population 15,527! World's largest buffalo, forty-six feet long!

The Sheyenne River!

*Valley City, population 6,826. The area offers camping, hiking, and picnicking, as
well as water sports!*

IN VALLEY CITY, WE STOP FOR GAS. We buy snacks—cheese, crackers,
jerky, and juices—and surmount a middle-of-the-country language barrier.

"Would you like a *beag*?"

"Pardon me?" my daughter says politely.

"A *big*?" my son says.

"A *beag*!" the woman says, frustrated.

"Oh, a *bag*!" says my daughter, cheerfully. "Yes, thanks!"

"Thanks," says my son.

In the car again, my daughter says, "So that worked out pretty nicely."

BOOKING AHEAD

ACROSS THE RED RIVER, through the Red River Valley, and into Minnesota, and for once, as far as lodging goes, I have it my way. I call ahead, to book a room in advance, or at least a couple of hours in advance. We call ahead not to a motel but a hotel. Yes, once each trip we offer the kids a nice place to stay, this time in the more-expensive-than-a-motel-but-not-outrageously-priced Saint Paul Hotel. And when we call, it is booked. So we stay at a hotel that costs more, significantly more, twice as much more, in Minneapolis instead, almost not getting a room there because our cell phone reception keeps cutting out: when I call back, I have to say, "But I'm the guy you just talked to, when there *was* a room available." Thus, we book this room in advance, a luxury in itself for the kind of cross-country travelers we are. At last a feeling of calm enfolds me, having just some idea of what is ahead, as far as lodging goes. The mere idea of sleep sustains me.

We are leaving the Plains; we are in the lake- and pond-filled farm-covered prairie of Minnesota, of green, green Minnesota, though, as on the Great Plains, we see a few more dead tractor trailer trucks being used as billboards, one in particular advertising elk meat. We pass the blue interstate highway signs, sanctioned by the Federal Highway Administration, that note food, lodging, and places of one kind or another in Sauk Center, Minnesota, home of Sinclair Lewis, author of *Main Street*, the novel. There's a sign for the Sinclair Lewis Interpretive Center beside a sign for a restaurant called Funky. We pass Fergus Falls, where in the summer of 2000 we all pulled over in our ailing station wagon and found a little park downtown and sat there eating a dinner of cheese and apples and thought we were going to melt it was so hot—our car had no air-conditioning to speak of. We pass through Saint Cloud, a name that, for me, has an ethereal quality, a genius to it in that it seems to canonize the already heavenly, white-appearing water-laden particles floating around beautifully here toward sunset. Regarding Saint Cloud, the AAA guide is naturally elusive: *Saint Cloud! Population 37,600! Especially noted for the fine-grained, many-hued granite quarries in the vicinity!*

THE END OF THE WEST

IT IS THE END of the West, the end of the Great Plains, of rivers that run out of the Rockies, of places where buffalo recently roamed, as we enter the area of Minneapolis and Saint Paul, the Twin Cities: in Minneapolis, we first pick up the scent of the East, and glimpse just vaguely our days-away return. And we enter in the glow of the suburbs and the suburban strip malls and the aptly named megamalls. We see the sun set over one particular mall, Albertville Crossing, that is a semicircle of brightly lit stores, of so-called outlet stores, the outlet being an aspect of modern tourism, the visit to the place to shop on what seems like the cheap. The neon reds of Albertville Crossing combine with the reds of the sunset to make for an overall highway-side effect that is dramatic by the standards of any strip mall. We have crossed the Great Plains. We have now left the West. Tomorrow we will cross the Mississippi, a great river that separates Minneapolis from Saint Paul, that gathers the waters of the Plains and of the great Missouri Uplift—a great river that signals to us eastbound cross-country drivers that we are nearly there.

We make it downtown. We check in. The place is nice, as in really nice—the opposite of the basement we stayed in the night before. At around ten, when the kids ask about room service, we say, "Sure." Because how often do you cross the country and actually book a place in advance, after having stayed in a pit the night before? The room service cart comes and won't fit down our hallway, for some reason. I aid the waiter, who apologizes profusely. "It's no problem," I say. We proceed to eat way too much while watching late-night comedy television.* My son laughs loudly, which makes my wife and me very happy. My daughter laughs and laughs. She's giddy. She gets to stay up too late. "So that worked out pretty nicely," she says.

---

* Including David Letterman, the TV host, who also hails from Indianapolis and also is known to drop things off buildings, just like the founder of the first cross-country highway, Carl Fisher.

PART V

Minneapolis, Minnesota, to Beloit, Wisconsin

INTO THE EAST

SLEEP DISPATCHED HIS SON, Morpheus, to inspire dreams through the night, and in the hotel bed in Minneapolis, I am in deep communication with Morpheus. In the morning Minnesota light, in a bed that is perfect in all the ways that the sheet-covered board the previous night was not, I am King Muchukunda, asleep forever in his quiet cave. I am Rip van Winkle, napping into another time, yet to be shocked by reentry. By seven A.M., my dream is a waking dream, and I dream of staying in Minneapolis and Saint Paul, of passing time sitting still, for hours on end, of not turning the ignition key. I feel the druglike power of this circle of snoozing expedition mates, sound asleep, in beds and foldout but still comfortable cots, unconscious in this hour near seven A.M., breathing slowly, deeply, sleeping.

And slowly, I feel too the dark power of the memory of my last time driving through Saint Paul. We will wake up very soon. We will spend a good portion of the day circling the Twin Cities, waiting for lunch with our friend just after noon, and yes, we will move on. But as we do, I will be haunted—or haunted a little, anyway—by my Minnesota breakdown. For it happened only a few years before and it was the time that I broke down and almost couldn't go on.

What happened? It is a difficult story for me to tell. It is a story of trials and tribulations, a story of a daunting return, of invaluable aid from a friend, of reuniting with my mother and father, of problems with a customer service hotline and furniture. It is a story that I am in many ways still dealing with, at least financially. Today, as I wake in Minneapolis and recall that here was where my trouble began, I am struck by the contrast between my present state (comfort) and my previous state while in the Mississippi River town (torturous and mind-numbing psychological trauma), and the jarring contrast rekindles my nerves, so that I am soon out of bed and in the excellent lobby drinking excellent coffee, which makes sense in that this room costs about twice as much as the room at the Miles City Super 8, about $120 bucks. My hand trembles the saucer as I slowly contaminate the black liquid with pure white cream. Unfortunately, much on this perfect blue-skied prairie city day reminds me of that cross-country breakdown.

So I head back to our room. I begin the long and arduous process of waking exhausted people sleeping comfortably for what I am hoping will be the next-to-last time on this trip, knowing that we are now beginning the most arduous leg. We are in Minneapolis and will today cross the river into Saint Paul, the river, as I mentioned, being the Mississippi, dramatic even in name. The old saying is true; we can sense it: Minneapolis is where the West ends and Saint Paul is where the East begins. Ergo, today we begin the eastern portion of the trip. When we entered the West with Lewis and Clark we were traveling way back in the history of America, as far as I was concerned, and now, entering the East, we are coming into the present.

AN IMAGINARY DOUGHBOY

BUT BEFORE WE GET ON THE ROAD, before I find my lanyard-bound key and place it around my neck, semi-ceremoniously, we visit the hotel's luxurious indoor pool, where our daughter learns to swim underwater; even now, I can still see her as she swims toward me in the invigorating bright blue. We walk through downtown Minneapolis, visiting the scene of a 1940s warehouse district labor riot, featured in a photograph on the front page of the *Star Tribune*, where we see the old warehouses being turned into condos. That was my idea. In the lobby of the Pillsbury Corporation, the Twin Cities–based foodstuffs company, which we came upon through happenstance, our son's idea is to imagine a cigar-smoking Doughboy, to picture the Doughboy striding into the steel and glass atrium of the corporate headquarters, chomping a cigar, accompanied by bodyguards, spotting us, shouting, "*Security!*" Lunch is with our friend Jim, a Saint Paul native, who treats us to a classic Minnesota meal, walleye, at a fish-fry place on a

lake, where we eat as reverent Twin Cities tourists—where, in the consumption of the walleye, we experience Minnesota.*

Readers may again recall that we are in a hurry, because we have been on
the road too many days already this summer. Why then do we linger along
the banks of the Mississippi, with walleye, historic scenes of a labor battle,
with jokes regarding a large, puffy white Doughboy? In fact, long-distance
travel by car has at its heart a physical grammar that is like Newton's laws, the
first being that the longer you drive, the more difficult it is to keep going.

Consequently, on our way out of town that afternoon, we take yet another
of the smallest of detours, I promise. We take I-35 south, just for a few exits,
my idea as an interstate-interested tourist. I-35 is a so-called modern interstate, an interstate redesigned after people decided that interstates ruined the
cities. It's constructed with tire-soothing asphalt rather than concrete, surrounded almost completely by neighborhood-protecting sound barriers, and
for the most part it is depressed, sunken into the ground as it runs through
the city, the directional road signs sprouting like tree limbs from the shoulder
of the road rather than towering over it, a gently landscaped meridian divid-
ing the lanes. We drive it, exit it, enter it, exit it again, and then backtrack until we finally land on I-94, heading east, and I come to the seat-of-the-pants
opinion that I-35 is an interstate highway that acts as if it has been through
rehabilitation but is not cured. It is an interstate that is drinking decaf, for the
moment, anyway.

But I am happy to be on I-35, or any road, happy to be leaving Minnesota
safely, in light of that difficult past crossing that I have alluded to. After that particular crossing, I can't believe I am crossing the country at all.

---

* Walleye is to Minnesota as cheese is to Wisconsin, as beer is to Milwaukee, and bagels are to
New York, and that is why, Jim reported to us shortly after we left Minneapolis, a television news
exposé had used DNA testing to show that much of the fish passed off as walleye in Minneapolis
was not walleye at all, but zander, a European cousin that was being illegally billed as walleye.
"Minnesota consumes more walleye than any other state. Walleye is Minnesota's state fish," a
KARE television news report said. "But KARE 11 has learned the fish being advertised as walleye on the menus of several Twin Cities restaurants isn't walleye at all, but a related species from
eastern Europe called *zander*." Fortunately, the restaurant that we ate at on Lake Calhoun passed
the television station's DNA testing.

THE WORST CROSS-COUNTRY TRIP EVER, PART I

EVEN NOW AS I TYPE and recall that particular five-day crossing, even as I look at the notes that I scribbled to myself in the truck, I close my eyes, shudder, shake my head.

The trip began late in the afternoon on a crisp October day, in Oregon, beside a storage space that was filled with our things—a depressingly large portion of which had been damaged by a sprinkler that was designed to water the storage space grass but missed. Once again, we were moving, packing up, attempting to reconvene on the East Coast after having just reconvened on the West Coast—and, as I say, if I could tell you exactly why we were constantly reconvening then we probably wouldn't have to have been reconvening at all. My wife and the kids were following me across by train; they were to leave the following day. But on that afternoon, we loaded everything into a twenty-five-foot rental truck, the largest size available to us, our usual. We drove our used-but-new-to-us station wagon onto a trailer that attached to the rear of the twenty-five-foot truck, making for the combined total length of the vehicle I was about to attempt to "drive" something like fifty feet, a length that felt to me, a novice truck driver, like the length of Delaware. I was concerned, to say the least, about driving the truck and trailer at a speed over five miles an hour; I convinced my wife to follow me to the interstate in her mother's car. I had a big lump in my throat when I hugged my son and daughter and my wife and took the paper bag with a sandwich in it, my supper. It was already dark, and as soon as I got on the highway it began to rain. My wife called me on the cell phone and I saw her wave to me in the giant-truck-size door mirrors on the door as she exited, as she pulled off the road and I pulled away. "Be careful," she said, something, as you might imagine, she often says.

Driving across the country solo in a truck with all your stuff in it and the family car attached to the back, in a vehicle that is actually pretty close in length to the second-smallest state in America, is completely different from driving across the country in a family vehicle with your family. Driving alone across the country in a truck as described above is like driving in a hybrid version of solitary confinement: you are secluded in the quiet of the truck's cab, confined to one long bench seat with maps and snacks and a cell phone and a crappy radio, but at the same time you are completely unconfined, unsolitary,

River and into Wisconsin, a few minutes away, and we are like Odysseus' sailors, after visiting with the Lotus-eaters, drugged by the idea of rest, by the notion of stopping; we have momentarily lost our traveling desire. With a long day of driving ahead, I forgo my best judgment and decide to pull off. Our goal this afternoon and evening: to reach a point past Chicago, best-case, in Indiana. From the other side of Chicago, we can make it to the East in a day—it's a long ride, but we have done it before. Right now, I am looking for the Wisconsin Welcome Center and a cup of coffee.

I LOVE WELCOME CENTERS. I love them for their free state highway maps, for their general tourist info, for their institutionalized graciousness. And as should be extremely clear by now, I love coffee.

According to the TripTik, the Wisconsin Welcome Center is in Hudson, a mere nine miles from Saint Paul. But after having taken what I thought was the correct exit and in hindsight know was not, we arrive in Hudson and can-not find the welcome center. Hudson does not seem to be the Hudson de-scribed in the AAA TripTik: "Hudson's mid-19th–Century prosperity as a river port and lumbering center is reflected in its renovated Victorian down-town and residential areas. The grand houses along Third and Vine streets once were the showplaces of wealthy merchants and lumber barons." Hudson is street after street of low but giant box-shaped stores, interspersed with gas stations. It is a newly fabricated town, not at all Victorian. It is vast sports-stadium-sized parking lot after sports-stadium-sized parking lot, and the parking lots do not seem to connect: after searching the edges of one parking lot, I have to exit to get to the adjacent parking lot. In terms of not wasting time, this is not the easy-stop-at-a-welcome-center that I had imagined; in terms of not wasting time, it is something of a nightmare, and I begin to un-derstand that this may be one of our most stop-filled trips ever. (The most stop-filled trips were surely when the children were very young and we made many stops during the day and drove, drove, drove late at night, making up miles late into the cool summer nights.) In an act of logistical triage, we decide to find a place to shop for small, not too terribly disgusting snacks that might constitute a late light dinner, as well as last us through Wisconsin and Illinois.

This is when traveling with our particular son becomes problematic.

Once, our son was a six-month-old who giggled at the lights in stores when we first crossed the country, who said *moo* when we saw a cow. He is now officially a teenager, who reads the paper from time to time, who has an e-mail address, who has checked out Web pages and home pages and blogs, and as a result, has definite opinions about the world at large, the world we are traveling through. One of those opinions has to do with the most prominent of the box stores. Wal-Mart's business model is, as he sees it, flawed. He believes that aside from offering cheap prices to consumers, Wal-Mart inadvertently ends up contributing to lower wages for the people who make the goods—as companies attempt to find cheaper and cheaper labor in order to manufacture products at prices pleasing to Wal-Mart. He is not convinced that low prices alone help the American consumer. Americans either like Wal-Mart or they don't, and a large percentage of those who don't still go there anyway. Our son does not. "Do you want there to be any jobs left?" he asks semi-rhetorically.

Meanwhile, there are Wal-Marts everywhere in cross-country America; to travel the country over the past ten years has been to watch the slow demise of what was once called simply the market, and even the supermarket. And yet the last time we ended up in front of a Wal-Mart, in Ohio, the last time we were in the middle of an interstate area that seemed to have no other store options besides the Wal-Mart brand of box store, our son would not set foot in it. He sat in protest in the car in the parking lot, strumming his mandolin, me pleading with him for mercy, for one free trip. I pointed out to him that I have never gone to one in my non-country-crossing life. "We're just trying to get some yogurt," I said.

"I'll wait here," he said.

We went inside with my daughter, who looked back at her brother and up at us and was somewhere between happy and concerned. Inside we were greeted by a woman in her seventies who ushered us into the airport-hangar-like space that made me feel sad even after we got out and ate yogurt. In the car, our son didn't speak for a long while, and in that while, I realized that he had been right, that I never should have gone in. We think we're different from everyone else, so apart from the masses and their trends, especially when we cross the county, but we are not. We are just riding along with the traffic. We are just looking for a better price because a company has caused us to think that that's what we want even if it's more likely merely what the company wants. That was the last time we went to a Wal-Mart.

Today, we see a Wal-Mart, but we stop at a Kwik Trip for a snack instead.

THIS LAND IS YOUR LAND

AS OPPOSED TO THE CALL OF A WAL-MART, the call of the large well-advertised corporation, the Siren song of some places that we pass on our trips across the country is often too much to ignore. On one cross-country trip, we stopped to see the hometown of Woody Guthrie, the singer and author of "This Land Is Your Land." I'd read about the town in a lot of places, many of them mentioning that some people were still against memorializing Guthrie, calling him a communist. Our daughter was listening to a lot of Woody Guthrie songs at the time, as was our son, and our son thought it would be a great place to maybe find an old guitar to buy, a great old guitar being his cross-country Holy Grail. My wife likes birthplaces in general, in addition to burial sites and presidential birthplaces; once, when she went across the country with my son and her mother and sister, they visited the burial site of Stonewall Jackson's arm, a visit that required that they sign in and traverse private property in Ellwood, Virginia, and walk through fields to an old private cemetery, to view the alleged final resting place of the arm.

To visit Woody Guthrie's birthplace, all we had to do was drive to Okemah, Oklahoma, in Okfuskee County, about fifty miles east of Oklahoma City, just off Interstate 40—we were on our way cross-country through Texas. Okemah is a little town, cleaned out once by the dust storms during the Great Depression and now seeming a little tired but still making it. Woody Guthrie talks about people getting on the road, about people leaving the Dust Bowl, in the songs "So Long (It's Been Good to Know You)" and "Goin' down the Road Feeling Bad."

We pulled into Okemah's downtown area, a street of old brick buildings, still in good shape, if quiet. It was not what it was after oil was found in the area, in the early nineteen hundreds, when it was, according to Woody Guthrie, "one of the singiest, square dancingest, drinkingest, yellingest, preachingest, walkingest, talkingest, laughingest, cryingest, shootingest, fist fightingest, bleedingest, gamblingest, gun, club and razor carryingest of our ranch towns and farm towns." It was a hot summer afternoon; no one was around. For me, it was the opposite of a box store experience.

We found a little park in between two old buildings with a statue of Guthrie and a mural. (Since we stopped in Okemah, the Oklahoma state capital finally put up a painting of Woody Guthrie, author of the state folk song, "Oklahoma Hills.") A few stores down, we went into an antique store to look for a guitar, and our son found one but bought some guitar strings instead. I ended up talking to the owner of the store, who was nice.

We told her we were in town to see the house Woody Guthrie was born in, on July 14, 1912. She told us that she and her family like to travel to Springfield, Illinois, to see the re-creation of Abraham Lincoln's birthplace. "It's good to know what it was like back then," she said. And then she proceeded to tell us about how Woody Guthrie was born in the town and even continued living there after his parents left—when the so-called Okies used Route 66, what is today Interstate 40, to make their way to California. She explained how to get to the house Woody Guthrie grew up in, and then directed us to the sidewalk in town where he carved his name in wet concrete. "You can't miss it," she said.

Sure enough, we saw his name etched into the concrete near the old theater:

Woody

Likewise, we found the ruins of his old house, a grown-over lot with a wooden sculpture in the middle. Then, our son took out his mandolin from the back of the car and played "This Land Is Your Land," a song that Woody Guthrie apparently wrote in response to "America, the Beautiful," including the last verse that people hardly ever sing but that describes a guy who goes walking up to a No Trespassing sign, a verse our son likes: "But on the other side it didn't say nothing. That side was made for you and me." Woody Guthrie traveled with the Okies and the construction workers building the dams on the Columbia River and with migrant farm workers all over, as well as with Pete Seeger, the other great American folk singer—together Seeger and Guthrie traveled cross-country from Oregon to the East, singing at union halls and wherever. Guthrie traveled up and down the Columbia and wrote about Lewis and Clark and migrant farmers and people who come into a town not knowing anyone—the path of the stranger. Singing "This Land Is Your Land" was my idea, as the reader will no doubt have surmised, and I didn't know if the kids were going to do it, even with my wife seconding me.

But our daughter sang, belting it out good and loud, right there on the street in front of the weed- and tree-covered ruins of the house where Woody

Guthrie was born, and then our son jumped in. Sitting there, I felt as if it was the first time anyone had ever sung it and, at the same time, as if a hundred thousand people had sung it on that spot a hundred thousand times before, which maybe they have.

Then we were back on the road, stopping at a convenience store owned by an Oklahoma Indian tribe—I bought a Coke and a postcard that listed many of the original Indian tribes homes in North America, a continent referred to by some tribes as Turtle Island. Boy, was I happy, sitting in the car, driving along after hearing our kids sing that old song. My wife was smiling too. I wonder if the kids noticed how happy we were. "Did you hear them?" she asked me a couple of times.

COFFEE

ON THIS ROAD CALLED GATE AVENUE, in Hudson, Wisconsin, passing drive-through restaurant after drive-through restaurant, we hit the Kwik Trip and stop just to get a few things, essentials:

1 Urge stck prtzls		0.99
6 Ntch wtr 20 oz		3.96
1 103 bananas dept		0.09
1 Lfsvrs wnt—grn		0.79
2 Tootsie pop asst		0.30
2 16 oz coffee		1.78
	Subtotal	7.91
	Tax	0.16
	Balance Due	8.07

COFFEE IS GERMANE TO MY RECOUNTING of this portion of our cross-country trip because I am planning on making it with coffee tonight—I am counting on coffee, in other words. On the road, I treat coffee as if it were a magical power, a mystical force that must be handled with care and respect, a certain amount of reverence. While it may sound as if I have been pouring a steady stream of coffee down my gullet throughout the course of this trip, in fact, I try to drink it only at key moments and not to rely on it too much, lest it lose its power to enervate. Morning is a key moment. If I have a couple of cups of coffee on the first night of cross-country driving, I will be awake long after we park at a motel, long after I begin to fall asleep at the wheel, ironically. Most likely, I will only drink a cup or so in the afternoon, especially in the first few days of a cross-country trip. Even when I was young and could drink coffee all day long and never have to worry about not sleeping, I would conserve my coffee usage so as to get its full impact when necessary. I fear building up an immunity, the way cockroaches become immune to poisons. And I try never to cross the power of coffee with the power of beer. I like beer. But I can't have a beer while I'm traveling anymore. If I have a beer on the road—in the motel room, say, after a long day at the wheel—and hope to break six or seven hundred miles, then I am sure to succumb to the power of sleep, even with the power of coffee.

Today, except for that hour this morning in which I was chugging the fancy hotel's delicious complimentary coffee, I have been coffee-free; I have been waiting all day to call upon the power of coffee and now I am calling. Thus, I am pleased to see an excellent selection of the magical dark liquid at Kwik Trip; it is a bank of coffee, in tall pump-on-the-top, self-service receptacles: nonflavored and flavored coffees, caffeinated and noncaffeinated, "Cinnful Cinnamon" flavored coffee, "Irish Creme Swirl" flavored coffee, "Hawaiian Chocolate" flavored coffee—it's a flavored and not-flavored highway coffee oasis. The coffee norm on cross-country trips is well known: a clear glass coffeepot with a brown top or orange top, with a pool of blackness, simmering since hours before you arrived and in the hours after you leave, coffee that might be run through your car engine for lubrication, if your car engine were not so particular.

As I stand before the bank of coffee dispensers, another Kwik Trip patron approaches; he too smiles, seeming pleased with the selection as well.

We stand still for a moment, staring straight ahead in coffee fulfillment unison.

Finally, the other Kwik Trip patron takes a step forward, reaches out his arms—huge, Styrofoam twenty-ounce cup in one hand, fingers ready to depress a coffee dispenser on the other. He depresses the dispenser on the container marked "Macadamia Nut."

Nothing.

He depresses again but the Macadamia Nut dispenser is empty. He takes a step back, resumes staring, as if he never depressed.

He tries again, this time choosing the so-called Dark Roast, which he successfully decants.

I watch, concentrating. At last I choose Italian Roast. I depress slowly, feeling a warm pressure in my cup, which builds until my cup is filled pleasingly with the streaming black liquid. I repeat the decanting process for my wife.

SLOWLY, I BACK OUT OF THE KWIK TRIP PARKING SPOT, careful of the coffee in my hand. After we find the interstate on-ramp, our son reads to us from a *Time* magazine article about sodas and teeth.

"A&W root beer is the *least* bad for your teeth," he says.

I nod, take a sip of coffee, look in the rearview mirror, and notice my teeth.

THE WORST CROSS-COUNTRY TRIP EVER, PART II

IN THE MORNING ON THE THIRD DAY of my worst cross-country trip ever, I had a cup of coffee in my hand as I filled the gas tank of the truck. It was just after dawn in Red Lodge, Montana, and I looked down into the cup to see the first raindrops of the day fall like depth charges into the milky coffeeness. I had stayed at a motel in Deer Lodge, in the glorious part of the state, amid the easy-to-love valleys of snow-capped vistas, a town where, when not carrying our entire life including our car attached by a trailer to a twenty-five-foot long truck, we had stopped as a family, to tour the old prison. But on that day of the worst trip ever, I was just moving, just pressing on, so far not having to worry about backing up.

The rest of the day it rained on and off, and vast fields of dark, low, woolly clouds followed me through Livingston and Bozeman, the valley that I knew to be so postcard-worthy on sunny days—watching the Weather Channel on TV in the morning, I saw that I was traveling in the only place that the American radar screen showed clouds. The wind blew the truck. In the record of my trip, I made sketches while driving that are now almost illegible to me partly because of the truck's jerky wheel, partly because, as is evident, when it comes to sketching, I am no Lewis, much less a Clark.

I wrote this: "A thrill." Since the OIL-WATER light episode, the truck had been fine; I had checked the oil and the water, and everything looked OK to me, a certified non-truck-mechanic. When I got sleepy, I sang songs at the top of my lungs and rolled the windows down. I was gaining in solo rental-truck-driving confidence. I was thinking, *I'm gonna make this trip!* My mood changed when I heard a radio announcer say, "There's a winter weather advisory."

By lunchtime, the rain had turned to mushy flakes and I got worried about ice again. I was coming close to having to make a decision—I was planning on going through Saint Paul to pick up my friend Jim, because I was leery of driving alone through the Chicago area and even all of the East in a giant truck pulling a car. I came to a fork in the interstate and had to decide which interstate would I take: I-94 to the north, through North Dakota, or I-90 to the south, through Wyoming and South Dakota. Aside from ice, I was worried about snow.

I got off of I-90 one exit before the fork in the interstate—at exit 452, where the map said there was gas and food. I went to a gas station, stood in the coffee area in the back, near the hot dogs that had been rolling over and over probably since the last time I had driven across the country, only a month before. Two truck drivers were talking over coffee. I paced around. I screwed up the courage to talk to them—me in my faux packed-with-our-life truck attached to the family car, them with God knows what in their trailers. The two truckers suggested I drive north. That seemed counterintuitive to me, but they thought the storm was going to be down in the passes in Wyoming. I listened to them. I got back in the truck, hit the interstate, saw the giant green overhead highway sign, and went north. That night, in Miles City, Montana, I parked the truck in a big empty parking lot under a clear sky. A full moon slipped in and out of clouds. On the TV in the Holiday Inn Express, after I walked under the interstate to a roadside restaurant for dinner, I saw that there was snow in the passes just south of Miles City. I was glad that I had listened to the truckers.

In the morning, the truck still seemed fine, until, when I began to climb a rise of land near the Painted Canyon in North Dakota, the blinking lights and beeping began again. Heading downhill, the beeping stopped. I drove slowly, or more slowly, never breaking 55 m.p.h., doing more like 50. I figured I'd just take my time getting to Saint Paul. I drove and I drove. I am not an artist, but I was so inspired by the gloomy, windblown landscape, by the marbled gray clouds, that I continued to make sketch after sketch after sketch on the legal pad sitting on the truck's big bench seat.

Only once did I think that the station wagon I was carrying had become unattached from the back of the truck, a nightmarish thought that I had previously suppressed. When I pulled off the interstate to inspect the hookup, everything looked fine.

That night, I slept in Fergus Falls—not in the charming old Minnesota downtown that my friend Jim had suggested I stay in, but the Fergus Falls near the highway. I slept in a tired bedraggled motel, watched a TV with bad reception—I felt like I was seeing the America that an actual trucker mostly sees. "Fergus Falls is rich in history and recreational opportunities," I read in the AAA TourBook. I was hoping I could find a place in the charming downtown to get a good breakfast in the morning, thinking I probably wouldn't have to back up.

THE REAL AMERICA

MY WIFE BEGINS A GUIDEBOOK ANALYSIS of our trip as we pull out of Hudson, as we enter Wisconsin way too late for any self-respecting cross-countriers, as I say, on this fourth day across the country, a setting out that is now coffee-fortified but also our second setting-out in less than an hour. A pattern is now established: one day traveling a lot, one day not traveling a lot. Nonetheless, we must make up some miles today—we are about to go crazy with being on the road. In addition to planning on driving late into the evening, we are changing guidebook zones, switching from the maps and books that navigate us through what AAA calls North Central—Iowa, Minnesota, Nebraska, North Dakota, and South Dakota—and moving into the maps and book that cover Illinois, Indiana, and Ohio, the heart of the cross-country trip. As a result, my wife has the half-finished TripTik in one hand, the Rand McNally Dist-O-Map in her lap, and, in her other hand, a fresh, never-before-opened, newly printed AAA TourBook, the best guide to highway-side accommodations and a distant relative of what is thought to be the very first travel guide printed in America, *Appleton's Hand-Book Through the United States*.

A planned two-part series published in 1846, *Hand-Book* only ever had one part published, the New York part, which referred to New York City as "the metropolis of the United States." In the mid-1800s, touring America was an oxymoron, and *Appleton's Illustrated Hand-Book of American Travel*, published in 1857, was written for Americans "accustomed to European habits." The early guidebook *Picturesque America; or The Land We Live In: A Delineation by Pen and Pencil of the Mountains, Rivers, Lakes, Forests, Water-Falls, Shores, Canons, Valleys, Cities and Other Picturesque Features of Our Country*, was the first coffee-table travel book of America; aside from being illustrated by some of the great American artists of the day—S. R. Gifford, Worthington Whittredge, and Thomas Moran—it featured the writing of William Cullen Bryant, Washington Irving, and James Fenimore Cooper, each of them arguing for America's scenic advantages over the scenery of the rest of the world, all seeing America's visual splendor as part of its nationhood, a regional exceptionalism that was its reason for being a nation and its reason for being God's chosen nation. "On the two great oceans which border our league of States, and in the vast space between them, we find a variety of scenery which no other single country can boast of," William Cullen Bryant writes in his opening. Bryant even instructed tourists how to look at America, how to see it. "People in search of the picturesque should understand the importance of selecting suitable points of view," he said. "No indifferent glances will suffice." Viewpoints such as those we see on the side of highways today—the kind marked by little blue camera signs—were what he called "sacred places."

In 1914 a Boston company published the See America First series, and throughout the twenties the federal government published guides and books about the national parks, but the first—and last—attempt to publish extensive guides to the roads and histories of all the states in America occurred in the 1930s, under the auspices of the Federal Writer's Project, a part of the Works Progress Administration, which put writers to work documenting the country and describing driving tours. It was state-sanctioned tourism, at a time when

Americans were trying to figure out what exactly was an American way of life. The guides employed writers including John Cheever, Richard Wright, Saul Bellow, Ralph Ellison, and Conrad Aiken, as well as a lot of other writers who had very little experience, and even some teachers, lawyers, and businesspeople. The material was collected by correspondents in the states and sent to an office in Washington, D.C.

Because it was a time when the political arena was full of arguments over who should get to be an American—immigration laws all but shut down the borders in the 1930s—there were immediately arguments between the editors in Washington and the editors in the various states. The Washington office wanted legends, social customs, "Negro lore," quilting styles, marriage customs, jokes. The D.C.-based directors of the guides looked at roads as a way to see the country but also as paths of historical significance, or just significance: "Roads have not developed by accident," wrote Katherine Kellock, one of the directors of the guides, who called the guides "a public Baedeker." "The general course of all routes of importance has been worn by the movement of large numbers of people who wanted to go from one place to another. Many routes were developed by migrating hordes." The directions from D.C. to the writers in the various states were a series of questions: "How do people take their politics, do they have election fights, have a liking for strange electioneering tactics, do they unite in non-sectarian religious groups or do they support a dozen churches in small towns?" Reporters were told not to exclude "certain distasteful phases" regarding Chicago's past, such as the Haymarket riot, the labor action that the directors of the guides felt had a great influence on the establishment of the eight-hour workday. They told reporters not to call Indian military victories "a cruel massacre of whites" while labeling white settlers' aggression as "a courageous and noble defense of homes." They suggested reporters listen for accents in neighborhoods everywhere. The director of the WPA said the editors were looking for "the real America."

The arguments between the Washington, D.C.-based editors and the state-based editors ended up being a travel-guide-editing version of the states' rights arguments that have roiled American politics since the country was founded. States demanded the right to define regions, the right to set the tone and to chose tourist routes. The Idaho correspondent wrote about only outdoor activities, skipped mining and any mention of Native American history; the Mississippi draft came in filled with racial slurs. In the end, in the war over what was "the real America," the WPA editors in Washington lost. Though they did win some battles: in addition to the inclusion of a recipe for huckleberry pancakes in the Oregon guide, the Ohio series featured Ben Shahn's photographs of small-town life, the New Mexico guide listed a Mexican-American glossary, and the Alabama guide printed photos of scenes of Southern poverty during the Depression. The guides were shut down, though, after investigations in 1938 by the House Un-American Activities Committee, which claimed that "Communist phraseology had been inserted in guides from the states and here in Washington." In 1939, the guides were reorganized under state control, their funding cut. Lewis Mumford, the social critic, called the books that did come out "the finest contribution to American patriotism that has been made in our generation."

MORE THAN CHEESE

WE HAVE ENTERED A CHEESE CORRIDOR. In the very few hours before night descends, before the sun sets and the moon rises, we see signs, signs that in other places might say FUEL or FOOD or NUDE but here say CHEESE. The AAA guidebook features an essay on cheese in Wisconsin. It is titled "Say 'Cheese'," and while it mentions that a traveler's experience of Wisconsin is more than just a cheese experience, it nevertheless does so in a cheese-oriented manner. "Wisconsin," the essay reads, "It's whey more than dairy. Milk Wisconsin for more than it's worth and you end up with more than cheese."

Tonight, the sale of cheese reminds me of William Cullen Bryant's opening in *Picturesque America*. For just as Bryant instructed the American wanting to experience the God-given grandeur of America, the "Say 'Cheese'" essay offers the modern traveler guidance in experiencing Wisconsin at a *Little House on the Prairie* replica cabin, in Pepin, where Laura Ingalls Wilder was born; by drinking beer in Milwaukee; by gambling at casinos in Baraboo, Barter, Green Bay, and Kenosha. "Get back to nature," the guidebook suggests, and lists the scenic attractions—"rose-colored cliffs" and "weathered caves" at Apostle Islands National Lakeshore on the northern coast for instance. "When it comes to family fun, America's Dairyland may just be the cream of the crop," "Say 'Cheese'" concludes. "Did you knows" are peppered through the guide: "Famous Wisconsinites include actors Spencer Tracy, author Thornton Wilder, magician Harry Houdini and architect Frank Lloyd Wright." But the AAA TourBook is best at telling you about the prices, the cost of seeing America.

It's the end result of what William Cullen Bryant started. People went out en masse to See America First. When they got there, they bought things: postcards, dishware, art, mementos, relics. They bought the rooms and the views that allowed them to most effectively experience the picturesque. They ate salmon in the Pacific Northwest, as we, in Minnesota, ate walleye. National tourism became a kind of ritual of citizenship, albeit for the most well-off citizens—packaged as a two-week summer driving vacation. "Nature's Nation" was a destination that was sold. "Born of modern consumer capitalism," writes the historian Marguerite Shaffer, "tourism offered a paradoxical promise: a one-of-a kind personal experience as a mass-produced phenomenon. Because tourism trafficked in the sale of experiences and spectacles rather than objects, it could promise a singular, personal adventure for each individual."

Something that scholars of the history of travel have noticed is that in the years from 1880 to 1940, when Americans became tourists in their own country, when people began to tour the Grand Canyon in Model Ts—as they would eventually drive the family to Disneyland in California in a minivan—political participation began to decline. One argument is that consumerism replaced citizenship. Eventually, the words Americans used as citizens, such as *rights* and *just*, were replaced by the words we used as consumers, like *value* and *deal*. To tour was to vote, to get a good deal on a room, a right, or what ought to be. Tourism came to be not a communal experience, not camping in the woods with strangers, but an indulgence, like being on the road alone in a car with no traffic lights, nothing in your way, when you're hoping to find a cheap motel somewhere outside of Chicago.

SADLY, I WILL MISS THE WISCONSIN I always enjoy seeing from the interstate. It is one of the prettiest interstate views in the country, a view of rolling hills, a gentle landscape covered with the tool of that most gentle-seeming industry, farming. The view for me is usually a contrast to the traffic and congestion and many-laned under-construction roads of the Chicago area; it's a rest before the same kind of roads we will come upon on the East

Coast. While the number of farms in the United States continues to drop, I think of Wisconsin as a quintessential pastoral landscape, the forest turned into farm, which, despite its utility, is still useful as scenery to the driver hastening by. How pleasing it is to gaze out on lush green fields of corn, punctuated by cypress trees that break the wind for farmhouses, by green tree-covered hills. The barns are sometimes red, as my imagination believes they should be. The interstates divide farms in ways that appear seamless, casual, smooth, and sensible, even though the idea of the interstate is not.

Tonight, the sun is fading, rouging the sky, as we head east on I-94. And the reason we don't want to stay in a motel in Chicago is because we are the type of cost-conscious consumer that is so often the modern country-crossing American—and we just blew way too much money in Minneapolis.

Plus, we want to be in striking distance of New York on the fifth and what is at this moment still planned as the final day of our cross-country trip—though my wife, the navigator, is beginning to use phrases such as "we'll have to really push it" and "if we make really good time" and "if we can start really, really early."

I am hopeful. The young people in the back seat are currently not thinking about not making it.

BEFORE THE INTERSTATES

FARMERS STARTED OUT RETICENT ABOUT MODERN ROADS—the road was an extravagant expense that was most likely to lead young people to the city and, thus, away from the farm where they were needed. But after trucks were invented, farmers used them to carry goods to market. The dairy farmers of Wisconsin, not to mention the Wisconsin farmers growing snap peas, sweet corn, hay, oats, and potatoes, became one of the groups clamoring for modern roads, as were, thus, their congressional representatives. A study commissioned by Congress showed that a French farmer paid eight cents to carry a ton of produce over a road and an American farmer paid twenty-one cents. Another study showed that the price of shipping a bushel of peaches

from a Georgia farm to Atlanta by road was the same as the price a California farmer paid to ship a bushel by train across the country. A farm town that
ended up having a lot to do with the development of the roads was Montezuma, Iowa—a town that is two hundred miles due south from where we
are on I-94 today. Montezuma was the boyhood home of Thomas MacDonald, known in the Bureau of Public Roads as "the "Chief," a man who considered road building to be, after the education of a child, the "greatest
public responsibility."

Before concrete roads, Montezuma was isolated by mud for four months of
every year, a mud that residents described as similar in thickness to horse glue.
Thomas MacDonald worked at his father's grain store as a boy. He attended
the Iowa State College of Agriculture and Mechanic Arts, in Ames. At college,
MacDonald wrote his thesis on Iowa farmers' highway needs and, after gradu-
ation, became Iowa's chief highway engineer, at a time when most of the highways built only lasted a few months and then rutted and crumbled. In 1904, he
was put in charge of road building in Iowa and toured the state to teach road
drainage methods, to espouse concrete culverts, to recommend steel bridges.
He made his reputation attacking corruption in the road business—the business of making roads that were quickly useless just to get the construction fees
involved. "There has never been a straighter man," the Montezuma newspaper reported. Meanwhile, Iowans began purchasing a lot of cars. In 1914,
Iowa was the national leader in cars per capita, one for every 5.5 persons.

Slowly, MacDonald put together a national highway system. In 1915, Congress established the Office of Public Roads and Rural Engineering, and President Woodrow Wilson signed the Federal Road Act in 1916, authorizing a gas
tax to finance roads. Wilson—who enjoyed a daily automobile drive, for relaxation purposes—put MacDonald in charge. No roads were built under the
new funding, however, due to the commencement of World War I; by 1919,
only thirteen miles of federally funded highway had been constructed. The
war also changed the roads that already existed, both physically and conceptu-
ally. The military used trucks to transport supplies from factories in the Midwest to eastern ports, a trip that was slow-going but faster than trains; after
the war, businesses copied the military, also eschewing trains. Thus, the passenger train began to die after the war, and railroads began to cut back on track
miles. The increased truck traffic on the roads caused the existing eastern
roads to crumble. At the same time, manufacturers had become more adept at

manufacturing cars. In 1912, Ford produced 168,000 cars; in 1917, 730,000; and by 1923, 2,201,000—the assembly line, first called "progressive assembly," had been created. On July 17, 1919, just after World War I ended, a military convoy set out across the county to test the efficiency of the highways. The trip took sixty-two days, and volunteering to go along was a young officer just returned from Europe, Dwight Eisenhower.

In 1919, MacDonald moved to Washington, D.C., where he oversaw the national redesign of major rural roads. He eliminated many railroad crossings, for instance. On the road from Washington to Baltimore, engineers redesigned a dangerous turn where over the years thirty-five people had died. In 1922, states added ten thousand miles of roads, the equivalent, MacDonald reported, of three transcontinental roads. "My aim is this," he said in 1924, "we will be able to drive out of any county seat in the United States at thirty-five miles an hour and drive into any other county seat—and never crack a spring."

THOMAS MACDONALD DID NOT SMILE IN PUBLIC. He was five foot seven inches, always wore a suit, vest, and thin black tie, and even his wife referred to him as "Mr. MacDonald," yet he was the roads' cheerleader. He brought together road building associations and construction interests such as the Portland Cement Association, the American Automobile Association, the Rubber Manufacturers Association of America, the National Paving Brick Manufacturers Association, and the American Association of State Highway Officials—he brought business interests to government for the making of roads. MacDonald created the Highway Education Board, publishing booklets and films for schools and, with the Firestone tire company, sponsoring school essay contests—the subject: roads. He founded *Public Roads*, a journal that espoused the goodness of highways. He organized road research, testing road surfaces, mixing times for concrete, optimum pouring conditions. In 1933, sixty-three road surfaces were tested, the winner being steel-reinforced concrete with thickened edges and longitudinal centerline joints, to reduce cracking. When you drove on the first federally financed highways, your car went *thump-thump-thump* and your wheels tended to turn toward the shoulder, which was thought to make the road safer but in fact made it more dangerous. (Some of these roads still survive.) With General John Pershing, MacDonald created the Pershing Map, a map of the roads considered vital to military operations.

With his penchant for standardization, MacDonald oversaw the change from roads in America being roads in America to being the Roads of America, though a large percentage of this was a matter of official designation. In 1925, the American Association of State Highway Officials designated an 81,000-mile nationwide system, reduced it to 50,000 miles, then, after listening to chambers of commerce and historic trail associations, increased it to 75,800 miles. They were merely incorporating existing roads into the national roads system. In 1922, a national uniform design for highway signs was proposed by three state highway engineers—A. H. Hinkle of Indiana, W. F. Rosenwald of Minnesota, and J. T. Donaghey of Wisconsin. After touring their respective states, the engineers suggested rectangular black and white signs to post mileage to towns, circular signs to mark railroad crossings, and octagonal signs to indicate stops, a plan adopted nationally, except in yellow and black instead of black and white. "If each shape had a definite meaning," Rosenwald wrote, "it would be a great advantage for night driving as undoubtedly the shape could be distinguished long before the words could be."

The idea of marking all highways in the federally designated U.S. highway system with the federal shield and a route number was proposed by Lou A. Boulay, an Ohio highway official, at a meeting in Thomas MacDonald's office in Washington, D.C., in April 1925. At the same meeting, Frank F. Rogers of Michigan quickly drew a sketch of a six-pointed highway shield and it was approved. (Southern states were initially opposed to the sign saying only U.S.A. and not the name of the individual states but eventually dropped their objections.) That summer, a panel of highway engineers that included Missouri's B. H. Piepmeier and Illinois's Frank T. Sheets, proposed even-numbered east-west routes in multiples of ten and odd-numbered north-south routes using numbers ending in 1 or 5 for principal routes. Sometimes, the system did not work; there is a portion of U.S. Route 20 in Oregon that is north of U.S. Route 30. And cities fought over particular route numbers. Proponents of the road that was a combination of old trails—the Federal Wire Road in Missouri and the Osage Trail in Oklahoma—wanted it to be Route 60 but had to settle for Route 66.

IN THE TWENTIES AND THIRTIES, the car, like each piece of new technology accumulated throughout the twentieth century, went from being a phase America was going through to a way of life. Road building increased in the twenties, then slowed with the Great Depression, then increased again under the Works Progress Administration. Farmers were put to work on the roads with hand tools, though during the Depression in the eastern counties of New Mexico, road engineers had to feed the horses *and* the farmers before work could begin. Meanwhile, driving was becoming more and more dangerous, given the combination of the number of cars and the number of faster cars. In 1920, 9,130 people died in car accidents; in 1930, 29,080 died. Roads were rarely straight and often curved drastically and crossed railroad tracks. The first electronic red-yellow-and-green stoplights were introduced in the 1930s, as railroad crossing signals. Engineers noticed that most accidents occurred when cars made left-hand turns, or when cars entered from side streets, leading them to develop another kind of road that would have a lot to do with the development of the interstates: the parkway—a bucolic road with what was termed "limited access."

The first, the Bronx River Parkway, opened in 1923. The Taconic Parkway, built as an extension to the Taconic, ran through the Hudson River valley and inspired comparisons with works of art—touring the Hudson Valley, winding forested glens, climbing to vistas of the Catskills and beyond, it was a practical experience of the sublime, a drive through one of the Hudson River paintings that had inspired the early western migration of Americans. The federal government followed those first scenic roads with the Blue Ridge Parkway and the Natchez Trace Parkway, which ran over portions of the original Natchez Trace, the very trail that Meriwether Lewis was traveling the night he died. The freeways built in southern California were built to assuage what were some of America's earliest traffic jams; road construction could not keep up when the state's population nearly doubled in the forties. And some California freeways were also parkways, such as the Arroyo Seco Parkway, but the roads eventually ended up stressing the *way* over the *park*—a term overshadowed very soon by *freeway*. The terms *parkway* and *freeway* were distinguished by Edward M. Bassett, the lawyer said to have coined the latter term, in this way: a parkway was dedicated to recreation, a freeway to movement. One of the things that would distinguish all these modern roads from what would become the interstates was that they were all essentially local, not cross-country routes in themselves.

THE GREAT DEPRESSION CAN BE SEEN as a time when America broke down and decided to fix itself up, and, in so doing, President Franklin D.

Roosevelt designed one of the first cross-country systems—what Harold Ickes, the secretary of the interior, called "a high speed highway from the Atlantic to the Pacific." In the forties, planners talked about speed-limit-less roads, about a reorganization of the population, to counter the movement of people from the country to the city; Roosevelt considered using the government's power to appropriate land to build the road, half-mile-wide swaths of which, in some cases, would be leased back to businesses. Roosevelt was intimate with the geography of the country in a way that amazed the people who worked with him, and he followed road building with a Jeffersonian preoccupation for detail: in a two-page memo regarding construction of a bridge to Miami that he dictated in the midst of a reelection campaign and while preoccupied with events in Europe, he said things like this: "About 4,334 feet of truss can be made single. This would give a savings of $75.00 a foot or $325,050." Roosevelt himself had helped design the Taconic Parkway, in New York state, near his family's lands in Dutchess County—though he was also considered by his family to be a terrible driver, and his wife, Eleanor, would not drive with him at the wheel of the car that was specially equipped to accommodate his paralyzed legs.

In 1937, Roosevelt sketched six lines across the country, and presented the rough plan to MacDonald, the national road builder. The meeting was a situation in which a patrician hobbyist road builder who was president of the United States faced off against a professional road builder who grew up on a farm and considered himself president of the United States' roads. MacDonald studied the plan and months later came back with charts and graphs and a report titled "Toll Roads and Free Roads." With the support of state and local highway officials with whom he had been working for decades, MacDonald shot the president's plan down. MacDonald argued that interstates paid for by tolls were not economically practical. He claimed families would not be able to afford them nor would they want to travel very far—according to MacDonald, the longest distance the majority of people drove was about ninety miles.

Roosevelt lost interest, mostly because of the war with Germany. For his own part, MacDonald had recently met Hitler. In 1936, MacDonald had gone to see Hitler's new roadway, the Reichsautobahn. The German roads were fast roads, smooth and sleek with no intersections or stoplights, banded by strips of undeveloped land, and designed to move machinery and military equipment. They were roads designed where roads had not been before, where there had been no previous need for roads. They were also along the lines of what Roosevelt had envisioned. An engineer named Fritz Todt had attracted Hitler's attention with a paper titled "Proposals and Financial Plans for the Employment of One Million Men." Hitler enjoyed taking drives on his autobahn, his chauffeur pushing the speed. He loved to pass American-made cars. Hitler offered tours of the autobahn to foreign officials such as Thomas MacDonald. Zeppelins flew over the roads that wove through the German countryside, a land of fir trees and farms and meadows, a place that probably looks a lot like Wisconsin, come to think of it. MacDonald was not as impressed as some people might have been. Through the Office of Public Roads, MacDonald had built 225,000 miles of road and, by 1936, was adding about 12,000 a year. The autobahn was only 2,000 miles. Also MacDonald found the roads impractical—the autobahn skipped the cities entirely, for instance.

Hitler was building one road for a nation, more along the lines of what Roosevelt was thinking about, but MacDonald was still thinking about people traveling locally.

In blasé reports back from Germany, MacDonald referred to the German leader as "Mr. Hitler."

O EAU CLAIRE

SURROUNDED BY FARMLAND that we are less and less able to see as the afternoon fades, we move through pastures and fields and feel the enjoyment of passing farms.* We pass alongside Eau Claire, and see brand-new houses grow in a field that turns into a valley. We pass an Acura with Minnesota plates, a guy driving as a woman in the back seat reaches up and massages his shoulders. We see another giant sign marked CHEESE. We pass mile 100 on

---

* Our farm-passing experience is bucolic and pastoral. Do farmers have a sensation less bucolic and more related to work? My wife's mother grew up on a farm in Oregon but it is now covered in part with an interstate highway.

the Wisconsin section of I-94, and we pass Sparta, "The Bicycling Capital of America," though naturally we see no bicycles—bicycles aren't allowed on the interstates, even though way, way back bicycles are part of their genetic past. The sky darkens—a few feathery cirrus clouds, wisps of painted red, getting redder. We pass alongside a beautiful signless field, an absence of advertising making it exceptional. We cross the Black River about which I know nothing, about which our guidebook is mum. In the almost evening, we begin to see the outcroppings of rock that we know to mark our proximity to the Wisconsin Dells, a huge resort area on the Wisconsin River that we have seen but will not see this time, because it will be dark by the time we get there.

Suddenly, a crisis.

A certain member of our expedition is desirous of a rest stop. This certain member tells the front seat that she *"really, really, really"* needs a rest stop. "I have to go so badly," this party member says, "that I can't even yawn."

As so often happens in situations such as these, the leadership of the expedition asks this expedition member to note that an opportunity for relief had occurred just a short time earlier—in this case at the Kwik Trip.

But mercifully, a Wisconsin state interstate rest stop comes up just a few miles ahead.

And it is an excellent Wisconsin rest area: state-of-the-art washrooms, landscaped by native plants, a plaque describing the influence of a particular bog plant that, as the sign notes, travelers do not see when they are traveling through Wisconsin. It's the sphagnum moss area. "The invisible industry," the 1974 plaque declares. Because it holds twenty times its weight in water, sphagnum moss is used to ship plants, as well as in surgical dressing and seed germination; it is harvested from the marshes.

The person who cannot even yawn is quickly escorted into the women's rest room, her brother heading to the men's room, just in case. I wait outside, by the car, reading the plaque and saying those words aloud, so descriptive are they of what is unseen throughout the interstate experience: *invisible industry.*

THE MOON IS A CRESCENT, a golden sliver, that glows and, naturally, reminds us of cheese—as does the sign we pass, a few miles farther on, for the cheese museum. In the foyer of the great barnlike rest stop building, I pick up some literature regarding road rage: "You can't change the other driver's behavior but you can control yours. Let it ride." I return to the car. I scan the road atlas, a map of the country that is at once exciting, at once depressing, for we are in the middle. I check the TripTik. Being alone with the car makes me melancholy, the dusk makes me sentimental. Seeing the rest of our expeditionary team appear on the concrete walkway causes me happiness.

I inspect our pack, which is shredded even more, bug covered but otherwise holding on and strangely quiet this evening, as we strap into the Impala. We reverse, pausing for a car that is speeding into the rest area to rest—the transition from speeding interstate traveler to rest stop rester can be difficult, and though he nearly kills us, I let it ride. As we attempt to gain entrance to the interstate, we see a small-town-sized Wal-Mart; in the back seat, our son groans. A giant Wal-Mart truck passes us quickly, startling me. Our son groans.

I think we are all feeling the relentlessness of the interstate. In the rearview mirror, I can see our daughter is suddenly clutching her stuffed dog as she gazes out the window. The dog is apparently reminding her of the real dog she would like to one day own, a point she brings up, just as a reminder. We don't really know what to say. "Who would take care of the dog if we have to travel?" is what I come up with, and as I say this, I feel bad about us ever having been on the road at all. Our daughter says nothing, returns to gazing out the window.

The miles to go are before us in the road, their arms crossed, as if to say "I don't care," and stepping steadily away as we race to cross them, to stop, to end the day of driving, even today, when we have not yet been driving for so long, when we had happily forgotten that we have twelve hundred miles to go before we rest.

In the rearview mirror I look toward our daughter again. Still clutching her dog, still gazing out window, the swelling on the giant mosquito bite on her forehead that she got while on top of Pompey's Pillar in Montana beginning to go down. Her eyelids are heavy, her eyes sweet and wondering as she looks out at Wisconsin's deep-blue evening sky, as she stares into the immovable firmament. And as I spot the stark white reflective lettering on a sign marked EMERGENCY STOPPING ONLY, I recall traveling apart from her. I remember for about the millionth time my worst cross-country trip.

THE WORST CROSS-COUNTRY TRIP EVER, PART III

MY ALARM CLOCK WENT OFF at five in Fergus Falls, Minnesota, and I was in the truck by five thirty. And though I wasted half an hour in the pretty downtown area of old Fergus Falls trying to find a diner that was representative of the "real" Minnesota and got worried about having to back up and finally gave up and bought a coffee at the McDonald's with the giant parking lot near the interstate instead, I was able to get out of the cute downtown and not make too much noise on the local truck-free side streets. I drove into the sunrise, only a few hours from Minneapolis, only a few hours from picking up my friend Jim, who, as the plan went, would help me park in the East and help me move all my family's worldy goods, including the car, still firmly attached to my truck's rear.

I listened to the radio, sipped coffee slowly. With Styrofoam, I toasted the rising sun.

I was only about twenty miles from Saint Paul when the OIL-WATER light came on, when it again scared the hell out of me. "*Beeeeeeeeep!* it said. This time I was not on a hill. This time the *beeeeeeeep!* did not stop. It just kept going *beeeeeeeep!* I put on my blinker and tried slowing down. *Beeeeeeeeep!* I put the map on the steering wheel and looked for a place to pull over, a place listed with services, a gas station. The next exit looked good, a suburb of Minneapolis called Maple Grove. Just off the highway, I found a gas station, in a mall.

Up to that point in my driving life, I did not know that there were gas stations in malls.

The gas station looked more like a large discount shoe store or a record shop, but I pulled up and I opened the hood and looked in at the engine and I am certain the expression on my face said I did not know what I was looking at, because I didn't. I did recognize that there was oil everywhere inside the engine compartment. I went inside the store accompanying the gas station and realized that it had all kinds of food products (including yogurt) and a lot of convenience items but no one who knew anything about cars. It was a gas station in a mall. I bought some oil, even though I, like the staff people I consulted, had no idea what kind I should use. I poured oil into the engine, hoping it would get me to a service station of some kind. I got back in the truck, pulled out of the strip mall, and realized that the oil was not going to get me anywhere, because now not only was the beep still beeping, beeping kind of uncontrollably, but also the engine was making sounds that I had previously only associated with the demolition industry or plate tectonics.

I veered away from the on-ramp and proceeded back over the highway to another convenience store on the other side of the overpass and parked in the back, near a pay phone. I turned the *beeeeeeeeep!*-ing engine off and got out and looked at the truck and our car and what accounted for all our worldly goods and wondered what the hell I was going to do. I started making calls. "I'm running behind," I told Jim. He completely understood.

THE LIGHTS OF THE DELLS

WITH THE NAVIGATOR CALCULATING, with the other members of the expedition questioning, with me fearing—all of us are coming to the conclusion that we will not be passing Chicago tonight, as we are running behind, the story, obviously, of our life on the road, not to mention our life. Our daughter suggests stopping immediately.

"Why don't we find a motel with a nice pool, and then start out really, really early," she says. She is interested in swimming underwater again.

"We have to keep driving tonight," I say.

"We just stopped and had a lot of fun in Minnesota, and now we have to keep going," says my wife.

To non-cross-country travelers, this may sound like a cruel logic, and in a way it is a kind of penance—you pay in late-night car movement for your daytime digressions when you are crossing the country. Ultimately, the kids understand, the kids being great kids. They return to their reading, to journal writing, to looking sleepy, to window gazing, to looking into the face of the darkening sky.

What they see as they window gaze is the beginning of the Wisconsin Dells. Traveling the interstate is traveling through themes of marketing, and the marketing theme of the area we now enter is recreation—specifically water recreation, especially as it is related to water in the Wisconsin Dells, the long-time and famous-in-the-Midwest recreational area. The Dells were created by man and nature, in a one-sided commercial partnership. First the Wisconsin River carved the sandstone into dramatic cliffs. Then man dammed the river, affording a lakelike recreation area. In 1931, the name of the nearby town was changed from Kilbourn City to Wisconsin Dells to promote the water for play and relaxation and watery comfort, *Dells* apparently intending to make it sound exotic and watery.

It's an area that I myself have never recreated in, merely driven through or slept in overnight while passing through.

The roadside signs advertise various versions of family enjoyment and happiness at prices that are intended to seem reasonable. We see indoor water recreations—waterslides, pools, water fountains spraying little herds of frolicking people—that are covered in glass for all the passing world to see. Like sailors passing small islands, we see a sign for Jellystone Park, with a watery cartoon-character theme, and then Ho-Hunk Casino, with a watery gambling theme, and then another sky-scraping sign for cheese. We see an orb of recreation illumination, the Kalahari Resort. Hard by the highway, the Kalahari Indoor Water Park offers us views of itself; here late at night, as we go sixty-five-miles-an-houring by, we see people, mostly young people, in watery abandon. We are at sea on land on an interstate.

"America's largest indoor waterpark," says our AAA TourGuide.

"It's for trapping children inside," says our son, who is feeling a little trapped himself at the moment. He presses up against the Impala's rear window. "I'm looking for kids pressed up against the giant window."

The storytellers of the Winnebago tribe described the riverine curves through the carved valleys using stories of a giant snake. The resorts now tell of rides in giant boats and of boat races and, at the Kalahari, of a great water that showers all who are beneath the giant water-spewing totem. The also-huge Great Wolf Lodge calls itself "America's Premier Waterpark Resort." There, recreators partake in a Northwoods-themed water park resort—an indoor park that references the outdoors of where it is, a place that recreates and fabricates a place that currently exists. Also available for recreational purposes are the Loose Moose Bar & Grill, a four-story-tall Water Tree Fort, and the Great Wolf Lodge's concept spa, which presumably is a spa with a concept, perhaps a concept regarding Wisconsin or water or both.

At the Chula Vista Theme Resort, with its heated indoor pools, fifties musical revue, and indoor water park, the theme is—just as it was for William Cullen Bryant when he described the appropriate poses to take in viewing America—nature, though not nature in a standard sense, but nature in a heightened sense. "Our attraction is natural," Chula advertisements say.

SO MUCH LIGHT EMANATES from the Kalahari Indoor Water Park that I wonder if it can be seen from space, or from a zeppelin, or from a plane crossing Wisconsin. Between water parks, with the help of the water parks' glow and the light of the headlights, we can just make out those sandy, hogback escarpments that mark the cliffs along the road, the Dells' non-man-made landforms.

At least, I think that's what we're seeing. I try to look back as we pass each rock formation but when it gets dark, it's difficult to look back on the road. You are forced to face forward, to concentrate on the future, rather than the past. You are forced to gaze into the rows and rows of red taillights, which blink and pulse on what appear to be whims.

STREAMLINE

EACH TIME I CROSS THE COUNTRY, I become more convinced that at one point the United States had a choice as far as its roads went, that there was a time when America came to a fork in the road of road development. It was a choice that just happened in the way that a driver can miss an exit and take the next exit and end up on another highway that still gets him to his destination, there being so many interstates, so many highways, so many roads. The choice happened, and the next thing America knew, it was draping itself with interstates. When I think of that choice, I think of two people, whose lives and writings I often compare and contrast while I am on the road: Norman Bel Geddes and Benton MacKaye, two men who thought about where the roads in America were headed and did so in very different ways.

They were both born at the end of the 1800s, when horses were fading and cars were about to be invented. They both came from wealthy families whose wealth disappeared. They were both involved with imagining a future for the United States at the dawn of the automobile—Bel Geddes working on the side of industry and MacKaye working first on the side of the government and then on his own. They both came up with plans for the United States at the dawn of the car era and envisioned new ways that the country might be organized—the big difference being that Bel Geddes's plan was the one we went with.

NORMAN BEL GEDDES WAS BORN Norman Geddes in Adrian, Michigan, in 1893. In his autobiography, he recounts living in luxury but, out of sight of his parents, being tortured by a nanny with hot pans and scalding baths. His father lost the family fortune when Bel Geddes was seven; from the next room, he heard his father weep when word of the stock crash arrived. Bel Geddes moved with his mother to Cleveland, where they lived in a boardinghouse. As a teenager, he worked for his family's dry goods store as a delivery boy and, according to his telling, fought off the advances of housewives on his delivery routes. Bel Geddes enjoyed spending free time in museums, where he made sketches that impressed a noted comic strip artist who got him into the Chicago Art Institute, from which he dropped out. He went west and sketched Native Americans living on a reservation for a while. He married Helen Belle Sneider and incorporated one of her names into his own, becoming Norman Bel Geddes. He took a job in advertising, making posters for car companies. He claimed to have invented miniature golf, even though people don't give him credit for it, probably correctly.

He moved to New York where he became a theatrical designer, first designing huge stages that he claimed well-known theater designers stole from him and didn't give him credit for, then designing lots of stages that he was given credit for—stages that were huge spectacles. Bel Geddes designed the sets of plays and films by Cecil De Mille, D. W. Griffith, and Flo Ziegfeld. The set for the play *Dead End* was an exact replica of a Manhattan street that dead-ended on the East River. He designed a set for a play about the Virgin Mary coming to earth that involved making the theater seats into pews and the stage into a giant altar, and costumes so heavy that they had to be lowered onto the actors with a system of pulleys and chains. His designs were often touted more than the play. Brooks Atkinson wrote in the *Times*: "Not only in its accuracy of detail but in its perspective and its power, his setting is a practical masterpiece." In 1916, he invented a war game, inviting friends and clients and theater people over to play with troops at long tables. Once, he court-martialed a general during a game; the general never returned. He played the war game for years in his New York apartment, where he kept many animals, including snakes and rabbits. He enjoyed filming the animals as they mated, and when his rabbits became pregnant he gave them away as gifts, the recipient not knowing they were pregnant. In 1916, he also invented the modern spotlight.

After a while he began to design objects—he began to design just about everything, in fact, becoming one of the first well-known industrial designers. The list of things he designed includes airplanes, cars, war ships, airports, a mattress, a meat-slicing machine, a rum factory, a stapler, a cigarette vending machine, luggage, a self-camouflage technique for the U.S. Army, a nine-deck amphibious vehicle, a double-decker bus, a vacuum cleaner, the first gas station pump that automatically calculated the price of gas, and a refrigerator for General Electric. A more complete list of things he designed goes on for several pages in his autobiography, concluding with a note: "The foregoing is not an exhaustive list of the works and enterprises of the life of Norman Bel Geddes. It is offered here only to indicate the extraordinarily broad scope of his interests and talents, and to give some idea of the precise nature of his contribution to American art and industry."

AS AN INDUSTRIAL DESIGNER, Bel Geddes had a trademark, which was what he called streamlining. For him, streamlining reduced friction and increased speed. Streamlining was a way to move cars faster, but also a way to redesign the world, for efficiency. Streamlining was the future. All his designs were streamlined, and he proposed that the designer of the future would be responsible for streamlining life: for streamlining social structures to more fluidly organize people; for streamlining factories to, as he said, "remove drudgery." He proposed to streamline the arts. His ideas were consistent with the contemporary economic theories that claimed the Great Depression was a result of economic friction and that streamlining would erase the friction that prevented consumer demand from aligning smoothly with production. Most notably, Norman Bel Geddes proposed streamlining roads. On the streamlined roadway, the friction of intersections would be reduced, as would the friction of right-angle turns, the friction of traffic entering and exiting. Motorists would slip smoothly from the faraway country to the far-off city and back again every day. Bel Geddes called the frictionless highway of the future the Magic Motorway.

Bel Geddes's streamlined future was seen by ten million people when it was presented to the public in his exhibit at the 1939 World's Fair. The exhibit was called "Futurama" and was wildly popular. He had initially gone to Shell Oil with an idea for a streamlined city packed with streamlined highways but Shell declined and he went to General Motors, which funded him. "Futurama" was a highway-filled world, with lanes and lanes of smoothly moving traffic, passing orchards covered in glass, passing busy smooth-edged factories, passing over the land as if it weren't even there, as if it were an oxygenless moon. The fifty thousand cars on the five-lane radio-controlled highways were shaped like little teardrops. (Only occasionally was there a miniature, teardrop-shaped car pileup.) People toured the exhibit in an upholstered love seat that flew them above the streamlined highways; a voice came through a loud speaker behind their heads: "By means of ramped loops, cars can make right and left turns at rates of speed up to fifty miles per hour . . . Contrast the straight, unobstructed path of the motorway at the right with that of the twisting winding ordinary road to the left . . . A freeflowing movement of people and goods across our country is a requirement of modern living and prosperity."

Excited spectators passed above the exhibit in what was ironically a kind of mass transit system—amusement-park-ride-like cars that looked down on a revised version of Saint Louis and its surrounding territory, a streamlined landscape that would allow city workers to live far off in the country, that anticipated cars driving three hundred miles an hour—the speed threshold, the master designer believed, past which humans might lose control. (Bel Geddes predicted that by 1960 cars would travel from New York to Los Angeles in twenty-four hours.) At the end of the exhibit, visitors viewed the latest General Motors cars, and sometimes, the other exhibit Bel Geddes designed. The other exhibit was called the Crystal Gazing Palace, and it was a roomful of mirrors, a woman in the center dancing a striptease.

Bel Geddes saw streamlining as a style of design that evolved straight out of nature; his vision of nature seems to have been the windblown sand dunes and the glacially eroded and logged plains of Wisconsin, as opposed to the nature of igneous rocks, of crumbling shale, of Wisconsin sandstone. His iconic artistry is pure and unadulterated, along the lines of the Parthenon, as opposed to the relatively ornate Rospigliosi cup then thought designed by Benvenuto Cellini in 1560, which he disdained. "In the Parthenon you can find no detail of superfluous nature," Bel Geddes once wrote. A streamlining of the country would happen when the all-seeing designer, this new industrial artist, aligned with business. "The few artists who have devoted themselves to industrial design have done so with condescension, regarding it as a surrender to Mammon, a mere source of income to enable them to obtain time for creative work," he wrote. "On the other hand, I was drawn to industry by the great opportunities it offered creatively."

Robert Moses, the road builder who was designing what were thought to be state-of-the-art parkways and roads all around New York City and New York state, thought Bel Geddes's ideas were ridiculous and far-fetched. But in 1940, at the request of President Franklin D. Roosevelt, Bel Geddes designed a possible national motorway. Bel Geddes knew that Roosevelt loved boats. When he visited the White House, Bel Geddes brought the president a model of a streamlined yacht.

REVELATION

BENTON MACKAYE WAS BORN IN 1879, and, like Bel Geddes, he was born into wealth that petered out early. His father, Steele MacKaye, was an actor, writer, and director who produced huge historical pageants with elaborate machinery, on a Bel Geddes–like scale. Steele MacKaye was the first American actor to play Hamlet in London, and as a director created dramas that showed movements of social forces, such as the *Drama of Civilization*, a pageant that was a re-creation of westward expansion and performed in Madison Square Garden in New York City. Also like Bel Geddes, MacKaye was born into the time of road change in America. "I myself have seen the change from horse and mud to gas and cement," he later wrote. He grew up first in Manhattan, but as his father's money waned, his family moved to the country, to Shirley, Massachusetts, where he climbed mountains and learned the local history, and eventually climbed a peak in the White Mountains, which changed his life: "A second world—and promise!" he once recalled thinking at the summit.

MacKaye considered himself a disciple of Henry David Thoreau. He played the harmonica. He was described as a great friend but not very friendly. He loved maps and saw them as idealized but realizable sketches of how things could be natural and communal. One of his sayings was "Speak softly and carry a big map." He graduated from Harvard in 1900 and joined the U.S. Forest Service at a time when its mandate was shifting toward conservation and away from commercial logging. He was hired by Gifford Pinchot, who used this definition of conservation: the use of natural resources for the greatest good of the greatest number for the longest time. While with the Forest Service, MacKaye traveled through Wisconsin, Minnesota, the Dakotas, Montana, and Washington, surveying the land and natural resources for the government, and he visited Everett, Washington, at a time when striking workers were being killed during labor actions. He also worked in the Labor Department and for the Postal Service. He became a journalist, writing radical editorials and living in Washington, D.C., in a place he called "Hell House," where Sinclair Lewis, finishing *Main Street*, came by to sing made-up songs, entertaining John Reed, Louise Bryant, Dean Acheson, and Louis Brandeis. He cofounded the Regional Planning Association of America and, with Aldo Leopold, the Wilderness Society.

He married Jessie Hardy Stubbs, a suffragist, and moved to Milwaukee to write editorials for the *Milwaukee Leader*. His wife worked for disarmament and at one point called for women to strike in their marriages, to hold back companionship, which the press labeled a "bride strike." "The women of the world will disarm the males in every country since the men do not seem to be able to do it for themselves," she said. "They will refuse to bear children to be slaughtered by the tanks and odorless gases made by men." In 1921, they left Milwaukee and moved to New York, where his wife became depressed and then suicidal. She was in Grand Central with a friend, waiting to catch a train to Oscawanna, up the Hudson River, when she went to the restroom and disappeared. It was headline news. The *New York Journal*'s front page said: NOTED SUFFRAGIST VANISHES IN QUEST OF DEATH. Her body showed up in the East River. Police called MacKaye to identify his wife's body in Brooklyn, but he wouldn't look. He called hospitals all night, hoping she would turn up. Eventually, he scattered her remains in Staten Island, and noticed frogs peeping. From then on, he always thought of her when he heard frogs in the spring.

WHILE NORMAN BEL GEDDES emphasized the streamling of all American society—a frictionless combination of art and industry, the melding together of society's elements—Benton MacKaye sought to untangle the landscape as industry pushed farther and harder into it.

"Nature's mystery has in good part been conquered," he wrote in his book *The New Exploration: A Philosophy in Regional Planning*. "But alas! The very conquering of one wilderness has been the weaving of another. Mankind has cleared the jungle and replaced it with a labyrinth. Through the sudden potent operation of the industrial revolution a maze of iron bands has now been spun around the earth; this forms the modern labyrinth of 'industrialized civilization.' And the unraveling of this tangled web is the problem of our day."

As opposed to Bel Geddes, who saw highways as objects, MacKaye saw planning as a way of orchestrating movement. He did not look at the highway so much as the movement it inspired, of factory goods, of workers, of raw materials. He looked at the flow of money and people—a method he referred to as "liquid planning."

"Anybody who has ever been in the Times Square station of the subway knows that he has struck a 'stream,'" MacKaye wrote.

In the early days of road building, MacKaye proposed "roadless towns" and "townless roads." He sought to control cars as they increased rather than allow cars and traffic to control us. He proposed building highways on the disused train tracks of defunct railroad lines—he saw several hundred miles of existing roads between New York and Boston, for instance. In the *New York Times*, in 1933, he proposed the United States be rearranged by watershed and with industrial and commercial flow in mind, independent of state boundaries. He proposed cross-country highway systems, as well as highway systems that crossed the world, and considered train, boat, and plane traffic. He saw traditional landscape planning as the domain of those "who would cope with the problems of life's setting and background in terms of planting pansies" and most industrial planners, like Bel Geddes, as "practomaniacs," as "too high and mighty to think on the thing—human sensibility—that the whole damn show is about." America was changing rapidly between the world wars and he was trying to show people those changes. Regional planning was, in his words, "to render actual and evident that which is potential and inevident." If "Futurama" was the future as Bel Geddes imagined it could be, MacKaye's ideas were represented in a proposal he published in 1921, titled *An Appalachian Trail, a Project in Regional Planning.*

PEOPLE THINK OF THE APPALACHIAN TRAIL as a hiking trail, as a footpath through the woods, and it is, but it is also a way of thinking about how the United States might have been organized, or reorganized.

Whereas Bel Geddes sought to merge art and profit, MacKaye conceived of the trail as "a retreat from profit." He was not against profit; he was not a Luddite. He was for orchestrating its influences. He saw the trail as a way to influence urban growth: in the original proposal he envisioned the trail linking to cities, rural work camps, industrial regions, and farms. He saw it as a corridor of movement down the eastern seaboard, as it had always been—the trail itself paralleled an ancient foot trail. "The Appalachian Trail is to this Appalachian region what the Pacific Railway was to the Far West—a means of 'opening up' the country," MacKaye wrote. Clarence Stein, a friend and fellow planner, praised it as an antidote to what Stein called a "possible giant city." MacKaye did not think of wilderness sentimentally; he thought that wilderness was a resource in itself, a psychological resource that offered a happiness. He saw it as a way to avoid parkways in national parks, like the Blue Ridge Parkway and the parkways that were proposed and abandoned for the White Mountains and the Olympic National Forest. He saw the Appalachian

Trail as a West for the East, the equivalent to the western natural parks that might be accessible only to westerners or easterners who could afford to visit. In 1946, in an article in the inaugural issue of the Wilderness Society's magazine, *The Living Wilderness*, he argued that wilderness preservation must not turn elitist. "We must widen the access to the sources of life," he wrote. He argued that wilderness ought to be democratic, that the government should work not to, as he said, "grab off earldoms for *some* but to open up kingdoms for *all*."

When it came to building the Appalachian Trail, MacKaye allowed local organizations to execute the loosely sketched-out scheme, a strategy that David Brower, onetime head of the Sierra Club, described as "Benton MacKaye's Theory of How to Build Big by Starting Small." "In almost every locality along the Appalachian ranges a greater or less amount of trail-making is going on anyhow from year to year," MacKaye wrote. "Various local projects are being organized, and in one way or other financed, by the local outing groups. The bright idea, then, is to combine these local projects—to do one big job instead of forty small ones." He envisioned a scenario in which "cooperation replaces antagonism, trust replaces suspicion, emulation replaces competition." He considered the trail "a folk product pure and simple."

In the end, Lewis Mumford, a friend of MacKaye's, called the trail "one of the finest imaginative works of our generation." MacKaye's friends called him a Moses in reverse, a Pathfinder who would take them *out* of the wilderness of civilization. With Mumford's encouragement, MacKaye worked on his magnum opus, a book called *From Geography to Geotechnics*, for more than a decade, and when it was done, people couldn't really understand it. Even his friends didn't really get it. "If only he could write the way he talks, he would surpass Mark Twain," said Lewis Mumford. Back in Shirley, Massachusetts, where he was retired, he continued to draw maps of the past and possible futures, to write. In 1966, Stewart Udall, the secretary of the interior, visited MacKaye and gave him a plaque. In return, MacKaye gave Udall a map, a proposal for two more trails, the Continental Divide Trail and the Pacific Crest Trail, both of which now exist. In 1951, a hiker made the first complete hike of the Appalachian Trail. In 1973, 166 hikers a year hiked the length of the trial. MacKaye died in 1975, in Shirley, at the age of ninety-six. By 2004, there were 4 million hikers a year. It encompasses 160 million acres. It is 2,167 miles long and travels through fourteen states. It is a utopian vision that was implemented and, incredibly, it is a utopian vision that worked.

NOT SEEING WISCONSIN IN THE DARK

WE DRIVE THROUGH WHAT THE SIGN CALLS POYNETTE, Wisconsin, at ten forty-one P.M., according to the dashboard clock, and all I see is the dark. Oh, how I dread the darkness more and more each night as the trip across the country progresses, and as I take more and more trips across the country. When I was twenty-six, in the year that we first crossed the country, I could drive in the dark, and I could drive into the early hours of the morning—I drove all night, on occasion. When the kids were young, we drove late by talking late, by singing along with the radio, hunched near its lowered volume. We talked about where our lives would go, where the kids' lives would go, wondering what it would be like when they were teenagers. Now, with a teenager, I am seeing in the dark the day that he stays awake past me, when the roles are reversed, when I will be in the back seat of the car, if in the car at all. I can see the day when I am like the Toyota Camry we had that after hundreds of thousands of miles, just broke down, all of a sudden, without any warning.

Darkness is more daunting heading east, of course. Heading west, we cheat the dark, running away from the time zones, getting an hour to our credit every once in a while. Heading east, we face darkness head-on.

In the dark, the miles left to cover for the day begin to lengthen, to stretch, to feel completed even though they are not, a mirage. And yet, there is so much left to drive: this final portion of the cross-country trip is the most difficult, the most tiring.

I HAVE CROSSED WISCONSIN IN THE DAY, and I have crossed it in the evening, and I feel compelled to mention that a night crossing is by no means a loss. In the night, in the East, we see fireflies along the road—we do not see fireflies in the West, another thing that, like the Mississippi, divides the country. One summer night in Wisconsin, we paused in our crossing just after dusk. It was the Fourth of July. We made camp in a very white room in a Ramada Inn with an indoor pool; we ate sandwiches in an over-air-conditioned room. From our motel window, we happened to see people walking in droves, as if out of a scene from *Invasion of the Body Snatchers*, except seeming more positive and upbeat. We walked outside and began to follow them and, as more and more people caught up and walked, ended up a short way from the motel, at an old baseball stadium—a beautiful place, made of bricks through a Great Depression jobs program. We sat in the stadium, and when the fireworks exploded in the sky, the explosions all of a sudden revealed the most beautiful pines. On another Fourth of July, we were approaching Chicago, just past Milwaukee, an urban and suburban area, and each time we rose to the top of a long, low hill, we would see fireworks for miles, as well as thick smoke, smoke everywhere, smoke that made it look like the country was a big back room, with people smoking and drinking and having a party.

LIDS

I HAVE JUST BOUGHT A CUP OF COFFEE. We have just stopped at a convenience store, a fluorescent cave that was about to close up, a few miles off the interstate in I'm-not-sure-where. The kids bought candy, and my wife bought a cup of coffee too. My son discovered a copy of *Rolling Stone*, a task that only took about 1,800 miles. I filled up the gas tank, and noticed that the small car next to us was full of people, people just sitting there with the engine off and then laughing, laughing in a way that was obvious and audible, even with their windows rolled up, and a little disconcerting in that I had no idea what they were laughing about—when they peeled out, their laughing heads falling back with g-forces, I was relieved. And now I am sitting in the front seat looking at my lid, as in my coffee cup lid. I am staring at it. Indeed, it would be fair to say that I end up meditating on these lids. I drive and I sip and I hold the lid before my face as if it were a missal for obvious ease of consumption, a side result being my familiarity with the various shapes, my acquaintance with the dispensing ways of the coffee lid industry: a cross-country-sipping mindfulness.

As is always the case, just holding a newly bought coffee itself causes me to feel energized; I can sense the promise of the late-night coffee through the insulating squeakiness of a very large Styrofoam cup. When it comes to buying coffee late at night on the interstates at a convenience store that is open late, you never know what it is they will be calling coffee. I am not so much talking about the quality of the taste of the coffee; after nine o'clock, taste is of little concern and less likely to be a variable over which I have much control. I am talking about the coffee's power. When you step into an interstate-side store you have never been to (or alternately that you were in once years before, so that it is as if you are stepping into a dream), there is always a chance that you are about to buy coffee that is powerless, devoid of the magic of caffeine, not something I like to think about, to be honest.

For the coffee is so important to me at this point in the trip that I invariably look to the lid, as a predictor. I study it as I open it, if only briefly, with anticipation of rejuvenation, in the same way that I might look at a church door.

The vast majority of to-go coffee lids are referred to by the lid manufacturing industry as "drink-through lids." It is said that the first drink-through lid was patented in 1935, the so-called Stubblefield lid.

For the record, while plastic lids have existed for decades, a surge in their development coincided with our own cross-country travels, in the 1990s; for me, it was as if I were Meriwether Lewis and the evolution of a new North American species was happening on the continent as I traveled with the Corps of Discovery. But it is only now, years after I first opened a drink-through lid, that I realize I have been traveling the country in the golden age of coffee lid development.

The predominant lids of the seventies and eighties were often mere plastic tops, holeless. A drink aperture was gained by the coffee drinker ripping his or her own drinking hole—an act of dexterity that in the best circumstances ended in a small wedge of plastic that Phil Patton, the design historian, has termed "the guitar pick." Variations on the so-called peel-type lid advanced with the perforated peels that distinguished Patrick T. Boyle's Splash-Proof Drink-Through Beverage Container Lid, first patented in 1977; on this lid, the tear area was scored, an idea that evolved into the peel-and-lock lid, wherein the lid that is peeled back is "locked" into a docking area of plastic to allow the free flow of the magical fluid. Like the colorings of birds, the lids come with various markings. There are easy-to-read initials that are intended to be circled with pen: s, c, cs, and b. There are raised dots that are aligned with similar initials or abbreviations and are designed to be depressed accordingly: c, s, DECA, and OTHER. Additionally, there are coffee lid opening and drinking-assistance notes imprinted, directions which themselves can be fashioned to read like a concrete poem in a driplike shape:

DECAF

CAUTION

MAY   BE   HOT

SIP   WITH   CARE

FASTEN   TAB   HERE

DRINK   WITH   COVER   ON

CAUTION   HOT   CONTENTS

CAUTION MAY BE HOT SIP WITH CARE

PLACE DRINK HOLE OPPOSITE CUP SEAM

SIP   HERE   WITH   COVER   ON

DECAF   CREAM   BLACK

LOCK   TAB   IN

HOT

There are variations on the peel-and-lock system, the variations mostly be-ing in the design of the sipping hole shape, and in the configuration of the lock: the Sweetheart brand's DLX12R features a rectangular "hole" with a length longer than its height, a kind of garage-door-esque coffee release, as featured in the lid I bought in Raton, New Mexico, late one morning (along with a Fig Newton that was rotten). Meanwhile, the Dart brand's 8FTL model is a tall rectangle, like the front door of a home, open and welcoming, which I see now as I study the one I bought in Reynoldsburg, Ohio, in the Wal-Mart that our son did not want to go into. The so-called pinch lid is merely a variation on the peel-and-lock lid. One pinches the ridge bordering the depressed sipping area and pulls back the scored section. Like the differ-ence between lagamorphs and rodents, the distinction between pinch and peel, it might be argued, can seem academic.

In their seminal essay on lid design, Louise Harpman and Scott Specht, two lid collectors, identified what they called the "pucker" as the next devel-opmental step in the to-go lid: a plastic lid with a hole, the hole being in that portion of the lid that is constructed in an elevated, mountain-range-like shape. With the peel lids, the on-the-road coffee drinker drinks coffee through the cup, the lid opening to allow drinker-cup interaction. The arche-typal pucker is the Solo Traveler, manufactured by the Solo Cup Company and designed by Jack Clements in 1986. With the Solo Traveler, the coffee drinker drinks the quasi-mystical liquid *through* the lid, the hole straining the coffee, in a sense. The Solo Traveler took off in the mid-nineties. It was the lid used by the Starbuck's coffee company; *I.D.*, the design magazine, championed it, and it was included in the Museum of Modern Art's exhibition "Humble Masterpiece." It is a lid that handles fancier coffee-oriented drinks that I personally do not associate with cross-country driving, such as lattes. It reminds me of a child's sipping cup, or sippy cup. I watched when over the course of two cross-country drives this sippy-cup-like lid began in the Northwest and spread East, landing at last in Chicago and then New York.

The least successful design and most rarely seen, in my cross-country experience, is the puncture style, such as David Herbst's Push and Drink Lid, patented in 1990. This features a raised lid piece, often a kind of plastic sewer grate, that is depressed, thus puncturing the lid and allowing a flow of coffee. In the case of the Dart model, the grate is depressed anew each time the upper lip of the coffee imbiber seeks to gain access to the so-called coffee. I find them to be confusing, causing me to ask myself questions such as "Have I punctured sufficiently?" and "Is the coffee coming through, because I really, really need it to come through?" Often I will take the entire lid off and just admire it on the dashboard. This happened the last time I picked one up in Missoula, Montana, at Finnegan's, the restaurant over the creek where Lewis and Clark supposedly camped. The coffee, by the way, was very good.

Variations exist on all the basic lid typologies—there are pucker lids that are designed with sharp angles and puckers designed like the soft sand dunes of the Oregon coast. There are punctures that are puckers with perforated holes, such as the one I bought on the Massachusetts Turnpike, which, I believe, caused me to spill the coffee on my jeans. Likewise, there are lids that fall into no particular category. The Solo Traveler Plus features a small lever that shifts a piece of plastic back and forth to open and close the sipping hole. I have read of but never seen the lid that features two holes, set one inch below the height of the cup, through which coffee flows; it features a drainage ditch that allows overflow coffee to run back down into the cup. (It is said to be especially useful on ferries, where spillage can be more of an issue than in automobiles.)

A new lid that has spread quickly in the past few years is a reclosable lid by Dart. Called the Optima, it is a pucker lid that is like a peel lid in that you lift a piece of plastic up to begin drinking the road-spirit-enhancing fluid, and it is further akin to a peel lid in that you can "lock" back the peeled plastic, but it is significantly more complicated in design and construction, a long thin arm of plastic covering the hole or bending back into the plastic locking area. I kind of like it, and I am certainly fascinated by it, but I also feel as if it is like the interstate itself—i.e., too much—and so I often take it off, and pour the coffee, for instance, into my porcelain Lewis and Clark mug.

Plastic coffee lids represent an area in the cross-country world where streamlined uniformity has not yet prevailed—they are the last vestiges of differentiation. I don't like to think that we would ever be a one-lid nation, though that day may come.*

---

* Conversely, in Europe, the American plastic to-go coffee lid is like an invasive species. Harpman and Specht report that a graduate student doing coffee lid fieldwork in Europe asked for a to-go lid in a French café and was handed a large porcelain cup, the waitress saying, "Go with it, but bring back the cup."

LIDS AGAIN

THE LID THAT I BOUGHT with the coffee at the place where my son finally found an issue of *Rolling Stone*, after nearly two thousand miles, is a puncture lid, a sewer-grate variation. The coffee tastes like nothing, but the caffeine may be working. I can't tell yet, and it is difficult to devote the concentration I would like to devote to monitoring caffeine uptake because there's an argument in the back seat. An argument wakes me up for the moment, even if, in a daylong cumulative sense, it will wear me down. The argument is one of aesthetics. The song is "Big Yellow Taxi," famous for its chorus: "You pave paradise and put up a parking lot." In the back seat, one member of our party is praising the original and disparaging the remake. The other member of our party is saying that the remake we are now listening to on a Madison, Wisconsin–based radio station is just fine. The back-and-forth continues. The arguers call for parental adjudication. The argument does not appear to be subsiding despite intercessions by both leaders of the expedition. For my part, the argument is making me feel claustrophobic and impatient and itchy, something that happens on cross-country trips, as well as, I would imagine, in space capsules. I feel like I am going to get upset in the darkness, with trucks passing, with lights all around us, with the pack on top all of a sudden, after hundreds of miles of relative quietness, starting to make that long low moaning noise again. I feel as if I am going to blow my lid.

TURNPIKES

SMOOTH, UNHINDERED, FRICTION-FREE, Bel Geddes as opposed to MacKaye—choosing thusly is the easy choice, the no-brainer, and around the time of World War II, this was the choice that we (as in all of us in the nation, whether we knew it or not) made when it came to building a new national highway system, a new network of new roads. And the road that paved the way for the interstate system that was about to be built was the modern turnpike.

There had always been turnpikes—the word comes from the oldest toll roads, whereupon a toll taker moved a pike, or road-crossing stick, so that a traveler, having paid the toll, might continue on. But Pennsylvania built the first modern turnpike, along the lines of what Norman Bel Geddes had been thinking about when he talked about streamlined roads. When the Pennsylvania Turnpike opened in 1940, publicists were calling it "America's Dream Road." As if nodding to Bel Geddes, the *New York Times* called it "magic." It was also called a "superhighway."

One of the things that differentiated the new turnpike was that its course was almost indifferent to its geography—tunneling through mountains, blasting out hills, bridging rivers. (To cut through the Alleghenies at one point, the Pennsylvania Turnpike employed a railroad tunnel built by Cornelius Vanderbilt and abandoned after construction stopped during the Civil War.) There were no more traffic lights; the turnpike was not concerned with the flow of traffic in and out of cities; it was concerned with the fastest travel across the state. On the turnpike, in fact, the time it took for a truck to cross the state was cut in half. The turnpike had four lanes: two on each side, divided by a grassy median. There would be no more steep grades and time and gas would be saved by keeping grades smooth and easy, or easy compared to what they were on the Lincoln Highway, which could be severe. As opposed to traffic pileups on the Lincoln Highway, as cars waited to get through traffic lights in cities and towns, the only stops on the turnpike were for tolls. There was no speed limit initially, though the governor set one at 35 m.p.h. to save gas and tires once America entered World War II. People ate at the first service areas, rest stops with food and gas, little villages on the self-sufficient world of the superhighway.

It was built by a private entity, the Pennsylvania Turnpike Commission, which floated bonds to build the road, and then Franklin Roosevelt put in money through the New Deal's Reconstruction Finance Corporation and the Works Progress Administration—aside from being a driving enthusiast, Roosevelt was up for reelection and wanted Pennsylvania's many electoral votes in a year when much of Pennsylvania was unemployed. The speed with which the road was built was phenomenal at the time—almost a quarter of a mile of four-lane highway a day. During construction, there were deaths, and even race riots, and workers raped women in the valleys. But the public forgot all that when the road was done. This too would become a characteristic of the modern road: when the new road is built, it puts us in a trance, like driving late at night, and we forget what used to be there and how it all happened. The superhighway disdains history.

OTHER TURNPIKES WERE BUILT in the east and midwest after the Pennsylvania Turnpike, turnpikes such as the New York State Thruway, the Maine Turnpike, the Kansas Turnpike, the Ohio Turnpike, and the Indiana Turnpike; tomorrow morning, our expedition in the Impala will be on the North-West Tollway, a turnpike to Chicago. Also at this time came what is in my mind the mightiest of turnpikes: the New Jersey Turnpike, with its airport-terminal-sized service plazas, with its bridges designed specifically to ignore the rivers that they cross, with its stories of gangsters getting lost or dumping bodies, with its special rules (no photographs allowed on the New Jersey Turnpike), with its pay phones at the service area that ring all the time, with its sheer Mob- and popular-song-related notoriety.

Yes, one day people would tire of the dullness that streamlining eventually conjured, but the significance of the Pennsylvania Turnpike to the transcontinentalist is that it showed the road builders and politicians and car drivers of America what roads could be—not to mention military planners: as soon as the turnpike was completed, and before it was open to the public, General John Pershing began using it for military maneuvers, noting that it was wide enough and big enough and of course streamlined enough to accommodate small planes. Also, it proved that Thomas MacDonald, the preeminent builder of hundreds of thousands of miles of America's roads was wrong, that his figures no longer lined up, that people *would* travel farther, given a streamlined chance. In its calculations, MacDonald's Bureau of Public Roads had predicted the Pennsylvania Turnpike would carry 715 cars a day, but within a year it was carrying nearly ten thousand.

As the interstates began to be constructed, over MacDonald's objections, he was phased out, quietly unreappointed by President Harry Truman, after serving since the time of Woodrow Wilson. It was the end of a long chapter in road building. On that day, he walked into his office, turned to his secretary, the only person allowed to ride in an elevator with him at his offices in the Bureau of Public Roads, and said, "Well, I've just been fired. We might as well get married."

PASSING MADISON

THE EXPEDITIONARY TEAM IS SLEEPY. The expeditionary team is very sleepy. There is no more arguing among its members. There is music, the sound of my open window closing, and then the sound of me turning down the music a little, and then the sound of the music turning off. My wife's eyes are closed, but every time I move suddenly, she jerks awake. "Are you OK?" she keeps asking. I am for the moment, but I am beginning to get sleepy, a feeling I dread. Within the expedition, discussion has begun as to the whereabouts and type of this evening's lodging. As usual, the expeditionary leaders, are desirous of getting as far as we possibly can, and the other members of the team, while understanding the value of such a move, are nonetheless still voicing support for a position that is more flexible in terms of stopping time and considering prospective stopping time options that include right now, which would mean Madison, Wisconsin.

How many times have I passed Madison, Wisconsin? How many times have I gotten home and read about interesting things going on in Madison, such as the event in town where people get together with old-fashioned push lawn mowers and cut grass without utilizing fossil fuels? Or the invention of a satirical newspaper with headlines such as REPORT: 98 PERCENT OF U.S. COMMUTERS FAVOR PUBLIC TRANSPORTATION FOR OTHERS? How many times have I driven through the outskirts of town and not stopped and really looked at the place—except for the one time I was on my worst cross-country trip ever with my friend Jim and (not to give anything away as to what happened after I was towed to a part of Saint Paul that he, a Saint Paul native, had never been to) we pulled into a strip mall in the truck with a car trailer on it and tried to find a restaurant that was better than something near the interstate but it ended up being like something near the interstate (i.e., bad)?

No, we will not stop in Madison, Wisconsin, for the reason that we had our nice stop in a nice town in a nice hotel and now it is time to press forward into the deteriorating time zones. We see the lights on the Wisconsin capitol building out the window, but we are looking at the outskirts of Chicago on our maps. We are looking for a motel that is close to the highway, that is in a city in between cities, that is maybe a Holiday Inn Express, which is the kind of motel I am thinking about obsessively, for no really good reason, especially since I didn't get to stay in the Holiday Inn Express in Miles City, Montana, two nights ago—which brings me to the origin of the Holiday Inn Express and the Holiday Inn, and of the motel.

THE FIRST MOTEL

IT HELPS ME TO REMEMBER—when I am checking in to, say, a really crappy room in a basement late at night, or when checking in to a motel that is clean and new but feels hermetically sealed—that motels are not so much related to hotels as they are to tents.

Recall, if you will, that when cars were first invented and popularized, people drove them into the hills to camp, to retreat from the city, to commune with nature with the aid of their new machine. Initially, as we have already noted, they camped where they pleased, or in some cases, on the land of farmers looking to make an extra buck. Soon, larger private pay camps popped up. Californians are said to have taken the lead in building cabins for car campers in the early 1920s. Often these were just canvas tents with wooden floors. It was in this time, in the era of the early pay camp, that camp owners around the country began using the cutesy spellings that still characterize roadside travel today, seen in names such as Kamp Kozy Kabins, U-Smile Camp, Dew Drop Inn, U Pop Inn, U Wanna Kum Inn, You Wanna Kum Back. Eventually tents gave way to buildings, usually cabins, often bungalows. Bungalow architecture gave way to English Tudor architecture and then to Spanish colonial and New England colonial. Bungalows prospered because car campers realized they did not like camping as much as they thought they would. "We are not a knapsack, open-air people," a traveler wrote in *Harper's*. "We like nature, but must have our roads straight and smooth, and we want to view the scenery through the windows (usually closed) of a two-door sedan." People decided that instead of luxuriating in the woods, they preferred what was soon described as "getting there." While in the process of "getting there," they still wanted to be able to stay somewhere convenient—i.e., they wanted to be able to stay anywhere they wanted. Thus, being on the road began to have less to do with communing with nature and more to do with a kind of logistical freedom, a freedom that was associated with the great outdoors but didn't think the great outdoors was so great.

As camps grew and offered more services, travelers were willing to pay more and more, and thus went from hitting the road to escape from commercialism to being consumers on the road, where they did more consuming. This, in turn, caused motel owners to offer even more services for even more fees—sheets, blankets, soaps, radios, food, showers. The resulting lodging places were variously called motor courts, motor hotels, tourist courts, cottages, hotel courts, auto hotels, and until just around the time when the word *motel* took over, *autel*. The first use of the term *motel* is said to have occurred in San Luis Obispo, California, at Arthur Heinman's Milestone Mo-tel, opened in 1926. A phrase that popped up in motel advertising around this time was "home away from home." "Home away from home" sounds quaint and cozy now, but at the time, it was an almost futuristic idea. In 1930, it was predicted that Americans of even modest means would one day be able to drive cross-country with just one suitcase.

In the thirties, the motel business blossomed, motels (being cheaper) benefiting from hard times, to the chagrin of hotel owners, who lost customers. Thus, hotel owners harassed motel owners: the president of the American Hotel Association charged that 75 percent of the sixty-two camps in New Jersey were "an assortment of dime dance halls, beer joints, disorderly houses, and criminal hangouts." (Other people harassed motel owners too; in 1940, J. Edgar Hoover, the FBI director, called motels "dens of vice and corruption.") But Americans in general liked motels, for motels offered Americans a transitory freedom. Even wealthy people liked to go to motels, to bargain prices down for sport, to the chagrin of motel owners. Starting in the twenties, garages were built alongside cabins—at the time, tourists wanted their cars covered. "Proud of their new acquisition and jealous of its delicate finish, tourists of the 1920s would walk a hundred yards through the rain to get to a pit toilet, but they would not let their cars get wet," one historian writes.

Motel owners began to build motels that were distinguishable from all the other motels—motels shaped like teepees, for instance, such as Wigwam Village near Bardstown, Kentucky. The number of motels went from 3,000 in 1928, to 13,521 in 1939, to 25,874 in 1948, to 56,248 in 1957. As more and more roads were constructed, Americans drove more. In the 1920s, the average worker worked all year without a vacation; in the 1960s, workers earned eight paid vacation days. In 1967, the average American household covered six thousand miles of driving in one year, the equivalent of two cross-country trips. If you were an African American, you did not partake in the abundance of motels as small motels popped up everwhere in the twenties, thirties, and forties; motels were essentially for the white middle class. A directory published by the Department of the Interior under the Franklin Roosevelt administration, titled *Directory of Negro Hotels and Guest Houses in the United States* listed no motels and mostly included old hotels and private homes and Young Men's and Young Women's Christian Associations.

In the forties, construction costs forced motel owners to get rid of garages. The modern L-shaped and U-shaped collection of motel units began to appear. In 1951, *Fortune* wrote: "There was a time when the sailor home from the sea went chicken farming. Nowadays, he buys a motel by the side of the road." (People who wanted the community that old motor camps used to offer turned to trailer camps, a kind of camping that got a lot of attention in the forties, as cities grew once again; *Reader's Digest* published a series of trailer camp articles, including one titled "Back to the Covered Wagon.") In the fifties, as parkways and then expressways and then at last interstate highways were constructed, the first motel chains appeared. By the forties, you were not only buying a room when you stayed in a motel. You were buying a room with all the accoutrements of modern life. In the fifties, motels went from looking like a version of your grandmother's living room to being a modernist vision. Simultaneously, motels became showrooms for products. Manufacturing companies worked with motel companies to highlight goods in the home-away-from-home for the traveling consumer: air-conditioning, wall-to-wall carpeting, soaps and shampoos, and, eventually, coffeemakers first appeared in motel rooms. Staying in a motel room became akin to visiting a department store, if only subconsciously.

WHEN I THINK of all the motels that we have stayed in after a decade and a half of cross-country travel, when I close my eyes and see the faux-pine paneling in the motel room on the edge of Little Rock or the white stucco walls in our room in Amarillo or the log cabin on a mountain road in Wyoming or all the rooms in all the Motel 6s, the Lamplighters, and the Days Inns, the Fairfield Inns and the AmeriInns, the Best Westerns, the Budget Inns, the

Ramada Inns, and even the lesser-known Drury Inns; when I imagine pulling back the heavy, flame-retardant curtains that keep out the light from the nearby neon signs, I can recall the fatigued excitement of turning the doorknob time and time again.

Sure, we've had to change rooms occasionally, for nonsmoking rooms that actually have not been smoked in or, in one case in Indiana, for a room that had not been painted a few minutes before or, as was the case in Ohio, for a room that was not occupied at the time that we opened the door and surprised the occupiers, who were apparently light sleepers. But generally speaking when you are driving cross-country, the room arrival is good even when it is not that good. It is the time when you are with a bag and your toothbrush, a time when the TV is on with a late-night comedian telling jokes or the scores for the baseball games being revealed or, sometimes, there is a huge national or international tragedy being televised and even though you are very much out in the world, traveling through it, you feel strangely separate, very far away. The best part is that you don't have to drive anywhere for a few hours.

I can only recall one time when we had a problem in the middle of the night in a motel room. It was in Youngstown, Ohio. It was at a big motel. We went to bed early, and in the middle of the night, there was a knock on the door. It was our son, who was around seven at the time and barely awake: he had gotten up and gone into the lobby looking for a restroom, an act that terrorized us for the rest of the trip. For the rest of that night, and on many subsequent nights in the remaining days of the trip, my wife wanted me to sleep by the door on the floor.

HOPING FOR HOLIDAY INN EXPRESS

AND TONIGHT, AS THE ROAD WEARS ME DOWN, as my eyes strain in the glare and weaken in the darkness, I am shooting again for Holiday Inn Express. Why? I'm not exactly certain. I thought the Holiday Inn Express in Miles City was clean and good and cheap and had everything I needed the night I stayed there a few years before, and I'm always looking to repeat good road experiences, even if that's an impossibility, something that, incredibly, I never seem to learn. In that way I resemble the 1950s traveler of America.

Another reason I am interested in booking a room at the Holiday Inn Express is that it is the latest incarnation of Holiday Inn, a huge, global lodging conglomerate that began when a guy went on a road trip with his family, something I can relate to. In 1951, Kemmons Wilson, a Memphis, Tennessee–based tract housing builder, went on a trip with his family only to discover that it was difficult to find a good, clean place to stay—a place where they didn't charge extra for kids and had a pool. Kemmons Wilson's trip that summer has been called "the vacation that changed the face of the American road."

KEMMONS WILSON WAS BORN IN OSCEOLA, Arkansas, in 1913. His father died when he was nine. His mother, a dental assistant, moved her son to Memphis, where he soon found work selling *Ladies Home Journal* and the *Saturday Evening Post*, and organized a group of boys on sales routes and took a percentage of their pay. At fourteen, he was hit by a car and told he would never walk again, but did walk again after eleven weeks in the hospital. He sold popcorn to movie theaters during the Depression, then made enough money to buy pinball machines and jukeboxes, as well as movie theaters— businesses that allowed him to build other businesses using debt. He became a home builder, mass-producing homes until he was known in as Mr. G.I. Housing. He once told graduating high school students this: "When you don't have an education, you have to use your brain. An opportunist is a man who meets the wolf at the door and the next day appears in a fur coat." He once advised a friend who had recorded a then-unknown singer named Elvis Presley to sell the contract that his friend had signed with Presley, and when Elvis Presley would see Wilson, Elvis would put his arm around the motelier and say, "Boss, you made a big mistake." On the vacation during which he came up with the idea of Holiday Inn, his son recalled that he drove too fast and talked his way out of speeding tickets.

When Wilson returned from that vacation, he decided to mass-produce modern-looking motels. He hired his mother, Ruby "Doll" Wilson, to decorate the rooms, every room in every motel the same. The first Holiday Inn opened in Memphis on U.S. Highway 70 in 1952; it offered free ice, free air-conditioning, and free parking, and children were allowed to stay for free. To keep down construction costs, the parking-lot-facing walls were made of large glass panels. To lower the risk of fires and, thus, lower insurance costs, floors were concrete slabs. Wilson built swimming pools at all his motels with the idea that if the children were happy, the parents would be happy. He hired IBM on credit to custom-design a computer for all Holiday Inns, the Holidex, the first computer used to track room sales around the country—desk clerks were encouraged to sign up people on the road for the next night. Wilson built a giant sign, known in the company as "The Great Sign," a fifty-foot-tall yellow and neon billboard reminiscent of a movie marquee. He sold franchises, often to locals who bought up the most traveler-convenient property before out-of-town competitor motel chains thought to. In 1960, two new Holiday Inns were opening a week, and by 1969 there were a thousand.

As far as building new motels went, Wilson just wouldn't stop. He kept building motels and buying related businesses, or semi-related businesses—Trailways buses, a cardboard manufacturer, a meatpacking company. He worked long days siting new motels, negotiating motel deals, and hosting dinners during which he talked motels. (He had a habit of ordering apple pie first, to get dessert out of the way while his steak was cooking.) He traveled overseas, eating only barbecued food or hamburgers, an aide telling his hosts he was too sick to eat the local cuisine. He once posed for a photo in a pool filled with money. Another time he printed fake million-dollar bills with his picture on them and then proposed to sell personalized money at Wal-Mart, the chain store of his close friend Bill Walton, until the Secret Service called him and asked him not to. Instead, he printed trillion-dollar and five-hundred-trillion-dollar bills with his face on them, and circulated the bills privately, mostly just to presidents and senators. On the back the bills said "Non-Negotiable" and "This Certificate Is Backed and Secured Only by Confidence in the American Dream."

A veteran World War II pilot, Wilson flew his own private plane, using it to site new motels. Once he accidentally flew into the restricted space over the White House, at which point the control tower radioed to say that he would be shot down. In his autobiography, he says he stepped down as chairman of Holiday Inn when he lost control of his board; many other accounts say Wilson stepped down when Holiday Inn had become unwieldy due to all the companies he had bought. Holiday Inn was sold to a British beer company, Bass, which in turn created Holiday Inn Garden Court, Holiday Inn Select, Holiday Inn Hotel & Suites, Holiday Inn SunSpree Resorts, and Holiday Inn Express—the place where, as I have mentioned on numerous occasions, I am hoping to stay tonight. Wilson and his associates kept the Embassy Suites, Hampton Inns, and Homewood Suites when they sold Holiday Inn. The state of Tennessee eventually erected a historical marker, identifying the site of the first Holiday Inn. The Smithsonian acquired an early Holiday Inn sign. When asked if he wanted to preserve the first Holiday Inn in Memphis, Kemmons Wilson said, "You can't make any money off of it. Bulldoze it."

TO BELOIT

AND NOW ON THE INTERSTATE, just outside Madison, the navigator, scanning the TripTik and TourBook and the atlas, has just informed me that there is a Holiday Inn Express in Beloit. I mention to the team that I would not be averse to staying there. I finish my coffee. I finish my wife's coffee. I ask for candy, hoping for a chemical reaction, a sugar burst, a confectioned blast that will allow me to coast into Beloit.

THE WORST CROSS-COUNTRY TRIP EVER, PART IV

I BOUGHT A CUP OF COFFEE at the convenience store that my truck had completely broken down in front of, where I was stranded while crossing the country in a giant truck with our station wagon on the back, and as I sipped pure burnt blackness, I was more awake then I wanted to be.

Adding to the moment of uncertainty—which, by the time the tow truck arrived, had stretched into about two hours of uncertainty—was the situation with the rental truck company, a company that did not seem to have a clear idea of what was going on; I was leaving messages with customer service representatives in a faraway state, people who took my phone number and told me to wait for someone to get back to me, which was getting more and more difficult to do as the guy in the convenience store was wondering why anyone would come back for more cups of the dark, burned, several-days-old-seeming stuff he was selling as coffee: it looked as if I was going to get kicked out soon. After several toll-free pay phone calls—I was trying to conserve my cell phone battery—I was able to make contact with a customer service representative who had great compassion for my situation and, as a result, gave me a direct number to stay in touch with her, and then called me on my cell phone to check on me.

The tow truck driver helped me unattach our station wagon, and I padlocked the back of the truck—locking all of our stuff up, as in every last thing. Sending it off with someone I did not know to a place I didn't know added a sinking feeling to the overall feeling of suffocation. I took the key to the truck off the lanyard around my neck and handed it to him, slowly. I was like a character in a fable or an epic tale who loses everything, and is separated from everyone he knows, only I was counting on it being temporary.

As the tow truck began to tow, I began breathing heavily. If you have ever watched a tow truck pulling a twenty-five-foot rental truck with everything of yours that you and your wife, though mostly your wife, have carefully packed not to break, then you know exactly how I felt. From our now unattached beat-up old station wagon, I watched as the driver nonchalantly towed all our belongings away, my life in stuff passing before me on the highway access road.

IT WAS A BEAUTIFUL AUTUMN DAY, the sky perfect, clear, crisp. In those days our old car had a nice new stereo. I drove into Saint Paul with Van Morrison cranked up as loud as I could stand it, to calm me, and up to Jim's apartment, where I found Jim waiting outside—he was to me what the loyal swineherd was to Odysseus, the guy who was going to help me through this somehow, though I didn't know how, and of course I only mean *swineherd* in the best possible sense. The nice customer service representative called me back to give me the phone number of the garage. I called the garage and a guy said that I had problems with my truck's rods, which was not good, even if I was only renting the rods. He told me it might take a long time to fix the rods, as in days. He told me to call back.

Jim and I hung out down by the Mississippi, hoping for a call. I phoned my wife on her cell phone, as she was crossing the country by train, to tell her what was going on. She too was concerned. She told me she was on the train in Montana, just past Kalispell, and that it was snowing there, and the kids were with her and the woman in front of them kept hitting her two kids and screaming at them.

In a few hours, the nice customer service representative called me. She told me that she had learned the truck's engine was not repairable and mentioned the rods, which she didn't know much about either. She told me that I was going to get another truck. I repeated what she said out loud, partly to inform Jim, who was standing near me, partly to process the information emotionally, given that it was one of the last things I wanted to hear. I thanked her, but I also mentioned that I really didn't want another truck, given that a new truck would mean repacking all my worldly goods. In considering such a scenario, I had one of those few seconds when all your bodily fluids do a quick lap around your body. She told me not to worry. She told me that moving men would be hired to do the job for me. She said that people switch trucks all the time, and she even had a name for it, a name that scared me with its casualness—a load swap. She said that the load swap would occur at eleven that evening. She gave me an address. It was in east Saint Paul. It was in a part of east Saint Paul that Jim, who was born and raised and spent a lot of his life roaming around Saint Paul, had never been to before—it sounded like we were involved in something shady. It sounded like, to use a patois often associated with the lot that we were about to visit, somebody was going to get taken out, like somebody might not get to make any cross-country trips anymore.

PSYCHEDELIC

I AM NOT IN A SPACESHIP, as I limp toward Beloit, Wisconsin, late on this summer evening on I-90 and I-94 combined with my family in the rented Impala, on the fourth day of this long, summer cross-country trip. But if I were in a spaceship, I would be losing my main thruster right now, or something along those lines. I would be coming out of hyperdrive.

I am still moving but I am just doing that—purely moving. I am purely getting there. Almost all of my interest in enjoying my surroundings, in experiencing the aesthetic pleasures afforded by my whereabouts, has disappeared. Indeed, I have little interest at this point in anything besides a motel and sleep, though mostly sleep. I have an emotional interest in coffee, but intellectually, I have now officially even given up on coffee. Coffee no longer seems to hold any power over me—I am temporarily immune. I must rely purely on the CD player or the radio, and on my window, which is open again. Tom Waits is playing right now, an old song from the seventies. I am singing loudly, the kids seemingly oblivious: "So goodbye, so long, the road calls me dear . . ." The lights of the roadside travel settlements that I do see—the fast-food signs, the motel signs, the lighted clusters of signs so many stories tall that boast of comfort and relaxation and charm in a trademark-strewn burlesque, against a backdrop of cheese advertisements—all mix together with all the lights I have seen on trips at night, a sunless sea of various pleasures through a measureless cavern of neon and halogen lights. OASIS-FOOD, says one, and then in an etymological car crash of food marketing and high-school-level eroticism, bizarre-seeming signs follow bizarre-seeming signs: FUDRUCKERS . . . HOOTERS . . .

To my wife, I utter the forbidden phrase: "How much longer?"

"We're almost there," she says.

Yes, I'm singing in the car right now, in our final miles on I-90, a tortured kind of singing because I am fighting off the song of sleep, because I am conscious of the threat of unconsciousness, the coffee having kept me just awake enough to drive and speak in long run-on sentences, like a bad and road-drunk beat poet. My wife, God bless her, is talking to me and I am talking to my wife, both of us talking to stay awake and keep the other awake, the kids beginning to pass out in the back—me talking about Jack Kerouac and coffee, about how Allen Ginsburg used to say that Jack Kerouac was wild on drugs while writing *On the Road*, but that Kerouac always insisted it was just coffee that kept him going, jazzed him up, while sitting in his mother's apartment, typing, sipping, scribbling. And then a reminiscence:

A REMINISCENCE, IN ONE LATE-NIGHT-DRIVING ACT

WIFE [*staring straight ahead, zombielike*]: Remember that bookstore in Boulder, Colorado?

HUSBAND [*staring straight ahead, zombielike*]: Remember the coffee place the guy at the bookstore took us to?

WIFE: Remember Jack Kerouac's gas station?

HUSBAND: Yes! Yes! Yes! Yes! Yes!

JACK KEROUAC'S GAS STATION

HOW IT HAPPENED THAT WE SAW Jack Kerouac's gas station is a story that goes like this:

We were about to drive across the country one summer when I happened to read in a newspaper that the manuscript of *On the Road* was on tour around the country in a traveling exhibition. *On the Road* was on the road. I knew already that *On the Road* was no ordinary manuscript, no sheaf of typed-up eight-and-a-half-by-eleven paper stacked neatly or even not neatly in a box, no handwritten pile of legal pads. No, the manuscript of *On the Road* was a scroll, a roll of paper, from a news agency's teletype machine reel or possibly an artist's roll. It was a typed-over, scribbled on, coffee-stained, ink-covered-hand-handled relic of a scroll. It is 120 feet long, and when a scholar finally rolled it out not too long ago, the ripped-off end gave credence to Kerouac's assertion that the end was bitten off by a dog.

On the Road was written in the time just before the interstates. Kerouac rode the roads moments before they were streamlined; he rode the original state highways and the old U.S. highway system highways built by Thomas MacDonald, the Chief. He took to the roads, in part, in defiance of the life that the interstate was about to put into high gear—the life with the house and the car in the suburbs—though he did not himself drive the roads. Jack Kerouac himself did not drive; other people did. And when he finally did learn to drive, he could not even keep a job as an attendant in a parking lot in Manhattan, or so the beat lore goes.

While we were on the road, the manuscript was to be exhibited at Boulder, Colorado's Naropa University, the Buddhist and beat-poet-associated home of the Jack Kerouac School of Disembodied Poetics—a school of poetry founded by poets and writers who wanted to have a place to get together and study that was not in New York City. At a meeting of the school's founders that included John Cage, Gregory Bateson, poet Jackson Mac Low, Allen Ginsberg, Diane di Prima, and Anne Waldman, they founded university chairs such as the Emily Dickinson Chair of Silent Scribbling and the Frank O'Hara Chair of Deep Gossip. Anne Waldman has written that she chose Kerouac's name for the school name because of his own search, his drive, both literal and figurative, physical and maybe metaphysical, or what she described as "the yearning of the North American 'soul' for higher consciousness or 'satori'—a poetic realization of the tenderness and emptiness and interconnectedness of all beings on the planet." Waldman also said of Kerouac: "He represented for me the genius-witness to both the decline of our Western civilization—its *cri de coeur*—as well as its outrageous wisdom and delight."

So we headed for Boulder, a cross-country point we'd never visited before. Just before we arived in Boulder, I called my home answering machine to check my messages; there was a message from a Naropa professor I had called before we left on our cross-country trip; I had left a message with him inquiring about the precise address of the scroll exhibit. His message said that the *On the Road* scroll exhibit had been cancelled, due to the high cost of insurance. We were crestfallen, but it was too late to turn around. We pulled into Boulder early one afternoon and found a restaurant that was running on wind-powered electricity, recycling its kitchen waste, and serving organic and locally grown food, a great place. I had a good cup of coffee and made some notes in my journal, luxuriating in the presence of food that was not fast, in the mere act of sitting still. Our daughter signed onto the restaurant's e-mail list, which to this day keeps us abreast of the restaurant's specials from a few thousand miles away. When we were talking to the waiter, I asked him if there was anywhere that Jack Kerouac was known to have hung out in Boulder. The waiter, who was in his twenties, had never heard of Jack Kerouac but he knew of a bookstore that might, he thought, be a good place for us to ask.

Thereupon, at the place in the continent where red cliffs rise up immediately from the flat Great Plains and announce the upcoming hundreds of miles of high-up western rocks, we came to the Beat Book Store and Tom Peters, the poet and bookstore owner who studied with the beats as a student at Naropa and once attended a lecture by Robert Creeley in which Creeley emphasized the need for poets to floss given that dental care would not be affordable—advice that Peters seems to have taken wholeheartedly given the way he responded when asked by a Boulder reporter how he had survived as a small-bookstore owner for over fifteen years. Indeed, he responded in a way that referenced the entire beat legacy. When I speak of the beat legacy, I speak of the days when the beat poets defined what *beat* was, which was *beat* as in *beat down*, as in beat down to the situation in which you just have what you have in life, which does not have to be much, materially speaking, the result being you can feel the world from the ground up, instead of feeling the world from where most Americans in the prosperous 1950s were hoping to feel it—with new cars, homes, and all the suddenly mass-produced consumer products. This *beat*, this kind of joyous broken-downness, is the beat that Kerouac and Ginsberg and William Burroughs and Herbert Huncke would talk about when they were sitting in Times Square eating fast food and not knowing they were creating beat but just planning on going west, on hitting the road.

When the reporter from the Boulder newspaper asked Tom Peters how he had survived as a small-bookstore owner for over fifteen years, he responded by saying, "Low aspirations."

"A lot of stores worry about making enough money," he went on to say, "but I just wanted to stay open. I've enjoyed it, and I've learned not to need many things."*

AS WE ALL WALKED UP to the Beat Book Store, Tom Peters was locking the place up, leaving, standing outside with another poet and her boyfriend-publisher, talking about going to the movies, trying to decide between *Shrek 2* and *The Breakfast Club*, what Peters described as "that high school Brat Pack movie."

I greeted Tom Peters and asked him if Jack Kerouac had been to Boulder.

"There is no evidence that Jack Kerouac was ever in Boulder," Tom said bluntly. Kerouac did go to Denver, where he famously visited Neal Cassidy, a driving companion, and Kerouac spent some time in Lakewood, which is not

---

* We learned that the Beat Book Store in itself is a road-trip destination for college students. Once, Peters had a visit from the Beastie Boys, rap artists from Brooklyn, New York, who bought a lot of LPs from the store and then proceeded to praise the store on a college radio station in Michigan, after which college students from Michigan began taking long road trips to the Beat Book Store.

that far away. In fact, Tom told us, the closest Jack Kerouac ever came to Boulder was the nap he took at a gas station in Longmont.

"Oh, well," I said. I didn't know what to say so I looked into the window of his shop without really looking. "Do you have any books by Jack Kerouac?" I asked, not knowing the extent of the ridiculousness of my question—not knowing for instance that, since opening the store in 1990, when he turned his personal collection into a bookshop, Tom had contacted Penguin, the publisher that owned the rights to many of Jack Kerouac's works, and persuaded it to reprint Kerouac books such as *Big Sur*, which has a lot to do with Kerouac's alcoholic breakdown.

"*Do I have any books by Jack Kerouac?*" he repeated, amazed, I think, that he would be asked such a question. "I have every book Jack Kerouac ever wrote!"

Tom turned around and unlocked the door, and the Beat Book Store was once again open. He ushered us in and began showing us all around the little store that was packed with books, books, books everywhere, in addition to posters, cards, and sheet music. I felt like I was in a large closet, albeit a closet stuffed with beat poetry books, with beat poets' prose, with relics, like some kind of dead plant or stick of some kind that had come from the apartment of Harry Smith, the folk song collector. Tom gave our kids a poster of Jack Kerouac, and he talked and talked to us, and I wanted to stay a long time. We bought a book of Jack Kerouac's haikus and a book of American folk songs, collected by Alan Lomax, at which point I wondered aloud if there were any old songs about Colorado. When Tom heard me wonder, he immediately closed up the store and took us all down the street to a coffeeshop where he pulled away a guy working the espresso machine—a guy who, he said, might know a Colorado folk song.

"I'm folk through and through," the guy said, "but I mostly write my own stuff." We waited as he stroked his chin and attempted to think of something but in the end he couldn't think of any old songs about Colorado. As we waited, a waitress began to act perturbed that we were standing along the bar not ordering anything while trying to think of a folk song. "Can I *get* somebody something here?" she said. I ordered coffee, to go. It came with a classic drink-though lid.

WE WENT BACK TO TOM'S STORE, a place that pleased me greatly, a place that I would have gladly stayed in for a while if driving home had not been on my mind at all. Naturally, I was feeling anxious about staying too long; I was beginning to rush us out. Tom was telling the kids more about the beats, and then telling how he was about to get married, and lamenting that he was forty, kind of sweating about being forty, actually. He showed us his poetry books—*Listen to My Machine*, published by Rodent Press, *over the roofs of the world*, published by Cityful Press and reprinted by Dead Metaphor in 2000, and *100 missed train stations*, published by Holy Mackerel Press and reprinted by far-falla press, which was, as I was understanding it, the press run by the guy who was debating between *Shrek 2* and *The Breakfast Club*. A poem in *100 missed train stations* begins:

> My heart can't imagine being thirty four
> though it will be in two weeks,
> my blood crawls like an old bus
> taking pensioners to south Florida

As we were leaving the store for approximately the third time, Tom gave us rough directions to get to the Longmont, home of the gas station where Jack Kerouac napped.

We also bought a book of poems from the poet who was waiting to go to the movies—she was very nice and very quiet, and her book was full of erotic imagery that was sometimes kind of rough and sometimes delicate, and she signed it for our children by writing "Blessings."

Then, Tom went and got us a copy of *100 missed train stations*, which is dedicated to his late father. He too signed it for our kids. He wrote: "From the author of this book at the beat book shop, boulder, Thomas J. Peters, Jr."

"Have a good trip," Tom said.

WHEN WE ARRIVED IN LONGMONT, we found the intersection where the gas station was supposed to be on U.S. Highway 287, but it appeared as if the gas station was missing. I found out later that it was being torn down to make way for a left-turn lane for Highway 119. We pulled over in traffic. I wanted to read the paragraph from *On the Road* wherein the narrator stops at the gas station aloud but there was too much traffic; I didn't dare. We drove back into the main shopping area of town, where I asked my wife to get out of the car to stop people in the street and ask them about the Jack Kerouac gas station.

She declined the opportunity, so I did it instead. Tom Peters had told us that it was a poured-concrete building of art deco pueblo style that was considered to be of architectural significance and, thus, a candidate for preservation, and I thought perhaps people would know. Most people did not know, of course, but then I found a man who seemed to recall a gas station up on blocks a few miles down the road, in the midst of a new housing development.

At an under-construction housing development called Solar Village, we found the gas station that Jack Kerouac had napped in front of, that he had apparently stepped inside, to use the restroom, if I am analyzing the text correctly. We saw it from the road as we turned onto the new and not-yet-lived-on theme-named streets: Tenacity Drive, Ionosphere Court, Neon Forest Circle. You couldn't miss the old gas station: it was a poured-concrete gas station that was up on wooden blocks, for it too had been on the road. In the window, a painted sign said, WE FINANCE AND NO CREDIT NEEDED. It was a floating gas station, set above the streets, above the highway. My wife got out of the car and took a picture, and I read aloud from the part of *On the Road* where the narrator, Sal Paradise, takes a nap at the gas station:

Under a tremendous old tree was a bed of green lawn-grass belonging to a gas station. I asked the attendant if I could sleep there, and he said sure; so I stretched out a wool shirt, laid my face flat on it, with an elbow out, and with one eye cocked at the snowy Rockies in the hot sun for just a moment. I fell asleep for two delicious hours, the only discomfort being an occasional Colorado ant. And here I am in Colorado! I kept thinking gleefully. Damn! damn! damn! I'm making it!

We piled in the car and got going quick—I was really revved up from that coffee that I got in the coffeeshop with Tom Peters—and then we got that same feeling that Jack Kerouac had after he woke up from his nap in Colorado and we just drove and drove and landed late in Wyoming and didn't stop once except for gas the next day and we made it to Oregon the next night. When I woke up the next day, I had this vision of the road that I couldn't shake from my head, so I painted it.

Looking down some
big hill, to see the
perfect 'cloverleaf'
exits on I-80 in
Wyoming

THE WORST CROSS-COUNTRY TRIP EVER, PART V

ON A NIGHT YEARS BEFORE OUR JACK KEROUAC ENCOUNTER, on the
night that I have been recalling in the midst of recounting our most recent trip
across the country, on a night that I thought for certain that I would not complete my cross-continent rental-truck-and-car-in-tow excursion, that there was
no way to move everything from my broken-down rented truck into another
truck, that I would somehow not *load swap*, in the parlance of the rental truck
company—on that night, Jim and I went to his house, grabbed some dinner,
waited around till eleven, and then drove over to the garage on the east side of
Saint Paul.

"I don't know about this neighborhood," Jim said as we drove in.

We saw junkyards with barking dogs, abandoned lots with barking dogs, barking dogs barking at barking dogs. As soon as we pulled up to the garage, I spotted our twenty-five-foot-long now officially broken-down truck in a muddy fenced-in field. The twenty-five-foot-long truck that worked was due to arrive soon—the really nice customer service person, working a late shift, had kindly called me again to make certain everything was OK. Then the moving crew pulled up, four guys from a suburb of Minneapolis, all anxious to get going, none of them very friendly. In a few minutes the "new" truck was there, and one of the movers backed it up to the broken-down truck. I unpadlocked the broken-down truck, and the two cargo areas faced each other, open back end to open back end. As I watched, the movers began to load swap. I had not hired a lot of movers in all my time moving, so I did not know what to expect, but these guys were fast all right, doing in minutes what my wife and I had sweated over for hours, as we worried about plates and glasses and old little fragile things that we loved.

Jim was telling me to relax, pointing out that my options were limited. Jim was an oracle. I stood with him by my car, in the yellow light of the garage in the junkyard area, watching for dogs. For a few minutes, I actually thought everything was going to work out, until one of the movers shouted over to me.

"It's not gonna fit," the mover said. He seemed sort of perturbed.

What he meant by "not fit" was that the "new" truck was smaller than the broken-down truck. What I found out when I got in touch with the customer service representative replacing the nice customer service representative who had left for the evening was that some twenty-five-foot-long trucks are smaller than other twenty-five-foot-long trucks. I quickly realized I had a problem that could only be solved by me leaving stuff forever in a junkyard in east Saint Paul, surrounded by dogs. I don't know how it works in everyone else's marriage, but in my marriage, furniture is not in my coverage area. My coverage area includes the stereo. In my marriage, one of the things you don't want to have to do is decide which pieces of your wife's furniture you should keep and which pieces you should leave to the dogs.

I stepped away for a second, asking for a minute to think. The moving guys growled. I felt beat—really, really beat.

What I decided to do was to strap as much of the furniture that would not fit as I could to the top of our car. Then, I stuffed the back seat of the car with more stuff. In order to keep me from breaking down completely right there in a beat-up lot in east Saint Paul, Jim was saying things like "Look, there's nothing you can do" and "just give it your best shot" and "she'll understand." Meanwhile, the movers were still "load swapping," tossing around boxes marked FRAGILE as if they were marked DESTROY and, in that sense, following directions to a T.

I tried to call my wife who was on the train crossing the country with the kids, but there was no getting through to her on the cell phone. I was in charge, and, as such, I chose to leave a giant planter, a few antique chairs, and some children's furniture, among other things. The movers said they would vouch for me; they said they would tell the rental truck company that the "new" truck was smaller than the broken-down truck. I took photos of the abandoned furniture, thinking the rental company would reimburse me, though it did not—the woman I eventually talked to said our furniture wasn't worth much anyway. The last time I took out those photos and looked at them, my wife said, "I *loved* that chair."*

LEAVING THE FURNITURE AND THE OLD TRUCK, putting the station wagon back on the back of the truck, putting the "new" truck's key on my key-protecting lanyard, Jim and I drove out of the lot. We went back to Jim's apartment and parked the truck and the car that it was towing in front of an old mansion, the home, it turned out, of James J. Hill, father of Louis H. Hill, the railroad magnate and national tourism enthusiast who once adver-tised Glacier National Park all over the Twin Cities, who was a huge propo-nent of the See America First campaign—part of the reason, if you think about it, I was living what I would call a nightmare. In the morning, we started up the truck and then waited a few hours more for the garage in east Saint Paul to send over someone to fix the broken taillights. In the meantime, I called the customer service person to thank her for all her help the day be-fore and she told me that her position was being cut the following week. She was being laid off, which was a lot worse than what was happening to me, I thought.

I got through to my wife in the morning. She did not have a sleeping car; she and the kids had been sitting up for several days, and now she was being

---

* Later, when I got settled and called the rental truck company and the rental truck company called the movers who said they'd vouch for me, the movers said they couldn't remember my move at all.

told that a chemical truck had overturned and, as a result, the train was not going to move for a long while. Meanwhile, Jim and I drove out of Minnesota on Highway 61, down the Mississippi, its beauty restorative. The next day we stopped in Toledo for dinner, at a German Mexican restaurant, where the owner told us he was a German boy who fell in love with a Mexican girl and subsequently opened a restaurant. For condiments we alternated between mustard and hot sauce.

ROAD ZERO

AS FOR OUR PRESENT CROSS-COUNTRY TRIP, as for us hoping we are close to Beloit, where we are precisely is described like this: we're driving beneath an underpass that says, COUNTY ROAD O.

We believe that we are very few miles from Beloit. Our navigational accuracy is waning, as it becomes more and more difficult to see and then add the tinier and tinier mileage numbers on the maps. Maybe we're there already. If there were one of those cameras in the car that they have in police cars when they are filming people being arrested on reality TV programs, I suppose you would see my eyes propped wide open, a big forced and tense-looking smile, then my eyes tightly squinting. I shake my head back and forth wildly if I dare blink. My wife: with the TripTik in her hand, her finger resting on our current position (as she understands it), her head facing forward, the picture of concentration, except that she's asleep and then awake and then asleep. The kids: asleep in their nest of pillows and sweatshirts and stuffed animals and alternative music magazines and notebooks and novels.

I had rolled the window up but now I am rolling it down again, and getting my face near the cool summer wind—like a dog we don't have because we travel—which is making it more necessary for me to shout, when and if I do speak. Suddenly, out of the blackness, I have just been hit by water, only it's not raining. The water has come from an agricultural irrigator of some kind, a farmer's oversized garden sprinkler, my face startled by the accidental blessing. A Wal-Mart tractor trailer passes us and its lights light up the Impala's interior, and then on the horizon, I see another giant cheese sign. With the sight of the cheese sign, hope fills my tired heart. I can see in the night an exit sparkling, the glow of an interchange. I can see the motels that are not our motel.

THE WORST CROSS-COUNTRY TRIP EVER, PART VI

AFTER MY SO FAITHFUL FRIEND Jim and I finally got going in the "new" rental truck carrying all my family's things including our car on a trailer, and after we drove from Saint Paul to New York (heading down the Mississippi through beautiful country on Highway 61 and then making it smoothly through Ohio and over the formidable Appalachians and into New Jersey), I proceeded to experience the worst moments of the worst cross-country trip.

They happened off the interstates, in fact. We had driven from I-80 to I-287, to a New Jersey suburb, a place where I had gone to high school, my family having moved out of the city, like so many American families. I knew this area, as in *really* knew it—theoretically, at least. I knew the roads and my thinking was that I would not get the truck in trouble anywhere because of that; I could leave it in New Jersey for a few days while our family found a place to live in New York City. (Did I mention that we were moving and had no place to move to? No actual address?) In New Jersey, the truck would be OK, I figured. Hence, Jim and I pulled into my parents' home, a condominium in a housing development a mile or so off an interstate, and reunited with my parents. My mother fed us lunch, while we listened to my father, who had this idea that we could store the truck at a gas station, a place where he knew a guy. It seemed like a good plan. Jim and I separated the truck from the car, leaving the car trailer on the truck, and went to the gas station—Jim driving my parents in my parents' car, all of us taking a main street on which large trucks with a trailer were permitted. At the station, my father got out of the car and, with his cane, walked slowly over to the owner of the station, shook hands with the guy, everyone smiling. As my father spoke, the station owner nodded his head. Then the station owner looked back at me waving to him from the cab of the twenty-five-foot truck with a car trailer attached to it. Now, the station owner was no longer nodding his head but shaking it. "You gotta be kidding me," my father said the station owner told him.

I got ready to drive the truck and the car trailer back to my parents' home. That was when I made my one truck-driving mistake.

AS I BEGAN TO DRIVE THROUGH THE TOWN I spent my high school years in—the town I learned to drive in, even—the automatic-pilot part of my brain suddenly took a route that was off the main street, a route that I would have taken had I been in high school or even later, a route that I would have taken millions of times, instinctively, a route on which trucks are not permitted. As I drove down this road, I relaxed, having that happy feeling of absolutely knowing deep in my driving bones precisely where I was going. I don't think I was even thinking that I was driving a truck at all. As I remember it now, I must have been looking at the railroad overpass for at least ten or twenty seconds, my face most likely smiling, my brain recognizing it as my brain would have recognized it when I was a high school driver with a station wagon that could easily clear twelve feet. I only began to read the railroad overpass as a guy driving a huge truck with a car trailer attached a few seconds before I reached it. When I did, I slammed on the brakes as much as I could slam them given my twenty-five-foot long vehicular condition, and I stopped about ten feet from having sheared off the top of the truck. Then I shouted a profanity, because I was upset, because I had traveled three thousand miles successfully through territory that was to me, a novice trucker-with-a-trailer attached, like territory at the middle of the map Lewis and Clark had set out with—blank, unknown, potentially treacherous, in light of my trucking skills—only to become trapped in the place I knew so well, perhaps better than anywhere, my teenage *terra cognita*.

I realized immediately that I would need to take drastic measures, especially since there was a car coming now on this road, which seemed a lot busier than I remembered it in high school. I realized that I would have to back up. I stepped down from the truck's cab. I would like to write that I did so carefully, but I am afraid I was frantic by now. I was out of patience and alone again—Jim was off ahead, driving my parents down the safe-for-trucks main street, unaware of my difficulties. I knew I had to move the truck fast.

I ran around to inspect the road and look to see if it would be safe for me to back up. I made hand signals that pleaded with the driver and the driver behind him to stop. I also said things that were attempts to be apologetic but in retrospect probably made little sense—frequently mentioning my children, my wife, and the "load swap." People stared at me, honked.

Then I got back in the truck. Dramatically, I put it in reverse and heard the ominous truck-reverse-gear beeping sound. A guy from a nearby auto repair shop had come out of the shop and volunteered to direct me.

It's one thing to back up a giant truck, I'll tell you, but a giant truck with a trailer is impossible to run in reverse without many hours spent in a truck-driving school. Turning the wheel is akin to shouting commands to a drunk. The guy from the auto repair shop was encouraging—"Come on, man, you can do it!"—and he eventually directed me into a driveway a few feet away that looked as if it would work for turning around. Unfortunately, the driveway ended up being on just enough of a hill to strand the car trailer, so that in a few seconds there were several people from the auto repair shop attempting to disengage the truck from the trailer—the truck was stuck. Pretty soon, the auto repair guys were disregarding the mechanisms designed to disengage the truck. They were using hammers.

Then, the cop came.

The cop was cool. My feeling now is that he could easily see that I was a truck-driving loser, or a truck-driving chicken with my chicken head sheered off by a low overpass.

"Let's get it out of here," he said, as he and another patrol car rerouted traffic in the town for the next twenty minutes.

We finally unattached the car trailer, freeing the truck to back up more easily. I backed up again, this time successfully. We had a lot of trouble reattaching the car trailer. But the auto repair guys seemed to think it would be OK, and it seemed to be when it was eventually hooked on. I proceeded on to my parents' house and took a street that, when I concentrated, I could see in my mind's road eye as being overpass-free.

I was driving along almost peacefully, but as soon as I relaxed again, I heard a horrible grinding sound. The car trailer had fallen off. I was completely unattached.

THE ROAD PROBLEM

BY THE WAY, there was traffic everywhere in America in the 1950s, after the U.S. highway system came into being and the federal government began to spend money on highways. The highways that existed were not capable of handling all the cars that were being produced—six thousand a day at the time of President Dwight D. Eisenhower's inauguration—and the roads were mostly two-lane highways. Magazines covers featured traffic jams; cartoons showed the government throwing money into ditches. More Americans were more mobile, which made for immobility on crowded roads, in new car-filled subdivisions, on roads that were choked with traffic as people began to choose cars over buses, as streetcars began to fade away. In the 1950s, the road situation was such that the roads were having their midlife crisis, a breakdown. Eisenhower referred to the traffic situation in America as "the road problem."

What Eisenhower did, in turn, was propose a large interstate road system. As a politician, he realized that the amount of jobs a national highway program would produce could only help him, not to mention the interest groups encouraging the construction of the interstates: the National Ready Mixed Concrete Association, the American Concrete Paving Association, the American Truckers Asssociation, the Rubber Manufacturers Association, and the National Automobile Dealers Association, to name a few. (Mamie Eisenhower marveled at the fur coats and jewels worn by the wives of the National Association of Car Dealers members, when the president held a reception for them at the White House.) Eisenhower's plan was vast, or as the critic Lewis Mumford said, "ill conceived and preposterously unbalanced." "When the American people, through their Congress, voted a little while ago . . . for a twenty six billion dollar highway program, the most charitable thing to assume about this action is that they hadn't the faintest notion of what they were doing. Within the next fifteen years they will doubtless find out; by that time it will be too late to correct all the damage to our cities and our countryside, not least to the efficient organization of industry and transportation." In building the interstate it was as if the country went out and bought a sports car that used lots of gas when what it really needed was a station wagon or something else a little more practical.

"If we are ever to solve our mounting traffic problem, the whole Interstate System must be authorized as one project, to be completed approximately within the specified time," Eisenhower wrote to Congress in 1956.

AS FAR AS CROSS-COUNTRY TRAVEL CREDENTIALS GO, Eisenhower, as I have already mentioned, had been on the military convoy across the country in 1919, as a young lieutenant, and, due to bad roads and broken bridges and vehicles that were continually getting stuck, the trip took two months—"through darkest America with truck and tank" is the phrase Eisenhower used to describe the adventure. During World War II, Eisenhower grew more impatient with the state of U.S. roads, especially after invading Germany and seeing the quality—and military application—of the roads that Hitler had built. "The obsolescence of the nation's highway system presents an appalling problem of waste, danger, and death," Eisenhower said while campaigning for the presidency.

"The failure a quarter century ago to anticipate the phenomenal growth of traffic volume, or the inability to provide for it, has brought about our present traffic chaos," the *New York Times* wrote in 1955.

The solution to the road problem was a modern, streamlined Norman Bel Geddes–esque interstate highway system—federally standardized roads that would bring, in Eisenhower's words, "greater convenience, greater happiness and greater standards of living." Even before the interstate system was completed, or especially before it was completed, the interstates represented the new America. They were the perfect plan for a superpower, forty thousand miles of smooth white-striped concrete that would link all states, that would unite Americans—though Eisenhower was insistent on the interstates bypassing the cities. (In designing the U.S. highway system in the late forties and early fifties, military leaders had sought loops around the cities, in order that cities destroyed by atomic bombs could be skirted.) That was the original plan, and he appears to not have noticed initially that the plan changed—that the Bureau of Public Roads in 1956 decided to designate 2,175 miles of interstates in cities and that in Congress, representatives who had previously been against the interstate program were now for it, with the promise of jobs and contracts in their vote-filled cities, with the promise of beltways and downtown exit ramps. (The only representative who voted against the bill was not reelected.)

Car- and road-related commercial interests, the good friends of the Bureau of Public Roads, were eager to see highways everywhere, especially in cities. According to *Automotive Industries* magazine, the interstate would change cities for the better. "The downtown commercial and industrial sites will become things of the past," *Automotive Industries* wrote. "In their place neighborhood units will spring up—pleasant residential areas, made up mostly of medium-sized apartment buildings located close to modern factories and office buildings, thus eliminating the need for a great deal of commuting . . . Transportation no longer will be a problem . . . Most people will be able to walk to work."

As far as the attitude of the country toward cars went, it was a time when people were crazy for cars. Sixty percent of the working populace drove and twelve million families already had two cars. It was a time when people paid to sit in a replica of James Dean's car after he was killed in a car crash. People were crazy for the things that cars brought, such as the suburbs; by the beginning of the 1960s, three thousand acres were being developed as suburbs every day. The interstates would feed the growth of the suburbs, those packets of houses, many built for returning-from-the-war soldiers, that spread out like mushrooms outside the city gates. In *Freedom of the American Road*, a book published by the Ford Motor Company in 1955 that offered examples of "enterprising civic-minded citizens" getting roads built in their communities, Henry Ford wrote: "We Americans always have liked plenty of elbow room—freedom to come and go as we please in this big country of ours." And in the craziness of war, in the craziness of a war between two nations that plotted to completely destroy each other and in so doing kept a peace, a nuclear peace, the interstates addressed the Soviet nuclear threat: it was the interstates that would provide a means of evacuating the population in case of Soviet attack. Eisenhower added the word *defense* to the name of the road system, the National System of Interstate and Defense Highways.

In his memoir, *Mandate for Change*, Eisenhower noted that the dirt and rock bulldozed to build the interstates would cover the entire state of Connecticut, that the amount of concrete would build six sidewalks to the moon. When Nikita Khrushchev visited the United States in 1959, Eisenhower insisted Khrushchev fly in a helicopter, though Khrushchev did not like to fly in helicopters. "If you are in the same helicopter, of course I will go," Khrushchev finally said. Eisenhower wanted Khrushchev to fly in a helicopter in order for Khrushchev to look down at afternoon rush-hour traffic, which, to Eisenhower, symbolized American success—Khrushchev had reportedly not believed Vice President Richard Nixon when Nixon told him that most Americans owned cars. "I would have given a great deal to know what he thought of the spectacular flow of thousands of automobiles so dramatically displayed below us," Eisenhower wrote in *Waging Peace*.

Khrushchev said nothing, returned to the Soviet Union, and bought three helicopters.

Despite his glee regarding Washington, D.C.'s rush-hour traffic, Eisenhower was worried about the government paying for the roads. In the years of negotiations, he talked about the highways being "self-liquidating," by which it was assumed he meant toll roads. What "self-liquidating" ended up meaning was a gas tax, and because gas was taxed per gallon, the gas tax was an incentive on the part of road builders to see cars drive more miles, consume more gallons of gas, the end result being that road builders would have more tax dollars with which to build more roads. The federal government would pay 90 percent of the costs of the interstates but the states would build them. The states would follow strict national standards: limited access, ten-foot-wide shoulders, pavement capable of handling cars traveling between fifty and seventy miles an hour, long sight distances and long, slow turns, and the complete elimination of the hills that once daunted travelers of all kinds. And the lanes would be, relatively speaking, huge. In 1928, when it was built, the Hutchinson River Parkway was a state-of-the-art road, with four nine-foot-wide lanes and no divider in the middle. In 1956, the standard was a twelve-foot-wide highway lane—the passing lane on the New York State Thruway, a turnpike.

Meanwhile, the roads on the new interstate system were to be organized like files in a well-run organization's filing cabinet—roads running north to south would have odd numbers (I-5, I-95), east-to-west interstates even numbers (I-70, I-80). Interstates that circled around cities would have an even number added (I-280), and interstates that were spur roads would take odd-numbered prefixes (I-180). The colors of the signs would be uniform throughout the United States—green for road signs, for instance, as mandated by a highway administrator who himself was color blind. Every mile of road would take fifty tons of cement, twenty tons of reinforcing steel, and would employ thousands and thousands of people, from the construction workers to the people working in restaurants and motels to the people researching the special reflective paint that was manufactured by the Minnesota Mining & Manufacturing Company. And they would build the roads anywhere, any way. In 1963, highway engineers planned to use a nuclear device to vaporize the abruptly rising, 1,200-foot-tall Bristol mountains standing in the way of the development of Interstate 40 as it passed across the Mojave Desert.

IT'S LATE RIGHT AT THIS SECOND in my particular interstate experience—all I can see of the land around me is what is lit up by the towers that light the parking lots of franchises, that cast that yellow sickly light, but what I see of the interstate is what it ended up becoming, is what Eisenhower's interstate system ended up becoming. It may have seemed at the time as if the United States was building roads for cars, but that was not all the United States was doing. If the first roads changed America, the interstates put that change into high gear.*

---

* The whereabouts of the very first interstate is a matter of dispute among highway afficionados. Some people claim that it is in Missouri, on I-44. Eisenhower signed the highway act on June 29, 1956, and on August 2, 1956, Missouri was the first state to award a contract utilizing the new funding. Some claim it is on I-70, which was then U.S. Highway 40, right near Saint Charles, also in Missouri, and just a few minutes from where Lewis and Clark took off. Kansas had already been working on a state highway but they paved it under the federal highway bill, so Kansas claims that I-70, just west of Topeka, is the first interstate. I tend to side with Missouri's second case, near Saint Charles, and on one trip across the country, we drove back and forth on it a few times. I was driving and I kept trying to get my wife to take pictures. There were a lot of lanes of traffic, so I was a little nervous about looking around, and we argued about the way I was directing the picture taking. But we thought we saw a sign that marked the strip as special, as far as interstates go; in the picture it is a blur. Mostly, though, the road just looked like an interstate highway anywhere at the edge of any city, surrounded by chain motels, office buildings, by streets to elsewhere. In a way, the argument over where the first interstate is is a moot point; in a way, the first interstate is everywhere. As Jean-Paul Sartre once said: "American streets are not sober little walks closed in between houses, but national highways. The moment you set foot on one of them, you understand that it has to go on to Boston or Chicago."

I CAN BARELY SEE

I'M SLAPPING MY FACE NOW. Things are bad. My wife knows this. "We have to stop," I tell my wife. She is also too sleepy to drive—in the old crossing-the-country days, we would just keep switching, keep driving, but now when one of us runs out of battery power, so does the other.

THE END OF THE WORST CROSS-COUNTRY TRIP EVER

WHEN THE CAR TRAILER FELL OFF the back of the truck, I couldn't believe it. When that happened, I was wondering how much worse things could get. Did I mention that we were moving and had no place to live? That I had no actual address, or no non-cell-phone number?

I knew the car trailer had fallen off the truck because the trailer was making a horrific grinding sound, and, when I first heard it, I said to no one in particular, "*Noooooooo!*" As the horrific grinding sound continued, I pulled to the side of the road—just a two-lane intratown road, a road that was a paved version of an old country road. In the first stage of me pulling over, the trailer's emergency hookup chain was holding; I was trying to pull over gradually. But in the second stage of me pulling over, after I had covered maybe half a block, the emergency hookup chain gave way. Thus, for a short time, my car trailer was a projectile in a suburban New Jersey town—something like a carless bomb just dropped from the bay door of a bomber. Fortunately, it didn't go very far, just up on somebody's lawn. And then, when the truck was stopped and off to the side of the town road, I was looking at my car trailer on somebody's lawn. With a Herculean effort that I was surprised to muster, I pulled and pulled the car trailer off the lawn. I assume that either no one was home or that the lawn owners were inside hunkered down, cowering at the site of a shaking, sometimes screaming, furiously perspiring novice truck driver on their lawn, though it wasn't like I was in the middle of their lawn. I was only a few yards from the street.

Meanwhile, as I struggled, people passed in cars, some hanging out their windows to stare at me. I kept thinking the cop who had seen me get the truck stuck under the bridge was going to drive by again and arrest me, or maybe shoot me to put me out of my misery. I struggled to lift the car trailer onto the truck hookup again. I was frantic again. I pulled and pulled but it was too much; I just couldn't do it. I pulled more and nothing happened except that my back felt as if it was losing in an Ironman competition. The car trailer barely moved. It was that point in the worst cross-country trip I have ever taken that I broke down, as in wept.*

I would say I wept openly except that no one seemed too concerned with me: I wept in the vacuum of the landscape that is the side of the road. At last, a man stopped to help me—at least I think he did. It sounds crazy but I have no recollection of what he looked like, and sometimes I think that maybe no one stopped and I imagined this person. But I remember someone faintly, and anyway, I don't think there is any way that I could have lifted the trailer back onto the truck alone.

I MET MY FRIEND JIM and my parents back at my parents' house. They had all been looking for me, driving around, wondering where I had gone with the truck and the car trailer. As soon as I saw Jim, I had him help me dump the car trailer off at the truck rental place—I never wanted to see that thing again. I left the truck at my parents' house—no one in their housing complex complained, after all—and drove the car to Brooklyn, to see my wife and kids, who had gotten in at two in the morning after the chemical spill had been cleared away. Eventually, we moved our things out of the truck and into an apartment, from which we would eventually move, of course, and drive across the country again, though I don't want to get into that. But on that morning, on the first morning I was safely across country and rendezvousing with my family in New York, I parked the station wagon for a few hours, during which time the car was hit by a truck. I know the car was hit by a truck because when I went to unpark the car, a note on the windshield said, "Your car was hit by a truck. I saw it happen." That was all the note said. That was enough.

---

* I am told that my son wrote a story about my breakdown for his English class, titled "A Writer in a Ryder."

EXITING

HER (as in my wife): Next exit.

HIM (as in me): This exit?

HER: *Next* exit!

HIM: OK, OK, you don't have to say it that way.

HER (who, by the way, as far as saying it *that* way goes, wasn't, it's just that, obviously, everyone's tired): This exit *here*!

HIM: OK, OK!

HER: OK, now, west.

HIM (scanning the horizon of signs): I see the sign over there.

HER: We made it.

CHECK-IN

TONIGHT WE ARE JUST A FEW MILES FROM ILLINOIS, not even out of Wisconsin, well short of our goal. As the car comes to a stop in the area reserved for people who are checking in, our daughter wakes, as if on cue. Without prompting, she begins preparing—unstrapping herself from her car seat so as to assist me in check-in, her self-assigned duty. We enter the lobby, which is brightly lit, notice the stylized Holiday Inn breakfast area, with its Holiday Inn Express breakfast area trademarks, a foreshadowing of tomorrow. We greet a clerk who is talking to an Eastern European woman, also in the middle of some kind of road trip, as my daughter stands on her tiptoes, so as to be seen by the clerks behind the front desk counter. Thankfully, there is a room—we had not called ahead. As we sign in, the clerk talks, and I wearily scan the lobby and think that this is the motel I had been hoping for, the Holiday Inn Express, and think that it is not exactly like the one I last stayed in, in Miles City, Montana, but similar.

We listen to the Eastern European woman, who is talking about her mother-in-law, who is confiding in the desk clerk, the clerk being busy, typing, sliding my credit card through a machine. "She is great," the traveler says to the clerk. "You would love her, but only for two and a half hours."

"Uh, huh," the clark manages to say.

The traveling woman shakes her head and begins to recount a recent moment on a previous trip to Europe, also apparently with her mother-in-law. "You know, we took her to Yugoslavia, where she's never been, and she compared a church built in 1400 with a church where she lives in Tennessee," the woman says. "She asked me if I thought they were the same, and I said, 'No!'"

SOLVING THE ROAD PROBLEM MADE FOR A BIGGER PROBLEM

NO, THE INTERSTATES DID NOT WORK AS PLANNED, or as they were thought to have been planned. It is not clear what President Eisenhower thought. It is said that in 1959 the former general (whose mother was a pacifist and cried when he decided to go to a war college) was stuck in traffic in the presidential motorcade while coming into Washington, D.C., this time observing traffic from the ground with his aides rather than from a helicopter with a Soviet leader he was hoping to impress. He did not understand how there could possibly be so much traffic. Calls were made, and it was explained to him that the traffic had to do with construction of a new inner-city interstate, which surprised him since he had not known that the interstates would run into cities. The president called for a study, and to oversee it appointed Major General John Stewart Bragdon, an old friend, a classmate from West Point who, during World War II, had built airbases around the world. Bragdon hired consultants and produced reports concluding that the interstates were working out to be something that Eisenhower—the so-called father of the interstate highway system—didn't plan on at all, really.

First of all, according to Bragdon's report, the defense highway system was, in 1959, not meeting defense needs—overpass and bridge clearances being too low, for instance, for an Atlas missile, and the cost of reengineering the bridges and overpasses was prohibitive. (Meanwhile, the also-new New Jersey Turnpike, a toll road, was bringing in 233 percent greater revenues than expected.) Bragdon hired consultants who showed that the interstate program had become merely about building roads, rather than moving people. "It is a highway program rather than a transportation program," wrote one consultant, "in danger of becoming a special-purpose, single-shot solution to problems that are much bigger than just highways." Bragdon also showed that the interstates were destroying cities, that land-eating superhighways—interstates required twenty-four acres of land per mile and eighty acres per interchange—were turning the downtowns of cities into deserts of concrete, wrapped in giant ribbons of more concrete, huge streamlined curves and clover leafs that could look beautiful from the air.

Eisenhower ignored his old colleague's report. In 1960, he called a meeting and was presented with the book of interstate highway maps that had been on the desk of legislators in 1956, the maps showing the intercity interstates that the Bureau of Public Roads had designated. "Are you sure this was on everybody's desk," the president asked.

When he left office in 1961, Eisenhower gave one of his most famous speeches: "In the councils of government we must guard against the acquisition of unwarranted influence, whether sought or unsought, by the military-industrial complex." And yet, by signing the legislation that began the construction of the interstate highway system, Eisenhower, in the words of one historian, "had done as much as anyone to extend the power of the military-industrial complex that so worried him in his farewell address."

Into the sixties, problems with the interstates multiplied. President John F. Kennedy appointed Rex Marion Whitton as the federal highway administrator, a highwayman's highwayman, a friend of the construction industry who sped up interstate building even if he himself preferred to drive the back roads. In many ways, Whitton reversed the philosophy of the old office of Thomas MacDonald. MacDonald was the engineer who built roads based on need. When it came to finishing the interstates, Whitton decided to built the rural routes first—the routes where there was *no* congestion, where the roads were not needed at all. Thus, Nebraska, one of the least populated states, was one of the first to finish its interstates. Meanwhile, the engine of interstate construction was the gasoline tax, and when for a time in the sixties Americans became interested in fuel-efficient cars—sales of low-fuel cars increased from 4 percent in 1957 to 16 percent in 1960, as Americans bought Volkswagens, Corvairs, and Falcons—the government increased the gas tax, President Kennedy, like his predecessor, citing national defense.

It was in the sixties that the interstates became known not for streamlined transportation but for corruption. In 1962, a one-hour NBC TV exposé cited what reporter David Brinkley called "swindles, fraud and thievery," and "the great highway robbery." Brinkley listed overvalued land, bad bridge supports, crumbling pavement, officials who testified that their families had been threatened if they ratted out corruption, and, in once case, highway officials who were paid three hundred thousand dollars to build an exit that reportedly led to nowhere. "The road goes one hundred feet into the desert and just stops," Brinkley said, the camera panning across New Mexico. The waste was not as bad as Brinkley made it out to be; the road actually led somewhere—to a water tank and a local road. The billions and billions of dollars that flowed legally to contractors and developers was corrupting in itself, unstoppable, something that a city or state had difficulty turning down. Daniel Patrick Moynihan, then a Harvard professor, noted: "The Interstate program is not a federal enterprise, it is only a federal expense."

In 1963, a television repairman named Joseph Linko began roaming the highways in his 1953 Jeep, photographing with one hand, driving with the other, pointing out that the interstates, rather than transporting people magically, were killing people. In 1967, Linko appeared before a congressional subcommittee in Washington, D.C., and showed thousands of slides of guardrails that guided out-of-control cars into bridge abutments, of barriers that protected exit signs and, when hit, rammed a car's engine back into the car's occupants, reminding Linko of military tank traps. All of these were built against federal highway standards, all imitated around the country, which he pointed out as he clicked through slides, as he commented in his Bronx accent, saying, for example, "Someone's going to have to get wiped out on that."

A REPORTER NAMED HELEN LEAVITT wrote a book about the interstate highway system after she discovered that a freeway was planned that would run through her town house in Washington, D.C. In it, Leavitt showed that the interstates, supposed to be completed in 1971, were, in 1970, only two thirds completed, and seven billion dollars over cost; that at peak commuting times, drivers could only drive up to twelve miles an hour, horse speed; that the speed in cities was 11.5 miles an hour, less than horse speed; that in 1969, the 86.5 million drivers on the highways drove an average trip that was only nine miles; that the interstates were not being built as a cross-country, long-haul tool but as a revenue scam; that it was road builders and their associates road building for the sake of road building; that the United States spent approximately a hundred billion dollars on automobile transportation every year, while it spent twenty-eight billion dollars on kindergarten through twelfth grade education; that trains and other forms of mass transportation were being abandoned, despite the fact that the average car carrying the average 1.6 persons carried less than five thousand people in an hour, as opposed to the fifty thousand people transported on a double-decker railway system. Leavitt titled her book *Superhighway—Superhoax.*

Mayors and city councils, Leavitt showed, could not resist the money, the millions and millions of dollars that a highway in their city would bring—the jobs, the construction, the baseless promise of no more congestion. And yet Leavitt showed that retail sales revenue fell when highways were built in downtowns. (In San Francisco, where a new highway was successfully opposed at the time, sales revenues increased.) "Critics who have questioned the wisdom of extending sections of the superhighway system into the cores of our cities, which fill up with commuter-trip automobiles, have been told by highway officials and highway boosters that these urban sections of interstate highways are essential to the economy, national defense, and safety of our transportation system," Leavitt wrote. "Persistent critics, those who question these premises, are dismissed by officials as fanatics, unpatriotic (since the highway boosters claim the highways serve national defense), or simply uninformed. Those who argue that the cities are being engulfed with commuter automobiles are told this is all the more proof that even more such highways are needed to alleviate congestion."

In 1970, of the five thousand miles of interstates in cities, most were built through black neighborhoods, the path of least political resistance—the new roads whisking people out to suburbs like Levittown, a town whose founder insisted it be all white. A letter to the presidential cabinet member on urban affairs unsigned and posted in Newark, New Jersey, read in part: "They are tearing down our homes and building up medical colleges and motor clubs and parking lots and we need decent private homes to live in." Leavitt wrote: "If the major growth in population occurs in our urban areas and the automobile remains the predominant method of transportation, all our large city centers will be huge concrete slabs with office buildings interspersed among parking lots and freeways, washed daily by the exhaust fumes of masses of internal combustion engines."

Another book that helped turn the tide against unmitigated superhighway building was *How to Halt a Highway*, by Ben Kelley. Kelley was a former member of the Road Gang, anti-highway-builder slang for highway builders and engineers. Specifically, Kelley was a former press officer for the Federal Highway Administration. Some of the headings in his how-to guide are "Avoid the Wait and See Approach" and "If Highway Officials Decide Against You, Consider Appealing to a Higher Authority." The book worked: highways were picketed in New Orleans, for example, where an elevated interstate was proposed for Jackson Square in the French Quarter; in Memphis, Tennessee, where Justice Thurgood Marshall eventually ruled against an interstate proposed to run through Overton Park; in Morristown, New Jersey, where, to slow a bulldozer wrecking houses for the construction of I-287, five women sat in a bulldozer, singing "When the Road Comes Barging In." It was a momentous occasion as far as U.S. road building went, because highways builders had never before faced public criticism. In the very beginning, farmers had opposed the roads, but then even the farmers had relented and hoped for better roads to market. Highway engineers had historically led people out of the muck. In the seventies, the public decided that highway builders were building people out of one mess and into another.

SLEEP

BACK IN THE CAR. Parking the car. Waking the teenager, which is like waking a bear, risky. Grabbing bags, sorting through luggage in the dimly lit trunk. Sleepwalking, the key to the Impala dangling from my lanyard, the flashlight in my wife's hand. Plastic magnetic key swiping once, twice, three, and then four times—we're in! The room is ablaze on our expectant arrival. Teeth brushing, pajama finding, my wife handing out supplies like military rations. The TV on and then, in a second, off, as people pass away to sleep in the dark, featureless room, the room that was not as cheery as I hoped it would be but is a first-floor room convenient to the parking lot, a luxury.

Somewhere around eleven thirty, I shuttle the last bags from the car to the room, until at last the room is asleep and I am outside taking the shredded pack off the top of the Impala. The parking lot is vast, like the parking lots beside it. To the south—if it is the south, for in the series of turns off the interstate, I have lost track of where I am once again—I see a pack of teenagers harassing the customers of the drive-through restaurant in the adjacent parking lot, what appears to be a McDonald's. Now, they are harassing the restaurant worker speaking through an intercom, the tired voice blasting from the giant speaker-equipped menu. Finished with the nighttime Impala-related logistics, I sit in the front seat for a moment, staring out at the kids as they run back and forth, from the large trash receptacles to the fast-food intercom, as they catch the attention of late-night customers. As I sit still in the not-moving car, I slowly realize that I am completely wired on coffee.

In the motel, I visit the lobby. I find an ice machine and, with a cream-colored bucket of ice, I wander back to the room. I walk down a forever hall, past a plant that resembles a giant marijuana plant but is not, along a corridor of creamy plastic wall paper—a design that seems as if it had hoped to be identified with a homey comforting feeling but ends up offering almost no feeling at all.

In an almost comfortable chair, with the TV volume on but nearly off, I change channels over and over, for who does not know the late-night feeling of being wired, wired, wired on coffee?

News, news, sports news, news of accidents, news of weather that, for us, shows cloudy but rainless skies, news of disasters, of wars, of weight loss. A history program on the History Channel, and then at last a concert: a concert in memory of George Harrison, one of the Beatles. His friends play, his son plays, and I watch and begin to feel less wired, though my eyes won't close. George Harrison's rock-and-roll friends look so happy playing George Harrison's songs alongside George Harrison's son, alongside surviving ex-Beatles. Everyone looks back and forth at each other, smiling, as I listen to the very low sound in a nondescript chair surrounded by nondescript walls and my sleeping family. My ears are still ringing, and, like the night before and the night before and the night before, I can still hear the highway rolling underneath the wheels of our rented car. And yet, when George Harrison's son and Paul McCartney and Ringo and Eric Clapton and a lot of other rock-and-roll guys from the sixties and seventies all play the old George Harrison song titled "All Things Must Pass," I get a little emotional. Eventually, I turned the TV off, the song still floating through my head: *"All things must pass away . . ."*

PART VI

Beloit, Wisconsin, to Bellafonte, Pennsylvania

AT THE START OF THE DAY WE ARE
SUPPOSED TO GET THERE

THE END HAS COME. We are finished, or believe we are about to finish. We are tired, dead tired, tiredness draping us like a shroud. We are done in by driving but the notion that we are nearing our last day, the very idea of an end of the miles and miles, will be the one incitement for us to arise one last time, for us to walk like the walking dead in our sealed-in motel room. Yes, we slept a little late in Missoula, played golf in Anaconda (for crying out loud), dillydallied in Minneapolis after a long day and a long night driving across the they-don't-call-them-"Great"-for-nothing plains, and, as a result, accomplished only the crossing of a mere two states in one day. Yes, the distance remaining stands before us like a great void that will take strength and perseverance and maybe even more coffee to cross.

But we will cross, because, oh, today will be different. After driving from the East to the West and then driving 2,028 miles on this trip back east again, we will be finished crossing the country for the time being. We have to finish. We need to get home, though I am less and less able to recall why exactly. At the same time, we *need* to stop. We need to wake up in the morning and not have to drive. We need to be outside of a moving vehicle and to not be calculating the miles lost each moment we are outside of a moving vehicle. The road has killed us, in the figurative sense, beat us down dead.

The phone rings, or more accurately, sounds, and I jump up and still feel asleep, and in the darkness maneuver around beds and bodies to answer the phone, and acknowledge what was possibly man, possibly machine, definitely a wake-up call.

"Thank you," I say either way.

I stand as if conscious. In the surgical light of the the Holiday Inn Express bathroom, I look in the mirror and see a blinking, shaking head. With the thrashing sound that accompanies the opening of the heavy motel curtain that is designed to shield us from parking lot floodlights and the clamor of slamming car doors, with the turning on of the TV that is soon to be greeting the day with televised baseball scores from around the nation and then cartoons, I suggest to the team that they awake, arise, bestir—that they do what they have to do to lift up their bodies one final time, even if they feel they cannot, for we are in striking distance of New York. We are in a place from which we have made it to New York before—albeit when "we" was just my wife and I and when "we" were young, or, from the perspective of how I feel at this moment, very young. More immediately, we are in the sway of the slogan of Beloit, which applies to us in reverse: "Beloit: Gateway to Wisconsin."

To the accompaniment of the grumbling and moaning and shouted mock-polite responses that accompany the waking up of young people on a three-thousand-mile trip by car ("OK, I'm *up!*" says my favorite daughter, and "*Aaaa-ugh,*" says my favorite son), I make complimentary coffee in a miniature electric coffeemaker—a quick coffee fix just intended to get me to the car with the luggage and then to the breakfast area for the real coffee fix. I pour the coffee into my Lewis and Clark coffee mug, which I use to celebrate the historic nature of the day—the completion of another crossing! As I sip from the Lewis and Clark mug, I welcome the warm bitter taste that has nearly lost its power over the past few days and weeks and, of course, years of driving. Surely, I have imbibed enough of the caffeine-laced warm liquid to kill an elephant, or at least that's how it feels this morning, when, as I sip, I vow to take a break from coffee once I arrive, once I stop driving, once I get off the road for a while. Semi-ceremonially, I don my car key lanyard.

Outside, the parking lot of the Holiday Inn Express this morning is like an old friend who has aged badly: a vast concrete steppe marked by fast-food restaurants that shoot up like groves of leafless trees, by tumbleweedlike bits of trash. I see now—as I lug the bags to the trunk and remove the rooftop pack that I believed would ease our trip but did not—that the drive-through restaurant where I watched a group of young people accost drive-throughers last night was actually farther away than I originally determined. Indeed, between my rented Impala and the McDonald's is a drive-through Wendy's, a Wendy's I completely missed, a Wendy's where, at this moment, a garbage truck is taking away the garbage—a tidal movement that makes me look around to suddenly see all the Dumpsters in my vicinity, and causes me to conjure all the Dumpsters at all the fast-food restaurants along the forty-three thousand miles of interstate highways. I stand alongside the car, the Impala key safely around my neck, and also notice a truck filled with fencing materials, a cargo of demarcation that pulled up alongside our rented Impala as I lay sort of sleeping last night. In this panorama that I have faced every morning over the past few crossing days, I see little variations of sameness, a view of the identical places differently arranged: Country Kitchen, Arby's, Econolodge, and next to McDonald's, a giant billboard as big as a motel swimming pool that says, "*Mmmmm . . .*"

Dreamy, dreary, and woozy, back in the motel room, showered and ready, our expeditionary team heads into the Holiday Inn Express breakfast area, where they eat breakfast.

THE MODERN BREAKFAST AREA

JUST AS TRAVELERS TRAVELING across the country by stagecoach stopped at inns and taverns alongside the road and were semi-forced into accidental comradeship, so we are forced into accidental comradeship with those who we meet or do not meet in the modern motel breakfast area. When I speak of the breakfast area, I speak of the portion of the motel that is set aside solely for breakfast. It is the place where the traveling people pause in their traveling, where they are in on-the-road limbo.

It is the nature of the modern motel that makes the breakfast area the standard interstate-side motel's only food area.* The breakfast area is likewise the main area for socializing in the modern motel, with the possible exception of the swimming pool area, which often includes the hot tub area. I am not a big hot-tub-area man. Once, however, while experimenting in Colorado with across-the-Rockies mileage on a state road through the middle of

---

* Sometimes, it is possible to discover snack-vending machines in a lobby area or, alternatively, in the vestibule between the front door and the lobby area, or in what I shall call the ice room that is a room on many motel floors, a room in which the ice machine clunks away angrily, alone forever in the smallest room of the motel.

the mountains, I passed the time easily with a man who, like me, was humoring his daughter, who, like my daughter, wanted to experience a hot tub, having already enjoyed the swimming pool. I was happy to converse with this father, as I needed a distraction from imagining the various microscopic animal life that might reside in a highway-side hot tub, and so I learned about that man's cross-country trip, which had brought him to the area of Olathe, Colorado, to experience a sweet-corn festival among his in-laws—a festival honoring the crop that saved the town when farmers could no longer make any money growing sugar beets and barley, a festival involving music and all the sweet corn one can eat. "Wow," I said, not exaggerating, as I sat in the hot tub.

But returning to the breakfast area, it should be noted that in the arc of time spent at the motel, breakfast is the most celebratory time, the retirement banquet of your seven- or eight-hour stay, the celebration at the end of your lifetime in the motel—for you are leaving now, passing on, most likely never to come through again.

TYPICAL INTERSTATE-SIDE BREAKFAST AREAS come in three general categories, the most basic version being the area directly before a counter or a table that is itself within the lobby area. The "food" that is offered in the basic breakfast area is usually small muffins or pastries or small doughnuts or some combination thereof. An example of this type of breakfast area would be the one in a motel on Route 66 in Missouri, where we ate breakfast on the edge of the lobby, in view of the inoperative historic 1950s-style gas pump. After each of our children found a plastic cup of watery orange juice, I advised them to take only one doughnut and then we watched a woman stack a small paper plate with three doughnuts, sit down, devour them, and get up for more.

The next version of the breakfast area is the entirely separate breakfast area—a situation in which, as the description implies, the motel sets up a breakfast area that is in a completely separate room near the lobby. Oftentimes, the food selection is more extensive in the entirely separate breakfast areas; there can be plastic bins that hold breakfast cereals, typically Rice Krispies or a generic puffed-rice stand-in, and bins or sometimes wicker baskets that hold different types of breads that are upon inspection extremely similar in appearance, such as whitish whole wheat and whole-wheat-looking white. The finest versions of the separate breakfast area serve yogurt and fresh fruits, though finding these items is a rare thing indeed. We once stayed in a motel in Little Rock, Arkansas, where the separate breakfast area was a small brick house, set off in the back of the parking lot. It was not a restaurant per se but a small, square one-room building with a long counter on one wall that was covered with breakfast foods. Inside, people sat together and quietly watched the *Today* show before getting into their cars and driving away.

Nearly universal to all of the above breakfast area situations is an inexpensive toaster that takes forever to toast toast. In using the breakfast area toaster, the breakfast area visitor is forced to return the slice or slices to the toaster repeatedly and seemingly in vain until at last the toast is warm and limp or burned. Rarely is perfect toasting attained.

The third motel breakfast area variation is an entirely separate restaurant, a breakfast accommodation that, of course, varies wildly. There is, for example, the little breakfast area in the back of the Irish Inn, an old motel that was also once on Route 66 and is still on Interstate 40, in Shamrock, Texas, where we stayed once while traveling through the Texas Panhandle. At the Irish Inn, the breakfast was served at a little diner out in back that was affiliated with the motel; when we were there, it was primarily a locals-only situation, as opposed to the motel, which was host to outsiders. Paying for a room at the Irish Inn allowed for toast and coffee in the diner, but we paid extra for the hot cinnamon rolls that were covered with syrupy sugar and simultaneously threatened our health and enervated us on an otherwise gray cross-country Texas Panhandle day. Then there was the restaurant connected to the motel in Idaho's section of the Bitterroot Mountains, just off I-90, where unbelievably I once had fresh brook trout and scrambled eggs.

As for myself, I prefer the separate breakfast area, such as is often featured at the typical Holiday Inn Express, such as the one we are breakfasting in this morning. In fact, part of the reason that I had been impressed with the Holiday Inn Express in Montana, which is where I last stayed in a Holiday Inn Express, was the breakfast area.

A SHORT DIGRESSION ON MEETING FELLOW
TRAVELERS IN A BREAKFAST AREA

IN THE BREAKFAST AREAS OF AMERICA at any given moment, there are people who are anxious for an early-morning conversation in the breakfast area, and there are people who are not. I fall into the former category, as you will by now have imagined—often embarrassingly so, as far as my family members are concerned. Once in a while, though, I meet someone who wants to talk more than me, amazing my family, as well as myself. Modern-day roadside pal-ship! The last time this happened was in Rawlins, Wyoming, at the Travelodge operated by Raj and Anila Patel and their family. The Travelodge was on Spruce Street, a road in a treeless, desertlike part of town, backed up against a small hill. The motel was adjacent to another hotel that had a large sign in front saying: AMERICAN OWNED, a sign that irritated me, as I recall. As I checked in, Raj noticed that I lived in New York. He seemed overjoyed. "You're from New York," he said. "I love New York. I love Chicago. I love L.A. I love the big cities."

"Then why are you in Wyoming?" I asked him. Wyoming, by the way, is the least densely populated state, the opposite of a big city.

"For a job," he said, "but next year, maybe my son will take over. Maybe my wife and I will go to L.A." He ran my credit card. "We'll see," he continued.

We had checked in late, and Raj, upon hearing me say that I had two children, was eager for a chance to impress the children by putting us in a room that was decorated with the Travelodge sleepy bear, a marketing icon I knew to be derived from the state flag of California, where the Travelodge company had begun. "I have the perfect room for you," Raj said. "The kids will love it." He was shaking his head. "Oh, you will see how the kids will love this room," he added.

This was not too long ago. Neither of the kids were young enough to be impressed with the sleepy bear motif per se. But the room was profusely decorated with sleepy bears and, thus, the children were entertained, in a way that perhaps Raj had not intended but worked out being great—a kind gesture.

Early the next morning, we headed to the breakfast area, a separate room

to the side of the lobby, all of us high on Travelodge sleepy bears. A family—
a man and a woman and their seventeen- or eighteen-year-old son—was already partaking in the breakfast area foods, coffee, juices, cereal in bins, and
breads of similar color for toasting, the mother at one table, the father and
son at the other. In an effort to break the breakfast area conversational ice,
the father made a general observation. "Ah, the smell of burnt toast!" he
said.

Everyone nodded, giggled, *mmmm*-ed. Liberated, the father proceeded to
ask us where we were headed and, after our brief response, told us of his trip
from Vancouver, Washington, back to Detroit, Michigan, returning home after a cruise to Alaska. The father was dressed in gray khaki shorts and a blue
T-shirt, and he had a mustache and shaggy graying hair. His son was dressed
in JNCO jeans, large baggy jeans designed to be worn down low, the crotch
at the knees. His son also wore a ribbed tank top, and a blue silk button-down
shirt that was not buttoned and was decorated with Asian-esque dragons; his
hair was short and bleached blond. The mother was eating a pastry at another
table, not saying much, in khaki shorts and a plain T-shirt. The son looked as
if he were asleep over his cereal, until his father talked about the cruise, at
which point the son jolted to life.

"We had one woman," the father explained, "and she came up to our table
and she said, 'Do you dance?' And then my son, next thing you knew, he was
dancing up a storm."

A broad smile spread across the face of the son.

"This woman," the father went on, "she said, 'Do you dance *salsa*?'" The
father made a salsa motion. The son leaned toward us across his small breakfast area table.

"I said, 'No,'" the son piped in.

The father continued speaking for the woman on the cruise ship. "Do you
want to *learn*?"

The son was beaming now. The son nodded.

"And so he danced with a senator's daughter," the father said. The father
looked at his son and then at us, the father now folding his arms. "That's
right, it turned out she was a senator's daughter!"

The father then explained that he and his wife were taking his son back to
Michigan, where they would see the son's daughter—and when the father said

that his son, who again was somewhere around eighteen, had a daughter, I saw my own daughter's eyes widen.

I nodded. I was happy to hear about the father's cross-country trip, even at six thirty in the morning; I felt like I was an explorer at a trading post swapping wilderness tales. Our children were nodding too as they sipped the watery juice and poured cereal. My wife was quietly toasting an English muffin.

The father, who seemed to have felt he'd established a rapport with us, which he had, began discussing the local prison; the breakfast area silence was unbearable for him, something I can understand, and his family, the people who were about to get in a minivan with him for at least a day, did not seem to have anything to say to him at that time.

"So, have you guys been to the prison yet?" he asked.

I wasn't certain if he was waiting for an answer. "No," I finally said.

"Well, we were at McDonald's last night, and I saw a sign that said 'Prison' and I thought, 'Wow! We have to go.' And we did, and it's a whole prison right there."

At this, the man's wife spoke up for the first and only time, as best I can remember. "You can go in it," she said.

The man looked away from me and over at his wife and paused for a second, and then nodded, finally looking back at me. "So then, when we were paying," he said, "I asked the lady at McDonald's if she had any half-price vouchers, and she said, 'I sure do!' And she handed me these half-price vouchers for the Six Flags Amusement Park in Denver. So we're on our way to Denver now with these vouchers."

To me, getting a bunch of half-price vouchers and just driving away to experience Six Flags seemed like a twenty-first-century American equivalent of Jack Kerouac going where the jazzed-up wind blew him, or of Emily Post taking a town as it came to her, or of Woody Guthrie boxcar-ing it, or just taking it.

I toasted the man in the breakfast area with my coffee cup and later lauded him in the car, though my daughter was focusing on his son, on the fact that the father's *son* was a father. "Remember when he said that his son who danced with the senator's daughter had a child?" my daughter said. "When I heard that, I was like, *What?*"

MY BREAKFAST IN THE BREAKFAST AREA

IN BELOIT THIS MORNING, breakfast area lightning is striking in the same motel chain twice in that there is a separate breakfast area. I drink pretty good coffee out of a fancy carafe. I eat a fine unmemorable pastry, as well as a bowl of cereal and a banana. I drink not-so-watery juice. The chain's breakfast area presentation, however, had been revamped since I last partook in it. It had been revamped, repackaged, and even reconceptualized. It was now called the Express Start® Breakfast Bar, and marketed with this as the thematic underpinning: "Quite possibly, the most rewarding experience you will have all day."

Holiday Inn Express, by the way, is the fastest-growing motel chain in the United States at the time we are staying there, and each and every location in North America is reported by the company to have a revamped breakfast area that, like this one, is a wall of breakfast stylings—stylings that I soon realize are, at the risk of sounding repetitive, streamlined: before a faux-wood backdrop decorated with handmade-looking drawings of muffins and fruit, the hard-boiled eggs sat beneath a plastic dome, the platters on varying levels of tall plastic stands displayed fruit advertised like exotic dancers in a futuristic strip club.

The cinnamon roll is described in the Holiday Inn Express literature as follows: "Arguably the best cinnamon roll this world has witnessed." In reality, the cinnamon roll is fine. I would call up the company later, when I got home, and though I could not convince anyone to call me back to discuss the breakfast bar, I read that every Holiday Inn Express breakfast bar in North America had been redesigned in order to present, in the words of a press release that I managed to find, "a refreshing, inviting breakfast experience to welcome any day." I learned as well that Holiday Inn Express had—in the tradition of motels teaming up with home product makers to sell home products to people who stay in motels—teamed up with Kohler, the plumbing supply company, to feature Kohler showerheads that were being marketed as shower heads exceptionally good at keeping you smart in the morning, exceptional smartness being something that I neither noticed nor felt after staying up late watching TV with coffee surging through my veins. The showerheads were called Stay Smart showerheads. The idea of being smart after using the showerheads was described by Holiday Inn Express as "the SimplySmart™ guest bath initiative."

AFTER BREAKFASTING, I exited the breakfast area and entered the front desk area to check out and, while doing so, learned from the motel staff that this particular motel had only recently become a Holiday Inn Express motel; it had been another motel entirely when it first opened, which was, they estimated, about twenty or so years before. Even more recent was the Express Start Breakfast Bar, which, when it had been brought in, necessitated the staff to throw out all of its old breakfast area china. As they were telling me this, I turned and looked over the lobby and suddenly realized that it was filled with charming old furniture, unstreamlined, untrademarked.

I also learned from the staff that the Angel Museum, the world's largest angel museum, which houses six thousand angels, including five hundred black angels donated by Oprah Winfrey, the television talk show host, was nearby. The museum, according to promotional information, "emphasizes angels as symbols for what is joyful, noble, and good." The museum, the museum's promotional information adds, "refrains from promoting religion or a theology of angels." Hearing about the museum reminded me of the *Wizard of Oz* museum we visited once in Indiana, where a gathering of the actors who played munchkins had been scheduled for two weeks before and then cancelled—our road memories are both entirely distinct and part of one long trip.

Just a few seconds after I learned about the Angel Museum, I heard a commotion. I turned and suddenly realized that there had been some kind of an incident, though I could not determine what kind exactly. In the space of a few more seconds, I scanned the lobby *and* breakfast area for our children and noticed them standing near a large empty birdcage alongside the CNN-playing TV. (I had become separated from my family during the breakfast area experience—they presumably moved on when I was sketching the breakfast bar.) I also noticed motel staff people running around the lobby and heading quickly toward the breakfast area. There was a franticness in the air, and as my wife and I reunited with our children, we determined that essentially everything was OK, even though something had obviously happened.

THE INCIDENT NEAR THE BREAKFAST AREA, IN RETROSPECT

BREAKFASTED, WE ARE IN THE CAR, pulling out of the motel parking lot, driving away from Beloit, thinking we are pulling out of the last motel parking lot we will pull out of before we get home. I gulp, considering how many miles we have to go, considering about 930 miles, thinking that in the old days it would have been no problem to drive 930 miles. Now, as I am driving again, as I am back on the interstate, as I take a deep breath in hopes that the coffee will soon take effect since I am feeling kind of out of it, kind of wasted away, I interrogate our son and daughter regarding the above-mentioned incident in the breakfast area:

DAUGHTER: I saw the parrot and I went over to the parrot, and [her brother] went over too.

SON: I was standing near the parrot looking at the parrot. We said "Hello" to the parrot.

DAUGHTER: The people at the motel were telling us to say hello to the parrot. It was sitting on top of its cage and we said "Hello," and it was saying "Hello" back.

SON: It was able to speak. We thought it was pretty funny.

FATHER: But you weren't touching the parrot, were you?

DAUGHTER: No.

FATHER: Were you bothering the parrot?

SON: No, we weren't *bothering* the parrot.

FATHER: Where were you when the incident happened?

SON: All I know is I wasn't in front of the parrot when it flew, because I remember turning around and seeing everything being knocked over. I saw the express check-in sign being knocked over, some sort of sign.

DAUGHTER: We had stopped speaking to the parrot by then.

SON: And the people at the motel were saying, "It's never done that before." I remember being confused as to what happened.

DAUGHTER: The woman ran around and started chasing the parrot.

SON: I think I stepped to the side.

THE FACE OF THE COUNTRY

AS WE ENTER THE CHICAGO AREA, an area spiderwebbed with interstate highways, I would like to reiterate that the interstates were supposed to skip the cities, to go around them, à la the German autobahn—that's the way that President Dwight Eisenhower, for whom the Dwight D. Eisenhower National System of Interstate and Defense Highways is named, apparently thought they were going to go. The old general was a detached executive and apparently never bothered to look at the maps in the manual passed out to Congress. Thus, to coarsely summarize the history of America in the sixties and seventies, with regards to its roads—to summarize, that is, in the manner of an interstate, which races by, disregarding the details of the landscape, the nuances of the place that it alters: the interstates moved into the cities and people in the cities drove off to the newly developing suburbs, which formed a ring around the cities, an ever-widening circle, sometimes referred to by planners as a dough-nut. In cities in the southern states and in California, the so-called Sunbelt, the suburbs were like desert flowers after a long rain, the suburbs blossoming with the arrival of the interstates. Suburbs themselves became huge new cities, though they did not look like the old cities in that they were based on people driving long distances in a car, as opposed to the old cities, which were based on people walking. At the same time that the cities of the Midwest and the East declined, in the Sunbelt, populations increased. It was as if a heart surgeon operated on the United States and executed bypass after bypass so that America's automotive blood, the traveling habits of the masses, the everyday human movement of America was rerouted and changed forever. Today, thanks to the interstates, Phoenix continues to develop its land at a rate of 1.2 acres per hour. Atlanta—its development nourished by the flow of I-20, I-85, I-75, I-16, and I-185—is suburb upon suburb: it is said by real estate developers that Atlanta is the fastest-growing human settlement in the history of human settlements.

IN HIS MEMOIR, *MANDATE FOR CHANGE*, President Eisenhower used the statistic that is religiously repeated in various books and articles and reports on the interstate: "The amount of concrete poured to form these roadways would build eighty Hoover Dams or six sidewalks to the moon. To build them, bulldozers and shovels would move enough dirt and rock to bury all of Connecticut two feet deep." The construction of the highway is equated with a moon project, with a voyage of discovery, like the Lewis and Clark expedition. The statistic that I see as more emblematic of the interstates' effect on the country is a statistic that is not nearly as dramatic, and might even seem unrelated. It is completely unexciting and banal and, in fact, perhaps even dangerous to ponder while attempting to stay awake on a long trip across the country. It is this: 7.5 percent. That is the percentage that Congress used when it changed the Internal Revenue Code in 1954 in hopes of spurring short-term construction—that is the statistic that, combined with the 1956 Federal-Aid Highway Act, made for America's face-lift.

Seven and a half percent meant that builders could write off buildings quickly, and thus more quickly begin accruing profits. The impetus in the

construction industry was put on building strip malls and inexpensively constructed regular malls and office buildings that were put up quickly on cheap
but accessible land, the land along the brand-new interstates. In turn, construction workers were, in the words of one historian, "de-skilled." The original owners of these cheaply constructed buildings then quickly sold the
buildings to new owners who quickly depreciated them—and were not economically interested in maintaining them. Subsequently, buildings were
abandoned, depreciated beyond any value at all. In the book *God's Own Junkyard*, the muckraking architect Peter Blake wrote: "All of a sudden an owner
was rewarded for selling out fast!" This government-mandated quick fix combined with the federal interstate project for statistically unexciting but quietly
dramatic effect. Mom-and-pop motels and restaurants did not benefit from
the tax change and, as a result, were replaced by Holiday Inns and McDonald's. The number of motels increased 50 percent in four years; a *Fortune*
magazine report compared the cheap real estate boom to a gold rush. "We are
not basically in the food business," said Harry Sonneborn, the partner of Ray
Kroc, McDonald's founder. "We are in the real estate business. The only reason we sell hamburgers is because they are the greatest producer of revenue
from which our tenants can pay us rent." At one point human settlements
were determined by proximity to food, to geological shelter, to the flow of
rivers. In the sixties, human developers began to build buildings outside of
the suburbs, on the unzoned edges of towns or in the unincorporated areas
where people were passing through but not necessarily stopping—especially
where there were interstates. It was a recipe for entropy.*

A half a century after the system was begun we see a new face on the country, a face that people who knew the face of the country fifty years ago probably would not recognize, even in Chicago, the place toward which we are
headed, the place that will dominate our view as the Impala crosses its roads

---

* It all created what Dolores Hayden, a landscape historian, has described as "edge nodes," those
places that are not near places and that characterize the view that we see today, now, on the road.
It was in the sixties that venture capitalists began to invest in cheap, quickly depreciating, poorly
built developments, an investment strategy that eventually cost the federal government a billion
dollars a year in tax losses by the time the 1970s arrived. The *Wall Street Journal* praised the phenomenon as "Profits in Loss." The interstate was encouraging business to move on. Thus, one
can think of the interstate as a coast-to-coast public works project or as the creator of state-
economy-sized piles of public debt.

during rush hour this morning. In the seventies and through to today, Chicago's population declined, while in the greater Chicago area between 1970 and 1990, land was developed for homes eleven times faster than the population increased. Land was developed for businesses eighteen times faster than the population grew. Commercial and industrial sites increased by 11 percent.

A statement that was understating all this, a statement that I think of as we pass the Dodge Neon manufacturing plant on I-90 (it used to manufacture the now-phased-out Dodge Dynasty and the Chrysler New Yorker) and that I will think of as we pass the completely disused factories we will see sporadically in the ring in between downtown Chicago and the suburbs of Chicago, was made by Bertram Tallamy, the highway builder: "Anyone who travels is aware that in building a new national highway system we are reworking the face of the country."

DRIVING IN THE EAST VS. DRIVING IN THE WEST

WHEN WE ENTER AND PASS through the area of Rockford, Illinois, we are in the gravitational pull of the interstates of Chicago, the crisscrossing knot of the interstate system in America. We are coming into superhighway country—into the often corroded road weavings that knit the Midwest and the East, that bind it up with these great concrete strips. In the West, we drove along the extremities of the interstate, its faraway and not-so-crowded limbs; in the West we drove through the vast land of one and only one road. Many writers have described the West in terms of aridity—most famously, John Wesley Powell, Walter Prescott Webb, and Wallace Stegner. Today, I would describe it in terms of relative lack of roads in respect to overall land area—though, due to the nature of interstates, that is changing.

In the West, little pockets of chain restaurants and chain motels and chain convenience stores selling food and gas pop up in exit-anchored patches of commerce; they are like the old railroad towns of the West, set up to handle a crew of workers or a new station and its anticipated passers-through, and they are exceptions to the vista of farms and grazing land and mines and mountains.

There, the interstate races across the country. Here, the pockets are the rule; the pockets are everywhere. It is as if the Midwest and much of the East and huge patches of the South—not to mention Eastlike western areas such as Salt Lake City and Las Vegas and much of the area between Denver and Colorado Springs—have become a highway exit writ large.

THIS MORNING WE ARE HEADING TOWARD or away from or crossing or sometimes utilizing, knowingly or not, the interstates numbered 90, 290, 294, 94, 88, 57, 355, and combinations thereof, and we sense a change in interstate demeanor immediately. No longer do we pass a driver alone or with one or two other passengers on a highway in the middle of an empty interstate at, say, ten in the morning. No longer do we note the farawayness, relatively speaking, of his or her license plates and then proceed to exchange gestures of greeting, gestures indicating that we are both cognizant of the extent of our respective trips. Cars and their license plates are like fish tagged by scientists for the purpose of studying their migration, and when we were in the West, we were crossing the country amid fish that lived locally and fish that traveled out to sea and eventually returned, like migrating Pacific salmon. Now we are traveling among huge populations of fish that swim back and forth in a confined area or just in circles on what is either a big work-proscribed lake or a small one, depending on how you look at it. We are crossing the country in the midst of traffic.

OVER THE ROAD

WHEN I LOOK AHEAD AT I-90, it is as if I am in the road, as if the road has swallowed me whole, the sound of the pack on the roof of the car now starting up, moaning, howling, wailing. My wife leans back in the passenger seat, sighs, shuts her eyes, exhausted from the logistics of bag packing, searching, lugging, of coordinating our every move. Thus, it is perhaps not surprising that I initially do not see the newly renovated service area on the North-West Tollway, or Illinois Tollway, a toll road financed, unlike most of the interstate system, through tolls. Federal interstate highway regulations prohibit commercial development of an interstate rest area, but it is OK to commercially develop a rest area on a toll road, and so this morning, excited to see this new service area design, excited, in fact, to see the first service area in this eastward march across the continent, I take the next exit, a nearby, no-big-deal turnaround, and pull into the newly yellow-striped parking lot, the drive-through restaurant not even open yet, and see the newly reopened Belvidere Travel Oasis.* As a native easterner, service areas remind me of home, not to mention my fast-food-on-the-road youth, the little gas stations built into the first parkways, the old service plazas on the New York State Thruway, the Massachusetts Turnpike with restrooms the size of the little house I grew up in: the clock in my head is rewinding as I hereby U-turn.

It is an over-the-road service area, designed in what is touted as stream-lined steel and glass, as opposed to the old concrete over-the-highway service area that I used to drive beneath while fearing its collapse. Inside, the service area is bright and shiny and people are walking in smiling and walking out with boxes of doughnuts and smiling even more, or so it seems to me as I enter, also smiling, excited for the newness: the frisson of the marble floors, the suspended-over-the-highway glass and steel, turning myself in a way that is in spirit like Julie Andrews's turning on top of the Alps in the opening of *The Sound of Music*, though without her style. People are lined up at the service area's McDonald's, lined up for espresso drinks, lined up for more doughnuts. People are not lined up at all for the Massage-a-Minute station. In the very middle of the place, there is a small child absorbed, like me, in the view from the over-the-highway service area. It is the view of a highway god, the view of an ancient poet on a mountaintop, the view into a flat gray-skied infinity, a view that hovers over the coming-and-going cars, that sees off into the for-ever kingdom of the east- and west-running river:

> A road, a stream of Illinois plates,
> Split: which way
> Is home?

---

* Toll roads being the most limited of limited-access roads, the rest areas on toll roads generally include services. But it does not always work the other way around. To wit, a service area is a rest stop but a rest stop is not a service area.

GO

SPEED, GET THERE, MOVE, GO, even though it seems as if you are not getting anywhere—don't let up on the pedal, don't relax, and then, the next thing you know, you've slipped from 65 to 70 m.p.h. or worse, something that is especially likely to happen in a rental car, in a car with an engine that actually works. You can't use cruise control. Your wife is against it for whatever reason that you do not understand, though it could be because you have those moments when you pull up behind a car and can't remember how to turn the cruise control off and end up suddenly hitting the brakes (*"You know I don't like cruise control . . ."*). Also, there are just too many people driving in the left lane, as usual, as is always the case crossing the country. The entire nation is passing; no one considers themselves "slower traffic." Ahead we see an overhead electronic sign, blinking, warning, indicating, in its words, TWENTY THREE MINUTES TO O'HARE TOLL. This must mean something to some of the cars that surround us, that pass us or that we pass, but means nothing to us— we are commuters in the grandest American sense, wagon train commuters, stagecoach followers, riding in the round-trip dust of Lewis and Clark.

NOW, SOMEWHERE NEAR THE MUNICIPALITY OF HOFFMAN ESTATES, I notice farm fields, or former farm fields, as well as farm fields that appear to be transitioning to former farm fields—fields once occupied by vegetables that might have been eaten by people in the area, fields that are being eaten up by houses, home developments, in addition to fields that are obviously old garbage dumps. Thus we witness the blooming of an edge city (so named by Joel Garreau, a writer who trademarked the term), and an edge city is an area that is not an old-style city with a downtown and not an old-fashioned garden suburb of the kind developed directly after World War II but a concentration of business offices and malls that grew out of a suburb or a rural area. It is sometimes defined also as the twentieth-century urban form, the model that all future cities will resemble. From here, we are very close to the giant shopping mall well marked on our map, the Woodfield Mall, the second-largest mall in America. From here, I know (from checking an Environmental Protection Agency map) that we are near the dozens of hazardous waste sites that sit at the intersection of I-90 and I-290 and that I cannot see. We can't see the

hazardous waste sites but we can see the crafted-from-the-earth sign that announces Prairie Stone, an environmentally sensitive business park that is,
from what I understand, the root of a lot of the area's local traffic problems,
problems that Prairie Stone is working on.

DEVELOPMENTS WITH NEW HOMES, developments with new office buildings, developments developing all along the highway, almost always with titles,
names. Meanwhile, hotels grow in size the closer we get to O'Hare airport. The
sky is now jet-streaked, landing gear deployed. The Hilton is really tall. The
Hampton Suites is really, really tall. The first corporate offices that we see on
our east-bound expedition act new, act oblivious to us, act as if they know something we don't, and could care less about what we know. The stories and stories
of glass on the corporate office windows reflect the low ceiling of gray clouds.

JUST PAST INTERSTATE 290, we see a medieval castle that we know to be
Medieval Times, a chain of Medieval-style restaurants that offers people an
opportunity to relax in a faux-Medieval setting and eat as people joust—a
chain that we have seen near airport-approximate interstates. The concrete
castle is beautiful, in a way, a spot of bland decoration in the monotony of
corporate headquarters.

A SIGN SAYS, 10 MINUTES TO O'HARE TOLL, and it is as if the buildings
themselves were racing to catch a plane, the pace of roadside corporate parks
picks up—big corporate parks for big corporations, bigger, taller, more expansive, and just plain *more*. A giant electronic McDonald's sign seems to say
something that I cannot read without swerving. Behind the giant McDonald's
sign is a hill that on second look is clearly waste, piled-up and grass-covered,
a garbage dump serenaded by advertising.

WE PASS ANOTHER OVER-THE-ROAD travel oasis that is under construction but will one day sell the same boxes of doughnuts to passengers in this
area of their trip across the country or, more likely, this portion of their
morning commute. We also pass our first limousine just before that travel oasis;
eighteen lanes, by my count, at the Irving Toll Plaza; another giant billboard
advertising a television program on the life of Evel Knievel; an erotic dancer
club and, right on cue, the strategic response of the not-so-erotic: JUST GIVE ME

JESUS, the sign says. I see a vista of signs that advertise the following: banking, beer, sex, a casino, more sex, and outlet shopping. Meanwhile, the speed limit is 55 m.p.h. I'm doing 70. I think my wife is not noticing. And yet everyone is going faster than me, as if they were racing.

CANNONBALL

IN BETWEEN THE TIME that the interstates were begun and the time that they were nearly finished, there was a last-ditch, underground effort to use the public roads for sport—indeed to turn highway driving into a sport, which, if you will recall, is how driving started out: not as something that anyone did to commute to work or to the market or because there just wasn't any other way to get there but as something that was fun. The Cannonball Run was created one day in 1971, a time when maps that you got at gas stations showed some interstates and then some interstates that were still dotted lines, still proposed. It was the day that Brock Yates, an editor at *Car and Driver* magazine, was walking to lunch at Brew's Pub on Thirty-fourth Street in New York City and, according to his own account, had the following thought: "Why the hell not run a race across the United States? A balls-out, shoot-the-moon, fuck-the-establishment rumble from New York to Los Angeles to prove what we had been harping about for years, for example, that good drivers in good automobiles could employ the American Interstate system the same way the Germans were using the autobahns? Yes, make high-speed travel by car a reality! Truth and justice affirmed by an overtly illegal act."

Yates named the race the Cannonball Baker Sea-to-Shining-Sea Memorial Trophy Dash in honor of Erwin George "Cannon Ball" Baker, who had beat the train from New York to Chicago in 1928, and in 1933 driven solo across the country in fifty-three-and-a-half hours, on roads that were paved and roads that were not. The rules consisted of no rules; contestants clocked out of the Red Ball parking garage, on Thirty-second Street, where *Car and Driver* kept its test fleet, and then clocked in at the Portofino Inn, a racers' hangout in Redondo Beach, California. For the first run, which he did without competition, Yates solicited two other drivers and a mechanic—Steve Smith, Jim Williams, and Chuck Kreuger. (He also solicited Robert Redford, who, according to a report that the Cannonball racers had read in *Rolling Stone* magazine, liked to drive really fast and indeed wanted to take part in the race but had to drop out at the last minute due to scheduling.) Yates also brought along his fourteen-year-old son, to watch for police.

Yates took off on May 3, 1971, in a 1971 Dodge Custom Sportsman van, with a 360-inch, 225-horsepower V-8 engine, dubbed Moon Trash II. It was outfitted with bucket seats; mag wheels; a roll of super tape; eight quarts of oil; a refrigerator; an early radar detector, which failed to detect police but detected dozens of high-power transmission lines; a sleeping bag; a foam mattress; a folding chair; a fire extinguisher; twenty-seven McIntosh apples; thirty-six Mounds bars; four Hershey bars; thirty-two garbage bags; twelve packets of Vivarin; twelve packets of Dentyne; two pounds of Jarlsberg cheese; and a roll of paper towels. The route of Moon Trash II roughly followed the Pennsylvania Turnpike, then, from Saint Louis, used as much of the still-unfinished interstate as possible.

Setting out through the Lincoln Tunnel, Moon Trash II averaged 70 miles an hour and entered the Pennsylvania Turnpike at 2:55 A.M. The team ran out of gas while trying to pass a truck on a two-lane road in Illinois. At 2:15 the next afternoon they crossed the Mississippi. They crossed Oklahoma going 90 miles an hour. Due to poor gas mileage—about three miles per gallon—they were stopping for gas a lot, though trying to make the trip in 40 hours. They crossed the California border cruising but then slowed down when they hit suburban sprawl in the desert, and then had to toss their apples before hitting the fruit inspection station at Needles, California—drivers behind them swerved to miss the fruit as it was squeezed out the small front vent windows that no longer exist in cars but that I loved for their ability to blow a little wind in your face (they had mostly eaten candy bars).

Moon Trash II pulled into Redondo Beach in 40 hours and 51 minutes, after driving 2,858 miles at an average speed of 70 and using 314 gallons of gas. Disappointed, they were convinced that the key to success lay in fewer, quicker stops and a better route. In his subsequent *Car and Driver* column, Yates described the run as "the first demonstration that some people are aware enough to handle their own destinies behind the wheel of an automobile."

"The other guys in the automotive press can sit around and recommend letter writing to your congressman," he continued, "but I've had it. From here on in, I am going to use the road according to my own skills and capabilities and not in conformity with a 49-year-old, cradle-to-grave, square-head bureaucrat who wouldn't know a good automobile if it ran over him," he said.

Yates saw the race in terms of resistance to authoritarianism, the interstate being a kind of rule. (In 1994, the landscape historian John Brinkerhoff Jackson, wrote, "Even during the 1992 Los Angeles riots the red traffic lights were respected: they represented an order transcending the political or economic order.") Yates was arguing that the interstates were not offering freedom but were closing us down, restricting us, restraining individual drivers so that they would stay with the rule-obeying herd. In closing his column he quoted Alexis de Toqueville's *Democracy in America*: "This sacrificing of rights becomes an indiscriminate passion and the members of the community are apt to conceive a most inordinate devotion to order."

THE NEXT YEAR, MORE DRIVERS SHOWED up to race, including an amateur sports car racer named Oscar Kovaleski, a professional driver named Tony Adamowicz, and a publicist named Brad Niemcek. Kovaleski, Adamowicz, and Niemcek drove a van filled with auxiliary gas tanks and, on the labels of their flame-retardant uniforms, announced themselves as the Polish Racing Drivers of America. They sent a telegram to Brock Yates announcing their challenge: "If we can find California, we'll beat you fair and square." A stock car driver showed up in a rented motor home with four other people inside. "We don't expect to beat all your guys, but we'll set a record for motor homes," one of its inhabitants said. A lawyer from Massachusetts found a car at the last minute in the classified section of the *New York Times*, a so-called drive-away—i.e., a car that the owner wanted transported from the East Coast to the West Coast, and thus the driver had to pay only expenses for the trip. In this case the car was a brand-new Cadillac Seville.

This time, Yates drove a Ferrari coupe—a 365 GTB/4, which was at the time considered to be the fastest road car ever built; he found a professional racer to drive it, Dan Gurney, one of only five American drivers to win a Formula One Grand Prix. Initially, Gurney demurred, citing lucrative promotional deals, but a day before the race, Gurney accepted the offer, saying, first, that his wife's father, who was dying at the time, asked Gurney what he had to lose and, second, that he had happened to read an essay by Ayn Rand titled "Moratorium on Brains." "So I said, to hell with it and decided to come," Gurney said.

Gurney and Yates drove I-80 west, across Pennsylvania, cut south through Columbus, Ohio. They drove 95 miles an hour starting out; Yates argued that the absence of speed limits in Europe meant that European cars were better engineered for faster speeds. In the Allegheny Moutains in Pennsylvania, a guy in his twenties passed them in a Camaro doing 100 miles an hour. Gurney let him pass at first and then went and passed him, Gurney exclaiming, "That's one fifty, just as steady as you please." Yates reported that Gurney's eyes were incredible, spotting highway patrolmen miles ahead and then, as Yates wrote, "falling obediently into his wake at 65 m.p.h." They hit ice in the mountains of Arizona and were passed by the three guys in the drive-away Cadillac Seville. "Our cockiness of a few miles back had given way to despair," Yates later recalled. Near Flagstaff the road was smooth but they could not drive over 125 miles an hour at night without outrunning the range of their headlights. They took a shortcut through Prescott National Forest, Gurney smoothly executing switchback after switchback. After they raced through Quartzite, Arizona, a cop chased them at 120 m.p.h.; they pulled over at a gas station where the cop, angry and wearing a helmet, gave Gurney a ninety-dollar ticket. "How fast does this thing go?" the cop asked them. To answer the question, Gurney took the engine up to 172 m.p.h. when they pulled away from the cop. They made the last 130 miles in under two hours, Yates watching out the back as Gurney cruised smoothly in and out of Los Angeles traffic. They punched in at the front desk of the Portofino Inn having driven 2,950 miles in 35 hours and 54 minutes. They were greeted by two reporters from the local paper, the *Daily Breeze*, and by Miss Redondo Beach. People thought Gurney was kidding when he later told the *Los Angeles Times* that they hadn't exceeded 175 miles an hour. The Polish Racing Drivers of America finished second, having stopped only once for gas. The new Cadillac Seville finished third, with five speeding tickets.

THE RACE WENT ON FOR A FEW MORE YEARS. "Seemingly every sports car nut, hot rodder, closet anarchist, and general Hell-raiser in the nation was ready to run if another race was organized," Yates wrote. In 1973, there were thirty-four entries, including writers for *Hot Rod*, the archrival of *Car and Driver*, who filled the back of an AMC Hornet with auxiliary gas tanks, and a stretch Cadillac limousine run by three women calling themselves the Right

Bra Racing Team, who turned the car over in Texas, totaling the car but only breaking the arm of one driver, a racer named Donna Mae Mims, who arrived at the emergency room colored blue from the portable toilet unit spill during the crash. The Flying Fathers were three men dressed as priests in order to win the sympathy of the police. Subsequent races included George Willig, the man who climbed the World Trade Center in New York, three guys in a government vehicle with Geiger counters that scared gas station workers in the area of the Three Mile Island nuclear power plant, and Hal Needham, who had directed *Cannonball Run*, a film based on the race. Needham drove an ambulance with Brock Yates. Pamela Yates, Brock Yates's second wife, lay on a stretcher in the back. Police stopped the ambulance on I-80 in New Jersey; a racer disguised as a doctor sat next to her, administering a fake IV unit.

"Why can't you fly her?" one cop asked alongside the road.

"She has a rare disease involving tiny lesions on the linings of her lungs," the fake doctor said. "She cannot survive in a pressured airplane."

The cops let the ambulance go.

The race stopped when the oil crisis made gas expensive.

"The secret route remains to be discovered," Yates wrote.

Years later, one Cannonball racer said: "I have had many people over the years say to me, 'Man, that sounds like great fun. Next time you run the Cannonball, I would sure like to drive with you.' My standard answer to them is, 'If you think you would really like to do that, I'd like for you to pick a weekend and sit in your car in the driveway. Don't drive it anywhere; don't run 120 miles per hour; just go sit in your car for 32 hours and 51 minutes. When you get out, call me and tell me if you think you would still like to run the Cannonball.'"

SLOW DOWN

MY SPEED IS SLOWLY INCREASING OUTSIDE CHICAGO. My speed is increasing when I stumble, jerk the car the slightest, littlest bit, so that my wife sewing peacefully in the drone of the ever-screaming expensive pack on top of the car, looks up, looks at the horizon, sees the traffic still passing but less so, strains to see the speedometer, suggests I slow down. "Could you slow down, please?" is how she puts it. Somewhat reluctantly, I do, and then a minute later, we see an Illinois state police car pull over a driver, the police car an unmarked Impala.

A vast billboard appears, offering a phone number: DATING OVER 40? WE NEED YOU . . .

And now, looking around I perceive that we are in Chicago. We see the cluster of tall buildings that are Chicago's downtown. On a previous cross-country trip by train, we stopped at the downtown train station and spent the day in Chicago—visiting the museum, buying fruit at a farmers market near the train station, eating a Polish sausage, having a great time. But today, though the interstate runs right through downtown, seeing Chicago from far away will be the extent of our Chicago experience. We're in a car! We're doing the speed limit, or maybe a little tiny bit better. *We're moving!*

WHERE WE ARE ON THE INTERSTATES

JUST AS ONE MIGHT WONDER if the cross-country trip described herein is really about over, as we are hoping it will be, so one might also wonder: is the interstate highway system finished? Originally, it was planned to be 41,000 miles long, and it was supposed to be completed in thirteen to fifteen years. By 1992, the interstate system was planned to be 45,500 miles and it was nearly complete. And by 2002, it was designated as 42,793 miles and reported to have 2.5 miles under construction and 3 miles not yet under construction. In the Federal Highway Administration's official fiftieth anniversary of the interstate publication, titled *The Interstate Is 50: Linking the Power of the Past to the Promise of the Future*, the Federal Highway Administration uses the number 46,773.

When the interstate system is completed, if it is ever completed, it will have cost something along the lines of 115 billion dollars, more than four times what it was originally supposed to cost—and the cost of the interstates does not include the cost to the communities that were destroyed, the small businesses that were closed, the old parks and neighborhoods that were ruined, the row of old oak trees lining Claiborne Avenue in downtown New Orleans, a street that was home to many African American professionals, which became what *Time* magazine eventually called "a seedy strip." When they were proposed, the interstates were often mentioned as a civil defense tool, as a way of evacuating citizens quickly from large cities in the event of a nuclear attack, but an astounding aspect of the hurricane that all but wiped out New Orleans in 2005 was that the interstates ended up being a not terribly effective way of evacuating people from a city at all. This was true for many reasons, one of which was that a lot of people did not have and couldn't afford a car.

The last time I was in New Orleans, driving through on an interstate, I happened to notice the sound barriers along the interstate—those giant two- or sometimes three-story walls that line highways and are said to prevent interstate-related sounds from disrupting interstate-adjacent neighborhoods. In New Orleans, I noticed that they were decorated with palm trees. Some states don't decorate their sound barriers at all, but some do. In Connecticut, they are made of wood, sometimes painted green. In New Jersey along I-80, the sound barriers are concrete and the concrete is decorated with giant tad-polelike creatures. In New Mexico, the decorations are reminiscent of those of the Anasazi, though they are not Anasazi, I don't think. The decorations are afterthoughts, pallid attempts to mollify the effects of a plan that obviously needs mitigating in a much larger, less cosmetic way.

WATER

ASIDE FROM THE SPINDLE of skyscrapers in the center of Chicago, we see the water towers that mark the skyline here in the Chicago area and all around the middle part of the country, as we drive, drive, drive, as I get a cramp in my gas pedal foot, and put on the cruise control, and then take it off due to the number of fast- and slow-going cars surrounding me, due to the unavailability of an even cruising speed, due to the fact that my wife knows I turned it on. Water towers are more prominent than at any other point in our trip, as they advertise a town ("The Friendly Village") or in the case of the one shaped like a tee with a golf ball, a golf course.

We are just stopping for absolute necessities; we are not exiting at all today. We are staying on the highways, utilizing only highway service areas, using the cross-country routes as they were imagined, as speedways across the nation. Thus, we stop for restroom usage at a temporary service area, a service area that temporarily replaces the usual over-the-road service area, which is being renovated to resemble the last over-the-road service area we stopped at. Despite its temporary nature, there is an impressively vast selection of bottled waters and a sign outside the rest stop that shows a man smiling as bottled water is poured onto his face, as he is doused with bottled water. In a heightened state of water awareness, I buy a water. A woman leaves the temporary service area with a dog bowl, a soda, and a bottled water and pours the bottle of bottled water into the dog bowl.

SLOGANS

AS WE PASS THROUGH INTERSTATE CHICAGO; as we stop at another highway service area, also under construction; as we leave interstate Chicago, which turns into interstate Illinois, which is (as I mentioned) characterized by frequent water tower sightings; in these last few Illinois moments, after experiencing the state purely by interstate-following car, I note a slogan on a billboard, an inscription, and point it out to my wife, pointing things out to each other being something we have done since our very first long road trip, before we crossed the country, when we were just dating:

Right Here. Right Now—Illinois

Seeing this slogan causes me to recall other slogans I have seen and noted while crossing the country, words that seek each person as they enter or exit the state—usually via an interstate, but do not do that, obviously:

America Starts Here—Pennsylvania
More Than Meets the Eye—Carbon County, Wyoming
Gateway to the Future—Reynoldsburg, Ohio
You Haven't Seen Colorado Until You've Seen Seven Falls—near Trinidad,
New Mexico
The Gateway to Cranberry Country—Tomah, Wisconsin
Just Happy to Be Here—Laramie, Wyoming
The Good life—Nebraska

I can't get the Illinois slogan out of my head, even after we cross the border in a few minutes and enter Indiana. Given that we are still on the road and given that no matter how much we want it to, the road won't end, this particular slogan is akin to a mental jail sentence, such that I am tempted, as I enter Indiana, to abandon all hope for making it today:

*Right Here. Right Now.**

PORTAGE

THE PLACE WHERE I-80 AND I-90 MELD into one road is a place called Portage, a place where, as it happens, I tend to get lost. Why do I tend to get lost in the Portage area? How does a person crossing the country on interstate highways get lost anyway, given the seamless, streamlined nature of interstate driving, which, come to think of it, requires nothing physically arduous, requires no actual portaging? Maybe it is because I am on the two longest interstates at the same time: I-90 leads a driver from Seattle, Washing

---

* From the April 2000 press conference at which the governor of Illinois introduced the slogan "Right Here. Right Now": "Governor George H. Ryan today announced a new marketing campaign for Illinois that will initially promote the state's tourism industry. The integrated campaign will also be used to tout the state's business climate and quality of life. 'The new theme we've adopted for Illinois is 'Right Here. Right Now,' which I believe captures the energy and forward-looking vision that my administration has taken in addressing the challenges and opportunities facing our great state,' Ryan said."

ton, to Boston, Massachusetts, 3,020 miles, while I-80 takes you from San Francisco to Teaneck, New Jersey, 2,899 miles.* Maybe it's because with all these interstates, with all this driving, I just always end up getting a little confused, especially today when I keep thinking we are going to make it home and then recalculate and am not so certain. I stayed in Portage once, and I couldn't make it out; I could not get any kind of a feel for it. When I think of the name Portage, I think, of course, of Lewis and Clark at the Great Falls of the Missouri in Montana, where they portaged over sharp rocks and plants with thin moccasins, where they ditched their big boat, where Lewis pulled out a special, high-tech, collapsible iron boat he had had made especially for the trip, a boat that, as soon as he put it in the water, sank—a boat that reminds me of my pack, which is moaning along with us now, which is shredding. "I need not add that this circumstance mortified me not a little," Lewis wrote.

Some things I know about Portage are that it has always been a place in between places, even for the native tribes that traveled the area, such as the Potawatomi, Miami, and Illinois; that it was once called Twenty Mile Prairie, a reference to its distance from Michigan City; that it was used as a stagecoach path between Detroit and Fort Dearborn; that the very first business in the town is thought to have been a notorious halfway house known as Curley's Tavern; that after the railroad came and little villages sprang up, people living in Portage sold farm products to Chicago, continuing past the streetcars that people in Portage could take to nearby Gary and even to east Chicago and, during the world wars, out to the steel mills, some of which still remain; that in the fifties Portage filled with people looking for mill jobs, people from Kentucky, southern Illinois, and Indiana; that the town doubled in population in the sixties, with people buying up cheap plots of land, moving into trailer courts; that, with no zoning ordinances, there was no downtown; that the slogans and sayings

---

* I-73 from Emery to Greensboro, North Carolina, and I-97 from Annapolis to Baltimore, Maryland, both of which together add up to a little under 15 miles, are the two shortest interstates. The interstate that takes a cross-country driver through the most states would be I-95, which goes through Florida, Georgia, South Carolina, North Carolina, Virginia, Washington, D.C., Maryland, Delaware, Pennsylvania, New Jersey, New York, Connecticut, Rhode Island, Massachusetts, New Hampshire, and Maine. The states with the most interstate miles built within their borders are Texas and California, given that they are the SUVs of state size—3,233 miles and 2,455 miles, respectively. But close behind them, in terms of interstate mileage, are the states that we are heading into today on what even in the footnotes I am still optimistically referring to as our last day on the road: Illinois, with 2,169 miles; Pennsylvania, with 1,759; and Ohio, with 1,572 miles.

applied to the town by itself or by others, in rough chronological order of when they were used, are as follows: City of Destiny, City of Pride, Country Style Living with City Advantages, and, most recently, City on the Edge.

CHILD CARE

NOW, IN INDIANA, AFTER NOON, after nearly five hours of driving, we are in a moving field of full-blown traffic, traffic caused by construction, traffic that is guided by the long strips of waist-high concrete that are named for New Jersey—Jersey barriers. Jersey barriers are ubiquitous here on the combined interstates, 80 and 90, and line the lane to my left and right. If a naturalist were to land on our shores from a distant place, he or she would think of the roads and the Jersey barriers the way David Douglas thought of the fir trees and basalt ridges that mark the Pacific Northwest, the way the pine trees and rocky cliffs mark the coast of Maine, the way dwarfed pines mark the Jersey shore. The Jersey barrier is named for its state of invention, much the way the lesser-known California-style barrier and Texas guardrails are named for the states where they first became known.

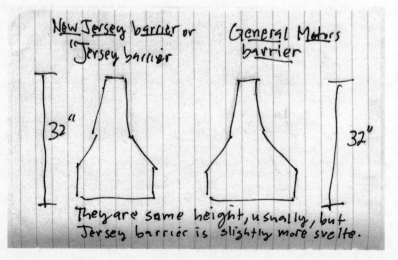

The Jersey barrier is a poured-concrete barrier that is anywhere from three to five feet tall and that is designed such that when a car's wheels hit the low-sloped bottom, the wheels turn back toward the driving lane, the car tilting up as its wheel rides the barrier, to minimize scraping. At higher car-impact speeds, the angles of the barrier are intended to cause the impacting car to be raised, the wheels denied friction from the road's surface, the car stopped. A truck that hits a Jersey barrier will proceed forward, its right or left wheel riding along the barrier for a time, until it is eventually redirected back to the lane, theoretically. Since the terrorist attacks on the United States, Jersey barriers have shown up in cities surrounding public buildings, are used as antiterrorism devices. This is a case of a piece of the interstate being used for defense, as originally proposed. Recently, however, public safety officials have reported that when a car hits a Jersey barrier at very high speed, it can shoot up and over it, soaring toward the building it is supposed to protect.

THE TRAFFIC THAT IS SURROUNDING ME (and is itself contained by miles of Jersey barriers) is intimidating from my point of view, the point of view of a guy coming into sixty-mile-an-hour-traffic from a two-thousand-mile place of no traffic at all—the point of view of a guy driving a little car as he passes large construction vehicles building the new interstate while the old interstate is still in use. Now, we're on one half of a half-dismantled bridge, the other half of the bridge dangling over us from a crane as we pass in a sixty-mile-an-hour herd. And in the middle of the three- or four-second panic I experience while driving beneath an unattached road, I see a handmade sign, somehow placed in the middle of the Jersey barrier holding us all in line—a sign that takes courage to read: CHILD CARE. I can't read the phone number that goes with it, not that I would not be interested to know (1) how they got that sign there, and (2) what kind of a child care giver advertises on a traffic median?

Meanwhile, an orange Caution sign warns of a $135 fine for reckless driving, speeding, or tailgating. At least I think it says $135: all the cars are packed so tightly together that it is as if we are all tailgating en masse, so I don't dare take my eyes off the road and the cars, which ends up being a good decision because now I see the car in front of me knocking over a large orange fifty-five-gallon drum-shaped traffic barrier, then swerving to miss another, then swerving to hit the following one. I experience a flashback to the time when, as a boy, I was riding copilot in the family station wagon when a man in front of us slumped over and went off the dark highway road as my father shouted and just avoided hitting him—I have always believed that we watched that man die. That was late at night and I don't recall there being other cars in the lanes on either side of us. At this moment in our particular cross-country excursion there are lots of cars around; the road is packed tight with cars. The guy is weaving in and out of the lane with orange traffic barriers, spitting them off the side of the road. I am attempting to slow down, but the guy behind me and the hundreds of cars behind him are, to use the driving vernacular, on my back. Is the guy in front of me dying? Or is something else happening? We have entered a driving hell, and all eyes in the back of my car are now concentrated on the road; there is no talking. I move closer to the wheel, while my wife's hand is on or near the dashboard.

He's doing it for fun!

Or what he seems to consider fun, because now he has pulled off the road and is driving on the shoulder, laughing along with his car mates, as they lean forward and back, which we see in a glance, in a flash that runs back slow motion in my brain. On the other hand, in this car-insulated world, who knows what is happening?

When I have a chance to sit with my journal for this day, I will note that, as I often am when driving in the area of Chicago, in that dense interstate-quilted land below the Great Lakes, I am pleased that we have not all died.

CROSSING THE FAWN RIVER

THE DAY WEARS ON, the sides of the roads changing to green fields, specifically cornfields. Beneath the green of cornfields, we see a sign with a kind of light beneath it. It is an animal detection system. If deer cross an infrared beam near the road, then the light will flash and alert drivers, who, like deer, are often injured when deer cross highways. Approximately one and a half million deer are hit every year, according to insurance reports, and, according to the American Automobile Society, twelve thousand humans are injured. Nobody knows how many deer are killed. According to an insurance company, most of the top states for deer-related accidents are in the area we are driving through now, in states such as Illinois, Indiana, Ohio, and Pennsylvania— Pennsylvania ranking first in deer accidents.

Ergo, we are now in the phase of our cross-country excursion where concern for non-automobile-driving creatures that might cause trouble for automobile users is at its highest.

There are other areas of course. Once, in Colorado, on I-70, a twelve-mile stretch of road was reconstructed with animals in mind. Previously, I-70 had been two lanes of winding, accident-causing mountain road that killed people and killed most of the local population of bighorn sheep—the remaining sheep were eventually flown out of the valley in the 1970s. The sheep were flown back by 1992, when the new road was rebuilt as a terrace, a four-lane series of bridges and aqueducts, an I-70 that was thought to be more sensitive to the flow of water around it, to the movement of animals. Guardrails were built abutting slopes of land that kept the sheep from entering the road.

But the one place where the nature of man and the automobile meets the nature of nature is often in the area of deer, of roadkill, of things that go bump in the early evening and kill people, or at least scratch up the car.

Now, there is an animal detection system on this run of interstate, and for whatever reason, it is not flashing: no animals are being detected.

Coincidentally, immediately after passing the deer detection signal and shortly before the exit for I-69, I see a sign suggesting that we are about to cross the Fawn River.

FORGIVE ME AS WE CROSS THE FAWN RIVER

FORGIVE ME IF I SEEM didactic or harsh at this halfway point in what I still pray will be the final day. Even when not crossing the country, we drive through an interstate world that is stuffed with automobiles, that seems designed by the car for the car, that can seem so unnatural when sitting in it for days on end, and so surely neither the cross-countrying reader or my fellow cross-country expedition members need to be lectured at this point on this long lifelike slog, especially now, in the monotony of a stopless day.

On the other hand, I would ask that the reader recall that I have just been nearly killed by a guy; like a deer in traffic, I have just seen the headlights.

And so I point out as we are about to cross the Fawn River that when I approach any river on a cross-country trip, I anticipate both happiness and dread. For rivers offer a promise, even today, even to the person traveling not in a covered wagon but in a rented Impala—if only a promise of the scenic. At the same time, rivers are a reminder of the consequences of the vast system of concrete and asphalt that is the world's largest public works project, the United States of America's Great Wall of China.

We do not see it on maps offered by the American Automobile Association, we do not read it in state travel literature, but the Environmental Protection Agency has rated half of the 3,662,255 miles of American rivers and streams as "good," half as "threatened" or "impaired." Likewise, of the forty-two million acres of lakes, reservoirs, and ponds, 54 percent are "threatened" or "impaired." Is the River Charon a thing of beauty or a horrific thing that eyes would dread or a sublime mixture of the two? Is the Fawn River a clear running stream? A smooth blue brown beneath the gray Indiana sky? Is it a stream unaffected by the things that seep from our 230 million vehicles? By the particles that rain from the smoke-tainted air? By the grasses and sedges, the marshes and meadows that are destroyed by the development inspired by the interstates? Is it similar in appearance to a sewer?

Again, I implore you to forgive the melancholy that hits me as I approach a river beneath a highway—I fear that in mentioning it I am merely encouraging midtrip napping. Forgive me too for quoting these mild-seeming but devastating words from one Richard Foreman, a landscape ecologist who has worked with road designers, who has sought out the affected and the last un-road-affected places in the country (a five-day hike into the Tetons in Wyoming, a mangrove swamp in the Florida Everglades): "The overall goal of transportation is safe and efficient mobility and the secondary goal is to minimize environmental devastation. The United States has done the first brilliantly and the second very poorly."

But as I say, I am eager to see the Fawn River, the problem being that, because of the way the highway was built, when we do finally cross it, I don't get much of a look at it.

LIFE LINE

A SIGN ADVERTISING CIGARETTES AND FIREWORKS marks Indiana's last exit—states' individual explosive and tobacco and alcohol laws define the interstate's borderlands. A large billboard marks Ohio's very first "WELCOME TO OHIO," and as I see it and scan the horizon, I glimpse suddenly laundry flying on a line, a stunning view, a kind of mundanely breathtaking view: the first emphatic sign of pure non-road-related life, of life not solely based on a car, that I have seen for hundreds and hundreds of miles. It is a note of stationary domesticity that is startling in its nontransitory nature, especially alongside a really big road. I pointed to it but I'm not sure anyone else saw it. I'm pretty sure I did not imagine it.

WE ENTER OHIO HEARING SPORTS TALK ON THE RADIO

MAN ON THE RADIO: But they've got [*inaudible*], though, still?

NEXT MAN: They've got [*inaudible*].

MAN: I think he's the best of the three.

NEXT MAN: He was the best of the three. He's the fastest.

MAN: He was the most all-around. He had more yardage.

NEXT MAN: Yes.

MAN: He was more consistent.

ANOTHER MAN: But they've also got a stud freshman coming in.

MAN: They've also got an excellent line.

ANOTHER MAN: They do.

MAN: They've had an excellent line for five years.

ANOTHER MAN: Well, they lost three of the five linemen this year. However, they've got big boys backing them up.

MAN: That's right.

ANOTHER MAN: Starting this year you've got . . .

MAN: [*inaudible*] is still there . . .

ANOTHER MAN: [*inaudible*] is still . . .

MAN: [*inaudible*] is huge.

IN NEED OF SERVICES

WE ARE IN NEED OF LATE-IN-THE-DAY SERVICES, as well as rest, thus, we seek a service area on the Ohio Turnpike. I know this road. As befits the driver of a limited-access highway, I know the Ohio Turnpike in a limited way. I know it like the back of the hands that I have been staring at for fifty-something hours since I left Portland, Oregon. We have in mind a particular service area, because for all the service areas and rest areas and parking areas we have ever stopped at—the rest area in Wyoming built on a bison refuge and utilizing solar power, the service area in Boston with a bank of Coca-Cola machines that are decorated with sections of a giant maplike display of Massachusetts, the rest areas in Wisconsin that are spacious and grand and exemplary in their use of native grasses—we inevitably become fixated on the service areas that are on the Ohio Turnpike, at least in our last few years of cross-countrying. The Ohio service area is a new service area—over the past few years all the Ohio Turnpike stops are being rebuilt. The particular service area in which we seek service and rest is the Commodore Perry Service Area, though we are not exactly certain which service area that is—as is well known, even to non-cross-country drivers, no matter how well you know the road, at certain points a lot of the road looks the same.

As we pull past the first service area that the toll road has to offer, we see it is not the Commodore Perry area. To see this, we slow the Impala. Almost suspiciously, we pull into the parking area. The rooftop-pack flapping sounds mercifully pause. We look, we linger for a moment, but then proceed on, hungry, unserviced, unrested, crestfallen.

I should say in passing that service areas are, for me, so bittersweet: comforting as places to pause the relentless driving but, like all stops, ultimately preventing you from arriving, from getting from sea to shining sea, from getting home. At a rest stop, you are in cross-country limbo, in a waiting room for another world. Some standard items at rest stops are soda dispensers, maps depicting the great bloodshot spread of roads in a given state, tourism literature, literature indicating the whereabouts of discount shopping malls, singles magazines, and cigarette butt holders, those tall plastic receptacles that can hold up to several thousand cigarette butts before being emptied, depending on their size—four gallons being the usual, rest area cigarette butt container size. (The cigarette butt receptacle is one of the newest features of the typical rest area, having shown up at most rest areas and outside of roadside convenience areas somewhere around 2000, by my calculation.)

As I said, we are hungry. The choice of food is like the choice of food along the road in general, limited. As is well known, the standard items at full-service service areas are, of course, hamburgers and fries.

HOW IT CAME TO BE THAT PEOPLE EAT HAMBURGERS AND FRIES WHILE DRIVING OR TAKING A BREAK FROM DRIVING ON THE MODERN INTERSTATE

IN THE EARLY DAYS OF DRIVING, drivers might picnic or camp but food was almost incidental. On long trips, drivers found food served at taverns or in homes. In 1915, Effie Gladdington, while driving cross-country on the Lincoln Highway, stopped in what was called a tearoom. "It's a charming little place, kept by a woman of taste and arranged for parties to sup in passing by," she wrote. "We admire the simple, dainty furniture, the home-like little parlor." People were treated like guests at roadside eateries partly because no one had much experience in being treated like anything else. Restaurants came slowly to highways, the idea of a restaurant being new to America in the first place, having only become commonplace after the Civil War.* As parkways became popular, with their scenic drives and scenic waysides, so did the restaurant with a roadside view. In the 1930s, the Grand View Hotel and Restaurant in the Tussey Mountains near Bedford, Pennsylvania, was decorated with a giant sign: SEE 3 STATES, 7 COUNTIES. Soon, of course, as cars became less bare-boned and even more luxurious, people began to eat in their cars. In the thirties and forties, the roadside stand grew into the drive-in, drive-ins competing with other drive-ins via gimmicks, such as the carhop, usually a female waitress who waited on cars. "That a dimpled knee, a shapely thigh, a fresh young mouth smiling prettily has a stimulating effect on the male appetite is a truism which has been practiced ever since eating in public became an accepted social custom," wrote *Time* in 1940, at the height of the carhop craze. "For centuries, kings and princes and men-in-the-money have mixed their gustatory pleasures with the visual delights of comely ladies."

Like motels, like gas stations, like cheaply built housing and offices, chain restaurants flourished in the seventies; the highway system was a greenhouse for chains and franchises. Examples include Kentucky Fried Chicken, begun in 1930 by Harlan Sanders, a foul-mouthed Kentuckian who was running a gas station and restaurant in Corbin, Kentucky, using his mother's seasonings to make a chicken recipe that, along with cleanliness, made his gas station a huge hit, a hit so huge that the governor of Kentucky made him an honorary colonel, around which time Sanders grew out his white hair and adopted his famous white suit and string tie, around which time the new highway bypassed his service station and, at sixty-six, he decided to sell his chicken recipe as a franchise. The franchise spread to four hundred locations around the United States and Canada, though eventually the colonel was bought out for two hundred million dollars, part of the agreement being that he have a job forever promoting the chicken he called "finger lickin' good." (Shortly after the buyout, it is said, Sanders gave up cussing.) There was the pecan farmer, William "Bill" Stuckey, who began selling pecans during the Depression

---

* *Restaurant* is a French word, initially used in 1765 to describe a soup of sheep's foot in white sauce that the chef called "restorative"—in French, a restaurant.

from a wooden shed on the side of the highway and then sold pecan rolls and pralines and souvenirs all along Route 66 and highways in the South, until his death in 1977, when the Stuckey's chain was bought by Pet Inc., which eventually sold it to Bill Stuckey Jr., who brought it back to life—today you can still buy pecan rolls from Stuckey's in twenty-three states.

To observe the dots that mark the location of Howard Johnson's, that mark the locations of Dog n Suds, Shoney's, or Big Boys—to see the country broken down by food franchise zone, is to see the dream of Thomas Jefferson come true, in a way. "Whoever takes control of the Ohio and the Lakes will become the sole and absolute lord of America," wrote James Maury, a tutor to the young Thomas Jefferson. And so it is with the interstates and with franchises and real estate and so on. And so it is that after five or six days of Seeing America, a cross-country traveler begins to believe that America's Manifest Destiny is to sell burgers, dogs, fries, chicken, even the Mexican-themed food sold by Glen Bell, who first opened Bell's Hamburgers and then Bell's Hamburgers and Hot Dogs and then "Taco-Tia" then Taco Bell then Hickory Bells, a barbecue place, which did not do well. For the interstates are the fast-food-oriented equivalent of the rivers of commerce that Thomas Jefferson sought to open with the mapping of the West. They are the promise of nineteenth-century exploration written with sales of burgers, shakes, and french fries.

THE REASON THAT IT IS HAMBURGERS that Americans prefer and not veal parmigian or sushi or beef souvlaki is in large part due to the failure of the hot dog as road food.

Hot dogs were introduced in 1893 by Anton Ludwig Feuchtwanger, a Bavarian sausage seller, who is believed to have served them either at the Columbian Exposition in Chicago of that year, or possibly at the Louisiana Purchase Exposition in Saint Louis in 1904, a point of debate. He lent out white gloves to hot dog eaters so they wouldn't burn their hands and then started giving out buns instead, since the gloves were frequently stolen. Some scholars speculate that the hot dog was too snacklike, too insignificant, not enough of a meal for Americans to take on as their national dish. But a big strike against the hot dog was that it was too regional, served differently everywhere it was eaten. In New York, people ate hot dogs with steamed onions and yellow mustard; in Kansas City, with sauerkraut and melted swiss cheese; in the South, with coleslaw; and in Chicago, with yellow mustard, chopped raw onion, sweet relish, dill pickles, tomato, and celery salt on a poppy seed bun. Even if people began setting out for adventure, to see something different, the road, as we have seen, eventually stimulated the desire for sameness.

Another strike against the hamburgerization of hot dogs was that hot dogs were a food of immigrants, specifically German immigrants, who ate them at immigrant gathering places, such as baseball games. Hot dog places were called "hot dog kennels." H. L. Mencken called hot dogs "a cartridge filled with the sweepings of abattoirs." (Nathan's, the still-prominent hot dog chain, hired people in surgeons' smocks to eat its hot dogs, to prove them safe.) Hot dogs had no cachet. Highway travelers, on the other hand, considered themselves part of the American elite, whether they were or not, much like the American elite today. Travelers liked that the hamburger was served without sauce and was, thus, presented uncovered—sauce, it was thought, hid bad beef and tricked customers. Travelers also liked beef in general. Beef, of course, in many places, remains a status symbol, or at least a symbol. Every time we drive through Amarillo, we pass numerous roadside signs advertising the free seventy-two-ounce steak served at the Big Texan Steakhouse. The steak is free if you can eat it with all the trimmings in an hour; in the restaurant, there is a table on an elevated stage, the backdrop a large electronic timer. Recently, we stopped at Cooper's Old Time Pit Bar-B-Que, a barbecue in the hill country of Texas, a ways off the interstate. Huge fans blew the smell of meat out on the road. We stopped. We looked into the huge barbecue pits. A man with a large knife and nearly pitchfork-sized fork asked us what we wanted. We pointed at a piece of meat. "Can I have just a little," my wife asked, politely. The man with the large knife and fork stopped cutting and looked at her as if she were from another planet.

HAMBURGERS MATCHED THE NATION'S METAPHORIC needs in other ways. Even though the British, who liked and wanted beef, initially helped fund western cattle raising and meat packing, by World War I the West was an American beef–oriented landscape. As Americans, even our palates have always wanted to head west on the road. While the origins of the hamburger are hotly disputed, the modern hamburger is thought to have first been served to a lot of people at the Louisiana Purchase Exposition in Saint Louis, in 1904 (possibly alongside the first modern hot dog). Even though the word *hamburger* probably came over with German immigrants, the hamburger itself was presented as a symbol of America, of homogeneity, of one nation full of people who seemed to like to eat the same thing, who wanted a choice but wanted it to be a choice to choose what everybody else was having. By the end of World War I, the beef industry worked happily with the automobile industry in establishing the modern beef-eating road experience. From 1910 to 1976, the amount of beef Americans ate increased by 72 percent.

The hot dog, meanwhile, did succeed in a few cases, such as when it was served with root beer at A&W or at a very successful roadside hot dog place called Dog n Suds. And the hot dog succeeds in California, a disproportionately highly-roaded state, where a disproportionately high number of fast-food stops are hot dog places, such as Der Wienerschnitzel, a restaurant that is also notable for being not a drive-up restaurant, where one parks and exits one's car to consume food indoors, or a drive-through restaurant, which might be more accurately described as a drive-near or drive-alongside restaurant. Der Wienerschnitzel is an A-frame through which customers drive their cars—literally, a drive-through restaurant.

AS FOR FRIES

AS FOR FRIES—CALLED french fries because of the julienne slicing, a French slicing style, not because they are French—these sliced and fried potatoes are noted in the United States as early as 1908, but the strong fry presence that characterizes the road today, and that characterizes the service area we will stop at here on the Ohio Turnpike, came late to the side of the hamburger. Indeed, it can be said that one of the great achievements of Ray Kroc, the onetime milkshake blender salesman who wanted to be a musician and failed and went on to create the McDonald's corporation and who gave money to conservative causes until he died, at which point his wife gave to liberal ones is this: Ray Kroc married the fry with the hamburger.

Fries, like hamburgers, began life on the road as exotics and then became staples of the road and subsequently of the home—because the road and home began to meld. The average American consumed 6.6 pounds of french fries a year in 1960, at the dawn of the modern road-food era. At about the midway point of the modern road-food era the average American ate 36.8 pounds of fries a year. Once, the road itself was exotic, or at least the long-distance car trip was, but as driving became more commonplace, as driving became something that everyone began to do, every day, road food became less exotic and more regular. Drive-through windows existed in the early days of driving when driving was for tourists, for Sunday drivers, but drive-through windows were reintroduced in the seventies by Wendy's, a hamburger-oriented chain that was not just selling to tourists but also to people going to work or to school. (Double drive-throughs were introduced by John Jay Hooker, founder of the Minnie Pearl chicken chain.) In the 1990s, restaurant companies began to develop more food that could be readily eaten while driving, as the average number of meals eaten in the car began to rise, as foods came packaged with utensils, as drinks were designed to fit in the road-food-friendly compartments of children's car seats, in the cup holders of cars. In the nineties, road food and home food were becoming more and more the same.

SNACKS

SOMEWHERE IN OHIO, at a point late into the afternoon, my wife turns to face the back seat. "We will have snacks for dinner," she announces, semi-dramatically.

"OK," says our son.

"OK," says our daughter, semi-cheerily, because they are in accord with the plan, they are extremely anxious to do whatever it takes to get home, such is the semi-torturous duration of the return cross-country trip.

Additionally, snacking is something they are used to. When we eat snacks for dinner, we mine the convenience stores for nuts and crackers and cheese, for peanut butter. As gas stations more frequently offer peanut butter from a tube, we are more and more likely to eat tube-squeezed peanut butter, like orbiting astronauts, only gazing at Earth. The peanut butter is squeezed in the front seat on crackers, specifically saltines. We eat a *lot* of saltines. We drink a lot of juices, some of which contain real juices. We drink water, which eventually will cause us to stop again of course. Upon entering a snack-selling store, our modus operandi is this: we fan out. We fan out, for instance, in a store attached to a Texaco in Utah and are lucky enough to find yogurt, an unroadly food.

"They have yogurt!" my wife says, always triumphantly, buying most of it up.

Our party of four fans out, for example, in a Love's Country Store, a Love's Country Store connected to a Hardee's, in Joplin, Missouri. Chances are we wouldn't stop at a Hardee's because I can't take so-called road food anymore; after fifteen years I am all road-hamburgered out—I am Herculean in my attempts to avoid the road-accompanying french fry. And at this Love's that I am recalling, as we drive up, as we get out, as we are greeted by a cloud of black soot that blew off the road on a gray day in Joplin, we immediately see the aisles of sugary snacks and truck repair items, of forever-turning hot dogs and automotive accessories, of men's and women's personal grooming items. We see the advertisements for the low-carb Thickburger and the low-carb Breakfast Bowl, and we see the staff, wearing Love's's headsets, communication devices that allow them, in this case, to talk to each other on Love's walkie-talkies as they search for a bag of candy, a candy that someone in the Hardee's apparently requested.*

ONCE, IN A GAS STATION OFF I-70 IN OKLAHOMA, I found a great snack, an amazing snack, a snack that belied everything I knew about the sameness of snacks and candies and sodas and foods in general as one crosses the country. It was a little package of beef jerky, the size of a flattened pack of cigarettes. It was called Mike's Famous Beef Jerky and it was so great I had to call Mike up.

---

* We have stopped at many of the Love's-related road-food-selling places, of which there are a lot—there seem to be circles upon circles of Love's-related businesses. The application for employment at Love's says: "HAVE YOU EVER BEEN EMPLOYED WITH LOVE'S TRAVEL STOPS AND COUNTRY STORES, INC. (LOVE'S AUTOGRAF, GRANDY'S MUSKET CORP., OKLAHOMA TRADING POST, TEXAS TRADING CO., COWBOY'S, OR CARL'S JR.) BEFORE?"

Mike was not there. I talked to his son, Mike, who makes the jerky with his father, as well as his own jerky, in Chickasha, Oklahoma. Mike told me about how his father bought an old grocery store and bought a jerky recipe and made jerky at the grocery store and, after just a few months, was selling more jerky than anything else at the grocery store; he eventually dropped the groceries. He told me about his own jerky, Jamie D's, which is mostly served in bars. "It's me and him, or mostly just me; he comes in the morning and helps me get it started up," he said. "We sell two to three thousand bags a week, and we just sell in Oklahoma."

He and his father were surprised to meet so many other jerky makers when they got into the business. "It's kind of like entering a society or something, a jerky community," the younger Mike said. He estimates that there are twelve other jerky makers in Oklahoma. "But I don't really eat any other jerky." They sell mostly in small shops, usually not even chain gas stations, in part due to the high insurance requirements that large stores require of jerky manufacturers, as well as all other manufacturers—I apparently lucked out finding him in a small-ish gas station.

"We're just in mom-and-pop stores," he says. "There's so much you have to do to get in stores like Love's and Wal-Mart."

Something about Mike's Famous Beef Jerky gives me hope, even in the midst of a terminal interstate trip.

NOT THE SERVICE AREA WE ARE HOPING TO STOP AT

WE DESCEND DEEPER in the Ohio Turnpike service area system. We pass an-other service area, and yet it is not the one we are excited for—we see the re-lieved souls as they are exiting, parking, leaving or reentering their cars, often with bags of food. Yes, we have stopped at this very service area. We stopped there once and bought gas and coffee and I played a video game, for in my early days of crossing the country, before video games were ubiquitous in the living rooms of America as well as the back seats of minivans and cars, they were mostly at arcades and at highway service areas and, yes, I played them there. And at this particular service area that we are not stopping at, I played a video game because I felt video games increased my adrenaline, hyped me up, gave me a little more time awake behind the wheel—in the case of the game I played at this rest area in particular, it gave me about forty minutes more time, allow-ing my wife and I to pull off exit 118 of the Ohio Turnpike at one o'clock in the morning, when we began to search for a motel in Huron, Ohio, and then got lost, and then asked for directions, and then followed a woman who thought it was easier to take us to the motel than to give us directions and seemed to go a long way out of her way, until she stopped, pointed, smiled, and waved. We checked in in the dark, not knowing where we were, and then woke up along-side Lake Erie, an orange-in-the-morning sun, a lake-sized surprise!

WE CROSS THE MAUMEE RIVER, the river of Toledo, and we look left and see Toledo's downtown bristle, and after a stretch of pretty much flat but sometimes rolling Ohio of the turnpike, we pass several men dressed in black T-shirts with cutoff sleeves, black pants, and silver belts, all surrounding a broken-down van, inspecting the engine that had broken down on the Sandusky County line.

A WOMAN IN A CONVERTIBLE JAGUAR, her long blond hair blowing back, passes us, racing, racing, her license plate personalized: Z-RAAD. And then another car races past, a man and two women in burkas, in a Nissan Maxima. Their license plate: 5-RAAD.

THE COMMODORE PERRY SERVICE AREA

I AM NOT EXAGGERATING when I say that we are close to ecstatic at having landed at the Commodore Perry Service Area. I suppose a measure of the extent of this ecstasy should consider that we have done nothing but sit in a car for about ten hours today. We ate a not totally crappy breakfast in a motel breakfast area and got in a car and drove all day, so that even though it feels as if time does not exist, as if we are in a land of eternal movement that has no beginning or end, the day is in fact passing and it is around four.

For what feels simultaneously like the millionth time and first time, we enter the Commodore Perry Service Area—we decelerate past an artificial hill, and while in the gradual turn, we see farms. We see a farm on the left and a farm on the right, and the service area itself seems like a farm of sorts, or maybe a trough—a brand-new food-producing, trash-making, gasoline-pumping, state-of-the-art service area bounded by a green corn-growing green. As we pull into the angled parking spot, we see it straight on. There are touches of Frank Lloyd Wright in the Prairie-style design, and it looks a lot like an airport terminal without the runways, an obelisk making it feel like something picked up off the Mall in Washington, D.C., and put on the road in Ohio. There is the Ohio state flag, the American flag, the six fast-food logos. Entering the service area via a walkway, I feel as if I am entering a town hall in a suburb. We pass a mailbox, look over to see pets frolicking in the pet area, hold the door for travelers exiting the plaza, and then, as we enter its grand foyer, the Commodore Perry Service Area speaks to us.

THE COMMODORE PERRY SERVICE AREA doesn't speak to us about Commodore Oliver Hazard Perry, who commanded the American naval ships that left Put-in-Bay, just off the coast of Sandusky and, though sailing a newly built and hastily equipped fleet, forced the British fleet to surrender on Lake Erie, helping pave the way for victory in the War of 1812. The Commodore Perry doesn't speak to us with the semi-immortal words that Commodore Perry is quoted as saying: "We have met the enemy and they are ours!"

What the Commodore Perry Service Area speaks to me about is the nature of the road at the dawn of the twenty-first century, which pushes us on, which continues to express an optimism that may or may not be rooted in reality: the optimism that comes from the America that bows to the god that it sometimes believes has suggested it press on, the god that is sometimes substituted with the god of technology, the notion that finite can be reengineered into the infinite, that stresses, no matter what, that there is more than enough space, more than enough room, that there is more.

That's what I hear the Commodore Perry Service Area saying, anyway, and as we enter it, as we are immediately consumed by the giant foyer, the neoclassical dome that houses the attendant, a rack displaying sunglasses for sale, Ohio-themed souvenirs, an offering of tourist literature, and fliers for the National Inventor's Hall of Fame, where I kind of wanted to go in Akron, and for the Rock and Roll Hall of Fame, where my son was saying he would go if, in his words, "we happened to be driving through Cleveland," which I didn't get—does that mean he wants to go or what? In the foyer, we are in sight of the Travel Mart, the video arcade, the restrooms, the truckers' lounge, and, most prominent and looming large, the food court. Immediately, we raid the snack area, finding saltines, peanut butter, juices, water, yogurt, and an extra, extra large coffee. With my coffee, I walk to the border of the food court. I look to the lines of people waiting for burgers and fries, among other road-adapted food items. Inhaling the greasy fast-food smell, I turn away.

*   *   *

THE KIDS HAVE MOVED TO THE VIDEO AREA—we must give them a few moments of nondriving time, even if we are only snacking for dinner. The video area is between the Travel Mart and the truckers' lounge. I join them and after a while take my turn in a chair that uses sounds and vibrations to simulate me driving really fast. After winning extended time, I stand quasi-triumphantly for a time in the foyer, watching people walk in, look up into the dome that is the foyer, then split into groups headed to the restroom and groups headed for food. I take a picture of the foyer—and subsequently fear that the attendant behind the desk that guards the entrance might give me a hard time for taking a photo, for some security reason or another, but he looks at me, pauses, then continues to clip his nails.

I greet the attendant at the front desk and remark on the largeness of the Commodore Perry Service Area. He responds, saying that older travelers on their way to and from casinos on buses gaze into the foyer of the service area, not in awe of the pseudo-Jeffersonian dome, but at the distance they will have to march to get fast food. "They drop their jaws," he says.

In speaking to me, the attendant expresses a strong affinity for the Commodore Perry Service Area. "I love being here," he says.

YES, I TOO ENJOY BEING AT THE COMMODORE PERRY, with one exception. As I walked through the service area, I began to sense the onset of tiredness. Sleep! Sleep licking like a flame at the souls of my nearly numb feet! The dreaded wash of tiredness lapping at my so-sick-of-driving heart! My legs were beginning to feel heavy, my eyes loosening in focus, just slightly, a strain. I want to shake it off as I return to the parking lot; I want to feel the rejuvenation associated with stopping, and fresh good coffee, but I cannot. Just thinking I am feeling tired is causing me to feel tired.

Entering the Impala, I check the straps on the nearly disintegrated pack once again. And then, as I turn the key and start the engine, as we pull out of our spot, I look back to see seagulls soaring over the service area in the breeze, as if we were at sea and passing a ship, as if we were setting sail one last time into the one-last night.

THE LAND BEYOND THE SERVICE AREA

THE LAND BEYOND THE SERVICE AREA as we drive east on what we still incredibly believed would be our final day is for me a dreamlike landscape: rolling hills, green trees, nearly uninhabited vistas. The green hills of the Appalachians are different from the plains of Nebraska, from the Rockies of Montana, from the prairies of Minnesota and the soft farmed hills I see in Wisconsin. The green hills of Appalachia are the hills of my past. They are the hills of the very beginning of our back-and-forth trip across the continent. They are the hills of the edge of the early United States. Oh, how beautiful is this heart of Ohio! We pass another renovated service area on the Ohio Turnpike, one where we once stopped to eat leftover pie that we had bought in Wisconsin. We pass the Black River now, entering the Cleveland area, where we will not pause. We see a drive-in theater that is empty, driverless. We cross the Cuyahoga County line and look into a valley that is like a movie screen, a large drive-in movie screen that is showing six lanes of winding highway passing through the mostly undeveloped hills, followed by power lines. The Cuyahoga River appears not at all like the river that once burned in downtown Cleveland, so polluted was it; it appears bucolic, pristine, except for our presence, the existence of the road. And then, all of a sudden, you cannot see much because a giant cement wall on the highway blocks the view, a large Jersey barrier. Now we are near Kent State, where, one night, while traveling across the country with a friend ten years ago, we ate her grandmother's eggplant Parmesan sandwiches; I can still remember the tangy taste of the Parmesan cheese, and I can remember how quiet everything seemed for a place where the military had once gunned down war protesters—we stayed in a ragtag motel near the Kent State campus. Now we are stopping at the Brady's Leap Service Plaza, a plaza named for a jump, a mythical jump in which a guy named Brady was running from pursuing Indians and jumped across the Cuyahoga and was subsequently called a turkey, a term meant as a compliment. We were hoping it was going to be another one of those newfangled service plazas, but we'll take any service area because the sound of the rooftop pack is just driving us nuts. (There seems to be a new bout of rooftop pack shredding.) The pack is just not working. Oh, why does it seem that so much of what I buy to reengineer my life doesn't actually reengineer my life? Oh, why does the pack suck?

A NIGHTMARE

COMING INTO YOUNGSTOWN, OHIO, the day further faded. We stayed at a motel on the outskirts of Youngstown once, checked in to the place early, as a person checked in alongside us, that person saying to the clerk: "Well, I'll bet nothing ever happened in Youngstown." The clerk said nothing about the first iron furnace, the old steel mills, the arrival of the Erie Canal and the cross-country railroad. Oh, historical malaise! We swam in the pool, snacked, all with the children, who were much younger then, little. We went to sleep, and woke up to be served breakfast by a waiter who knew all about the Revolutionary War and Youngstown—so much happened to us in Youngstown.

Passing Youngstown today, we're in the "Following Too Closely Target Enforcement Area," with a guy tailgating me. And then we pay a toll as the road changes from toll road that is interstate to simply interstate, as in I-80—$8.50. I pay a very nice guy, or a guy who is very nice to me. It is like paying the gatekeeper to a land of road delirium.

We pass a sign for the Meander Reservoir on I-80, though we will not have time for anything like meandering. Then a crop of signs, a crop as we have not seen for some time on the more-controlled Ohio Turnpike: SLEEP INN, WENDY'S, ARBY'S, DEERFIELD INN, SUBWAY, TACO BELL, MOTEL 6, TRAVELODGE, PERKINS, HAMPTON INN, BEST WESTERN, BP TRAVEL CENTER, COMFORT INN, SOUTH SEA PASS MEXICAN RESTAURANT, BURGER KING, MCDONALD'S. Then when the road splits in Pennsylvania a short time later, we spot a large interstate roadside directional sign. This is an especially large directional sign that is the official interstate green with white lettering—though maybe it merely looms large in my darkening imagination.

Darkening, or at least reversing, for I am thinking back to the origins of interstate signs, thinking first of reports of Indians leaving markings along trails—conflicting reports because some historians argue that they never marked the trees. I am thinking of the bark reportedly being stripped from a tree, the resulting patch of wood painted with red ochre and charcoal and recording attacks, hunting reports. Then there were the Moravian missionaries, who, in their attempts to convert the tribes to Christianity, left Bible passages on trees. A more recent event in the history of interstate road signs was sponsored by the Bureau of Public Roads in the 1950s, when a three-mile test road near Greenbelt, Maryland, was constructed with signs for an imaginary exit:

UTOPIA

TWO MILES

The bureau designed the signs in green, black, and blue and found hundreds of people to drive past the signs at 65 miles an hour, and, in the end, the majority of drivers were able to better recall green, followed by blue, followed by black. In 1972, words (NO LEFT TURN, NO TRUCKS, HILL) began to be replaced by symbols; interstate signs adopted the European symbol for "no," a red slash through a circle. Because by the 1970s, misreading of signs was a serious problem. In Omaha, Nebraska, so many travelers misread interstate signs on I-80 during the 1970s that the state had to build a sign that said LOST? on the north freeway, which branched off from I-80; beneath the sign were directions for U-turning. In California, the leading cause of death on highways was cars heading the wrong way on highway exit and entrance ramps. After exit and entrance ramp signage was improved, the leading cause of death on California highways was cars hitting an obstruction, often a sign.

But the sign that we see before us—this huge and for us especially notable sign, the sign that this evening seems greener than usual in the hypnotically green valley of greener and greener Pennsylvania—proclaims our goal, New York City, and it says that New York City is only about six more hours.

IN THE VALLEY OF OIL CITY

PENNSYLVANIA IS A STATE misplaced to us cross-countryers, a state that is so big, that takes so much mile-passing effort, it ought to be in the western half of the United States, or so it seems to us. It is the country's very first West, of course, and you can still feel that today, even on an interstate. The hills watching us feel old, even now, even while resting, or restrooming at I-80's first Pennsylvania rest stop, which is a small rest stop, a simple rest stop that is without major services, like gas and oil, hamburgers and french fries. It is a charmingly simple rest stop that is the epitome of the roadside as one with nature, a rest stop that is semi-bucolic, with the exception of the tractor trailers lined and resting, engines running, near the entrance. Indeed, as far as the hard-driving interstate of this morning, this is a primordial rest area, and I enjoy the lack of trademarks, the lack of people, come to think of it. The building is small and brown and clean; I compliment an attendant on the faucet fixtures, which, he explains, are new.

There is a simple map with a posted notice on road construction, so that as I chew on more saltines and drink warm juice, I once again think back to the early ancestors of rest stops. I think of what naturalist John Bertram described as the road food of the Iroquois, corn browned in hot ashes, cleaned, pounded, sifted, mixed with some sugar, and then, on the road, mixed with water and served. I think of the communal shelters along the path, sometimes stocked with beans and dried meat—the first fuel-and-food-service areas. I think of the road as a place that was personal, people interacting, rather than standing by cars, greeting, sizing each other up, noting temperament, posture, stance, voice, and expression. "[T]he road or path," writes landscape historian J. B. Jackson, becomes "the first most basic public space."

Coincidentally, the first footpaths on the American continent shared by Native Americans and European settlers were in the Appalachians that we are entering. And though they were, like interstates, designed to transport, they could not have been more indirect. Arthur Butler Hulbert, a geographer who charted the last of them, marveled at their relative circuitousness, at the walking required by the average traveler: crossing streams at their narrowest points regardless of the detour, walking around an obstruction no matter how far, avoiding all engineering. Hulbert noted that the only trail that *was* engineered was the warpath.

ASIDE FROM BEING THE FIRST INTERSTATE REST AREA we encounter in Pennsylvania, this, by the way, is the Oil City area rest area—it is only one mile from the exit for Oil City, the town named for the black liquid that was pulled from the earth at Oil Creek, another ten or so miles as the crow flies, outside of nearby Titusville. Frank Drake struck oil in the Pennsylvania hills in 1859, hit a pocket of what would one day be petroleum 69.5 feet below ground, the creamy dark liquid first used as a lubrication, an alternative to whale oil, since the whale oil supply, due to the world's overhunting of whales, was dwindling. Oil caught on. First, Russia led the world in oil production through the 1870s, followed by Romania and the then–Dutch East Indies and Mexico, and then after a gusher in east Texas, the leading oil producer was the United States, thanks to Texas, Oklahoma, and California. Then, the United States led the world in the shift from coal to oil, followed by western Europe and Japan. By the 1970s, due to the high price of oil, oil companies were looking for oil everywhere on the globe. Thus, the Oil City area is for me a rest area to rest while thinking about the far-flung results of oil: mechanized farming, plastics, revolutions in South American countries, hostage taking in the Middle East, tanker spills in the oceans, cars, war after war after war.*

But fear not, I did not ponder oil for long. No, mostly, I utilized the restroom, and checked out the new plumbing fixtures, as I have said. Then I did a bunch of jumping jacks alongside the car, accompanied by my daughter, and thought, "Damn, I'm tired."

Now, to the team, I exhort: "Let's go! Let's go! Let's get there. Let's go!" *Exheunt.*

DARKNESS

LIGHTS ARE ON, and not just the automatic always-on lights of rental cars and new cars; manual lights are on as we enter the thick of the Allegheny Mountains. Sometimes, interstate highways make mountains seem meaningless, especially so in a rental car, a working Impala. But my hands feel the engine working, and my hands recall trips in cars with weaker internal organs: I clench and turn up the dashboard lights, the brain floods with a recollection of

---

* From *Something New Under the Sun: An Environmental History of the Twentieth-Century World*, by J. R. McNeill: "This energy regime allowed wealth and ease on scales quite impossible in earlier centuries for a billion or two people. It had enormous social, economic, and geopolitical consequences for the twentieth century. It also polluted air and water and changed environments generally on scales equally impossible in earlier centuries. Oil, on one reckoning at least, was the single most important factor in shaping environmental history after the 1950s."

snow one cold winter night as I approached the Rockies in Wyoming, in a rented minivan, with my mother-in-law in the back with my daughter, both of them so far back, so far away from my wife and me in the front seat, that we did not see them much those three thousand miles—I will never rent a minivan again, driving already is too lonely.

We cross the Allegheny River. We pass towns I don't recognize, which startles me, so often have I driven this stretch of this road.

Here in Pennsylvania we see the phrase "All-American Plaza" on a giant sign towering over the woods. And my wife and I look at each other and think: what does that mean, "All-American Plaza?" This is just one reason we are still married, I believe, a deep-set interest in such matters.

We do not take the Punxsutawney exit, of course. We merely pass it, thinking of the groundhog that famously sees its shadow there, thinking of seasons, of passing of time. As I already mentioned, it's getting dark.

THE HIGHEST POINT IN THE CROSSING

UNDER THE BRIGHT-BURNING HALF MOON, beneath the darkening blue of the sky, in between the rows of reflective flames that burn in the headlights on the edge of the road, pursued by tractor trailers and following in their long, brightly lighted wake, we come now to the sign that marks the highest point on Interstate 80 east of the Mississippi. We come to an elevation of 2,250 feet. And at this highest point, I hereby look back very quickly, not at the West and all of America that we have traveled. Who would want to go through that again? No, I look back to the days when this road—Interstate 80, the first cross-country interstate—was about to be finished, was first near completion, a small finalizing patch put in place right here in Pennsylvania.

THE KEYSTONE SHORTWAY—a 313-mile run of interstate across north-central Pennsylvania, through beautiful lost-looking hills, rolling forest— opened in September 1970. Fred Waring, of Fred Waring and the

Pennsylvanians, conducted an orchestra of students from eighteen schools, and there were speeches and balloons—orange, blue, red, and green balloons were released, each with a tag good for one of two Shortway souvenirs, a book about the new road or an ashtray. The engineer who headed the job was seventy-six years old and about ready to retire ("to close up shop," he said), and he told people that he originally hoped to build the road in time for the 1939 World's Fair—it was named the Shortway because it would shave ninety miles off the trip from New York to Ohio, from the Delaware Water Gap to the Ohio border. When it opened, the corners at all the interchanges were immediately leased to motels and restaurants, and sixty-nine new factories were built in the fifteen counties that the Shortway crossed. Businesspeople praised the opportunities, nonbusinesspeople worried about crime, people just moving through.

Two thousand of the 2,900 miles of I-80 were open in 1970, and newspapers sent out reporters to inspect the nearly finished cross-country superroad. In 1965, *Engineering News-Record* predicted, "The motorist who zips across the country on I-80 will be able to sample a hefty slice of Americana."

The reporters met mechanics in Pennsylvania happy to have had their car repair work doubled; small-town grocers in Pennsylvania worried about competition; a Youngstown, Ohio, chamber of commerce president predicted fifty million dollars of development and called the road "the biggest gift"; a town in Illinois, Joliet, changed its slogan to "The Crossroads of America." Meanwhile, Omaha had ten thousand new jobs that had been manufactured since I-80 opened. Cheyenne had a new five-million-dollar motel. Reno, Nevada, had more tourists and a smog over Lake Tahoe that was not lifting— forest lookout stations were closed.*

In Brooklyn, Iowa, a doctor predicted that I-80 would put an end to the shortage of doctors in Iowa. A farmer broke up his one farm into an unfarmable two; another farmer refused to sell his land, so that in 1970, the exit

---

* I-80 was completed in its entirety on August 17, 1986. It was completed with a five-mile stretch outside of Salt Lake City, Utah. During the ceremony in Utah a few days after the stretch was opened, officials noted that they were only about fifty miles from Promontory Point, where, in 1869, the first transcontinental railroad was completed. Additionally, a regional federal highway administrator, Morris Reinhardt, made the following statement, a statement that I am not certain is true: "This will go down in history. You will be able to read about it in your history books."

that his farm surrounded had no motel, no restaurant, and no gas station, despite constant calls from oil companies, trying to get him to sell so a gas station could be built. "The trouble is, I'd have the darned thing under my nose," the farmer said.

The editor of the local weekly paper, the *Brooklyn Chronicle*, said: "One of the state patrolmen told me a while ago back that if people in Brooklyn had any idea of what was going by out there they'd be sitting with shot guns in their laps all the time."

"Reports from all the states through which Interstate 80 passes make it clear that not everyone loves the highway," a newspaper report said. "But the vast majority seem to view it with fondness and with hope."

What fondness and hope replaced, in the thinking of thinkers of the road, was nothingness, the only alternative to the road.

The *New York Times* wrote: "The Shortway, which was opposed in the beginning by Philadelphia, the Pennsylvania Turnpike Authority, and the Route 6 Association, opens up an area of Pennsylvania that has been rich in the rugged scenery of the Poconos and the Allegheny Mountains and the pleasant towns and the neat farms but not much else."*

NOT MUCH ELSE! COINCIDENTALLY, at this moment, at the highest point on I-80 East, we are on the very edge of not much else. In this case we are, as I-80 travelers, in Pennsylvania state lands that border a reserve that runs to the north and east, to where the Pine Creek runs down through the Grand Canyon of Pennsylvania, an area of the United States that is considered among the most pristine, among the least touched by humans—on par with the Jarbridge Wilderness in Nevada, the Central Idaho Wilderness, and parts of the Texas grasslands. The Endless Mountains are a capital of *not much else!*

Forgive me once again, for it is late in this trip, and I have obviously driven a few too many miles. Forgive me, for I have cruised the roads of the country

---

* Route 6 is the route that Jack Kerouac wanted to take but didn't, because it was raining and he couldn't hitch a ride. "I'd been poring over maps of the United States in Paterson for months," *On the Road* begins, "even reading books about the pioneers and savoring names like Platte and Cimarron and so on, and on the road-map was one long red line called Route 6 that led from the tip of Cape Cod clear to Ely, Nevada, and there dipped down to Los Angeles. I'll just stay on 6 all the way to Ely, I said to myself, and confidently started."

so often that I am now consumed with the contemplation of roads. Forgive me, for the road is devouring me, like a flame: I am burning in the fires of continual, relentless cross-country driving. But I must ask rhetorically now: what else is *not much else?*

THE NIGHT CLOSES DOWN ON US, and in the humbling dark, I too am hopeful but also gloomy about what cars and roads can do. In the closing-in aisles of tractor trailers, I am driving so much that I am beginning to forget that I am driving. I am thinking of the interstates and they are making me anxious and I need to get home, to get to one place and lie down for a few days.

In fact, the highest point is a low point for me, because it is pretty clear that I am losing it again.

ALL-KNOWING GUIDE

I TURN TO MY ALL-KNOWING GUIDE, who has geared herself up for the late-evening cross-countrying: the TripTik in one hand, the TourBook in the other, she calculates distances and exit numbers and motel details along the three hundred or so miles left to go—she calculates possibility. Three hundred miles! *Three hundred!* A number that is laughable in terms of how far we have come—twenty-five hundred on this trip and another four thousand coming out—and that would be like nothing were it nine o'clock in the morning, in the day, or earlier in my life on the road, when we were twentywhatever and coffee was new to my lips. If it were the morning, we would laugh at three hundred miles. Now, I cower at three hundred miles. Only four hours more, but it is now like a lump in our throat as we climb slowly through the Appalachians. I am afraid of falling asleep.

WAYS THE AUTHOR SEES THIS PARTICULAR SITUATION, THE SITUATION BEING HIM BEGINNING TO FALL ASLEEP BEHIND THE WHEEL AS HE CROSSES THE APPALACHIANS

FIRST, I SEE US WAY UP. I see us in the mountains, or the East Coast's version. I see us in the Alleghenies—part of the Appalachians, an old mountain range geologically speaking, older than the relatively newborn Rockies. These mountains are the mountains that separated the colonies from the frontier, from the physical country it felt it was destined to be. I see these mountains—the very mountains that I am dangerously close to falling asleep in—that America itself struggled through when it first became America.

The National Road, the very first U.S. highway, the genetic forebearer of our path tonight, began life because of these mountains: the road that Washington called for (after surveying parts of the Alleghenies, after struggling through them in the French and Indian War), the road that Jefferson, our national land envisioner, proposed as a link to the new Louisiana Purchase; the road that Congress subsequently commissioned in 1800. The National Road was surveyed in 1811; interrupted by the War of 1812; and completed from Cumberland, Maryland, to Wheeling, West Virginia, also in the heart of the Alleghenies, in 1818. It featured a surface of crushed stone, and it mostly followed an old Indian trail, Nemacolin's Path. The road moved west from 1825 to 1833 along the trail built by Ebenezer Zane, and then continued again to Vandalia, Illinois, and at last to Saint Louis, the eight-hundred-mile-long road eventually being a road used in the great western migration, when people sang:

> Droop not my brothers, as we go
> Over the mountain, westward, ho!

It is true, that the National Road began to fall apart by the 1830s, and the states had to take over its maintenance from the federal government and add tolls, a possible foreshadowing of what is ahead today for the national road system that has not already been converted to toll road. The National Road was the first giant national public works project, the road that Jefferson's allies saw as the "road cementing the union of our citizens located on the Western Waters with those of the Atlantic States," the road on which the troops set out for the West, to explore, to build, to take. That National Road was the road eventually known by one of its various nicknames: the Cumberland Road, the Ohio Road, Uncle Sam's Highway, the Great Western Turnpike, the United States Road, and simply, the Road. In 1815, it was eighty feet wide, a layer of broken stone, a foot thick in the best parts, on top of another layer of gravel. Jefferson predicted a six-day trip from Washington to Saint Louis, but it ended up being about ten. "Never," wrote one historian, "in all the world, since the great days of road-building by the Romans, had any government undertaken to construct such a highway."

IN THIS LONG AND GETTING LONGER NIGHT, I see crossing the mountains that Americans first crossed—and crossing them on the first cross-country interstate highway—as akin to approaching some giant space-time continuum that you see in science fiction films. I see it as symbolically difficult. In the light of the long line of tractor trailers, beneath a big moon in a clear late summer sky, Louis Armstrong, picked by our son for the car stereo, sings: "I'm so forlorn."

ON A LATE SUMMERY SATURDAY NIGHT with a nearly full moon, I see mountains and I see darkness and, in the flickering shine of the reflectors between which we drive, in the blinking reds of the trucks that race up to us, pass us, sometimes cutting us off, I see the fiery flames of car accidents. I'm afraid that I see the moment as a metaphor, as if an ancient poet sitting on the hood of the car would tell me not to go on, if I asked him—as if my wife is my Beatrice, my patron from another, higher world. I really do see this kind of thing, and if you don't believe me, you should talk to me after I've been in the car for five or six days just driving, driving, driving.

SOME QUESTIONS ABOUT DEATH
ON THE HIGHWAY

What is the deadliest month to drive, according to the National Highway Traffic Safety Administration?
August—i.e., the summer vacation month, because deaths of Americans on the highway are directly related to the number of miles that Americans drive. The more miles Americans drive, the more likely they are to die driving. And Americans drive the most during the summer, in the time of the summer vacation. After August comes October and then July, in terms of statistically deadliest months.

What are you, the author, doing driving again?
We are on summer vacation—a summer driving vacation.

What is the deadliest time of day to drive?
The end of the day, either between three and six P.M. or between six and nine P.M.

What time is it now, when you are in Pennsylvania?
The end of the day.

According to the National Highway Traffic Safety Administration, what is the deadliest day of the week to drive?
Saturday, which, yes, is what this day is.

From the point of view of a highway engineer, what are the technical reasons for an accident?
A road engineer sees an accident as most liable to happen in the moment when the driver's performance drops to a low point for any of a number of reasons (distraction, a failure in the vehicle, or sleepiness) at the same time that the road makes its highest demands on a driver (weather, turns, roadwork).

How do you feel as you drive now?
I feel tired, as in the walking-dead tired.

What is the condition of I-80 in Pennsylvania?
Bad, if you ask me. For years and years we have traveled through construction, horrendous construction on horrible roads—roads that inevitably end up forcing us into one lane, a lane in which we sit between trucks or large aggressive drivers and the trucks or the drivers encourage us to move forward and move faster in ways that are aggressive and rude.

Have there ever been any horrific accidents on this stretch of I-80?
Some months before our rented tires spin across this stretch of Pennsylvania, in the winter, there was a series of accidents on I-80, beginning at eleven in the morning, when a snow squall caused a whiteout, and cars and trucks began to crash into each other—sixty-three vehicles were reportedly involved, including a tractor trailer carrying flammable material, which exploded after the crash. There were crashes in both lanes. The man who was a passenger in the car that was second in the line of crashed cars said his wife attempted to avoid the swerving of the first car and got hit by a car behind them and then hit again into a guardrail. And then cars began hitting each other, one after the other. "It was like a chain reaction," his wife said.

"It was like, 'Boom! Boom!'" another woman in the accident said. "Every few seconds you could hear another car exploding."

Cars plunged into the ravine. Cars burned. Days later, when bodies were still being identified, people from around the country called the Pennsylvania State Police hoping to track down friends and relatives who had not yet returned home from the holidays.

The following Friday, another person died in a tractor trailer pileup. The next week there were three more multivehicle pileups in this area, just past the highest point on Interstate 80 in the East, in the space between the Allegheny and the Susquehanna rivers.

In the first accident, tractor trailers and twenty cars crashed and burned and killed six people, the crash again in the morning, though the vehicles burned through the night. "They can't get the fires out," a state trooped said.

The second accident involved three trucks, one pulling a prefabricated home, a so-called wide load.

The third accident involved twelve tractor trailers.

Because the area is so remote, during the following month, the Pennsylvania

Department of Transportation announced that it put emergency heart defib-rillators in the rest stops along the road.

Are you looking a lot at the white stripe down the middle of the highway, the one that you have been looking at for the past five days, the one that is your personal hell at this point?
Yes, and aside from looking at it I am recalling that there are a few theories as to where the white stripe came from but the most prevalent theory—and the one that I personally believe—is that the white stripe was developed by June McCarroll, a woman who was born in the East at the end of the nineteenth century and moved to California, near Palm Springs, when her husband de-veloped tuberculosis; who worked as a doctor for the Southern Pacific Rail-road and for the Native American tribes in the area; who was sideswiped and run off the road by a truck one day in 1917 as she was driving the road that would one day be U.S. 99; who painted a white stripe down the middle of the road and then, through the local Women's Club (and subsequently the Cali-fornia Federation of Women's Clubs), petitioned for the white stripe to be law, which it now is; who had a stretch of I-10 named after her, the Doctor June McCarroll Memorial Freeway.

What is happening now?
Oh boy, am I losing it. Am I ever feeling tired as I am herded into a single lane, behind a truck on a Saturday night late in the summer. I am slapping my face. I am slapping my face repeatedly.

A QUESTION FROM THE BACK SEAT

Are we going to make it home tonight?
We're trying but it will be very late if we do, so please, you can just go to sleep, please, I say.

A VISION

SUDDENLY, WE SEE SOMETHING. Ahead of us, ablaze in the beam of our lights, a vision. A vision that involves a van that is scribbled on with writing that is in its homemadeness more scary than quaint in the headlight-striped darkness. My wife and I hunch forward to read; the back seat jostles to see beyond the front seat's headrests. It is a word-covered truck, as in a Word-covered truck; it is a van painted with words that shout out about God and righteousness and sin, about love and marriage and more sin, about man and woman and sin again. The van is going very slowly. It is crawling. I am too quickly getting too close to it. I am hitting the brakes.

GOD ON THE ROAD

A PART OF US IS USED TO THIS—a part of us is used to seeing God-related signage on the road. Put another way, in our transcontinental experience, the frequency of God-related signage comes just after seeing signage for food and lodging, signage for directions, and signage for adult entertainment. There are signs for God saving, God damning, God watching, God choosing, and God caring; as far as iconic representations of God go, cross-country travelers most often see representations of the Virgin Mary* or the cross, with, in my own personal experience with the road and God, representations of Jesus Christ coming in around third.

Cross-country drivers see crosses in fields along roads, on tops of hills, on cars, on fences and towers, and once, while driving across Texas, we stopped at one of the largest roadside crosses that I know of—a 190-foot, metal-siding-covered cross in Groom, Texas, just off Interstate 40. It stands on a

---

* We saw a giant Virgin Mary in Montana, on Day Two of this particular cross-country trip, in the Rockies, if you will recall.

rise in the midst of the Texas Panhandle's flatness. You can see it for twenty miles in most directions, and, on an audiocassette for sale at the Giant Cross gift shop, you can hear the man who designed and built the giant cross, Steve Thomas, talk about its impact: he believes it is seen by ten million people a year as they drive by. "Some cry, some praise the Lord, and some try to ignore the message," he says. "But all are reminded of Jesus. This is spiritual food for the spiritually hungry."

We happened to see it on a gray, rainy day, when the sky seemed disappointed. When I saw it, I exited and followed a sign to the Giant Cross parking lot:

GIAN✝ CROSS

A sign promised what it called "an Amazing Spiritual Experience."

I DON'T KNOW IF IT WAS THE GRAY SKY or the fact that the cross was nearly twenty stories tall and the thickness of a house, but everyone else in the car was a little freaked out by the Giant Cross and didn't get out. I got out and went to the visitor's booth. A woman greeted me. "That's our visitor center over there," she said cheerily, "and those are the Stations of the Cross and then behind that there's Calvary and behind that is . . ." She paused and pointed to a kind of hill surrounded by construction material. "Oh, I'm brain dead today," she said. "That's the empty cave, that's right, and then if you could just sign our guest register."

I was the only visitor at that moment, and as I walked toward the Giant Cross, the place was quiet except for the whooooosh of car after car on the interstate and the crunch of my sandals on gravel. I walked slowly, not certain, unfamiliar with decorum at a roadside giant cross; the feeling of the place was an unsettling combination of service area and religious shrine. It was all a little eerie, actually, and I looked back at everyone in the car and even though they were watching me, no one smiled or waved.

I approached the Giant Cross slowly, and, when I was face-to-face with it and its smooth backyard-toolshed-like metal siding and the thousands of metal fasteners extending up into the gray highway-side sky, I didn't know what to do exactly, so I touched the Giant Cross. When I did, I realized there was a small door in the otherwise smooth surface of the cross—a Giant Cross maintenance access point, I assume. I looked at the door for a while, feeling self-conscious, and then I turned around and nearly tripped over a life-sized

Station of the Cross, a black metal sculpture of Christ lying down on a life-sized cross, a nail being hammered through his hand by a Roman soldier, the Roman soldier's arm back, caught in midswing. I looked around and realized I was encircled by a ring of about-to-be crucified Christs, and by more crosses, and then I saw that Calvary was a re-creation of the hill mentioned in the Bible, a hill with even more crosses, the re-created site of the Crucifixion with stairs for easy access by visitors.

I turned in a circle, seeing just beyond the site of the Giant Cross, seeing the town of Groom, Texas, and the flat, flat plains, the great mysterious flatness.

We drove back out on the interstate, and as we sped up to get on, we narrowly missed hitting a pickup truck that was pulling over suddenly, apparently to get a look at the Giant Cross.

PASSING

STILL BEHIND THE GOD-ADVERTISING VAN—behind it for a while now, its reflective glow slowing us, dragging us along slowly, dragging we who are physically dragging, we who are at the door of our mental motel rooms—we begin to contemplate passing. Meanwhile, as if to add to the bunker-under-fire atmosphere in the front of the Impala, trucks behind us are beginning to honk. They are beginning to blink their high beams, flashing their brightest lights. They are flashing at me, as well as the vehicle in front of me. We, the expeditionary leaders, are saying things to each other: *Be careful. I see it. It's slowing down more! What is he thinking! Look out for this truck! Look out!* Trucks are passing faster and faster now, trucks racing up behind us, slamming on their brakes and horns, and then passing, passing, passing. Finally, we summon the courage to do likewise, to pass this vehicle that is before us and glowing. A gap between trucks allows us to change lanes and, on an uphill run, pass, the passing being terrifying to me as now a truck is barreling up behind us. I begin, for one of the very last times on this trip, to think that the end is near, that a tractor trailer is about to charge the Impala and run it down and devour it as if it were an actual impala out on the African plains. I pass the God van.

THE FINAL QUESTION AND FINAL ANSWER

From the back seat: Are we going to make it home tonight?
From the from seat: We're figuring that out.

I OPEN THE WINDOW

SLEEP—JUST SAYING THE WORD while driving late, after days and days and days of driving, causes me to feel its dark power, causes me to feel the warmth of the car, which lures me, Siren-like, to that eyes-closed happiness. Concerned, I look to my wife, who is semi-asleep, her eyes closed, her lap covered in maps, the TripTik in hand. In semi-desperation, I open the window and the air races in, the sound of the disintegrating pack roaring, but in just a few seconds, in less than a minute, the fresh air too makes me sleepy, weary: *sleep.*

SWERVE

AND NOW, I AM ABOUT TO SWERVE, ever so slightly to the right. I am about to hit the so-called rumble strip. Or at least I think I hit a rumble strip, the rumble strip having been developed by the state highway department of Indiana, on rural roads, out where a person might miss a rural Stop sign. As my wheel hits the groove of the pavement, as the car stutters, I semi-jerk the car to the left.

"Are you alright?" my wife asks, suddenly jerking awake.

"We have to find a place," I say.

"OK," she says, startled back to map work.

She looks down, and looks back up immediately—she was ready for this moment, just one of the reasons I love her.

"Bellefante," she says. "Next exit. A Holiday Inn."

A VERY BAD DAY

I DRIVE INTO THE U-SHAPED ENTRANCE of a Holiday Inn built in the early days of the interstate. I fall out of the car, but my daughter follows me, fresh, napped, ready to greet the desk clerk kindly, as is her wont. A woman is before us, and as I attempt to summon the mental acumen necessary to speak while being so tired, I sense discord, discord connected somehow to a lack of rooms. I am terrified, frankly, at the thought of there being no rooms. I cannot return to the night. I can drive no more. I need this encounter with the desk clerk to proceed smoothly and efficiently, the end result being a room, any room. At last it is our turn. In the lobby, we are standing beside a small water fountain, the water trickling patiently.

"Hi, how are you?" I say to the clerk, smiling, my arms open, or at least not crossed.

The clerk says nothing. He is typing at his computer. Immediately, I am concerned. I pause. He looks at me; he almost stares.

"Hi, is it okay?" I say now—I am concerned that he is in the middle of something that cannot be interrupted. Again, he just looks at me and does not reply.

My daughter, whom I am not certain the clerk sees, for she is beneath the height of the counter, makes her own attempt to contact him.

"Hello, how are you?" she asks.

This breaks him, or appears to me to break him. Without skipping a beat, he addresses her. "Well, I've had a very bad day," he says. "A very bad day. Not that it matters."

"Sorry," she says, smiling, though nervously, on her toes.

"Sorry about that," I say. "I guess you're probably sold out then."

He shoots back. "No, we're not," he says curtly. "But the only rooms we have left have two queen beds, and they're a hundred dollars."

It's true. One hundred dollars is more than I had planned to spend, especially after the nice hotel in Minneapolis. I planned to be home this evening, to slip into New York late at night, too late for traffic.

"That's fine, great," I say. "We'll take one."

But then I pause, remembering how much my wife detests smoking rooms, how much my children detest them. "Oh, no, I'm sorry," I say. "Are they smoking or nonsmoking?"

He stops typing, and slowly looks up at me.

This is it, I think. *I am going to be asked to leave.*

"Well," he says, annoyed. "They're smoking, but since you have a child, you'll be getting nonsmoking, because smoke is not good for children."

I am flummoxed. "Oh, really," I say, "Uh . . ."

I look at my daughter. "Well, I don't smoke, so that works out pretty nicely," I say. My daughter looks up at me as the clerk returns to typing, and she discreetly smiles.

"Fine," he says and he gives us a room, a bright warm room.

PART VII

Getting Home

DID I EVER MENTION that part of the reason we embarked on this round-trip cross-country drive was to go to a wedding? We're talking about the wedding now, on this final morning in the car, on this last day to the sea, when our voyage across the continent is coming to an end. The car's trip meter says 3,117 miles, a distance that took us a little longer than we had expected, but still we are pleased and relaxed, smiling and reminiscing about past miles as we proceed down the eastern side of the Appalachians. We are on a downhill run out of the night that we have somehow survived and into the light that shines this morning on the eastern mountains—albeit a light that is not so focused. There is a haze, which in a short while burns away to reveal a thick fog, which in turn lifts to reveal the cloudy but bright white sky. There is no stopping today, not because we won't make it if we stop; there is no stopping because of the tantalizing anticipation of no longer having to sit in a car and drive. The expeditionary members' resistance to stopping is at its highest, as is illustrated by comments made when I pull over for gas in front of a convenience store in a small town in the Poconos, the coffee from Central America via Vermont fresh, the staff not at all talkative.

"Why are you stopping?" says our daughter. "Get back in the car. What are you doing?"

"Don't stop driving," says our son. "Do we really *have* to stop?"

At one point, in the jovial mood of a driver who can see the light at the end of the tunnel, or in this case, at the end of Interstate 80, I joke that I am going the wrong way. Our daughter does not think this joke is funny. She is serious about getting home now, focused.

"Dad, stop joking about things like that," she says.

The team is not reading. They are not asleep. They are sitting up, focused, looking out on almost-home. My wife is pleased to be finishing her quilt.

* * *

AND WE ARE REMEMBERING the wedding.

It was a wedding in the Cascade Mountains, the far north of the American Northwest, a remote corner of the country. It was my wife's cousin's wedding, and after resting the rented Impala for a few days in Portland, we headed north on Interstate 5 and then took a right turn east up into the mountains. We went up State Highway 20, through the fringe of interstate development and into smaller and smaller towns, including Sedro Woolley, an old logging town and an old Wobbly town, where workers making modular homes as well as convenience store clerks joined the Wobblies a few years ago, an old loggers' union returned to life. The Wobbly motto: "Forming the new society within the shell of the old."

We drove farther and farther into the higher and higher hills, some logged off, some with trees returned or returning, and eventually wound up skirting beautiful corners of peaks and daredevil cliffs and bottomless blue lakes in the North Casade National Park. After nine long, hard hours of slow, turn-after-turn driving, we wound down into a little town on a river plain where there were a few ranches and cabins. We found the lodge where we were staying, along with all the other people going to the wedding.

The next morning, we got up early to go on a hike in the North Cascade Mountains, the same mountains where some beat poets lived in the late fifties; Gary Snyder, Philp Whalen, and Jack Kerouac had all taken jobs as fire lookouts, all of them—in their correspondence, in their journals, in their writings from the time—frequently referencing Han Shan, the anonymous eight-century Chinese poet and mystic, who in his incarnation as folk hero, lived on Cold Mountain and poked fun at the self-important monks, the rushing and worrying in the world down below. "If I don't get a vision on Desolation Peak, my name ain't William Blake," Kerouac wrote to Lucien Carr just before he entered his mountaintop cabin. I would loved to have climbed to one of the beats' fire lookouts that afternoon, or at least to see one of the peaks they lived on, but we had to get to the wedding—time is elusive no matter where you are in the country. So after our hike, we raced back to the lodge, and everyone got dressed up for the wedding. For the first time on a driving trip in years, I even took off the car keys that I was wearing on my lanyard.

*   *   *

THE RECEPTION WAS BEING SET UP at a lodge down the road, and the wedding ceremony was a short walk from there, down alongside a fast-running little stream: people sat in a circle of chairs in the smooth stones and gravel. Our friend Carol played violin, and it was as if the air and the clear summer afternoon's light were a small, gentle choir quietly accompanying her. There was a point in the ceremony during which people were asked to speak if they felt so moved, and I decided to be quiet and let other people talk for a change—in the case of my wife and children, they'd had to listen to me talk all the way across the country. Then the couple were married, and we all walked back up to the lodge, where tables were set up, where behind the building the peak of the mountain that we had climbed that day was towering over us, an implausible sky-sized prop.

There was a fiddler and a woman was calling dances, simple old dances to simple old fiddle tunes, from the Colonial era, and the men lined up quickly to face a line of women—the fiddler had to leave early, so everyone started dancing right away. Our kids danced with each other and with their relatives, and my wife and I danced and we had a great time: it had been a long time since my wife and I had danced. The summer sun wasn't even thinking about setting, even at nine at night, and we danced and laughed, and at one point the caller asked couples to step down one at a time, depending on how long they had been married. Thus, the longest-married couples danced the longest, and we were excited to be nearly last on the dance floor, even after all our driving, all our moves—beaten only by the couple who had been married for twenty years. Finally, the fiddler left, though I could have kept dancing all night under that mountain.

The cake was cut and then we went back to the lodge and to bed. The next morning was crisp and clear, and I packed the car, patiently carrying bags across dry pine needles, relaxed in the alpine air. And then, when I finished packing the bags in the trunk, when I was feeling organized and purposeful, I locked the keys in the trunk. I realized that they were in the trunk during the half a second or so that it took for the trunk to slam down.

I went into the lodge's dining room and mentioned that I had locked the keys in the trunk to my wife, who was having coffee. I was pretty calm, I thought, considering that after years of worrying about locking my keys in the car, I had finally managed to do so in one of the most faraway parts of the country. I called a locksmith in the next town, a half hour away, and then sat down for breakfast. In about an hour, I was wearing my lanyard again. To get the key out of the trunk cost two hundred dollars.

As we reminisce now, in Pennsylvania, in our final three or so hours of our trip home, after we talked about how wonderful the wedding was and how much we enjoyed the dancing, the subject of me locking the keys in the car arises, as it will continue to do from time to time, by my own accord or that of others, even later when we are at home. "Remember when you locked the keys in the trunk?" my wife will later ask, for instance. "That was horrible."

"Aside from the two hundred dollars, what was so horrible about it?" I will respond.

WE HAVE GAS, and we have already had food. Lewis and Clark suffered in their last days of travel to the West Coast, nearly died. When they returned to Saint Louis, at the end of the summer of 1806, they were exhausted and, in Lewis's case, possibly lost somehow, confused. In contrast, on our last run, we are feeling pretty good, considering the night before. We are cruising up short hills and coasting down longer ones, as the Appalachians release us, as we cross the threshold and cross the Susquehanna, as we prepare to cross the Delaware.

We pass a woman in a car, hunched over, concentrating on the road straight ahead, oblivious to our wave.

"Her license plates are from Colorado," my daughter says.

"Look at her go," I say.

For me, crossing the Delaware is a big moment in the return cross-country trip. We greet the toll taker. We pay exact change, and then drive a long low bridge across a wide bend in the river, seeing boaters and fishermen or the occasional Sunday-morning hikers in the woods. We cross the Appalachian Trail, that utopian vision for America that, as I mentioned, didn't work quite as planned but worked. Additionally, I would argue that in crossing the Delaware we cross yet another metaphorical line, metaphorical lines being all I see after driving pretty much straight with the exception of a break for golf in Montana and that long day in Minneapolis.

Crossing the Delaware is crossing the river that was crossed by the founding father, George Washington. The crossing of the Delaware is a moment that, as historians currently recall it, the Revolutionary War began to turn in favor of the colonial army, when the United States was not just imagined but executed. Thus, in my now-frazzled mind, when we cross the Delaware, we are reborn. We are able to see the country at conception, at its philosophic origin. Or even if we are not reborn, I feel reborn when we cross it—especially when I see the Delaware Water Gap, that cut in the mountains that is, no matter how you look at it, the entrance to our return, the gate into the East Coast home country. We began our entry into the continent through the Columbia River Gorge, and we end it coming through this gorge on the eastern shore. In the forested Kittatinny Mountains that surround the Delaware Water Gap, I feel symmetry, I feel conclusive, I feel caffeine.

"I can see the Delaware Water Gap," I blurt out to everyone in the car.

The response is a question—a question that I have heard before and have been reluctant to respond to. Now, I am pleased to answer, the answer being sweet, mellifluous even. "How much longer?" my daughter asks.

"Not much," my wife says, nodding, smiling, turning the TripTik to the very last page. The very last page of the TripTik being a map of the last fifty-five miles, featuring the phrase "Approach Routes N.Y.C."

On this last page is the final green east-pointing arrow. *Home James!*

IN THE FIRST FIELD- AND FARM-BORDERED MILES of New Jersey's I-80, I risk an incident in the Impala and actually stop, just for a moment, at an interstate scenic viewpoint, in order to look back on the portal in the continent and on the horizon. From the top of a hill and with people antsy to get back in the car, I see a place between city and country, between development and national park, in this case the Delaware Water Gap National Recreation Area. I see the interstate running out of the West and the Plains and lands along the Mississippi and then through the old mountains of Pennsylvania. I see the interstate running out into the green of New Jersey and, as I do, I see an I-80 that is broken up in places, literally, which reminds me of what a trucker said about the state of the interstate—way back in 1978, when the interstates were only six hundred miles from being completed and twenty-two years old: "The whole interstate isn't worth the powder and lead you'd need to blow it apart."

Even today, the interstate is a utopian vision that is crumbling, that by nature will crumble, that at one point or another, after a million tourists like me, after billions of tons of truck cargo, after studded tires and rain and snow and salt and the road being what it is, will end—the interstate doesn't go on

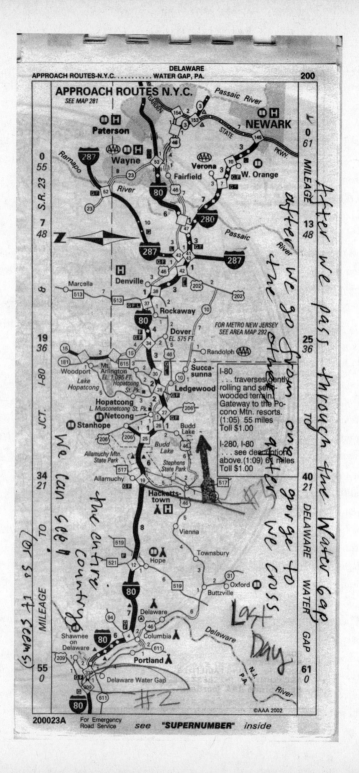

forever. It is like an invasive species, a path that is unflinching despite its uncertainty, that destroys as it manages to thrive.

AS IF IN SYNCH WITH MY PENCHANT for reverse imaginary time travel,
I-80 just into New Jersey is named in honor of Christopher Columbus, and
we travel it nearly alone, four empty lanes on either side of the grassy median.
The few miles that remain seem longer than the miles at our beginning—the
miles at the end of a country-crossing being the opposite of the gallons at the
end of a tank of gas. As far as the shredding, really expensive rooftop pack
goes, I almost don't notice the pack anymore. The pack is bearable now, for I
am rolling home.

We cross the Musconetcong River, described by the Musconetcong Watershed Association in a manner that is a beautiful combination of reverence
and humility, an attitude toward the land that is utopian in its practicality, inspired in its unexceptionalism: "The Musconetcong River valley is not a place
where great battles were fought or important treaties signed. No single historic feature found in the valley is by itself entirely unique to the history of
the region, state, or nation. Yet, few river valleys in New Jersey tell such a
compelling story of the interrelationships between humans and the natural
environment." After the Musconetcong, we notice I-80 is picking up a ragged-
ness, the road seeming worn. A caution sign says, MAINTAIN SPEED.

An hour and a half to go, and as we move away from the gap, we are officially heading into that settlement on the Atlantic side of the Appalachians
that runs from Maine to south of Washington, D.C., and is spreading. It is
the eastern seaboard's vast megalopolis, the assemblage of villages, towns,
cities, edge cities, suburbs, and ruburbs that stretches from Atlanta to Maine,
a five-hundred-mile stretch that contains forty-five million people, the
world's greatest concentration of urban areas. It seems quaint to look back on
what people thought the East would become, but in the case of development,
the past still seems prescient. "We are confronted with the prospect of a place
of business ten miles long," said a New York City newspaper, just after the
Civil War. "What must be the scale of expenses when such monstrous distances must be traveled in the transactions of business?" But the monstrous
distances have only increased, first with trains and now with cars and at last
with interstates. While traffic is slow on this Sunday morning, the road is
worn by the commuters who drive to New York City from old steel towns

behind the water gap, by people who travel for three hours on buses, two and three hours in cars, all so that they can own homes, a patch of land on the ever-expanding edge of the city. Of course, these "monstrous distances" repeat themselves around the country: in Washington, D.C., people travel I-270 from West Virginia; in northern California, commuters drive an hour and a half from Stockton; Boston commuters live hours from the city, in a less and less undeveloped New Hampshire.

Here in Rockaway Township the trees are still green and plentiful, but a highway-side sign offers services, a plethora of chain restaurants, the country's best-known same-everywhere names; we joke about the difficulties the sign maker might have faced in winnowing down the list. The next sign: RE-PORT AGGRESSIVE DRIVING. Then, in the town of New Hope, as we drive a mile or two an hour over the speed limit in the second to last lane on the right, a woman races past me in the so-called slow lane, startling me, a Native American dream catcher dangling from her window.

By this time, black asphalt fills the cracks in the concrete road. Sound barriers begin to rise past the shoulder of I-80. As I am closed in by concrete, I am reminded of driving near interstate-rich Chicago. I see a Holiday Inn that is designed with a brick that echoes the pattern of the road barriers, and then a truck from Springfield, Missouri, on our left, driving what seems like a thousand miles an hour, a sign on its bumper taunting us: IF YOU CAN'T SEE MY MIRRORS . . .

In general, the speed is really picking up on I-80—more cars pass us while simultaneously passing each other. Sound barriers are covered with an ivy of some kind as we near Interstate 287, and then as we pass some new housing developments and more new hotels, we suddenly cross through a swamp, the Great Piece Meadows. It's a semi-native landscape that is a pause in between the greater metropolitan area and the metropolitan area itself, a brief caesura in road-coveredness. The Great Piece Meadows, it has always seemed to me, is a marvel in itself, in that any part of it has avoided the hand of man.

OUR TRIP BEGAN WITH A GORGE AND A WATERFALL—a beautiful western waterfall that travelers on the road religiously stop to view—and, as our trip is less than an hour from its end, we again pass a gorge and a waterfall, but they can't be seen from the interstate: just beyond the Great Piece Swamp, just across the Passaic River, comes Patterson, crumbled city of industrial dreams, brainchild of Alexander Hamilton, Jefferson's archrival, who saw in Patterson's potential industry, and in the industry of the United States' young cities, a liberation from the world, a factory-made self-reliance. Hamilton started the mills that were followed by more mills and factories for fabrics and silk and planes and all kind of manufacturing goods that, like factories all along the Appalachians, saw stops and starts and eventually became great when American manufacturing swelled, during and after the Second World War, and then deflated, to what they are today. Patterson is a symbol of the eastern city un-reborn, still struggling, and the falls—racing, roaring four stories down into the crash of white water—are symbolic of themselves. The falls are falls. I've been off the highway on occasion and stood where there are no crowds and looked out over the raging water, eddies of fast-food litter at the top, and seen the greatness of the Great Falls. Unlike their counterparts on the Columbia River in Oregon, these falls don't draw highway crowds. They are frequently the scene of police activity.

In lieu of the Great Falls, our expedition sees the road, which is crumbling more, weeds waving through the cracks. They see old factory smokestacks, old warehouses, the Eagle Plastic Bag Company, maker of "the plastic bag for all purposes." They see decay. They see the abandonment of a city for the ideals of the rural and the suburban, cities moved to within easy commuting distance of the rural (or semirural) homes of CEOs. They see what looks like the Acropolis but is a not-so-proud-looking bank that holds the deposits of all the immigrants who fill the old stores in downtown Patterson, who play soccer on baseball fields, who save for a new life, which I know because, like I say, I have been there, I have walked around.

Trash is for me the defining note now as we pass Patterson and prepare to pass through the last low ripples of the Appalachian range: there is now an extensive selection of trash along the road, each piece telling a story the way that grasses and seeds tell the story along a western road. Trash is collected in clumps in the gutters. Truck tire shreddings line the left shoulder, the emergency breakdown lane that is bordered by a New Jersey–based Jersey barrier. We pass the Patterson Rod & Gun Club: "Protect your rights, protect your kids." We cross over the Garden State Parkway interchange. "We're going over the Garden State Parkway, guys. Isn't that exciting?" I say, because it kind of is. Marking the intersection of two historical themes of road thinking is a circular, modernist Holiday Inn. We see the interstate has widened, now to eight lanes. We pass over the Garden State Parkway. We switch to an I-80 express lane, passing alongside the spermlike pattern that decorates the walls of sound barriers. The sign dangling above us says, NEW YORK CITY, 10 MILES.

"THERE'S NEW YORK CITY, EVERYBODY!" This I announce, even though everyone has apparently already seen it, and in our through-the-front-windshield view, it is not a city on a hill, like Boston, or the figurative city of the Puritans. Rather it is a city that is surrounded by water and swamps, by fields of trucks and smokestacks, by hills of garbage.

As we see the bristlelike spine of Manhattan, we're in the express lanes to the upper level of the George Washington Bridge, and we're moving at a speed within reasonable distance of the legal speed limit, and yet we are being passed by fleets of people doing above and beyond 70 miles an hour. As we come over the final ridge, the median has gone to seed, making for an accidental kind of wildness. Also as this happens, I am noting things and shouting them out, and everyone seems cool with me doing this because, let's face it, we're just about there. Our goal is in sight, joy again fills the car.

"Okay, we've got one, two, three lanes, five, six, seven, eight, nine, ten . . ." I say. "Yes, *ten* lanes!"

Somebody, I think my son, puts on Frank Sinatra.

Once again, we are surrounded by advertising, though the view is still huge despite the billboards—like a moment on the interstate on the Plains when you are coming into, say, Sioux Falls. We see an advertisement for an instant coast-to-coast walkie-talkie, for four nights in the Caribbean, but mostly we see Manhattan, shaped itself by geology: the high rise on the bedrock in the south and middle, the swamp in the middle.

But then we're coming into more cars in the express lanes, and then, slowly, the euphoria slows. We are coming into traffic.

There is nothing like traffic to squash euphoria, I'll tell you. Highly audible sighs are voiced in the rear of the car. And it's a lot of traffic on I-80, megalopolis-worthy traffic in the roads over the swamps surrounding the city, a.k.a. the New Jersey Meadows or the Meadowlands. For a moment, even on Sunday, we slow nearly to a standstill—it's like traveling from one circle of traffic hell to the next. For the next few minutes, the slow-down persists, but then speed increases, through millions and millions of dollars of new construction, even in these swamps. This is a moment that could be had crossing the country anywhere in America: all over the United States, congestion continues to increase, in small cities and larger ones, in areas of all shapes and sizes. The time that traffic is considered to be "free-flowing," in the words of traffic analysts, is less than half what it was in 1982. The time that we as car-driving Americans spend in traffic that is not free-flowing has more than doubled.

Boldly, we ignore the bridge traffic information sign, the one saying, BEST ROUTE CARS, LOWER LEVEL. We want the upper level at whatever cost. Interstate 80 goes from coast to coast, and New York is an island, which means, in other words, that by the time we are on the George Washington Bridge, the first cross-country interstate will have ended and we will be thrust Evel Knievel–like into the air, if only on a bridge named for George Washington. When I-80 becomes I-95, that great north-south-running interstate, it is like the meeting of the Mississippi and the Missouri, a national juncture.

We proceed at 40 miles an hour, a good-enough speed, until we come to the tollbooths, and find ourselves in a lane behind a broken-down car. Next, we proceed on at 6 miles an hour. Next, we come to a complete standstill— we're like the members of the Corps of Discovery at the moment on their return when they had to pull over their canoes to let a herd of buffalo cross the Missouri. We're behind a Wendy's Old-Fashioned Hamburgers truck and a B&B Produce Yams truck from North Carolina ("Microwavable Sweet Potatoes"). And we've accidentally broken into some kind of convoy of cars with little white ribbons on their antennas. We're frustrated but holding the expedition together. We eat some leftover peanut butter on crackers to get us to the toll. Once we made it all the way across without any traffic then sat for an hour waiting to pay the toll at the George Washington Bridge. It was midnight and it was raining.

THE TRIP OUT OF THE TOLL GATE on the upper deck of the George Washington Bridge is the adult-driving-a-rented-Impala's version of a child setting off from the top of a tall playground slide. We pay our six dollars and then we are zipping (safely, but zipping) down through the cut in the dark cliffs that face the Hudson River.

And then, after seven days and so many thousands of miles, after sights and smells and parking lots and wake-up calls and deliriums and dances and hugging and slamming the key in the trunk of the car, we are over the Hudson, at the east edge of America, the first edge as far as the European settlement of the continent goes, though the last edge if you go the other way. We are in the place where Europeans first got a look at the land that they quickly assumed was theirs. We are in a place where you can see why people would want to live and settle. The Hudson, so wide and blue in the canyon of these palisades, takes over as tour guide, as host, pointing left to the hills of the North Country, pointing right to the tired but still great city, pointing to the gates of the harbor and the sea.

"It's amazing," I am saying over and over, once again and, once again, meaning it.

It's amazing to think of the country when you are done with the interstates and suspended over a mile-wide river. It's amazing to think of the first trips in canoes and by foot through the old mountains behind us. It's amazing to again imagine people crossing the continent in wagons, their entire families, with all their belongings. It's amazing to picture the first cars and the first roads and to picture the first raceways and speedways and parkways and highways and eventually the first interstates. It's amazing to imagine how different the country is due to the development of its roads, it's amazing to picture America seeing America and, in so doing, seeing it change the face of itself.

It's incredible to imagine that in this moment on the bridge, when I feel so perfectly alive and inspired and fulfilled while exhausted and ultimately somehow at one with all my fellow Americans in all the states that I have ever crossed, I at the same time am absolutely apart from the thousands of people around me who have just paid six bucks, with the exception of my wife and two children. On this bridge, in this daredevil-like moment of multilane over-the-river traffic, I can see that the modern American road is a common space where people share nothing. It is the thing that, while separating us, we all have in common.

WHEN I WONDER ABOUT THE FUTURE of the interstates, of these things that cross and bind and rush-hour America into a stupor of convenience and aggravation, and when I think of what seems so unlikely to change, I think again of how quickly things came to be—of the generation of my parents, who saw the birth of the interstates, of the generation of their parents, who saw the birth of the car, of the generation of their parents, who rode the first railroads. Technology is a gift, a nightmare, an illusion, a transitory thing.

Change is well known to be constant, especially to those who have spent a
week on the road, and, after a week, and after fifteen years, I can envision the
roads changing the land *or* the land changing. I can envision farms in the city
and cities in farms. I can envision orchards on Park Avenue and windmills
along the city's outside ridge. I can envision trains running from new small
town to new small town in Montana and regions of various types of cleanly
redesigned industry on the Great Plains. I see suburbs that are developed and
redeveloped to look like something I can't even imagine, something that
mends the division between urban and rural, that somehow heals. I can see
something new built on or alongside or even on top of the interstates, and I
can imagine interstates looking like something I can't imagine, like things
taken out of my wife's cross-country sketchbook.

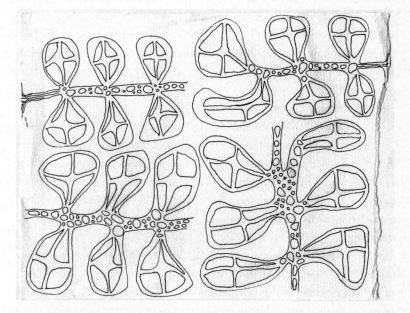

I can envision a future built on history, a path unengineered, unstreamlined—a path mostly just considered. I can envision all kinds of things
happening in and to and on the country, especially after crossing the country
via road.

Then again, I'm just a driver driving the same roads over and over, and I've probably been driving too long. I'm no clairvoyant. I'm a guy in a car with his wife who has been in the car with him many, many times. Maybe too many time, though I hope not. I'm just a dad trying not to drive his wife and his kids crazy. I'm just another driver.

I WOULD MENTION IN CLOSING that during the summer that followed the one I have just finished recounting, we did not drive across the country. We flew. We thought we were going to drive and then we started feeling as if we needed some time off from the road, and, well, we booked some cheap tickets well in advance and flew.

Nobody liked flying. Of course, we liked the *idea* that we could get to Oregon in the space of a day, and I personally liked looking down on the land that we have crossed so many times—to see the lonely interstate runs, to see the development clusters, to see the grid first drawn by the 1785 land survey, to see the Missouri River that Lewis and Clark followed, to cross the Rockies during the course of a videotaped news program shown on an overhead monitor, to cross the Bitterroot Mountains in the time it takes to drink a small cup of lidless coffee.

"I feel cheated," my son said.

"I want to go to New Mexico," said my daughter.

But we really were tired of driving, and after a long series of life-related events, we ended up moving again, as usual—as I have noted time and time again, we are most American in that we are always moving to the next place. In this case, we moved from the suburbs back to the city, where, I am pleased to report, we no longer drive very much at all. We might drive up north to the country, or out to the suburbs to see my parents once in a while, or for some other special occasion, but mostly we walk, an undervalued luxury in our car-oriented world—an extravagance in a country where three quarters of all short trips are made by car, where only 6 percent of daily trips by Americans, according to the Federal Highway Administration, are made on foot. I move our car to the other side of the street once or twice a week when the street cleaner comes.

Now, perhaps perversely, perhaps not, we are thinking that next time, if we can work it out, we are going to drive.

AFTERWORD

OF COURSE, THE ROAD NEVER ENDS. If the road had ended—if I may be simultaneously literal and metaphoric about it—then you wouldn't be reading this, or I wouldn't be typing. This particular road book, however, is now officially over, and at this point, many of you readers are probably relieved or at least excited to grab some sleep or maybe even some coffee, if I haven't scared you away from coffee forever. And then, I imagine, you will set out on another book, maybe something that doesn't move around so much, something contemplative and still, like a book of ancient Chinese nature poetry, the kind of poetry that I have ended up reading upon wrapping up our last few cross-country trips. They ground me, no coffee pun intended, being as they are free of mileage or any idea of, to use a road term that has always seemed to me an oxymoron, "making time."

> The car sits in the driveway,
> wind blowing through the open window,
> rain soaking the maps.
> But I don't care
> Until tomorrow.

After the road trip recounted in the preceding pages, my family and I were pretty tired of traveling. In fact, we worked hard at not going anywhere for a while, a difficult feat in this country that is laced with roads, that is all car all the time. We ate dinner at the neighbors'; we walked around a lot; we took trains.

But after a couple of weeks, we finally ventured out, driving from the house we were then renting in New York up to Rhode Island to go to the Newport Folk Festival. (Yes, we have a folk problem, and my kids would say it's me.) And, as I mentioned in the very first pages of this book, our actual car, as opposed to rental car, broke down, sure enough, pretty much forever. It was difficult to say goodbye to that car. It was a car that we had crossed the country with, and, thus, was a car that was more than a car to us; it was a rattling chunk of metal and plastic that seemed to have soaked up some cross-country anxiety, some vista-viewing excitement, some knowledge of our beginnings and ends: a road-transformed thing.* After that, we moved—packed everything in a truck and set up in a new place. Moving is still one of the things we do best, unfortunately. (My great hope always is that moving will one day become something we *used* to do well.) Specifically, we moved to a place where I don't have to drive as much as I used to: New York City, the city of my birth, as well as a city where, for the price of a cup of fancy, non-road coffee, I can ride forever beneath the streets, reading, relaxing, writing more found concrete poems (see page 242)†—I'm talking about the subway. What happened next, roughly, aside from the kids getting even older and my wife and I celebrating our fifteenth anniversary on the road of married life, was that the company that published this book sent me on the road.

That's right, sent me on the road. In a car. Don't worry. I didn't take it personally. They meant it as a positive thing. Authors know about the mixed blessing of the "tour." I am thinking of Emerson striking out first to New En-

---

*When we broke down, we were in Connecticut and headed to the Newport Folk Festival. We were going there to see some musicians I have mentioned in this book, players we listened to a lot while crossing: in particular, a band called Wilco, a singer named Rufus Wainwright, and a singer and fiddler named Carrie Rodriguez, whose CD we'd bought on a trip through Austin, Texas. We were on the Merritt Parkway, in Connecticut, a beautiful ride, and yet breaking down was obviously extremely disappointing: it was as if the road were telling us that it didn't like us anymore, as if we should just stay home. For a second, we thought we would not make the concert in time. But somehow, using the experience that my wife and I have garnered from so many years of traveling and breaking down in various fashions, we managed to get the car to an exit and then roll it into a gas station. Next, a cab to a rental car place in nearby Fairfield, where I rented a car (again!), and we hurried on to Newport, our hopes rising, even though we were very late. Things were fine until we hit—what do you know?—a highway-long line of traffic and began to not move at all. Now, another idea. On the edge of Newport, we dumped the rental car in a parking lot and grabbed a ferry, which took us right to the festival, flying across the water, beneath a blue ocean sky. The ferry let us off right at the entrance to the festival—like much of life, it seemed as if everything that had happened up to that moment was as fate would have had it, fate being a drunken prankster. When we walked in, my son and I stood for a moment listening to a band called the Mammals, and in a second I realized that we were standing right next to the lead singer of Wilco, who was with *his* son, so I knew we were OK, that we had made it. Like many people, I am happiest when my family is happy, even though I have a tendency to get confused about who knows best about what makes them happy, especially on the road.

†OK, so I am a lousy poet. But let me just say that when we were in Mississippi, a poet came to one of my readings, an actual published poet whose name I won't mention for fear of associating his work with my work. While he in no way complimented me on my "poetry," he did say that he had never seen a found concrete poem before. While there might be several interpretations of this statement, I take it to mean that I am one of perhaps a handful of people working in that genre today.

gland and the Middle Atlantic on the Lyceum circuit of the 1850s and then missing trains in Ohio; of Melville not going over well in the 1850s when he was talking about what he wanted to talk about (nationalism, philosophy, etc.) instead of what people wanted to hear about, which was cannibals. I am thinking of Mark Twain, after coming up with another get-rich scheme that had bankrupted him, inevitably, so that he was back on the road, filling auditoriums with hilarity, to get himself solvent again. From the beginning, the act of authorial touring in America has been a mixture of positive, ego-boosting interactions with the reading public and exhausting, quasi-humiliating races to places where, as happened to me once in Pittsburgh, the "crowd" walks in, alone, looking for something else, apparently, stumbles upon me at a table idly sipping free author-only water, picks up a book—*Rats*, for example—looks at me, looks at the book, and says, incredulously, "This is *you*?"

"Yes," I say.

"Why should I read *this*?"

A question for which I really have no good answer, a question that I have heard often, a question that immediately causes me to feel as if I am suddenly part of a play by Samuel Beckett. I'm sure nobody wants to read a lot of inside baseball about writers out on the road, but in my experience, many people have the wrong idea about book tours. Many people think of room service, escorts, champagne toasts, late nights drinking, or maybe rock-and-roll bands, broken-up hotel rooms, and police dogs. These sorts of things have not been my experience. Sure, an argument could be made that it's good for me (and my family) to get out of the home and home office, respectively, whether the home office be the kitchen or the basement. But mostly book tours don't happen during summer vacation, and I spend a lot of time calling home and feeling bad about not being there when it's a Wednesday night and my wife is attempting to persuade people to do their history homework. Thus, my potentially great idea: Combine the book tour with the family cross-country vacation. I thought, in other words, that my work life and familial vacation needs might, for the first time in recorded human history, align.

As I have stated on numerous occasions, our usual family summer cross-country trip is between three thousand and four thousand miles. But on the book tour–vacation summer, we would, in the end, accrue eight thousand miles. We would, moreover, travel the outer edges of the country. Like

Magellan, the sixteenth-century Portuguese explorer, we would be circum-navigating, except with a minivan.

With the minivan, I was making a concession to the other members of the expedition, given that not all of them saw the genius of combining intensive authorial work and relaxed family vacation. The other members were pro-minivan for a long trip, because of the additional room. My feeling, on the other hand, is that we don't need that much room. And besides, it's difficult for me to make myself heard all the way in the back. (Come to think of it, this is probably a big reason why the other members of the expedition are pro-minivan.) I was also worried about the price of gas, which was rising that summer and was expected to continue to rise, which it did—oh boy, did it rise.

WAS IT THE WORST ROAD TRIP OF OUR LIVES? What is a bad road trip? Had we merely had too much of a good thing, or of the road? Is there such a thing as a bad road trip? Were we all out of our minds when it was nearly over? Once again, I turn the words of Emily Post for solace and hope: "It is your troubles on the road, your bad meals in queer places, your unexpected stops at people's houses; in short your misadventures that afterwards become your most treasured memories." This particular trip, in other words, is one of our most treasured memories.

The biggest difference between this cross-country trip and all our previous cross-country trips: this trip was planned, and we never plan trips. I was to read passages of the book at bookstores around the country—à la your typical book tour—and we had to coordinate our driving accordingly, which meant taking as much time as possible between Washington, D.C., and Oxford, Mississippi, for instance, and racing as fast as we could between Jackson, Mississippi, and Austin, Texas, or between Portland, Oregon, and Saint Paul, Minnesota. Normally, we take our time one way across the country, dawdling where possible, and then hightailing. On this trip, hightailing so often felt like being stuck in a perpetual fire drill; dawdling when we did not wish to dawdle made for existential moments of crisis, as when we were stuck in Chicago in a scorching heat wave and standing out on the street because there was no air-conditioning in our (tiny) hotel room and wondering if we could make a lunch in a restaurant stretch for three or four hours, until dinner, which we would stretch until we returned to the hotel and went to bed, to be awoken by the fraternity boys in the adjacent room, who slept by day and went in and out of their room by night, drunker and louder after each outing. You can only kill time so long before it begins to kill you.

But that makes it sound all bad, or worse than it was, which is not to say it was a dream vacation or a dream. It was more like a sugar-coated nightmare. Looking back, I would certainly not want to do it again, but at the same time, of course, I wouldn't have missed it for anything.

THE LAST THING ANY READER NEEDS from me at this point is more about road tripping, but if I were to name just a few highlights, I might mention stopping in Tennessee, just off the old Natchez Trace, a beautiful old two-lane highway that's older than the country, and, in a clearing in the woods just off the road, seeing the burial site of Meriwether Lewis, an exquisitely sad spot marked by a broken pillar; touring William Faulkner's home in Oxford, Mississippi, or Eudora Welty's house in Jackson, Mississippi, or Elvis's birthplace in Tupelo, Mississippi; taking a tour of the sixty-thousand-acre art ranch in Marfa, created by Donald Judd and covered with giant sculptures and other kinds of art, when a young artist from France leading the tour said to me, "I don't think Americans understand European humor"; sneaking the kids into a bar in the Tenderloin in San Francisco so they could lead the book-reading audience in song, in particular "Don't Fence Me In" and "Farther Along" (people love to sing, I don't care what anybody says); eating at the Pine Top Club, in Dayton, Ohio, a place that looked like it was 1958, where I had a steak that was so good I haven't had one since and have no immediate plans to.

And there were abundant not so highlights, which I don't want to dwell on, so I will just quickly mention the motel room in Oxford that was as dark as night all of our three days. And the drive from Jackson to Austin, Texas, via Louisiana, in one long day, not knowing if we would make the seven hundred miles to the reading, at Book People, but then making it, just barely, my heart panting, everyone beseeching me to calm down as we raced out of the minivan and into the quiet store, a mental rest stop, a haven. Or driving the thousand or so miles through the desert Southwest during a road-melting heat wave, through days so hot that I thought I could smell my skin burning when I de-minivanned, when we got out of the car at an all-but-abandoned rest stop, the wind whipping through a break in the Santa Rosa Mountains, a breeze like something from a hair dryer—people looked at us as if we were crazy to kick a soccer ball, which maybe we were. Or driving from Portland to Minnesota, racing across Montana and the Dakotas, and then taking a state highway, a road so small on the map that our son, who was by now fifteen, looked around and took the map from us and said, "Wait a minute. Why are we on *this* road?" He said it in a way that caused me to realize that we had gone from playtime with the map to him wondering about the navigational savvy of his elders. (From then on, our son watched the maps closely, rarely allowing us to stray from the most direct interstate routes. "We're going to get there," he said at one point.) Or driving that same back road very late that night and not finding any motels with rooms, on account of the fires in the area, so that it was necessary to keep driving, through packs of pronghorns, which crossed the road at random, jumping up from the ditch suddenly, as I attempted to get us to a lodging, any lodging, anywhere.

I would say that the hard part was just driving for a month straight— driving early, driving late, driving until I didn't want to hold the steering wheel anymore. And then, after driving, staying in another motel, all of us on the verge of motel mutiny, tired of putting ice in plastic bags in little plastic ice buckets, tired of being barely able to sleep until just before the wake-up call (*"Hello, this is your wake-up call!"*), tired of motel laundry rooms, with their harsh bright lights, their dryers that bake the clothes dry, your zippers transmuting into dangerous weapons. It is sometimes said that James Joyce's favorite story was "How Much Land Does a Man Need?" by Leo Tolstoy. A contemporary version of such a fable might be: "How Much Time Can a Man Spend in a Minivan?" or "How Far Can a Man in a Minivan with His Family Drive in One Shot?" The answer: a little less than eight thousand miles.

AS FOR THE ATTEMPTED MIXTURE OF WORK and "vacation," the opera- tive question for me, as I ponder it all again now, is this: What was I thinking?

From my perspective, book tours turn out to be enough to worry about without dragging your family along. From my family's perspective, traveling on their author father/husband's book tour is tantamount to having a fa- ther/husband broker, perhaps, and sitting in his office to quietly watch him make phone calls—and then to maybe sleep in the office for a month, or at twenty or thirty different offices, never knowing which office will be next, or if there will be food, or potable water. From their point of view (and please note that I am not the best source for information on their point of view) the book tour was, in some ways, a little like a hostage situation—despite the great bookstores; despite our successful adventures; despite the people we ran into who were, as is often the case, very kind to us; despite, of course, the books. My daughter's economic activity was probably noticed by the Federal Reserve Board given the number of young adult novels purchased and devoured on the trip, and my wife inevitably left each bookstore with armfuls of large art books, so that by the time we got to Oregon, the minivan might have weighed as much as a tractor trailer. My son, meanwhile, found a beautiful Gibson mandolin from 1905 at Willie's American Guitars, a great store in Saint Paul.

But what I remember most about the book tour is my wife's face. I would be up at the podium or table or desk or whatever the particular bookstore was offering to me as protection, and my wife would be in the audience, usually working on her cross-country quilt, my son and daughter either roaming the shelves or sitting alongside her. I could see her anxiously scanning the room. I could see the attendance figures in her eyes. I can tell you that I personally am very happy if one person shows up at a reading, even if they're lost, so eternally amazed am I that anyone would stop to read what somebody else wrote, much less come to hear him have, in my case, a kind of public nervous breakdown. (My readings tend to be a little caffeinated, to stick with the theme.) However, I could see the low attendance was tough on my wife. I didn't expect anybody on Fourth of July weekend in Oxford, Mississippi—the streets were nearly empty, and I was pleased with the first-row-only enthusiasm, my family taking up maybe half the seats. I was mostly happy to finally get to visit what I'd always heard to be a great store. (Greatness confirmed.) But as the attendance grew from reading to reading, the expression on my wife's face grew more satisfied, and she would work more energetically on her cross-country quilt, stitching happiness.

By the time we were in Portland, Oregon, her hometown, at Powell's Books, a bookstore that I almost have to be forcibly removed from each time I visit, she was beaming. The room was packed—mostly, I would argue, because I hired a band, a great old-time music band called Foghorn Stringband. They played before I read a couple of pages, and then after I read a couple of pages, and during the awkward post-reading signing time. They even played while I read, which was for me a beat-poet-like experience, and for them was probably something they'd rather not go through again. But they were good sports, and the crowd loved the music, or so it seemed to me. I was certainly happy—some of our old friends and family were nearly dancing. Mostly, I was happy to see my wife so pleased, our fifteenth summer on the road crossing the country, and nowhere to drive that evening.

THE SUMMER OF 2006 WAS A SUMMER OF ANNIVERSARIES. It was the two hundredth anniversary of the *return* of the Lewis and Clark expedition, and it was also the interstate highway system's fiftieth anniversary. And in celebration of the interstate's birthday, a convoy pulled into Washington, D.C., after driving I-80 across the country. It began in San Francisco and consisted of ecstatic highway engineers and road historians; automobile club representatives eager to build more interstate highways; a leader of the "Go RVing" campaign, which serves the nation's eight million recreational-vehicle users; a descendant of President Dwight Eisenhower, who rode in another convoy as a young army officer in 1919, when he saw firsthand how ineffective the roads were; and Andrew Firestone, a descendant of the tire magnate Harvey Firestone. The original two-month-long convoy was sponsored by the United States Army. This one, expected to last thirteen days, was sponsored by Bridgestone Americas, the tire company, and the American Association of State Highway and Transportation Officials, known in the road business as Aashto (pronounced ASH-toe); Bridgestone was calling it the "greatest road trip in history."

Which can't be true. Just think of Jack Kerouac or Ken Kesey and the Merry Pranksters (in their psychedelic school bus, christened *Further*) or Odysseus or the Cannonball Run or even Lewis and Clark, just to name a few. Also arguable is Aashto's description of the interstate as a "symbol of freedom." A point I have attempted to make—probably too subtly, a problem of mine that is perhaps a little surprising given how talkative a companion I am while driving cross country in a car—is that the interstate is no longer about just freedom. In 2006, with congestion and traffic delays increasing nationwide, it also symbolizes a kind of commercial and personal and possibly even national strangulation.

At least since the sixties, the interstate has been the system that all state roads and, more recently, many local suburban roads have sought to emulate.

Why have a two-lane, easy-moving local road, in other words, when you can have something fast and frenetic and, well, like an *interstate!* And, frankly, the interstate system is amazing. Just look at how it has moved us; according to the Automobile Association of America, in 1956, Americans drove 628 million miles, in 2004, 2.8 billion. The even bigger story is trucks. In 1997, according to the Department of Transportation, the interstate system handled more than 1 trillion ton-miles of stuff, a feat executed by 21 million truckers driving approximately 412 billion miles. Sometimes I think of the interstate as a giant, 80 m.p.h. conveyor belt for trucks.

But the interstate system has also given us a lot that we didn't expect. While building it during the sixties, the United States destroyed nearly as much public housing as it constructed. Then again, in a backhanded way, the interstate system helped spawn the modern environmental movement, with the battle over I-40 through Overton Park in Memphis, for example, and the fight over I-75 though the Everglades. It gave us historic preservation, only after wiping out middle-class black neighborhoods in New Orleans. It also gave us sprawl. It gave us Atlanta. It gave us the modern South.

The first Bush administration's plan for a *second* interstate system, thankfully, never took off—it's tough enough having one interstate system to deal with. And the alternative has become new state-grown plans to build different kinds of roads. The interstate as a model is fading away, in a sort of parallel move to its physical deterioration. State highway departments have been taking big roads and narrowing them, adding bike lanes and trails. In the last ten years, engineers have increasingly looked for ways not to speed cars along but to slow them down. "You can design a road that addresses mobility but also makes them want to get out of the car." Tom Warne, a former state highway engineer in Utah who is working with New Hampshire's Department of Transportation, said to me. "It's the stuff that's along the street—windows, benches, street furniture, greenery. There's meandering." In Pennsylvania, where general traffic increased by 63 percent and truck traffic by 82 percent between 1984 and 2004, there are plans to make communities across the state more walkable, to build new highways at grade rather than elevate them, to build on Route 202 in the eastern part of the state what looks less like a multilane seventy-five-mile-per-hour superhighway and more like an old, slow-curved parkway. The idea is to get back to seeing America, or even sitting still in America, as opposed to racing through it.

In a nation where the average number of people in a household (1.8) was recently passed by the average number of cars (1.9), this is revolutionary—a change in decades-old policies that put speed first on the list of road-building requirements. New Hampshire has been retraining state transportation engineers and inviting community members to training courses. In Meredith, N.H., the state recently threw out plans for a one-million-dollar engineer devised widening of route 25, which backs up each summer with tourists headed to Lake Winnipesaukee and the White Mountains. "Are we going to design a road that stops traffic from backing up on the Fourth of July?" Carol Murray, the New Hampshire commissioner of transportation, asked me. "No, but if you're stuck in traffic, you're going to have something to look at besides pavement." Lewis Feldstein, president of the New Hampshire Charitable Foundation, says, "I think what we're seeing is transportation is too important to be left to the transportation planners." Feldstein was chairman of the panel that wrote the state's next ten-year transportation plan—alongside representatives from the health-care industry, children's-services providers, environmentalists, and business promoters.

Some road engineers remain territorial, but many of them are suddenly showing up at meetings to listen to issues besides congestion—especially as planners and politicians are seeing the cul-de-sac off on the edge of town, far from existing roads and services, not just as one person's quality-of-life choice but as a strain on the existing municipal infrastructure. In general the definition of what a road engineer does is expanding. "They are realizing," says Andy Wiley-Schwartz, vice president for transportation for the Project for Public Places, a group facilitating the planner-community dialogue, "that they are in the community-development business and not just in the facilities-development business."

Call it the Slow Road movement, but not the No Road movement, because the crumbling of the fifty-year-old interstate system brings an opportunity, a chance for a giant retrofit. The entire system might be regeared for rapid-transit buses (see Bogotá, Columbia) or for regional trains (see China) or for light rail (see Los Angeles, where they're not quite sure what to do with the system just yet, and Denver and Phoenix). In Indianapolis, where the old Lincoln Highway crosses the White River, the road is now a park, alongside a proposed walking trail that will be partly supported by state money devoted to fighting obesity. Roads are even being promoted by environmentalists as opportunities to fix the American landscape, for while the interstate unites human population centers, it divides everything else. "What we've done is cut the land into these little pieces—it's almost like a megazoo," says Richard Forman, the author of *Road Ecology* and a landscape ecologist at Harvard University. Smaller and smaller communities of road-bound plant and animal life are being reconnected by means of wildlife over- and underpasses in Canada, Holland, and—are you ready?—Florida and New Jersey. In Maryland, stormwater runoff has been tied to road reconstruction in the Anacostia watershed. "I think we're on the verge of understanding not only the impact of roads but how to eventually restore the watersheds," says Neil Weinstein, director of the Low Impact Development Center, a nonprofit engineering and sustainable-planning organization.

It was a historic summer all right, because soon after the Aashto convoy finished its trip, the re-creators of Lewis and Clark's 1804 to 1806 Corps of Discovery convoy pulled into Saint Louis. (There was a low spectator turnout, possibly because of the price of gas.) Now, two hundred years after the Lewis and Clark trip laid the groundwork for the interstate, we have to decide whether our roads will continue to strangle us, to drive us crazy, to pollute and poison our air and water, or maybe to slow us down in a good way and give us a chance to enjoy everything we still have left and have worked so hard to build.

FOR WHAT IT'S WORTH, I have decided to try and use the roads less, decrease demand a little. Maybe not coincidentally, the summer that this book was published also marked what my family is calling our last cross-country trip. I should point out that this would not be the first time that we have called the most recent trip our last trip. But, as I have tried to indicate, this last trip was a doozy. We may have changed, as sad as that is for me to think about. This summer we may need to just sit around somewhere for a couple of weeks. We may need to camp and hike and try the things we never really have because of driving obligations. I don't know if I'll have the nerve to do it, but I'm thinking that my new year's resolution is to sell my car, which, I'm thinking, may change my way of life a little, which, in the grand macroeconomic scheme of things, is a lot.

The road is metaphor a lot of times, and it's not difficult to see why, especially after crossing the country. The road can change a country, and it can change you, or at least me. There's the road to Mecca, Moses' flight from Egypt, Saint Paul's road to Damascus. In Caravaggio's *The Conversion of Saint Paul*, the saint-to-be is struck off his horse by a flash of lightninglike power, an automatic change of heart, and I think that's the kind of thing people are looking for on the road, though without quite Caravaggio's life-threatening drama. In fact, in his letters, Paul himself talks about a slower conversion, a more mundane, gradual change. He spent his life on the road, walking, historians estimate, somewhere along the lines of ten thousand miles, working things out, one letter at a time, one moment illuminating all the others.

Speaking of which, the other night I was thinking about the moment late one evening when we were driving though the Alleghenies, on the last night of the last trip, when we were all so exhausted as to be punch drunk, when the kids had just finished detailing (accurately) many of the drawbacks of traveling around the country on their father's book tour. At the end of that discourse, our son pulled out the new-to-him mandolin and began singing an old song and then his sister joined in, and, although we are parents and, as such, our opinions ought to be completely discounted, it sounded great to us. I'm remembering this now on this winter afternoon at our dining room table, its legs worn from frequent moves, its sides scratched, and the memory is sending some kind of convoy up to my tear ducts, to get metaphorical again. Then again, maybe I'm just happy not to be driving.

Many, many times people stopped me on the trip and said, "You traveled eight thousand miles in a car with your *kids*?" It was the thing most said to me on the trip, in fact. I'd just like to wrap up by saying that this question irritates me for many reasons, the least of which is that, as a question, it has it all backward. Our kids are more likely to suffer, being kids and having to be with us, the so-called adults. We're lucky we get to be with the kids, that we are legally capable of forcing them to go along with us, even though it may seem at times as if nobody is going along with anything. Despite the fact that the road is very, very long, there's only so much time. By the way, one of the songs our kids were singing on that last night is that old Irish song "The Wild Rover."

> I've been a wild rover for many's the year
> I've spent all me money on whiskey and beer
> But now I'm returning with gold in great store
> And I never will play the wild rover no more

And it's no, nay, never,
No, nay never no more
Will I play the wild rover,
No never no more

I went in to an alehouse I used to frequent
And I told the landlady me money was spent.
I asked her for credit, she answered me, "Nay
Such custom as yours I can have any day."

I took up from my pocket, ten sovereigns bright
And the landlady's eyes opened wide with delight.
She says, "I have whiskeys and wines of the best
And the words that I told you were only in jest."

I'll go home to my parents, confess what I've done
And I'll ask them to pardon their prodigal son
And, when they've caressed me as oft times before
I never will play the wild rover no more.

And it's no, nay, never,
No, nay never no more
Will I play the wild rover,
No never no more.

If you drive around the country for about fifteen years, if you rack up a hundred thousand miles or so, if you have kids and they grow up and then sing you that song in the back of a minivan, then that song will blow you away.

NOTES

PART I

I rented the Impala from Avis; got the TripTik at the Manhattan branch of the American Automobile Association; and had the car that we didn't take and that died fixed at Straub's Auto Repair, in Hastings-on-Hudson. My rooftop pack was by Kanga, and I bought it at Campmoor, where I go before I write every book I've ever written and will go again, though I will not be buying that pack. Information about Mount Hood and about other Oregon place names came from *Oregon Geographic Names*, sixth edition, by Lewis A. McArthur (Oregon Historical Society Press, 1992).

PART II

In studying the Lewis and Clark expedition, I relied heavily on the books of James P. Ronda, especially *Finding the West: Explorations with Lewis and Clark*, a luxuriously nuanced explanation of the ideas that defined the expedition, and *Lewis and Clark Among the Indians*, which gives a detailed analysis of their time in all the nations they passed through and helps you realize that expedition was less like a wilderness adventure and more like a trip through Europe in the tourist season. The edition of the Lewis and Clark journals we carried was edited by Frank Bergon and published by Penguin Classics. Jefferson's "unspeakable joy" is mentioned in Willard Sterne Randall's *Thomas Jefferson: A Life*. I first learned about Thomas Jefferson writing a letter to Catherine the Great asking for permission for Ledyard to cross Russia in *Great Plains*, by Ian Frazier, one of the best road books ever, as well as best books ever; Frazier neatly sums up the Russian queen's reaction: "Catherine hit the ceiling." That Jefferson taught Meriwether Lewis comes from *Thomas Jefferson: An Intimate History*, by Fawn Brodie.

A book that examines America's mythic interpretation of Sacagawea and York is *Exploring Lewis and Clark: Reflections on Men and Wilderness*, by Thomas Slaughter. Critics of Slaughter argue that he demeans the accomplishments of the Lewis and Clark expedition by pointing out, for instance, that Saca-gawea was a slave, that York was treated like an animal by Clark; I think he puts them in context and in so doing gives them greater depth. " 'Sacajawea' is a creation of twentieth century American culture," Slaughter writes. "Our history made her up. She is our national Indian, our founding princess, and a symbol of what our interracial history might have been. By turning her from a slave into a leader of the Lewis and Clark Expedition, we have fabricated heroic qualities that our culture needs. . . . Climbing through mountains, paddling long and sometimes rough rivers, and seeing the ocean and a whale were thrilling experiences. By making it back she was also part of an amazing collective accomplishment. Nonetheless, her most remarkable achievements may have come after she left Lewis and Clark."

I learned about the near-disastrous ending of the expedition's trip west in Rex Ziak's *In Full View: A True and Accurate Account of Lewis and Clark's Arrival at the Pacific Ocean, and Their Search for a Winter Camp Along the Lower Columbia River*. Ziak, a native of the Gray's Harbor area at the mouth of the Columbia, reckoned Clark's maps with modern-day locations, with photo-graphs and painted maps. A great essay about the history of the perception of Lewis and Clark is "Making History: Why Bother with the Lewis and Clark Bicentennial?" by Mark Spence in *Oregon Humanities*, Spring 2004. Details about the fate of the journals after the return of the expedition are from "The Perilous Afterlife of the Lewis and Clark Expedition," an article by Anthony Brandt, editor of National Geographic's edition of the journals, that was in the June–July 2004 *American Heritage*. I read about Lewis's suicide in, among other places, an article titled "What Really Happened to Meriwether Lewis?" by Dee Brown, in *Columbia*, Winter 1988.

The Mineral County Historical Society's *Pioneer*, Volume 6, featured an article titled "Blazing the Mullan Road." An article titled "Captain John Mul-lan," by Addison Howard, which first appeared in the *Washington Historical Quarterly*, July 1934, was included in a special report to the *Missoulan*, cover-ing the cleanup of sediments at the Milltown Dam, a federal Superfund site at the confluence of the Clark Fork and the Blackfoot rivers. There is a me-morial to Mullan at Fourth of July Pass, right about where my rental truck first began to break down on my worst cross-country trip ever, and parts of the old Mullan Road can still be seen—for instance, off State Route 26, just east of Washtucna. In December 2003, David Sarasohn wrote "Bring Your

Mule (or SUV) When Trying Corps' Trek over Lolo Pass," an article in the
Oregonian about traveling Lewis and Clark's Lolo Trail that I clipped out before I tried to travel the Lolo Trail but only read *after*. The *New York Times*
covered the opening of Route 26 on August 12, 1962, in "New Highway
Along Historical Western Trail," by Jeanne K. Beaty. Richard Neuberger
wrote "Along the 150-Year-Old Lewis and Clark Trail" in the July 4, 1954,
Times. Some of the information about Celilo village came from the Center
for Columbia River History. At Harvard University's Peabody Museum of
Archaeology and Ethnology, I learned that Lewis and Clark wore waterproof
whaling hats on their way back, in 1806. They got them from a Clatsop
woman who had gotten them from a whaling tribe living to the north of the
Clatsop—the Makah.

I read about the modern Lewis and Clark reenactment in the following
places: "Reliving Lewis and Clark: Conflicts with the Sioux," by Anthony
Brandt, for *National Geographic News*; "Indians Condemn Expedition Re-
Enactment," by Joe Kafka, an Associated Press reporter, who filed on September 24, 2004; "Paddling in Lewis' Wake Brings Sense of Awe," in the
Billings Gazette, on June 17, 2005; and "Willamette Week's Guide to Lewis
and Clark Re-enactors," by Emily Cooper, an article in *Willamette Week* that
compared what ended up being the rival expeditions that camped near each
other at the western terminus of the Lewis and Clark trail. When I called to
interview Scott Mandrell, I got the spokesperson for the reenactors, who was
a police officer and took calls on his cell phone on breaks from police work,
and when I visited Saint Louis, I stayed at the Cheshire Lodge, an old motel
on Route 66 that was designed with a medieval theme and had a medieval-
themed bar called the Fox and Hounds Tavern. Everyone I met in Saint
Louis had a story about the Fox and Hounds, several of which featured their
car and the police.

For traveling along the reverse trail, I utilized *Along the Trail with Lewis and
Clark: Travel Planner and Guide*, published by *Montana Magazine*; Falcon
Guide's *Traveling the Lewis and Clark Trail*, by Julie Fanselow; and Greg Mac-
Gregor's *Lewis & Clark Revisited: A Photographer's Trail*, which has photos of
sights along the trail as they appear today. In the introduction to MacGregor's
book, James P. Ronda notes that Jefferson assigned Lewis and Clark to describe "the face of the country," the phrase that Bertram Tallamy would use
150 years later to describe the impact of the interstates. "Rather than artfully

screening out dams, powerlines, and amusement parks," Ronda writes of MacGregor, "his images challenge us to confront our romantic notions about the West. These photographs call out to us, asking us to move beyond nostalgia for an imaginary past or bitterness about a seemingly cluttered present to acknowledge the presence of the daily ordinary—what historian John Brinkerhoff Jackson describes as 'the vernacular landscape.'"

Bernard DeVoto's cross-country trips are discussed in *The Western Paradox: A Conservation Reader*, by Bernard DeVoto, edited by Douglas Brinkley and Patricia Nelson Limerick, and with a forward by Arthur Schlesinger Jr., who traveled cross-country with DeVoto. ("Driving Benn's Buick with that best-informed and most zestful of guides resurrected the dusty past," Schlesinger said.) They are also discussed in *The Uneasy Chair: A Biography of Bernard DeVoto*, by Wallace Stegner, a student of DeVoto's at Breadloaf. "[DeVoto] inspected with interest the new caravanserais, the motel strips, whose food he found calamitous, and he recommended instead the corner drugstore of any town, which at least understood how to make a sandwich," Stegner writes. "He dismissed the folklore that said any truck stop was a place where the food could be depended on. He praised the roads and the highway commissions in general, and the Michigan roadsides and the Montana historical markers in particular. He found the western drivers fast and dangerous, thereby demonstrating that in fifteen years he had ceased to be a Westerner and had lost his casualness about speed and distance." The quote from DeVoto comes from *The Course of Empire*.

PART III

The bookstore in Missoula we bought too many books at is Shakespeare and Company. *A Field Guide to Sprawl* is by Dolores Hayden. I read about mountain men in *Frontier Skills: The Tactics and Weapons That Won the American West*, by William C. Davis, and in Robert Utley's *A Life Wild and Perilous: Mountain Men and the Paths to the Pacific*. I read Marcus Daly's obituary in the *New York Times* and the Butte *Miner*, and I read about Frank Little in *Wobblies!: A Graphic History of the Industrial Workers of the World*, an illustrated nonfiction work that is one of my favorite books and was edited by Paul Buhle and Nicole Schulman, and published by Verso in 2005. For information about Montana's environmental history, I referred to *The Natural West:*

Environmental History in the Great Plains and Rocky Mountains, by Dan Flores. I got information about the Berkeley Pit from the Montana Bureau of Mines and Geology. Most of what I know about Evel Knievel's life comes from an excellent article by Tom Zoellner in the November 24, 2003, edition of *High Country News*, titled "Butte Ponders the Power of Evel." Additionally, I read Evel Knievel's biography, which can be seen at www.evelknievel.com, Knievel's official Web site.

I read about the overland migrations in *Women's Diaries of the Westward Journey*, by Lilian Schlissel. The book includes portraits of settlers who posed with the bodies of children who died; it also says this about Native Americans attacking the settlers while in transit: "The evidence is that the Indians were universally feared, only sporadically hostile during the most important years of emigration, and more or less continually the guides and purveyors of vital services to the emigrants." I learned about stagecoach crossings in *Stagecoach East*, by Oliver Wendell Holmes and Peter T. Rohrbach; *Stagecoach: The Ride of the Century*, by A. Richard Mansir (which included the list of things a stagecoach passenger should not do on a stagecoach); and from Mark Twain's *Roughing It*, a book that every cross-country traveler should read before crossing the country, if not during and after—especially the chapter in which he describes having coffee with a famous vicious murderer. The history of gas stations came from John A. Jakle and Keith A. Sculle's *The Gas Station in America*.

PART IV

Charles Preuss and John Charles Frémont are featured in James P. Ronda's *Beyond Lewis and Clark: The Army Explores the West*, a companion volume to an exhibit of the same name that I (as well as the rest of my expeditionary team) visited at the Washington Historical Society—an exhibit that later traveled to historical societies in Virginia, Kansas, and Missouri. The Enchanted Highway has been covered by the *Wall Street Journal*, Salon.com, *People* magazine, and National Public Radio; and Gary Greff maintains an Enchanted Highway Web site.

The book that I relied on most heavily for information about early American tourists and the early American tourism industry is *See America First: Tourism and National Identity, 1840–1940*, by Marguerite S. Shaffer. This is an excellent book about how art and commerce and citizenship got all mixed up in the formation of the American identity; it shows that what Americans were doing when they were vacationing was forming what they were thinking of when they were thinking of themselves as Americans. Of the beginning of cross-country travel, Shaffer writes: "Transcontinental travel came to be understood as an extension of Manifest Destiny." Of the end of cross-country travel, a moment she aligns with the publication of Kerouac's *On the Road*, Shaffer writes: "[Kerouac] built on the legacy of escape that had been laid by Dustbowl refugees and transformed it into a quest for personal freedom that tapped the alienation and restlessness of white suburban youth. In so doing, he helped transform the road into a liminal countercultural space at odds with the marketed tourist landscape and mainstream American culture." Eventually, she writes, tourism itself became a contradictory act: "It simultaneously reaffirmed the triumph of mass consumer culture and provided an antidote to it."

I read about the Blackfeet camp on the roof of the New York City hotel in the *New York Times* of March 19, 1913.

When I played the Super 8 film of the first cross-country trip that my wife and I took for our children, they couldn't believe how much hair I had back then and how much my wife still looks the same.

The history of our Impala is drawn from several sources, including *The American Highway: The History and Culture of Roads in the United States*, by William Kaszynski; the Duryea brothers obituaries in the *New York Times*; the Wayne State University Digital Repository; and the historical resources of musclecar.net, which apparently was once a group of muscle car club Web sites but then got together as one muscle car club Web site, called musclecarclub.com, which was sold during the time between when we returned from our last cross-country drive, in 2004, and the time I completed writing this account. From musclecarclub.com: "In April of 2005, MCC was acquired by Classicmusclecars.com. Its owner, Tony Begley, had a vision to unify all muscle car owners worldwide via the internet through a worldwide muscle car registry. This will allow owners, prospective buyers, insurance companies, finance companies, and law enforcement agencies the ability to track and help preserve muscle cars and their history. This will be the first time that any internet site dedicated to muscle cars has undertaken such a task."

Carl Fisher's life is covered in *The Pacesetter: The Untold Story of Carl G.*

Fisher, by Jerry M. Fisher," a relative of Carl. Information about the Lincoln Highway came from Shaffer's *See America First* and from Drake Hokanson's *The Lincoln Highway: Main Street Across America*, as well as the Lincoln Highway Association. *Get Up and Go: The History of American Road Travel*, by Sylvia Whitman, includes information on the first cross-country drivers, including Alice Ramsey, as well as information about early roads. Most of the references to the accounts of the first cross-country trips come from *See America First* and from Warren James Belasco's *Americans on the Road: From Autocamp to Motel, 1910–1945*, which captures the moment that Americans went from not having or loving cars to having and loving cars. Belasco notes in his preface that he began his research by trying to write about the automobile as it related to contemporary society, especially in relation to its destruction of our natural habitat, such as cities; he ended up writing about our earliest relationship with the machine that, as I see it, sought to give us freedom from machinery, from what can sometimes seem like the drudgery of a modern-convenience-filled life. "Like the car, the motel did not fulfill the dreams that created it," Belasco writes. "Thus my journey ended with a feeling of frustration, a sense that for all this movement, basic needs remained unsatisfied. Maybe motorists took the wrong path. Instead of escaping to the road, perhaps they should have looked for answers closer to home."

Emily Post's book *By Motor to the Golden Gate*, is mentioned in Belasco and Shaffer. I read a first edition that I found in the Westchester County Public Library System; a new edition, complete with all of Emily Post's original maps, comes with an excellent introduction and extensive annotations (which I relied on) by Jane Lancaster.

A great old folk song about the way that roads were kind of welcome and kind of unwelcome in America in the early days of the car is "Jordan Is a Hard Road to Travel," and it includes these verses:

> The public schools and the highways
> are causing quite an alarm
> Get a country boy educated just a little
> and he won't work on the farm

> Now I don't know but I believe I'm right
> the auto's ruined the country

Let's get back to the horse and buggy
and try to save some money.

Information regarding the development of the enMotion paper towel dispenser came from Tom Banks at Georgia Pacific, the paper company, based
in Atlanta. John Collier's life is covered in the *Journal of American Indian Education*, May 1986; "Twentieth-Century American Indian History: Achievements, Needs, and Problems," and an article in the fall 1994 issue of the
Organization of American Historians' *A Magazine of History*, and from several books on the history of Native American law. Matt Shanandore's CD can
be purchased in Five Nations Arts store in Mandan. His playing was mentioned in the April 20, 2005, *McKenzie County Farmer*, the newspaper of
McKenzie County (population 5,700, with a median income of $27,000, and
the second highest arrest rate for methamphetamine production in the state,
even before federal money was shifted from drug-crime prevention to home-
land security work in the state). The news article, which references the high
winds being experienced on the Great Plains that April, stated: "Sharing the
legacy of both the original Corps and the Corps of Discovery II was McKenzie County's honor and privilege. The wind continues to blow here, and the
wind of time moves every moment into a state of flux and change. But for a
moment, a week, time stood still and people from anywhere, including 1,900
students from area schools, were able to meet the profound experience of
Lewis and Clark, as well as their neighbor."

PART V

I first learned about Minnesota's I-35 in *The American Highway*, by William
Kaszynski, a Saint Paul, Minnesota, lawyer, who, in fact, covers nearly every
aspect of the highway in America, using his own photos and memorabilia and,
in the end, "leaving," as the *Library Journal* noted, "no pothole unfilled."

I have read about Woody Guthrie's hometown in many places, including
the excellent biography *Ramblin' Man: The Life and Times of Woody Guthrie*, by
Ed Cray, and I have visited the Woody Guthrie Archives in New York City on
many occasions. Guthrie is being remembered more and more as a writer and
a visual artist, and a good place to see some of the drawings that Guthrie went
on to do after sketching his name in the sidewalk is *Woody Guthrie Artworks:*

The Journals, Drawings and Sketchbooks of an American Original, by Steven Brower and Nora Guthrie, with contributions from Billy Bragg and Jeff Tweedy, published by Rizzoli. An early article about the controversy over Woody Guthrie in his hometown is "Woody Guthrie's Home Town Is Divided on Paying Him Homage," written by B. Drummond Ayres Jr., on December 14, 1972; the town was divided about the third of three water towers having been painted to read "Birthplace of Woody Guthrie." (The other two towers were painted to read "hot" and "cold," respectively): "Before persuading the water board to act, Mr. Walker joined with some of Woody's second cousins—the only kin left here—and led the fight that forced the local library to accept the collection of Guthrie records and books. Initially the library board flatly refused, relenting only in the face of Mr. Walker's pressure and when Woody's widow, Marjorie, and his son, Arlo, also a folk singer, showed up in Okemah to hand over the gift in person." There has since been established an annual Woody Guthrie Festival. I saw the quote about Okemah in the Woody Guthrie Archives, which sells his recordings and artwork and continues to publish his lyrics and writings and artwork, more and more of which has been rediscovered. At Guthrie's homesite, we saw a memorial, a standing tree carved by Justin Osborn, a local chain saw artist, and then after we got in the car, we stopped later that day at Cadillac Ranch. As soon as we looked at the Cadillacs, we saw that one had been spray painted *Woody*.

I read about the early history of guidebooks in Shaffer and Belasco. I read about Thomas MacDonald, the early highway builder, in Kaszynski, as well as in Phil Patton's excellent investigation of the American road, *Open Road: A Celebration of the American Highway*. This book looks extensively at the aesthetics of the interstate, as well as roadside architecture and the literature of the road; it presents Vladimir Nabokov's *Lolita* as a road book, for instance, right alongside *Travels with Charley*, by John Steinbeck, and *Blue Highways: A Journey into America*, by William Least Heat-Moon. Both Kaszynski and Patton cover the modern turnpikes, as well as Norman Bel Geddes, the industrial designer whose aesthetic—or selling of his aesthetic—so influenced American roads and design.

The book that I relied on most heavily for an explanation of the politics of the interstate and the history of its slowly evolving conception was *Divided Highways: Building the Interstate Highways, Transforming American Life*, by Tom Lewis—a book that I recommend everyone read in this year, the fiftieth anniversary of the interstate highway system. He makes Eisenhower out to have sort of missed what the interstates were, and President Nixon as the first president in the interstate era to attempt to assuage the devastating effects of the intestate in the inner cities. Lewis puts the end of the age of the interstate at 1991, the year Congress passed the Intermodal Surface Transportation Efficiency Act, which mandated a less interstate-centric approach to transportation planning. However, when you drive across the country, you get a feeling that a lot of state planning departments haven't yet heard about that Intermodal Surface Transportation Efficiency Act.

A thorough comparison of Norman Bel Geddes and Benton MacKaye and their design theories is found in *Organization Space: Landscapes, Highways, and Houses in America*, by Keller Easterling. I also read Norman Bel Geddes's book on his theory of industrial design, *Horizons*, and autobiography, *Miracle in the Evening*, coauthored (or edited, as the book's title page puts it) by William Kelley, who wasn't paid enough, I just have a feeling.

In addition to MacKaye's proposal for the Appalachian Trail and several other of his articles on roads and planning, I read his book *The New Exploration: A Philosophy of Regional Planning*, which the writer Tony Hiss has called "a long lost classic." I referred mostly to Larry Anderson's biography of Benton MacKaye, *Benton MacKaye: Conservationist, Planner, and Creator of the Appalachian Trail*. MacKaye was an artist in engineer's clothing and vice versa, especially when he defined the qualities of what he called "the New Explorer," in 1928, a definition I think of when I cross or am about to cross the country: "The new explorer, of this 'volcanic' country of America, must first of all be fit for all-round action: he must combine the engineer, the artist, and the military general. It is not for him to 'make the country,' but it is for him to know the country and the trenchant flows that are taking place upon it. . . . His place is in the frontier—within life's 'cambium layer'—the fluid twilight zone of all creative action in which the flickering thoughts of future are woven in the structure of the past. . . . And our last instruction to our new explorer and frontiersman is to hold ever in sight of his final goal—to reveal within our innate country, despite fogs and chaos of cacophonous mechanization *a land in which to live*—a symphonious environment of melody and mystery in which, throughout all ages, we shall 'learn to reawaken and keep ourselves awake, not by mechanical aids,' but by that 'infinite expectation of the dawn' which faces the horizon of an ever-widening vision."

Phil Patton wrote an article for *I.D.* magazine in 1996 on the subject of coffee cup lids. The article "Peel, Pucker, Pinch, Puncture," by Louise Harpman and Scott Sprecht, was published in *Cabinet*, Issue 19. Harpman and Sprecht are partners in the architectural firm Sprecht Harpman, in New York City and Austin, and in their lid treatise they mention a coffee lid used at a deli across from the ferry in Iselboro, Maine, which I hope to someday visit. The 1986 patent, number 4,589,569, for a Solo drink-through lid describes the lid: "A lid for a drinking includes an annular mounting portion for engaging the lip of the cup, an annular side wall extending upwardly from the mounting portion, and a top wall having a drinking opening formed in it. In the preferred embodiment, the top wall of the lid has a recess formed in it adjacent the drinking opening to accommodate the upper lip of the user." I like it when they use the term *user* for coffee drinker. The humorous headline about Americans wanting others to use public transportation comes from *Dispatches from the Tenth Circle: The Best of the Onion.*

The history of the motel comes from Belasco, Kaszynski, and especially from *The Motel in America*, by John A. Jakle, Keith A. Sculle, and Jefferson S. Rogers. I read the Kemmons Wilson autobiography, cowritten by Robert Kerr, *Half Luck and Half Brains: The Kemmons Wilson, Holiday Inn Story.* David Halberstam was the writer who called the Kemmons family vacation "the vacation that changed the face of the American road."

I read about Jack Kerouac not being a good parking attendant in *Car and Driver*, the magazine of the American Automobile Association. I read about Kerouac's quests in *Kerouac, the Word and the Way: Prose Artist as Spiritual Quester*, by Ben Giamo, which says: "Kerouac's lasting appeal to readers, young and old, corresponds with Merton's assessment of Pasternak's attraction: 'it is the man himself, the truth that he is full of the only revolutionary force that is capable of producing anything new: he is full of love.'" Giamo also quotes Kerouac's letter to Malcolm Cowley, his editor: "I'm mighty proud to let you know that I have just finished a new novel, written like *On the Road* on a 100 foot roll of paper, single space, cup after cup of coffee." I also referred to *Departed Angels*, a book of Jack Kerouac's artwork that features photographs of his journals—mostly to show the kids after we missed seeing the scroll. Anne Waldman talked about the names of the chairs at Naropa in "Anne Waldman: 1945–," in the *Contemporary Authors Autobiography Series*, Gale Research Series, Volume 17, 1993, which I saw referred to on www.poetspath.com, the Web page of the Museum of American Poetics, or MAP. The restaurant we ate at in Boulder is called the Kitchen. I learned about the Beat Book Store in a column in the *Daily Camera*, the Boulder newspaper, by Clay Evans, titled "Locals Survive Corporate Onslaught" and published May 1, 2005. I read about the gas station in the *Boulder Weekly*—"Longmont Gas Station Faces Demolition: Residents Rally to Save Historic Building," an article by John Peabody that ran on June 6, 2002. Tom Peters allowed me to use his poem. Solar Village, the unfinished development where Jack Kerouac's gas station was parked, was selling one- or two-bedroom condos for between $142,000 and $370,000 when we were there.

The quote regarding traffic chaos in America came from a December 9, 1956, *Times* article by Joseph C. Ingraham titled "Highways v. Cars: Road-Building Has Lapsed Far Behind Demands of the Modern Motorist." Lewis Mumford calls the interstate system "ill conceived and preposterously unbalanced" in the title essay of *The Highway and the City*, his still prescient 1964 collection of writings. Information about Eisenhower comes from Lewis and from *The Man Who Changed America, Parts I and II*, by Richard F. Weingroff, a historian for the Federal Highway Administration who has written many great reports on the history of the highway and, among other things, has debunked the highway myth that states that the highway was built to accommodate airplane landings every five miles. "As with Dracula, it is very difficult to put a stake through the heart of this 'fact,'" Weingroff writes. I read the quote from Jean-Paul Sartre in *Divided Highways*. Joseph Linko is mentioned in Helen Leavitt's book, *Superhighway—Superhoax*, and in "House Gets a Look at Road Dangers," by Nan Robertson, published May 25, 1967, in the *New York Times*.

PART VI

The history of development is covered in Dolores Hayden's *Building Suburbia: Green Fields and Urban Growth, 1820–2000*. Pace of growth comes from a Natural Resources Defense Council report titled "Once There Were Greenfields: How Urban Sprawl Is Undermining America's Environment, Ecology and Social Fabric" by F. Kaid Benfield, Matthew D. Raimi, Donald D. T. Chen. Information about the Cannonball Run came from news clippings and from *Cannonball! World's Greatest Outlaw Road Race* by Brock Yates—a collection of Yates's *Car and Driver* columns on the Cannonball and stories and reminiscences by many of the participants. Information about the history of Portage comes from the *Encyclopedia of Chicago*. In *The Interstate Is 50: Linking the Power of the Past to the Promise of the Future*, the Federal Highway Administration describes the interstate system as being 46,773 miles, as I note. I could not get them to confirm that fact. The neighborhood in New Orleans was called "seedy" in a *Time* article from January 10, 1983: "Down a Ribbon of Highway."

A Joyce Purnick column in the *New York Times* discussed Jersey barriers as antiterrorism devices: "One test showed that a Ford Festiva easily hurled itself right over one. 'Jersey barriers, pinned or not, are useless in the long run as a terror-interdicting device,' said [John Colgan, a deputy chief who leads the New York Police Department's counterterrorism unit]. 'They are an urban blight.'" The Jersey barrier is discussed in "Basics of Concrete Barriers," by Charles F. McDevitt, published in the March–April 2000 *Public Roads*, the magazine of the Federal Highway Administration. A 2005 State Farm Insurance report ranked Pennsylvania as the first among places with the largest number of deer and car accidents. Water pollution figures are according to the National Water Quality Inventory, a 1998 report to Congress. Richard Foreman's work on road ecology is featured in the *Harvard Gazette* from June 14, 2001, and I read his book *Road Ecology*. "Right of Way," a report on highway and wildlife, ran in *Audubon* in June 2003.

Much of the history of restaurants on the road comes from *Fast Food: Roadside Restaurants in the Automobile Age*, by John A. Jakle and Keith A. Sculle, as well as Kaszynski's *The American Highway*. Carhops are described in the February 26, 1940, *Life*. A 2004 article in *Newsweek* reported that American households took out an average of 118 meals annually from restaurants, up by 64 percent from 20 years ago. That the Brady of Brady's Leap service area was referred to as a turkey comes from the Kent Historical Society, in Kent, Ohio, the offices of which are above the Pufferbelly restaurant and bar, which is, like so many restaurants that you see when you drive across the country, in an old train station. I referred to Phil Patton's article about the Commodore Perry service area, which appeared in the *New York Times* Design Notebook, under the headline "Turnpike Stops Worth the Trip" on July

27, 2000. Signs development is discussed in *Divided Highways*, as well as in "Signs of Progress—Road Symbols Guiding Traffic," by Robert Lindsay, a *New York Times* article from April 23, 1972. Early communal rest stops are noted in *Get Up and Go!* The environmental history of oil is discussed in *Something New Under the Sun: An Environmental History of the Twentieth-Century World*," by J. R. McNeill. The California legislature's bill referring to June McCarroll, the early proponent of the white line on the road, is viewable on the state government's Web site; it mentions that, as a doctor, she used to operate on people on tables in their homes.

The description of the opening of the Pennsylvania Shortway is covered in "Interstate Highways: Life Changes in Their Paths," a *New York Times* article published on September 21, 1970, and the classification of the Endless Mountains as relatively untouched comes from research conducted by the Wildlife Conservation Society and the Center for International Earth Science Information Network at Columbia University. The report and maps showed that 17 percent of the world is untouched and that in areas capable of supporting crops and thus people, 2 percent of the land is untouched. Some of the maps appeared in the *Times* on July 31, 2005. The historian who compares the National Road to Roman roads is Olive Woolley Burt in her 1968 book *The National Road: How America's Vision of a Transcontinental Highway Grew Through Three Centuries to Become a Reality*.

Dangerous times and days to drive are noted by the National Highway Traffic Safety Administration, and I learned about how highway engineers think of accidents in *Highway Engineering*, by Paul H. Wright, the sixth edition, published in 1996, which I also referred to on the history of highway legislation. Details about the accidents on I-80 in Pennsylvania come from local news reports and Pennsylvania Highways pahighways.com, an amazing Web site that covers every detail of the Pennsylvania highways system. It includes photos of the accidents I refer to, as well as photos of all the interchanges along I-80, and it is maintained by Jeffrey J. Kitsko.

PART VII

When we flew in the plane and I looked down on the country while crossing, I carried *Window Seat: Reading the Landscape from the Air*, by Gregory Dictum (which I also referred to while crossing the Great Plains by car). The time that the beat poets—Gary Snyder, Philip Whalen, and Jack Kerouac—spent in the North Cascades is covered in *Poets on the Peaks*, by John Suiter, a writer and photographer who photographed all the places mentioned in the writers' works and journals, as well as the writers involved, including Gary Snyder, the poet who grew up as a logger and, in a sense, worked his way up the mountain. For Kerouac, it was the opposite of running around on the road for inspiration—and *Dharma Bums* worked (synchronistically, as Suiter says) to inspire the conservationists, early members of the Sierra Club, and members of the Mazamas, one of the Northwest's oldest climbing clubs, to create the North Cascades National Park. It is a good thing I did not try and visit his fire lookout with my family and my wife's relatives; it sounds like a difficult climb, though people do it all the time and, according to Suiter, leave little notes, happy to see the view and the place that inspired Snyder's poems: "One turns and sees what the poet saw on those transparent mornings fifty years ago, when Desolation called to welcome him, for then and ever, to the 'community of lookouts.'" A good place to find some of the Northwest fiddle tunes we danced to in the North Cascades is *The Portland Collection: Contra Dance Music in the Pacific Northwest*, by Susan Songer with Clyde Curley.

The truck driver's quote about the state of the interstate comes from the *New York Times* of June 18, 1978: "Deteriorating I-80 Typifies Ailments of Interstate System," by Grace Lichtenstein. A report in the *Journal of Urban Economics* showed that highway spending has increased national productivity—getting goods to market, for instance—but that the returns have diminished in the past twenty years, in part, it is theorized, because more money is spent on maintaining the roads that were, for instance, rushed into place to finish the system. Virginia Postrel, an economic columnist for the *Times*, argued on May 20, 2004, that spending on the interstate offers fewer and fewer returns: one dollar of annual highway spending reduces congestion costs to highway users by only eight cents, and that dollar must keep being spent, the user being caught in the highway system.

The Musconetcong valley article, "A Cultural Landscape Still in the

Making," was written by John P. Brunner. "Shaking Off the Rust: New Suburbs Are Born," an article from the December 22, 2005, *Times*, describes the extension of the length of commuting. William Whtye first noted the desire of the corporate executive for a short commute from a semirural setting as the basis for headquarters location. Information on national road congestion came from the 2004 Urban Mobility Report, published by the Texas Transportation Institute at Texas A&M University. The newspaper quote regarding the extent of the city is from *American Space: The Centennial Years*, by John Brinkerhoff Jackson, whose writings I carried with me while crossing the country over the years, and who asks in his 1994 essay "Roads Belong in the Landscape," "Which do we value more, a sense of place or a sense of freedom?" His response: "The answer will come when we define or redefine the road as it exists in the contemporary world; when we recognize that roads and streets and alleys and trails can no longer be identified solely with movement from one place to another. Increasingly they are the scene of work and leisure and social intercourse and excitement. Indeed, they have often become for many the last resort for privacy and solitude and contact with nature. Roads no longer merely lead to places; they are places. . . . As with Saul of Tarsus, the road to Damascus may lie straight ahead, but it is only in the course of the journey that we discover our true destination."

I decided not to renew my AAA membership when I heard AAA criticized on *Car Talk*, the NPR program, and when I discovered that AAA supports the building of more roads to relieve traffic everywhere—I believe the opposite is necessary.

Something I purchased after our last cross-country trip and before I began typing up this account is a thirty-seven-inch-by-fifty-eight-inch map of the United States by Raven Maps and Images, a mapmaking company in Medford, Oregon. When we first got back, I bought it and put it up on the wall and put on some music and got a drink and just sat there enjoying it for a long time. I packed it up last time we moved, and I haven't found it yet, but when I do, I plan to repeat the process, because it's an amazing map of a vast and, even with the interstate system, unexplored and amazing place.

ACKNOWLEDGMENTS

Gillian Blake; Sara Mercurio; Greg Villepique; Amy King; Benjamin Adams; Alona Fryman; Amanda Katz; Maureen Klier; Karen Rinaldi; Jin Auh; Sara Chalfant; Andrew Wylie; Tim Farrington; Anna Wintour; Sally Singer; Jay Fielden; Ned Martel; Laurie Jones; Nick Paumgarten; Kate Browne and Eric Etheridge; Meg Lamason; Greg Radich and Camille Schwae; Satoru Igarashi; Hastings-on-Hudson Public Library; Two for the Pot; the Arrowhead Lodge; John Laursen; Jerry O'Sullivan; Dana Lyn; Tara Circle; Sister Breda Galavin; Mary and Joe Perillo, Skip McPherson; Jacqueline and Dudley Laufman; the Multnomah County Library; Scoops on Hudson; Irene Schneider, Joyce Pendola, and Jay Merritt; Gully Wells; the Zanes family; the Mockler family; Anthony Andreassi; Megan Liberman; Deborah and Jeff Cole; the Kaplan family; the Spieler family; the Shaeffer family; Nancy Balaban; Ray and Beth Smith; Will and Betty Gaylin; the Marzorati family; the Barry family; the Quinn family; the other Quinn family; Jill and Dan Bauer; the Sullivan families; the Diehl family; Foghorn Stringband; James Leinfelder; Matthew "Matt" Sharpe; Linda and Donald Desimini; Mary Elizabeth and Robert Sullivan; and Suzanne.

A NOTE ON THE AUTHOR

Robert Sullivan is the author of *The Meadowlands*, *A Whale Hunt*, *How Not to Get Rich*, and the national bestseller *Rats*. He is a contributing editor to *Vogue* and his writing has appeared in the *New Yorker*, the *New York Times*, and *Dwell*. He lives in Brooklyn, New York, with his wife and their two children.